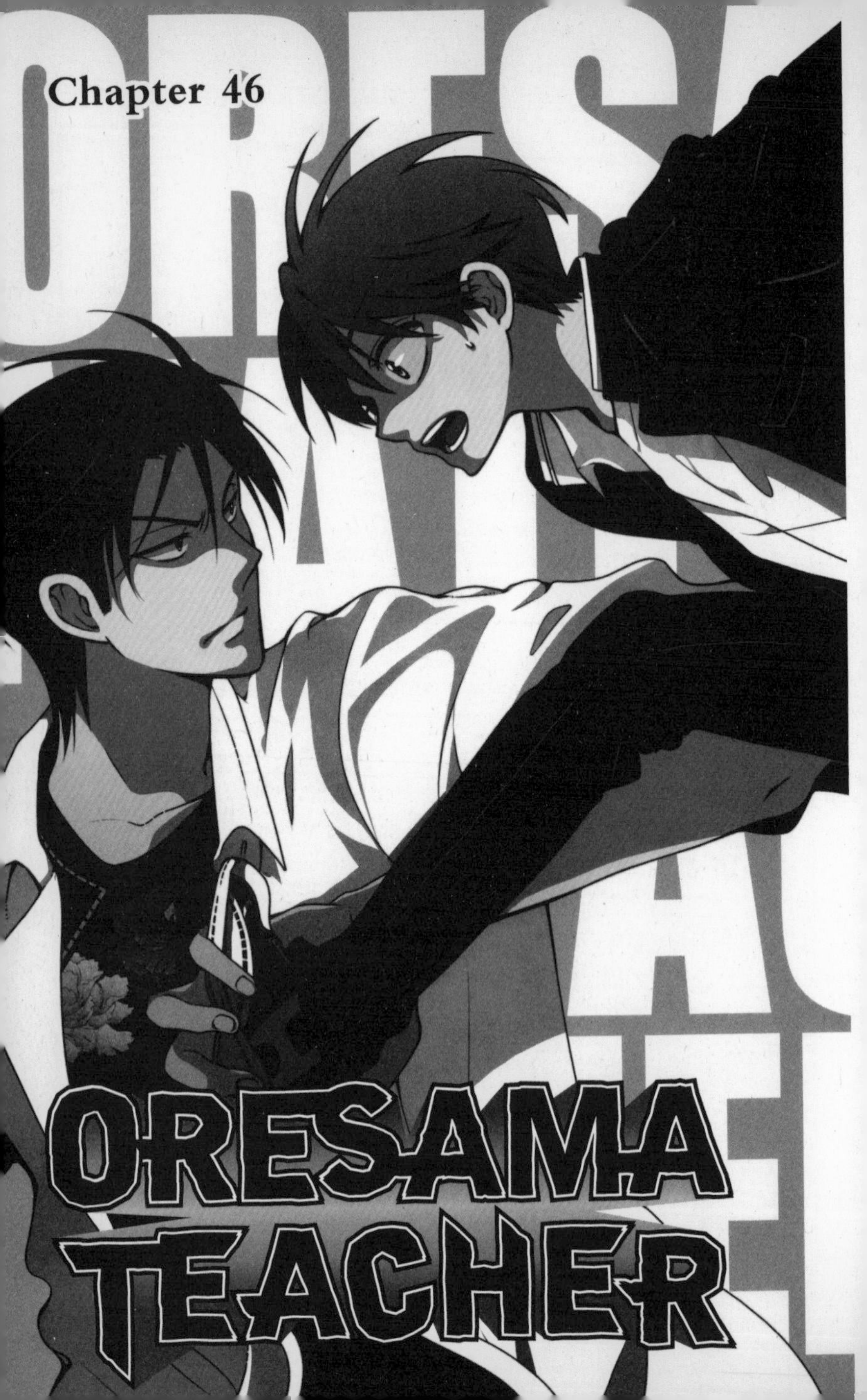
Chapter 46
ORESAMA TEACHER

QUANTITY OVER QUALITY

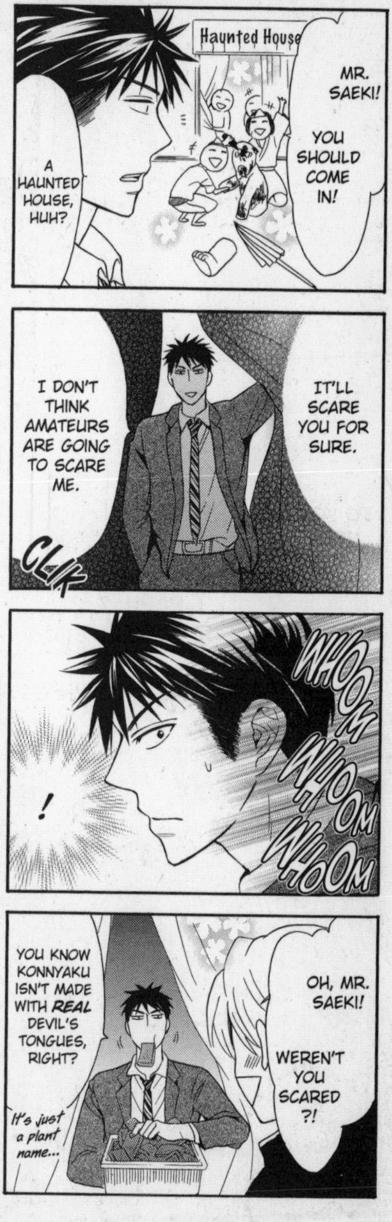
Haunted House
MR. SAEKI!
YOU SHOULD COME IN!
A HAUNTED HOUSE, HUH?
IT'LL SCARE YOU FOR SURE.
I DON'T THINK AMATEURS ARE GOING TO SCARE ME.
CLIK
WHOOM WHOOM WHOOM WHOOM
!
OH, MR. SAEKI!
WEREN'T YOU SCARED?!
YOU KNOW KONNYAKU ISN'T MADE WITH ***REAL*** DEVIL'S TONGUES, RIGHT?
It's just a plant name...

WELCOME TO THE NINJA CAFE!

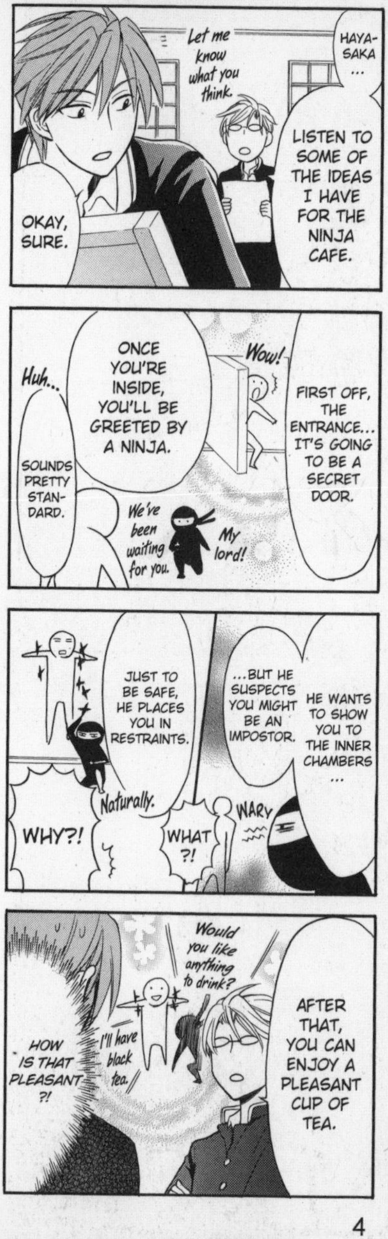
HAYA-SAKA...
LISTEN TO SOME OF THE IDEAS I HAVE FOR THE NINJA CAFE.
Let me know what you think.
OKAY, SURE.
FIRST OFF, THE ENTRANCE... IT'S GOING TO BE A SECRET DOOR.
Wow!
ONCE YOU'RE INSIDE, YOU'LL BE GREETED BY A NINJA.
Huh...
SOUNDS PRETTY STAN-DARD.
My lord!
We've been waiting for you.
HE WANTS TO SHOW YOU TO THE INNER CHAMBERS...
...BUT HE SUSPECTS YOU MIGHT BE AN IMPOSTOR.
JUST TO BE SAFE, HE PLACES YOU IN RESTRAINTS.
WARY
WHAT?!
Naturally.
WHY?!
AFTER THAT, YOU CAN ENJOY A PLEASANT CUP OF TEA.
Would you like anything to drink?
I'll have black tea.
HOW IS THAT PLEASANT?!

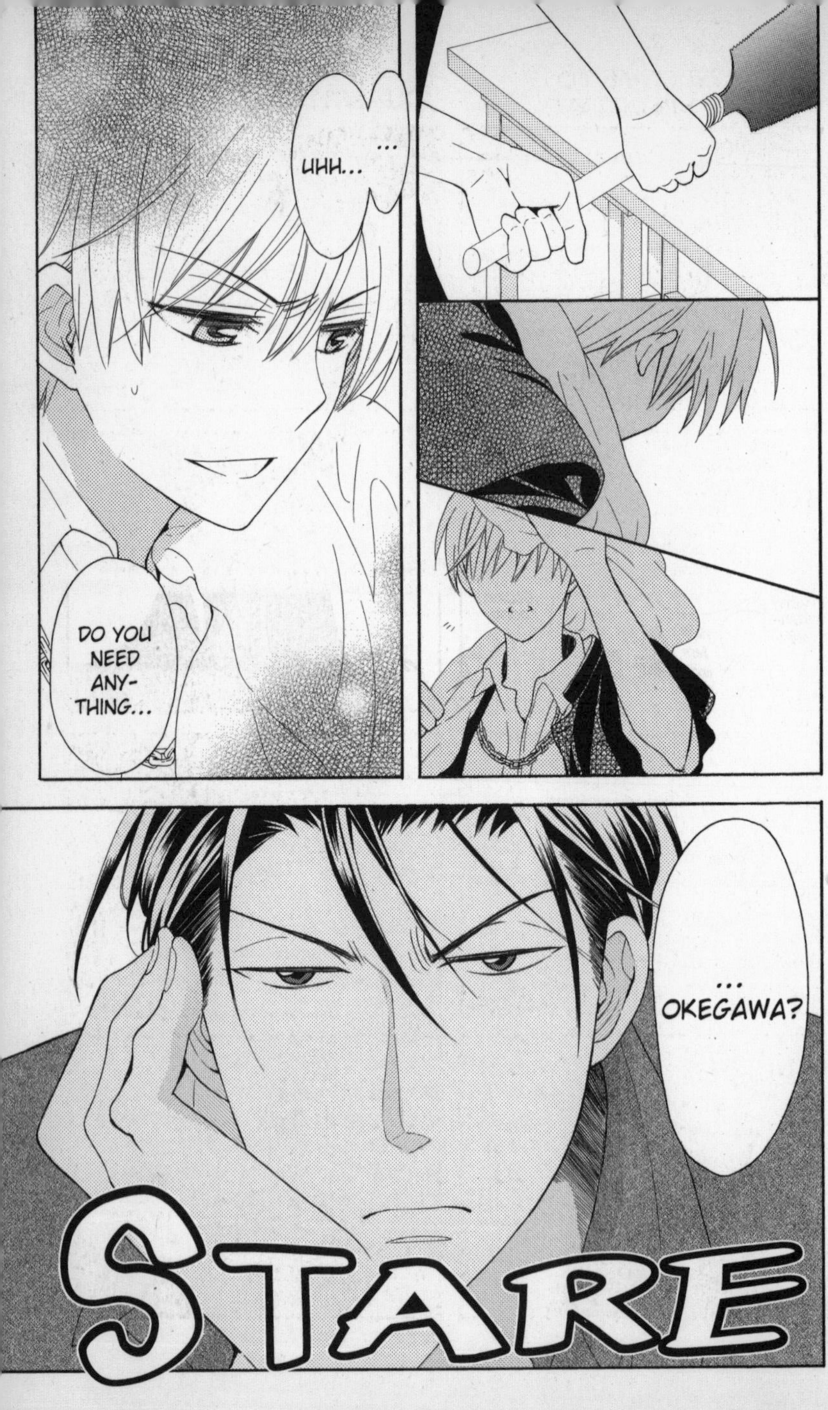
... UHH...
DO YOU NEED ANY-THING...
... OKEGAWA?
STARE

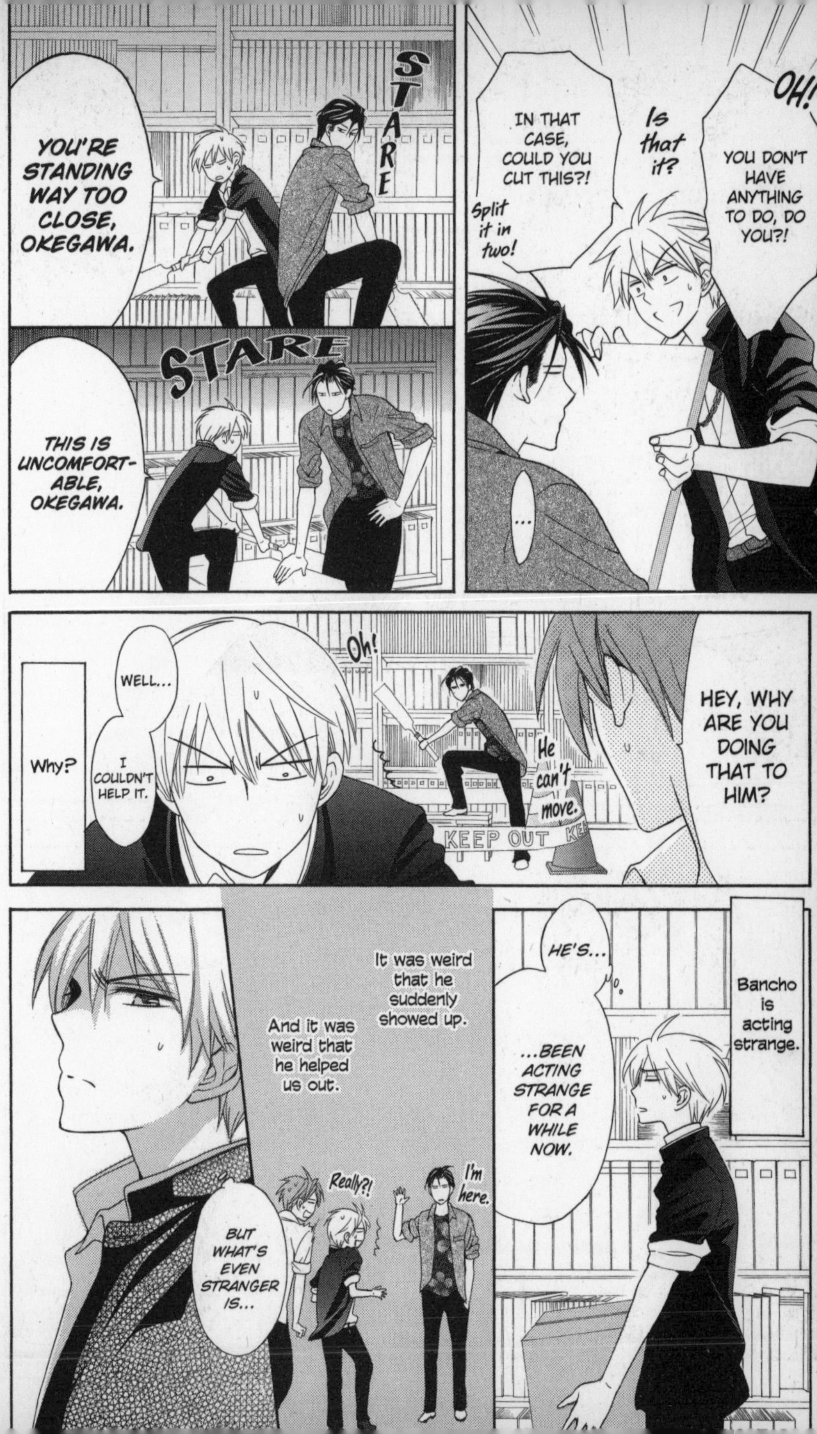
OH!
YOU DON'T HAVE ANYTHING TO DO, DO YOU?!
Is that it?
IN THAT CASE, COULD YOU CUT THIS?!
Split it in two!
...
STARE
YOU'RE STANDING WAY TOO CLOSE, OKEGAWA.
STARE
THIS IS UNCOMFORT-ABLE, OKEGAWA.
HEY, WHY ARE YOU DOING THAT TO HIM?
Oh!
He can't move.
KEEP OUT
WELL...
I COULDN'T HELP IT.
Why?
Bancho is acting strange.
HE'S...
...BEEN ACTING STRANGE FOR A WHILE NOW.
It was weird that he suddenly showed up.
And it was weird that he helped us out.
I'm here.
Really?!
BUT WHAT'S EVEN STRANGER IS...

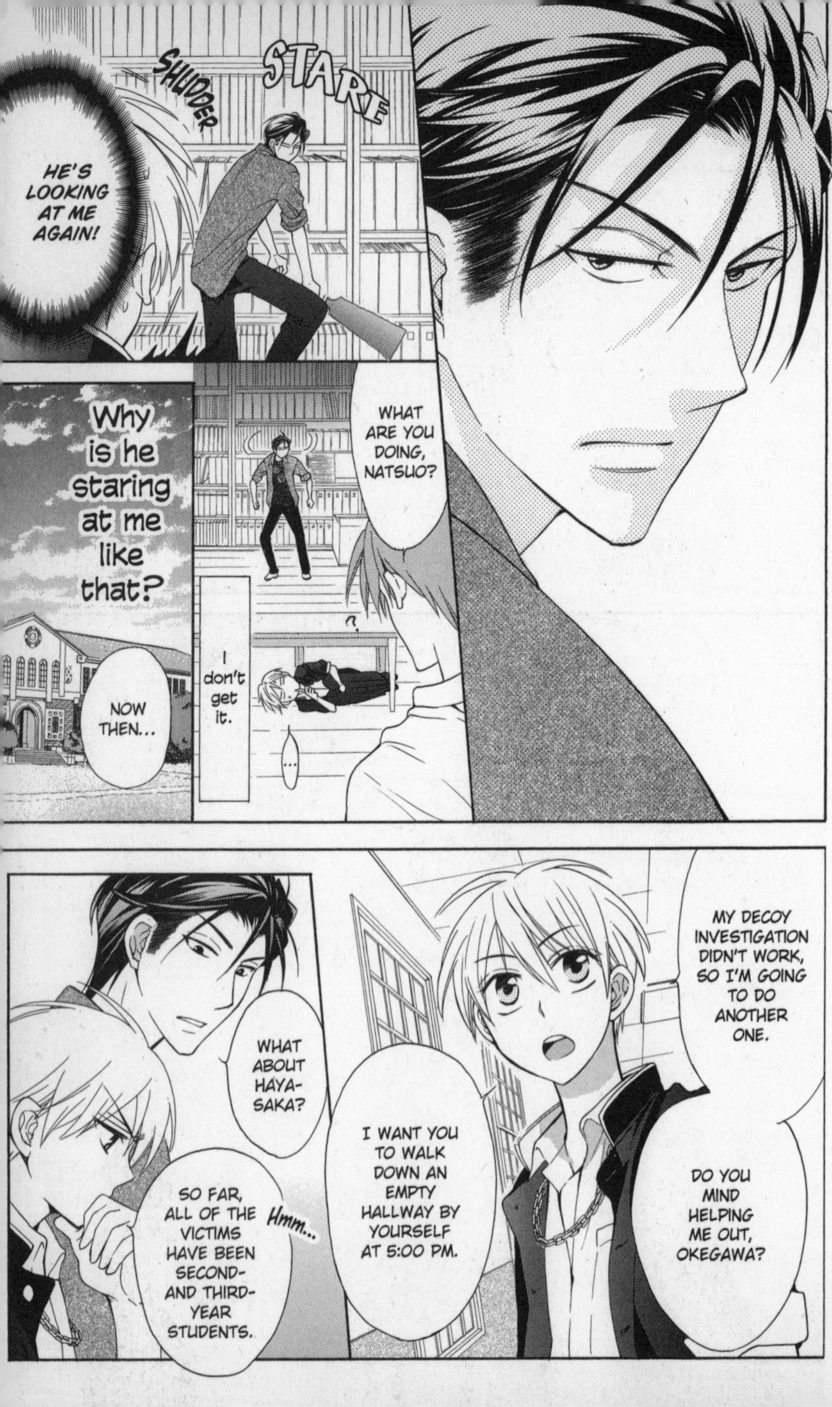
STARE
SHUDDER
HE'S LOOKING AT ME AGAIN!
WHAT ARE YOU DOING, NATSUO?
?
I don't get it.
...
Why is he staring at me like that?
NOW THEN...
MY DECOY INVESTIGATION DIDN'T WORK, SO I'M GOING TO DO ANOTHER ONE.
DO YOU MIND HELPING ME OUT, OKEGAWA?
I WANT YOU TO WALK DOWN AN EMPTY HALLWAY BY YOURSELF AT 5:00 PM.
WHAT ABOUT HAYA-SAKA?
Hmm...
SO FAR, ALL OF THE VICTIMS HAVE BEEN SECOND- AND THIRD-YEAR STUDENTS.

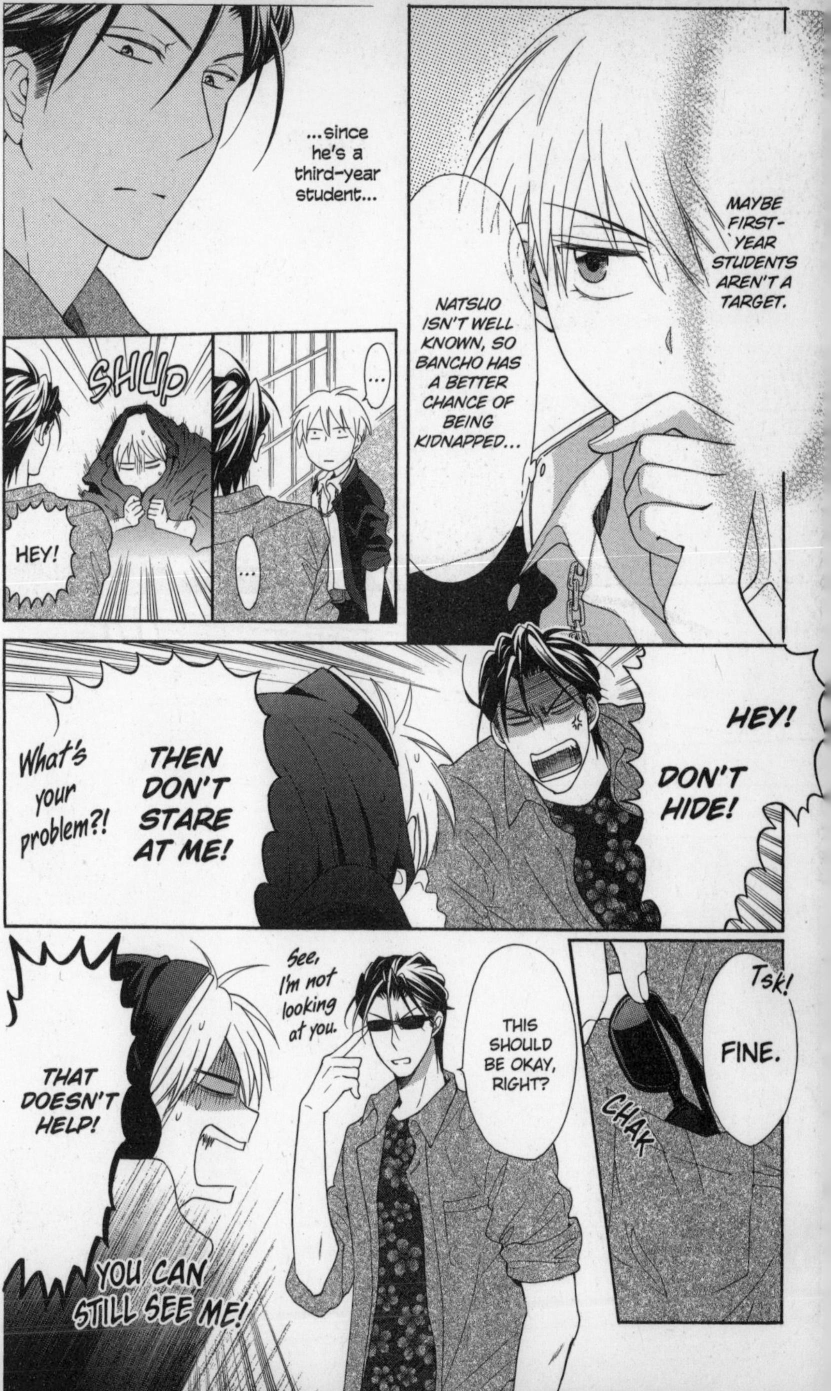
MAYBE FIRST-YEAR STUDENTS AREN'T A TARGET.
NATSUO ISN'T WELL KNOWN, SO BANCHO HAS A BETTER CHANCE OF BEING KIDNAPPED...
...since he's a third-year student...
...
...
SHUP
HEY!
HEY!
DON'T HIDE!
THEN DON'T STARE AT ME!
What's your problem?!
Tsk!
FINE.
CHAK
THIS SHOULD BE OKAY, RIGHT?
See, I'm not looking at you.
THAT DOESN'T HELP!
YOU CAN STILL SEE ME!

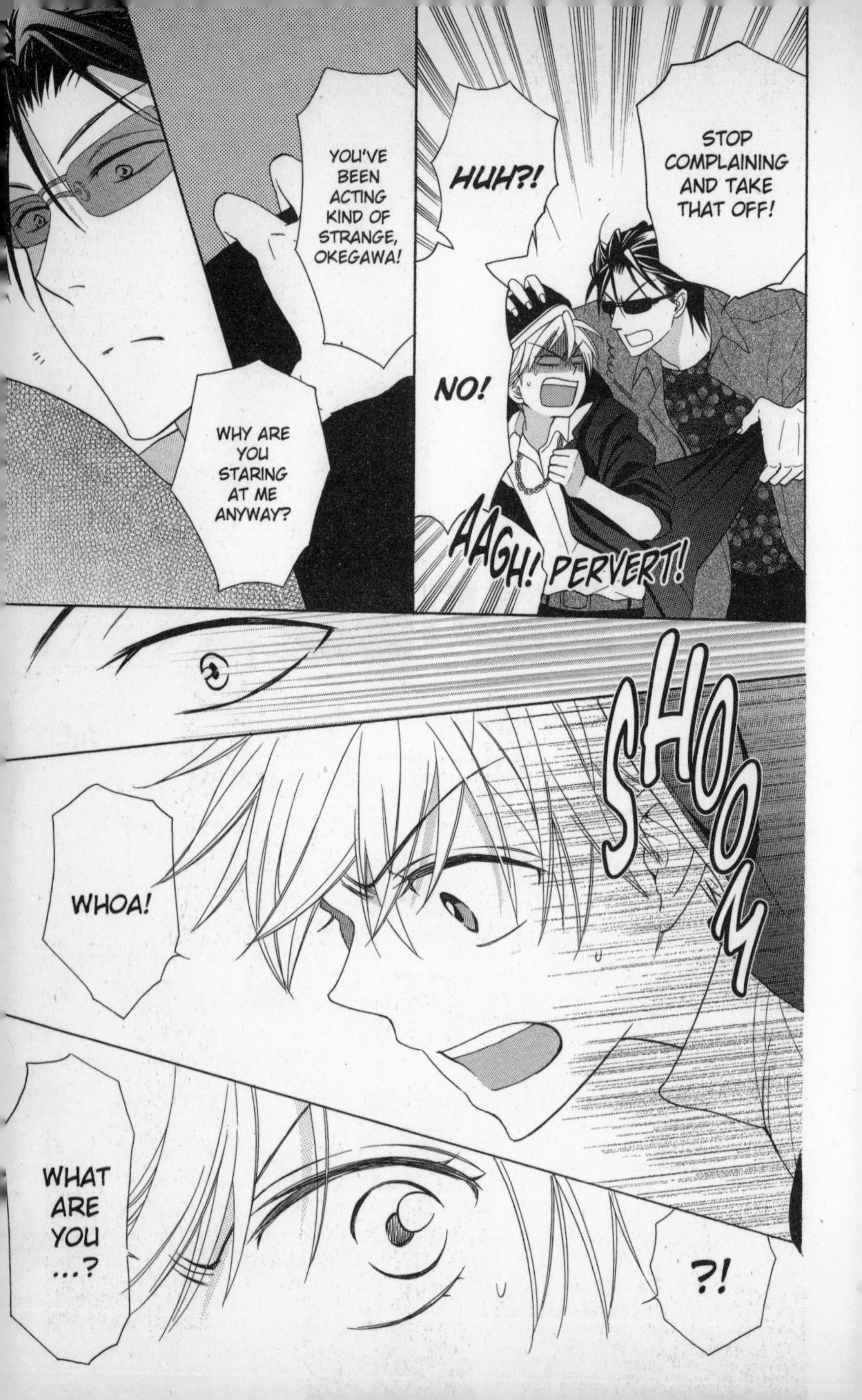
STOP COMPLAINING AND TAKE THAT OFF!
HUH?!
NO!
AAGH! PERVERT!
YOU'VE BEEN ACTING KIND OF STRANGE, OKEGAWA!
WHY ARE YOU STARING AT ME ANYWAY?
SHOOM
WHOA!
?!
WHAT ARE YOU ...?

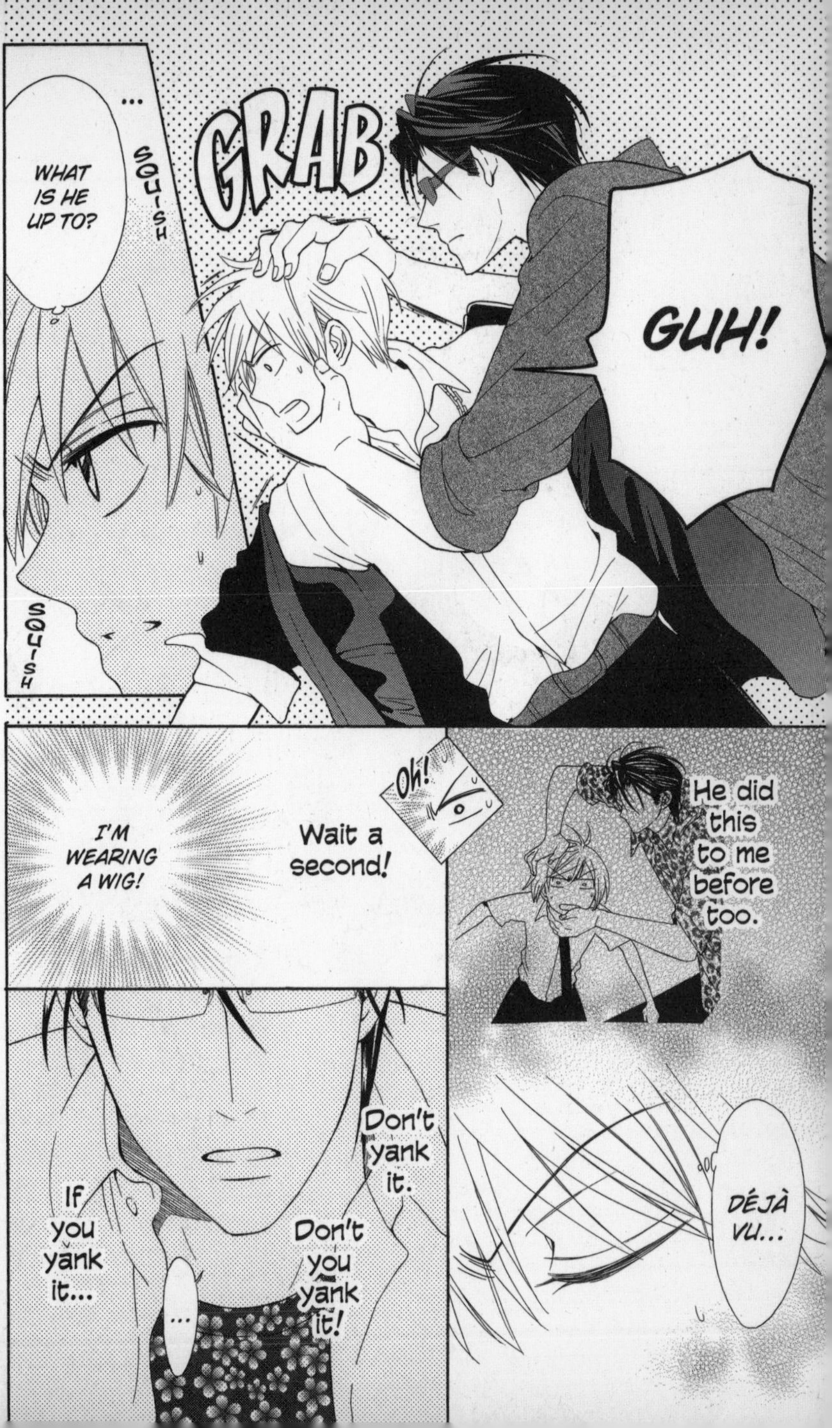
GRAB
GUH!
...
WHAT IS HE UP TO?
SQUISH
SQUISH
He did this to me before too.
DÉJÀ VU...
Oh!
Wait a second!
I'M WEARING A WIG!
Don't yank it.
Don't you yank it!
If you yank it...
...

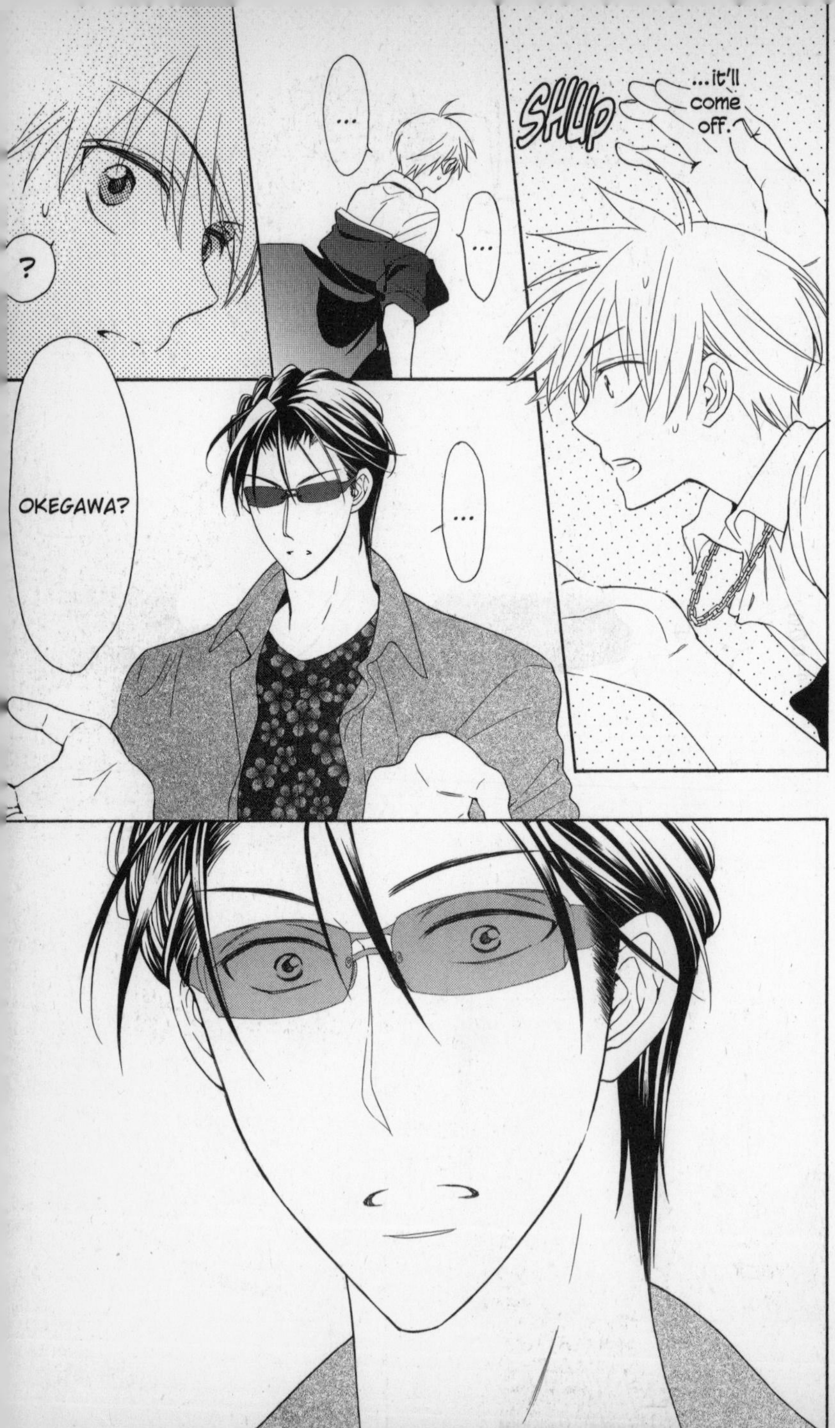
SHUP
...it'll come off.
...
...
?
...
OKEGAWA?

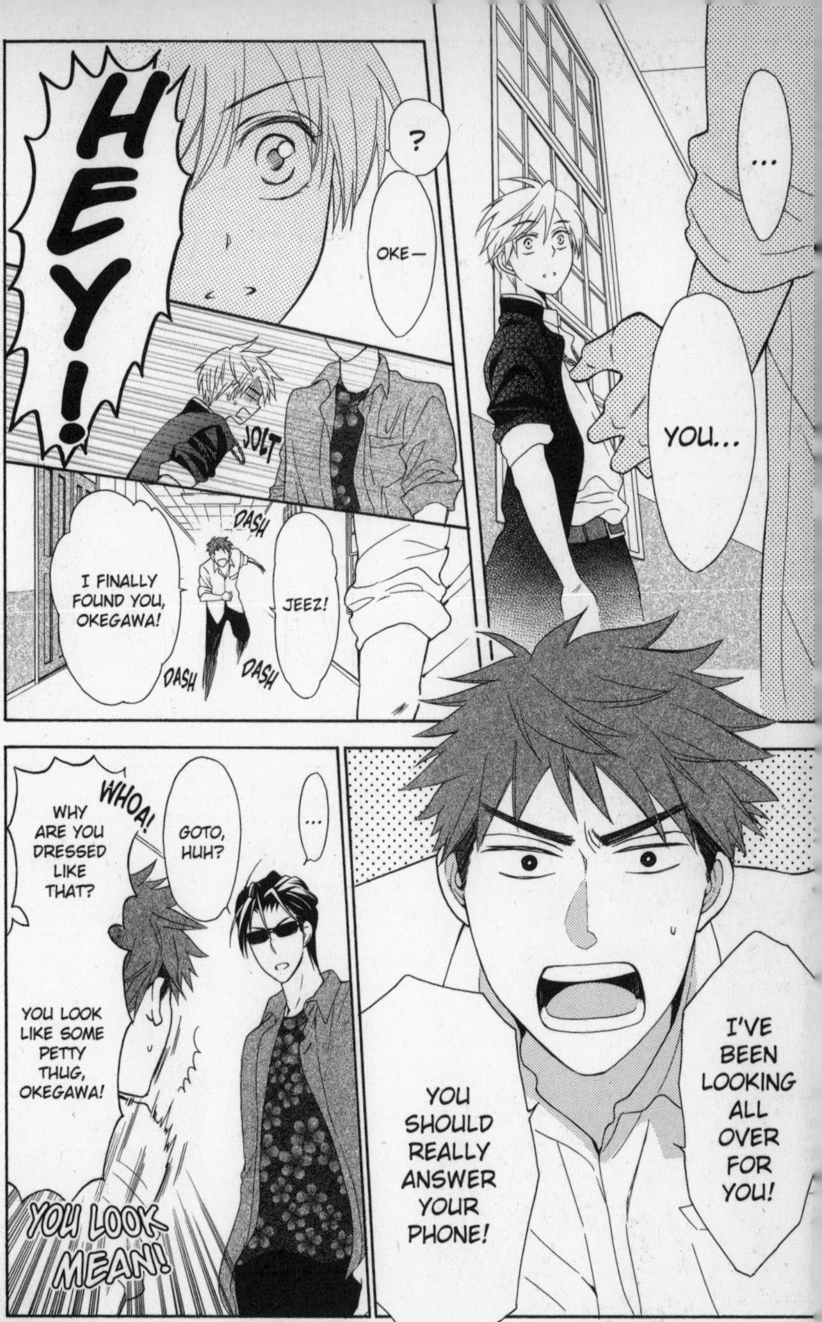
...
YOU...
?
OKE—
HEY!
JOLT
JEEZ!
DASH DASH
I FINALLY FOUND YOU, OKEGAWA!
DASH
I'VE BEEN LOOKING ALL OVER FOR YOU!
YOU SHOULD REALLY ANSWER YOUR PHONE!
...
GOTO, HUH?
WHOA!
WHY ARE YOU DRESSED LIKE THAT?
YOU LOOK LIKE SOME PETTY THUG, OKEGAWA!
YOU LOOK MEAN!

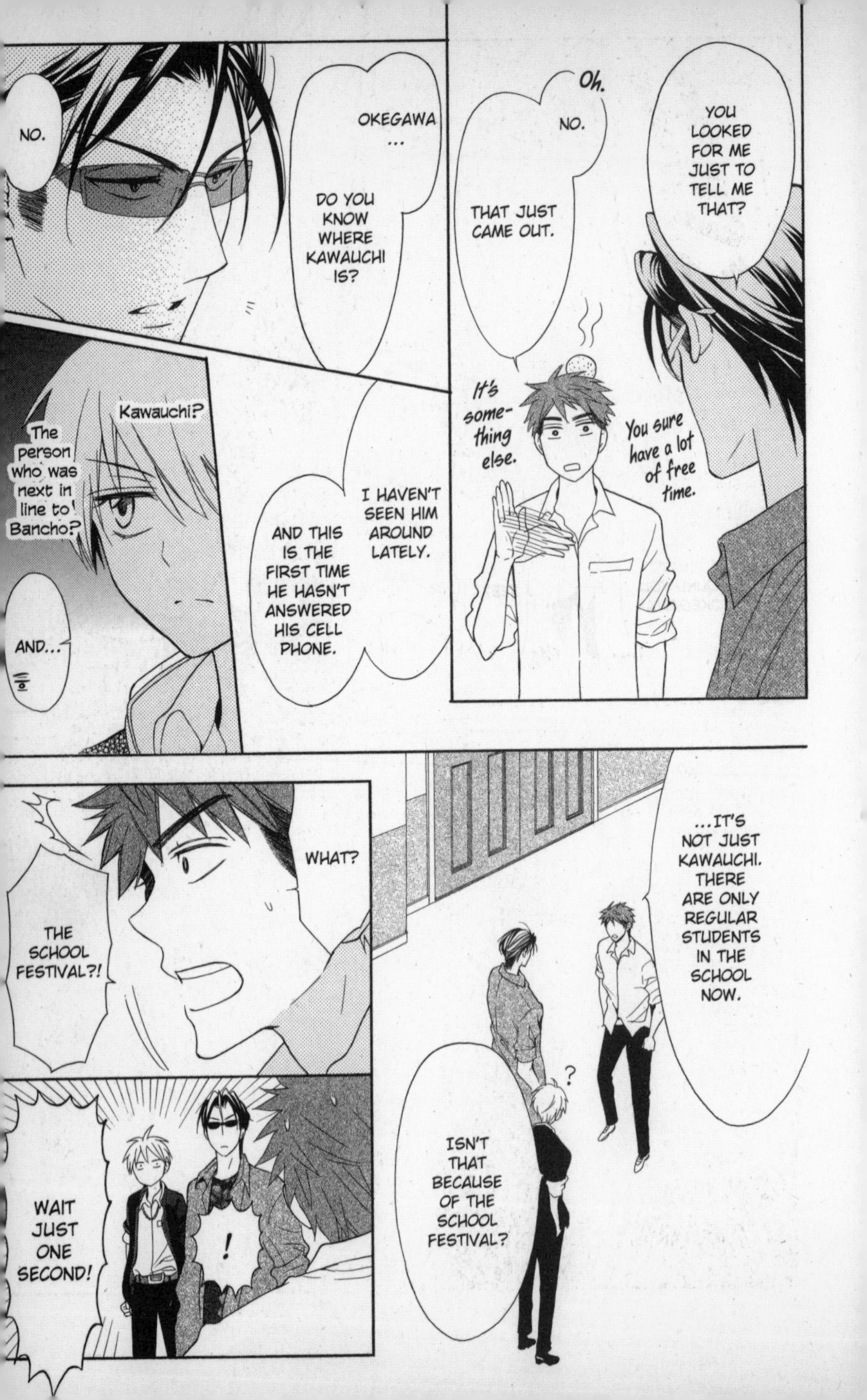
YOU LOOKED FOR ME JUST TO TELL ME THAT?
Oh.
NO.
THAT JUST CAME OUT.
It's something else.
You sure have a lot of free time.
OKEGAWA...
DO YOU KNOW WHERE KAWAUCHI IS?
NO.
I HAVEN'T SEEN HIM AROUND LATELY.
AND THIS IS THE FIRST TIME HE HASN'T ANSWERED HIS CELL PHONE.
Kawauchi?
The person who was next in line to Bancho?
AND...
...IT'S NOT JUST KAWAUCHI. THERE ARE ONLY REGULAR STUDENTS IN THE SCHOOL NOW.
?
ISN'T THAT BECAUSE OF THE SCHOOL FESTIVAL?
WHAT?
THE SCHOOL FESTIVAL?!
!
WAIT JUST ONE SECOND!

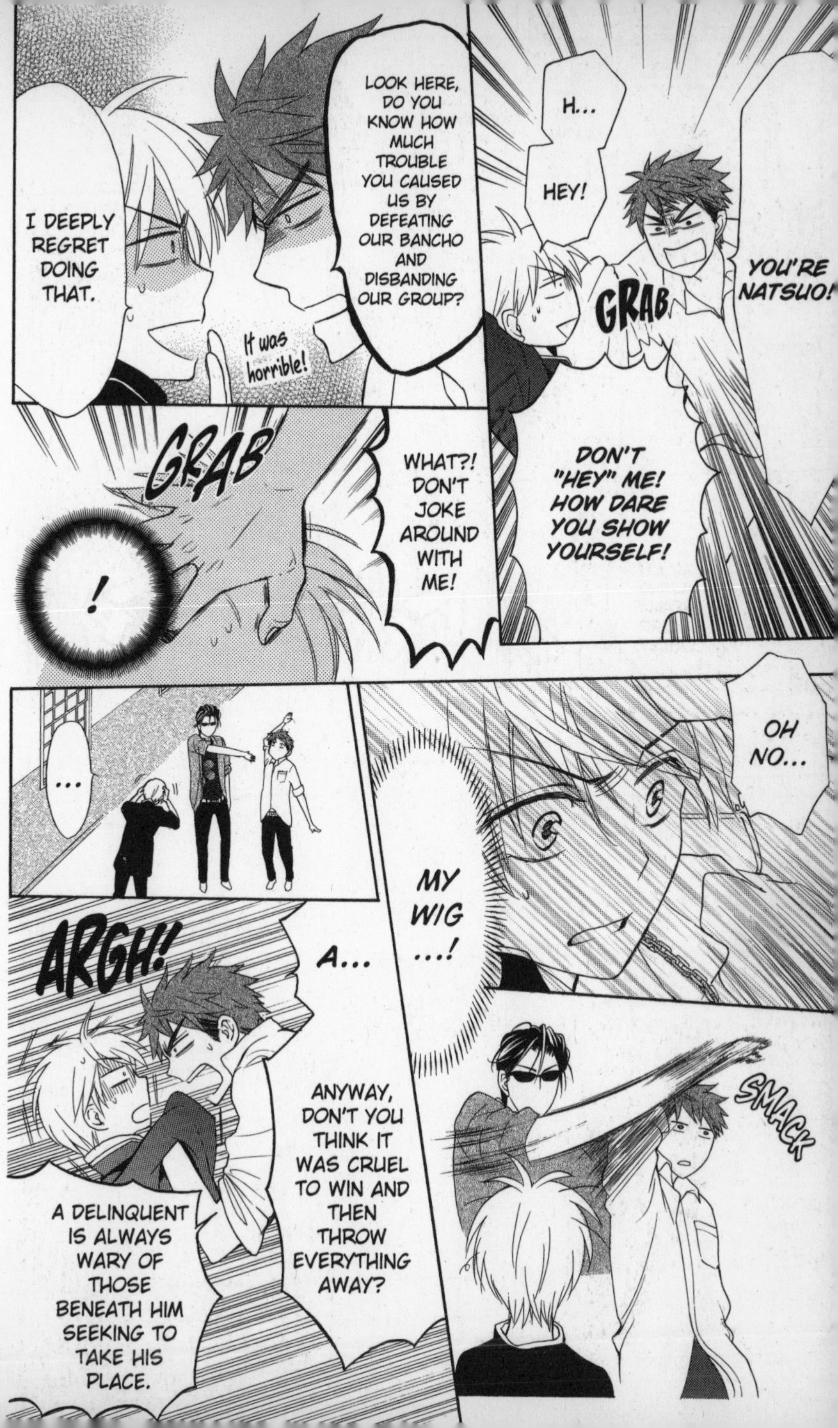
H...
HEY!
GRAB
YOU'RE NATSUO!
DON'T "HEY" ME! HOW DARE YOU SHOW YOURSELF!
LOOK HERE, DO YOU KNOW HOW MUCH TROUBLE YOU CAUSED US BY DEFEATING OUR BANCHO AND DISBANDING OUR GROUP?
It was horrible!
I DEEPLY REGRET DOING THAT.
WHAT?! DON'T JOKE AROUND WITH ME!
GRAB
!
OH NO...
MY WIG ...!
SMACK
...
A...
ARGH!
ANYWAY, DON'T YOU THINK IT WAS CRUEL TO WIN AND THEN THROW EVERYTHING AWAY?
A DELINQUENT IS ALWAYS WARY OF THOSE BENEATH HIM SEEKING TO TAKE HIS PLACE.

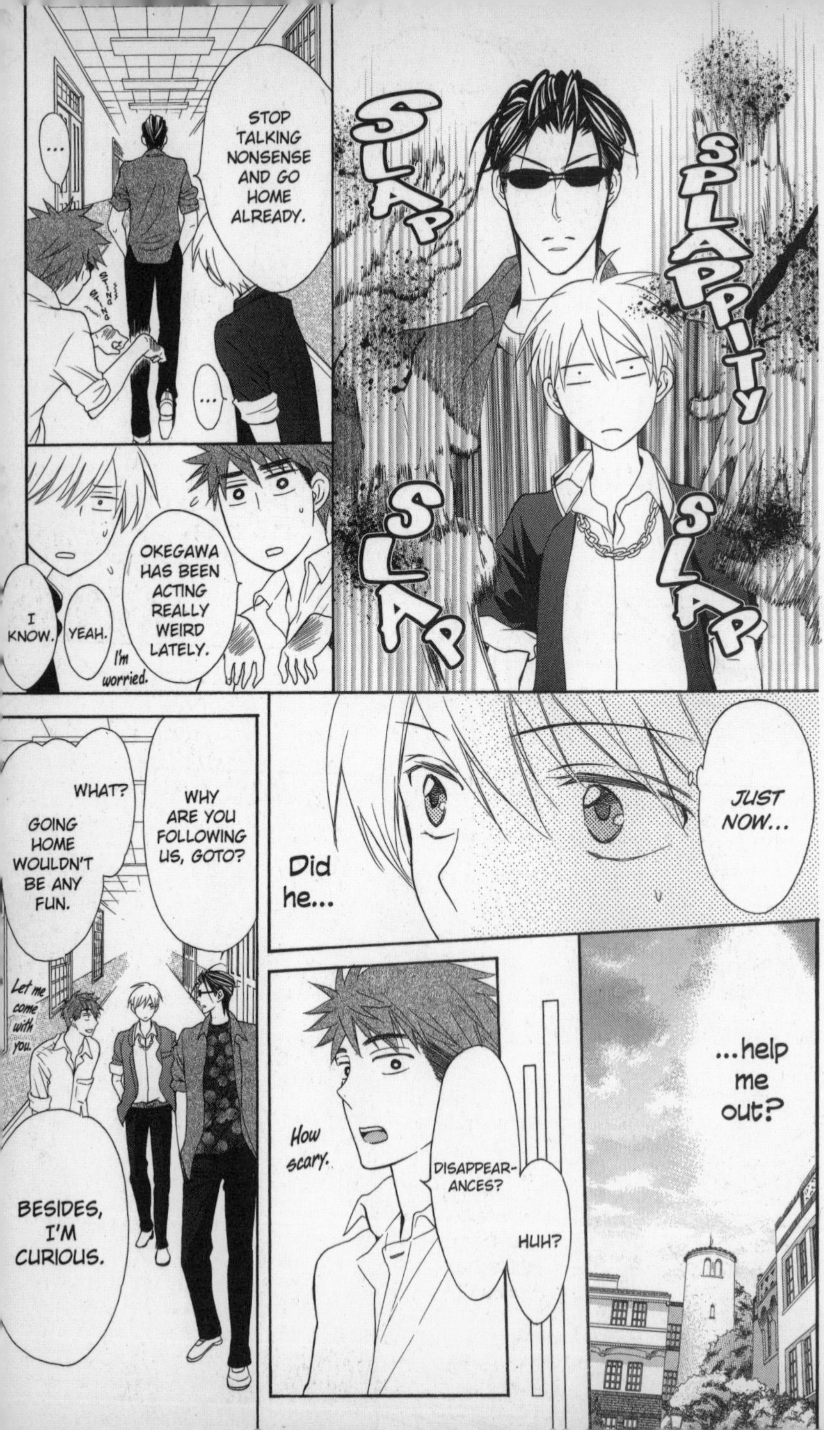
SLAPPITY
SLAP
SLAP
SLAP
STOP TALKING NONSENSE AND GO HOME ALREADY.
...
...
STING STING
OKEGAWA HAS BEEN ACTING REALLY WEIRD LATELY.
I'm worried.
YEAH.
I KNOW.
JUST NOW...
Did he...
...help me out?
HUH?
DISAPPEAR-ANCES?
How scary.
WHY ARE YOU FOLLOWING US, GOTO?
WHAT? GOING HOME WOULDN'T BE ANY FUN.
Let me come with you.
BESIDES, I'M CURIOUS.

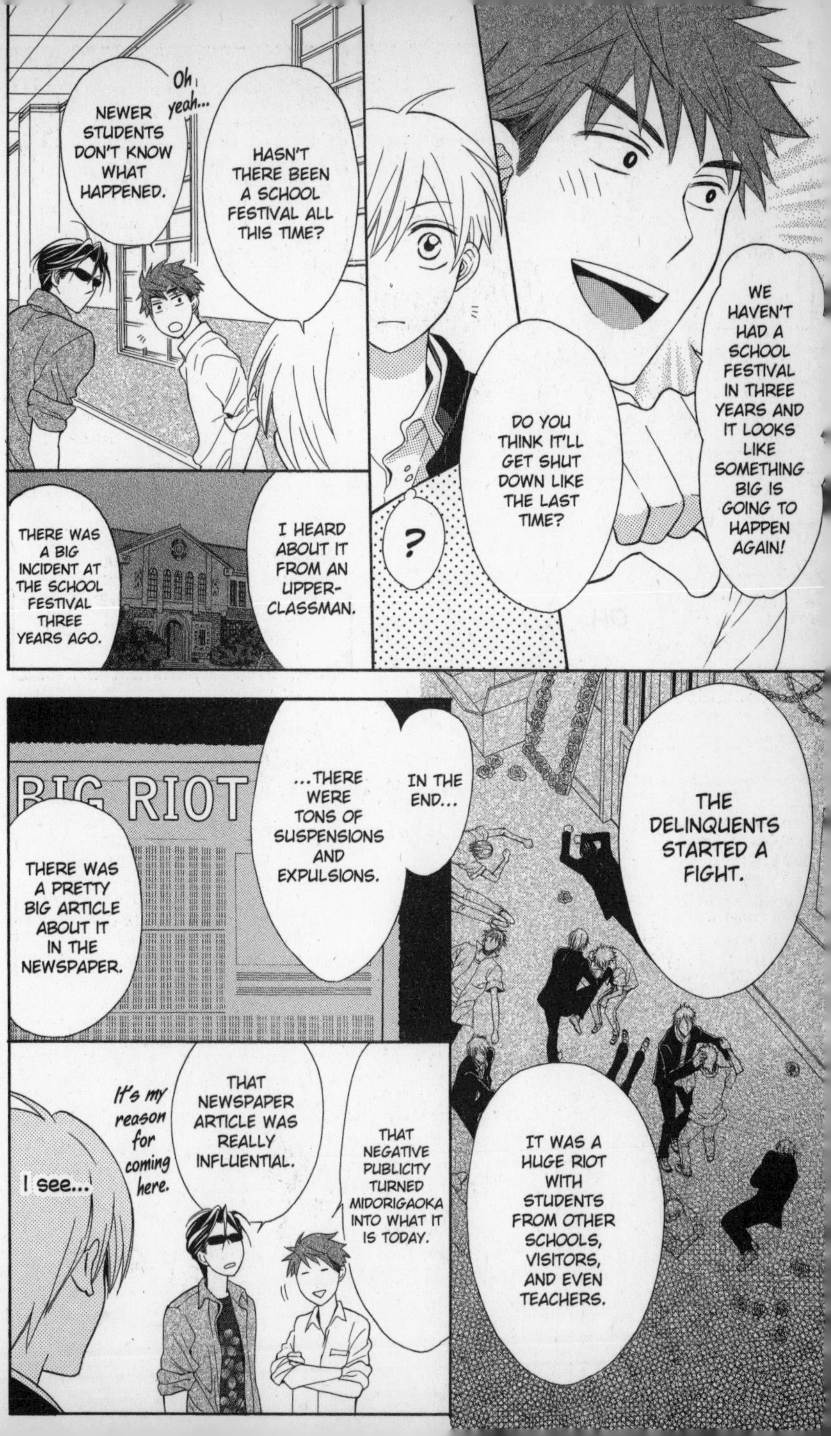
WE HAVEN'T HAD A SCHOOL FESTIVAL IN THREE YEARS AND IT LOOKS LIKE SOMETHING BIG IS GOING TO HAPPEN AGAIN!
DO YOU THINK IT'LL GET SHUT DOWN LIKE THE LAST TIME?
?
HASN'T THERE BEEN A SCHOOL FESTIVAL ALL THIS TIME?
Oh yeah...
NEWER STUDENTS DON'T KNOW WHAT HAPPENED.
I HEARD ABOUT IT FROM AN UPPER-CLASSMAN.
THERE WAS A BIG INCIDENT AT THE SCHOOL FESTIVAL THREE YEARS AGO.
THE DELINQUENTS STARTED A FIGHT.
IT WAS A HUGE RIOT WITH STUDENTS FROM OTHER SCHOOLS, VISITORS, AND EVEN TEACHERS.
IN THE END...
...THERE WERE TONS OF SUSPENSIONS AND EXPULSIONS.
BIG RIOT
THERE WAS A PRETTY BIG ARTICLE ABOUT IT IN THE NEWSPAPER.
THAT NEGATIVE PUBLICITY TURNED MIDORIGAOKA INTO WHAT IT IS TODAY.
THAT NEWSPAPER ARTICLE WAS REALLY INFLUENTIAL.
It's my reason for coming here.
I see...

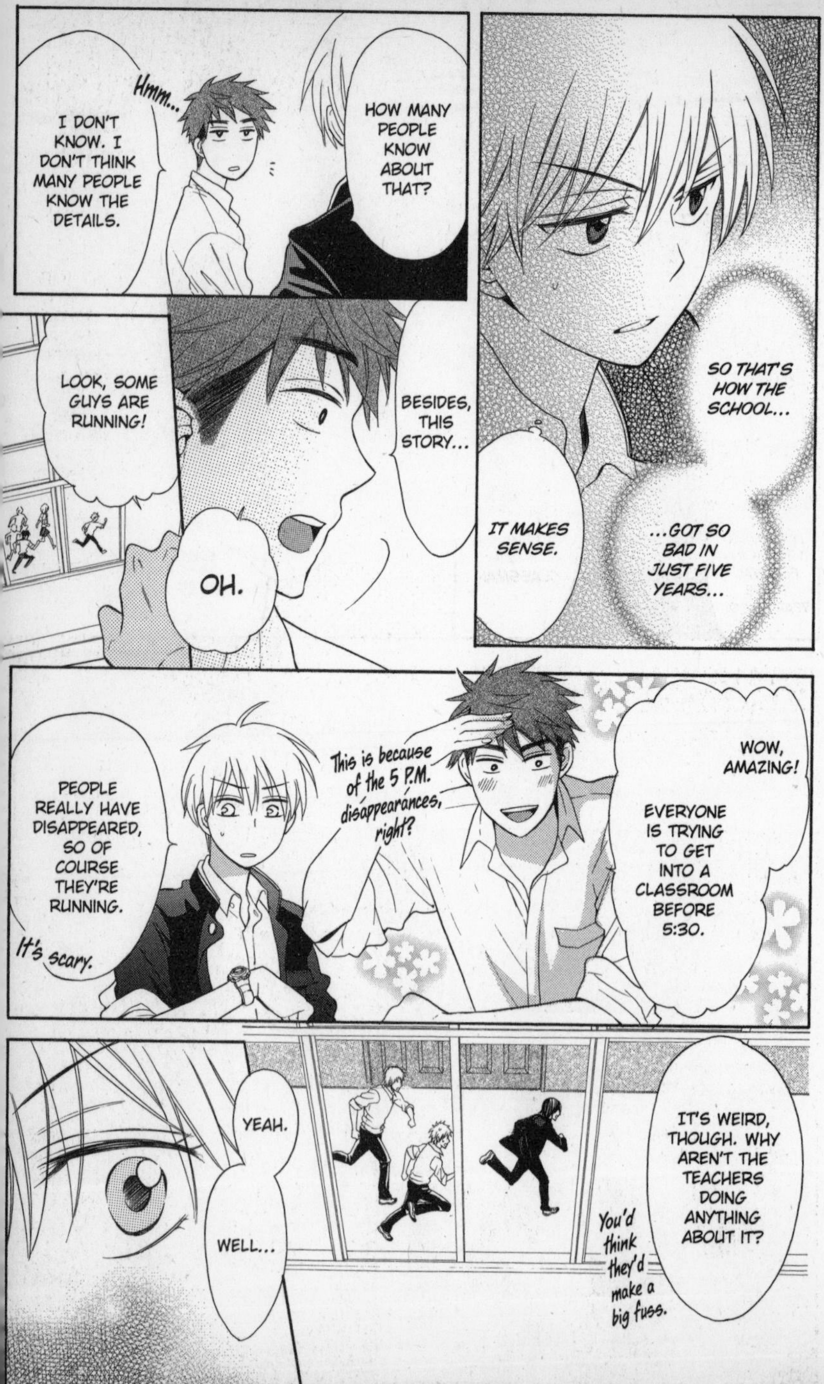
SO THAT'S HOW THE SCHOOL...
...GOT SO BAD IN JUST FIVE YEARS...
IT MAKES SENSE.
HOW MANY PEOPLE KNOW ABOUT THAT?
Hmm...
I DON'T KNOW. I DON'T THINK MANY PEOPLE KNOW THE DETAILS.
BESIDES, THIS STORY...
LOOK, SOME GUYS ARE RUNNING!
OH.
WOW, AMAZING!
EVERYONE IS TRYING TO GET INTO A CLASSROOM BEFORE 5:30.
This is because of the 5 P.M. disappearances, right?
PEOPLE REALLY HAVE DISAPPEARED, SO OF COURSE THEY'RE RUNNING.
It's scary.
IT'S WEIRD, THOUGH. WHY AREN'T THE TEACHERS DOING ANYTHING ABOUT IT?
You'd think they'd make a big fuss.
YEAH.
WELL...

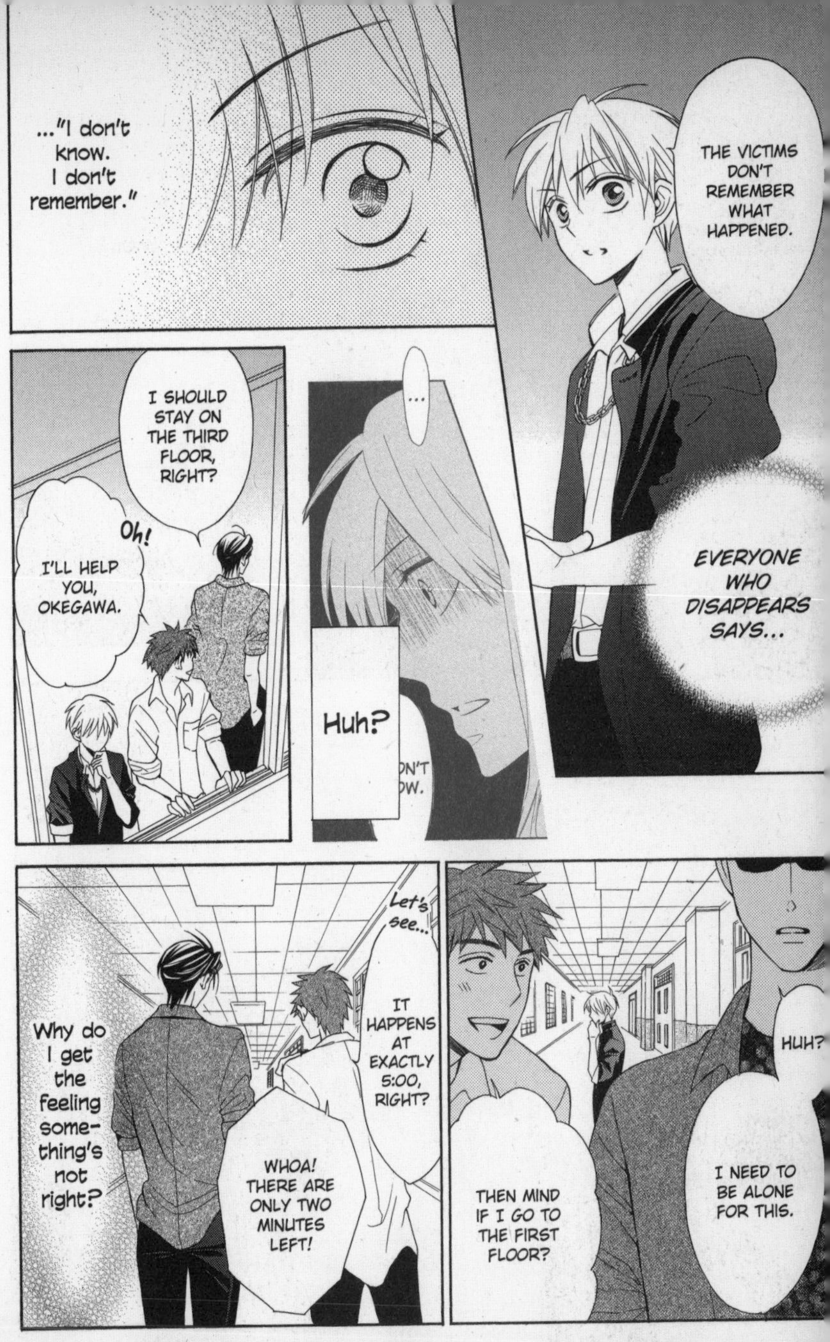
THE VICTIMS DON'T REMEMBER WHAT HAPPENED.
EVERYONE WHO DISAPPEARS SAYS...
..."I don't know. I don't remember."
...
Huh?
I SHOULD STAY ON THE THIRD FLOOR, RIGHT?
Oh!
I'LL HELP YOU, OKEGAWA.
HUH?
I NEED TO BE ALONE FOR THIS.
THEN MIND IF I GO TO THE FIRST FLOOR?
Let's see...
IT HAPPENS AT EXACTLY 5:00, RIGHT?
WHOA! THERE ARE ONLY TWO MINUTES LEFT!
Why do I get the feeling some-thing's not right?

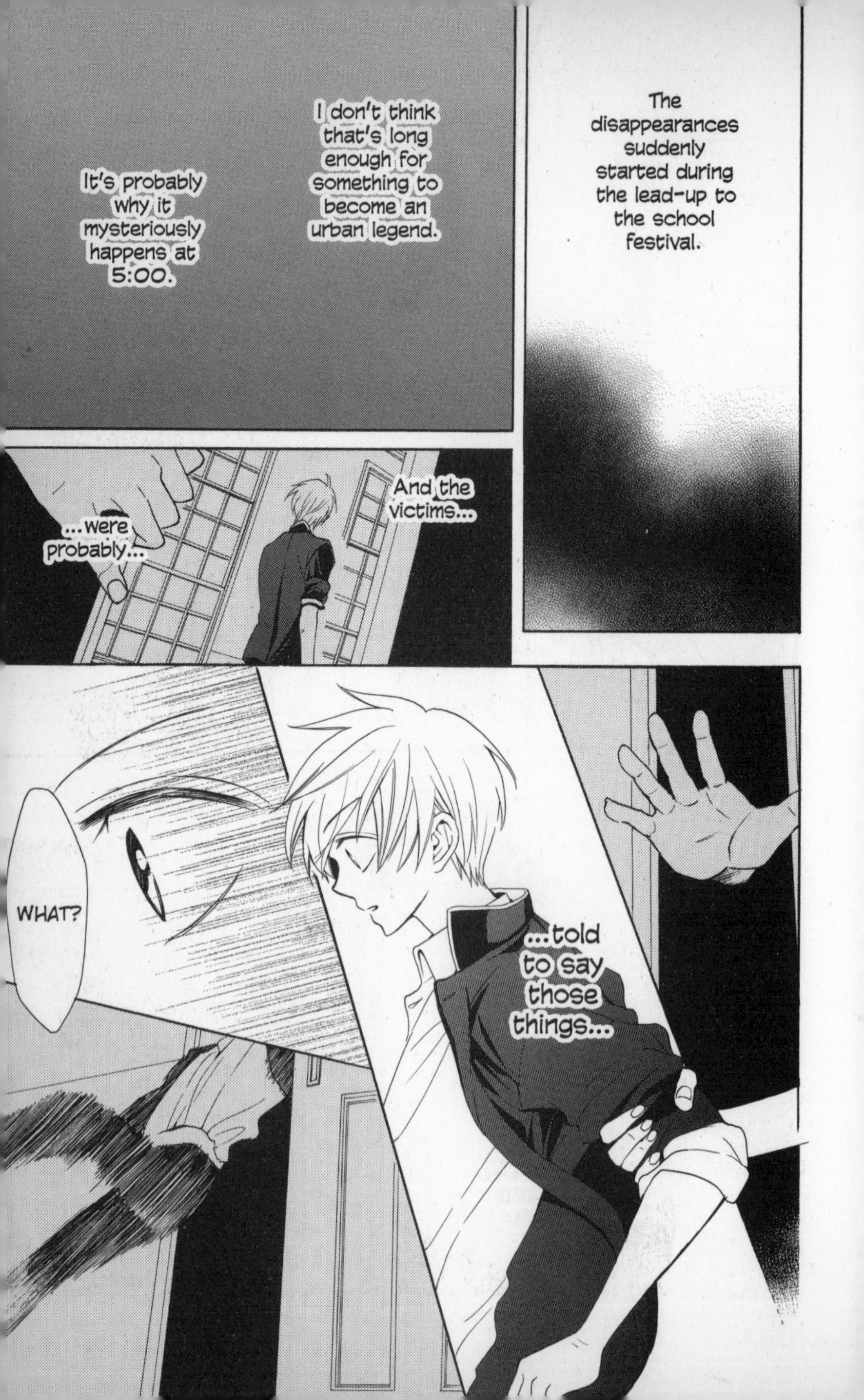

The disappearances suddenly started during the lead-up to the school festival.
I don't think that's long enough for something to become an urban legend.
It's probably why it mysteriously happens at 5:00.
And the victims...
...were probably...
...told to say those things...
WHAT?

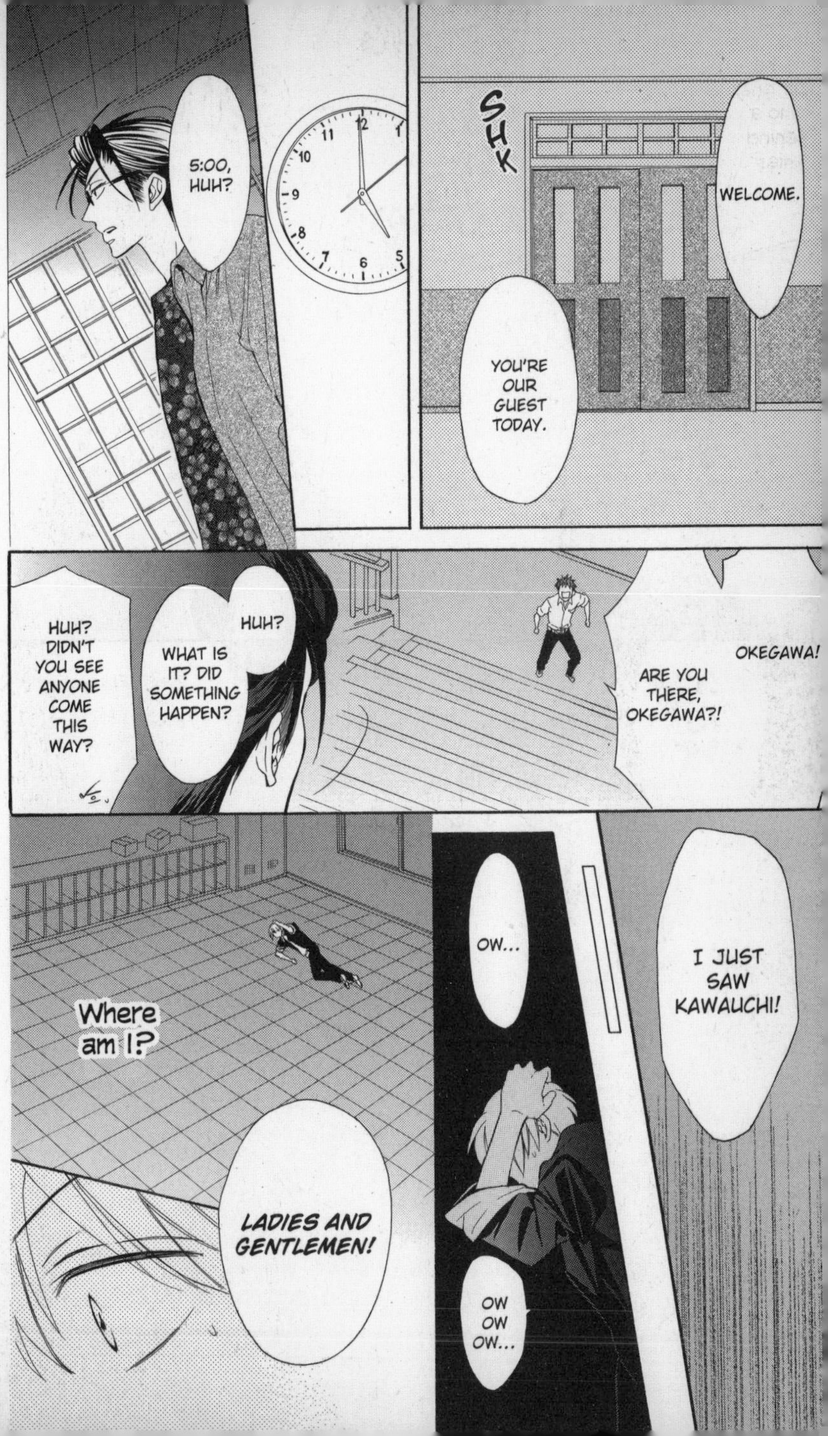
SHK
WELCOME.
YOU'RE OUR GUEST TODAY.
5:00, HUH?
OKEGAWA!
ARE YOU THERE, OKEGAWA?!
HUH?
WHAT IS IT? DID SOMETHING HAPPEN?
HUH? DIDN'T YOU SEE ANYONE COME THIS WAY?
I JUST SAW KAWAUCHI!
OW...
OW OW OW...
Where am I?
LADIES AND GENTLEMEN!

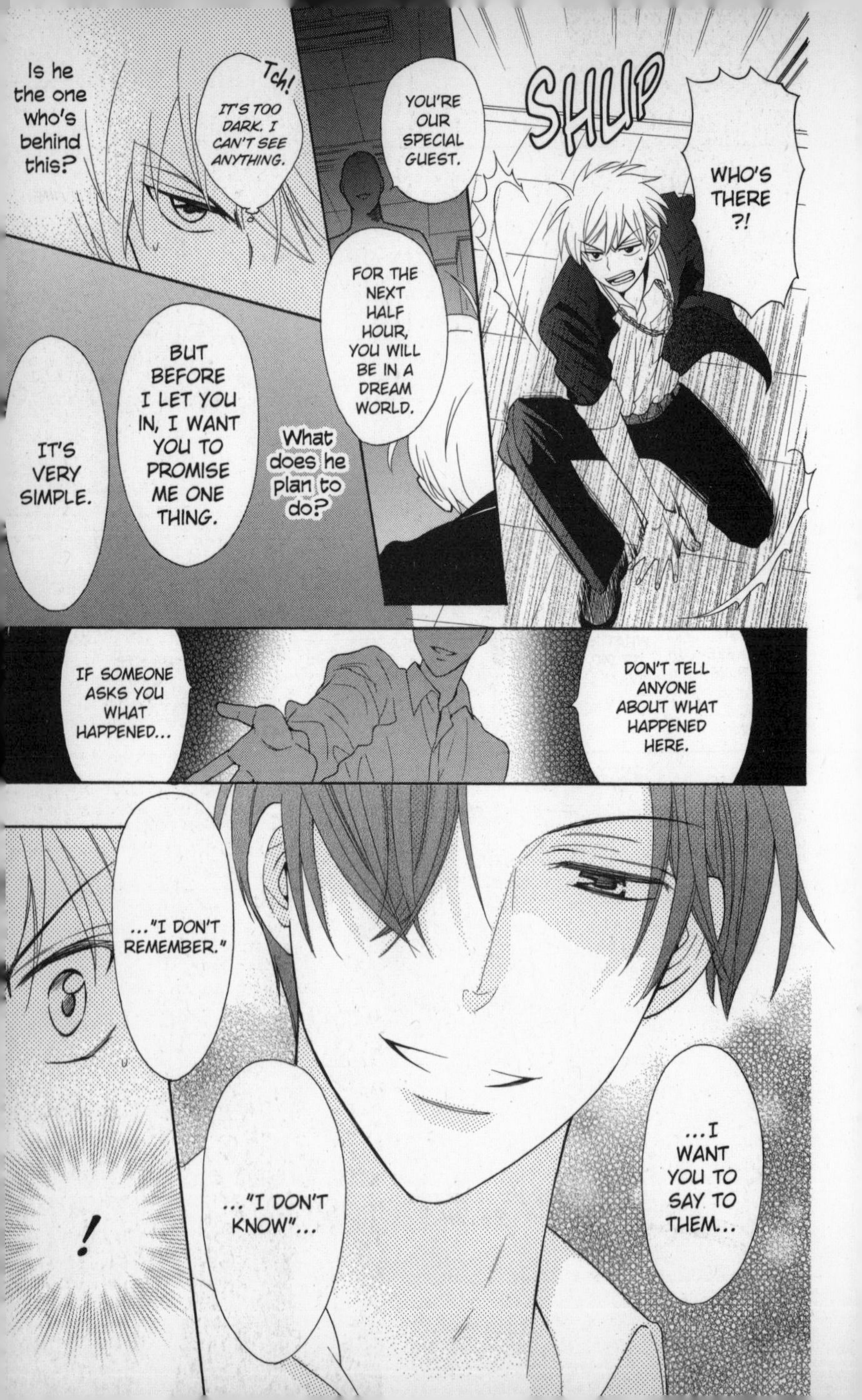
SHUP
WHO'S THERE ?!
YOU'RE OUR SPECIAL GUEST.
Tch!
IT'S TOO DARK. I CAN'T SEE ANYTHING.
Is he the one who's behind this?
FOR THE NEXT HALF HOUR, YOU WILL BE IN A DREAM WORLD.
What does he plan to do?
BUT BEFORE I LET YOU IN, I WANT YOU TO PROMISE ME ONE THING.
IT'S VERY SIMPLE.
DON'T TELL ANYONE ABOUT WHAT HAPPENED HERE.
IF SOMEONE ASKS YOU WHAT HAPPENED...
...I WANT YOU TO SAY TO THEM...
..."I DON'T REMEMBER."
..."I DON'T KNOW"...
!

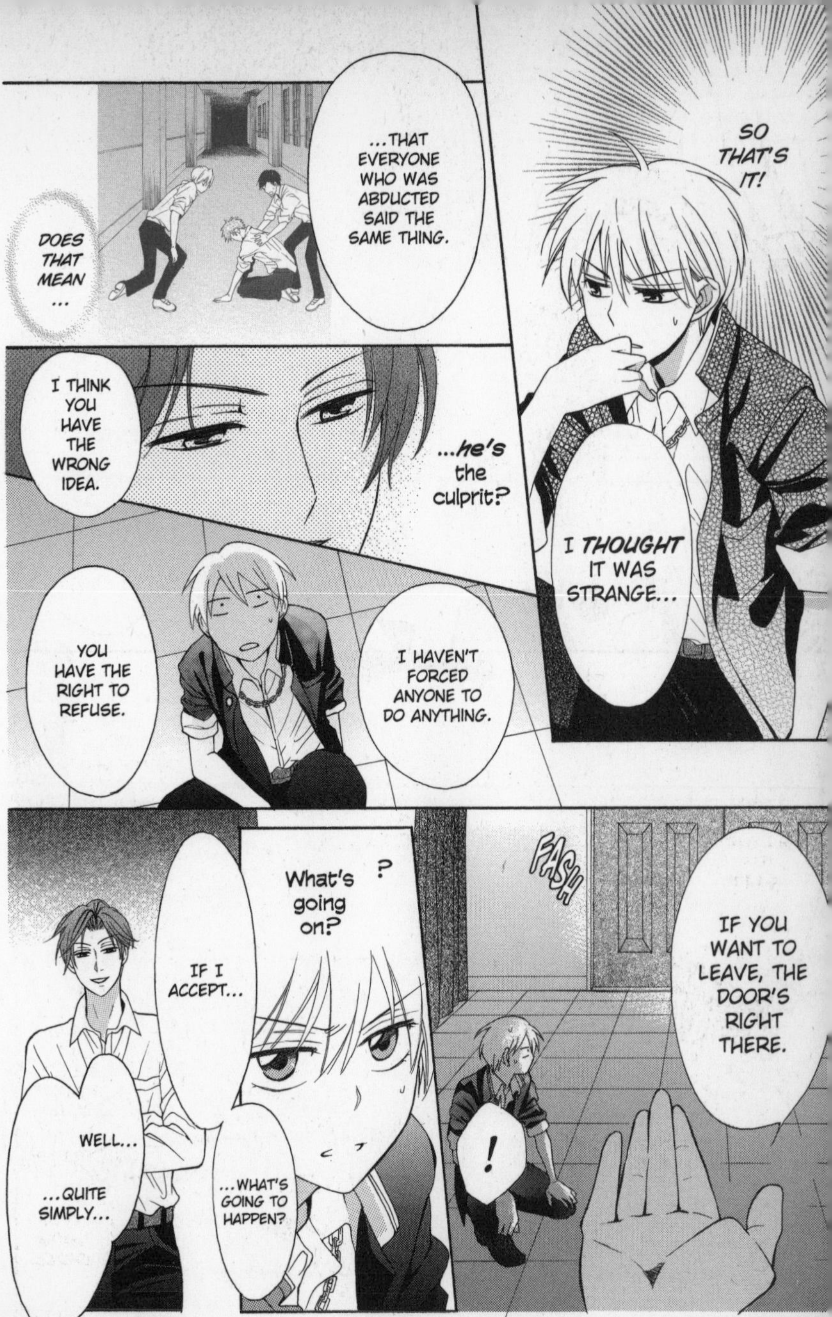
SO THAT'S IT!
I THOUGHT IT WAS STRANGE...
...THAT EVERYONE WHO WAS ABDUCTED SAID THE SAME THING.
DOES THAT MEAN...
...he's the culprit?
I THINK YOU HAVE THE WRONG IDEA.
I HAVEN'T FORCED ANYONE TO DO ANYTHING.
YOU HAVE THE RIGHT TO REFUSE.
FASH
IF YOU WANT TO LEAVE, THE DOOR'S RIGHT THERE.
!
What's going on?
?
IF I ACCEPT...
...WHAT'S GOING TO HAPPEN?
WELL...
...QUITE SIMPLY...

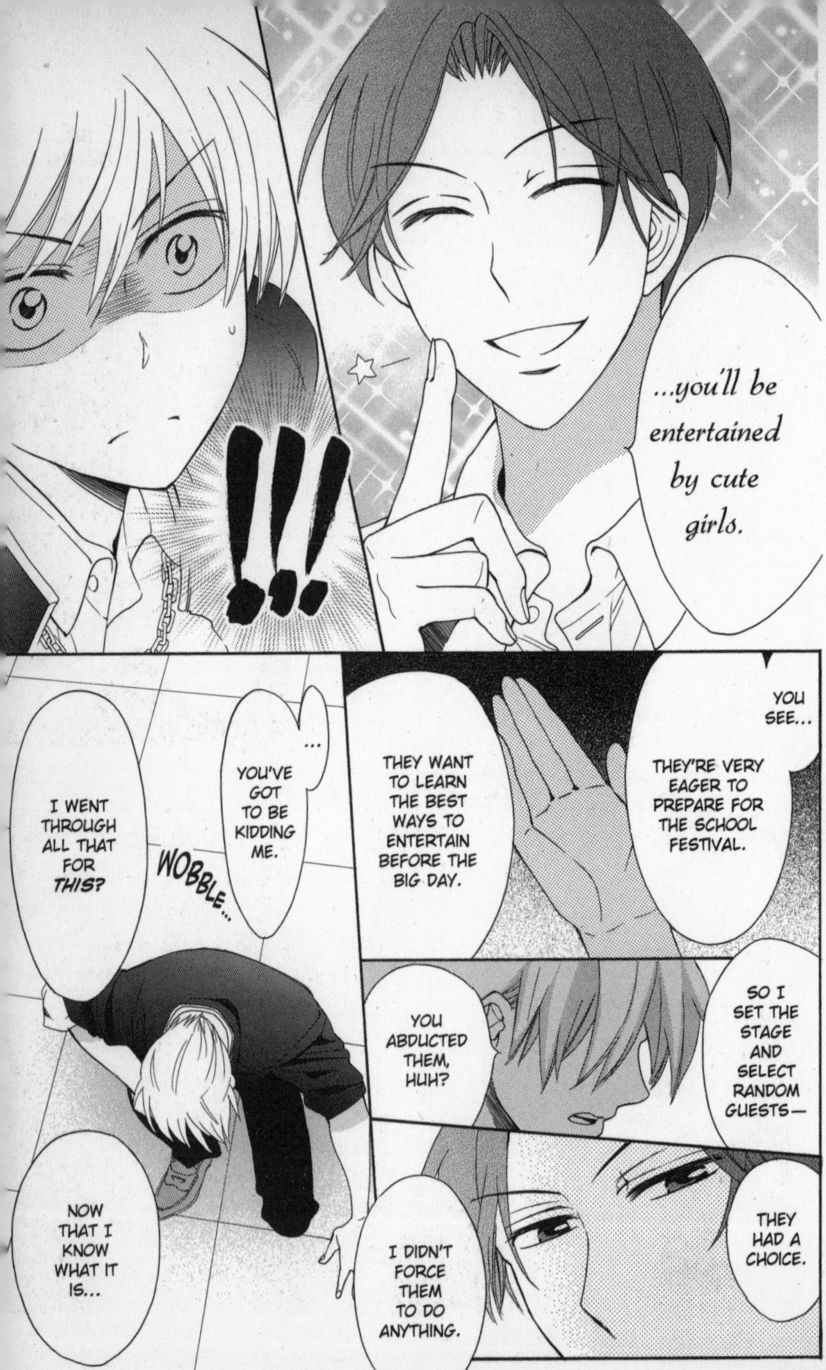
...you'll be entertained by cute girls.
!!!
YOU SEE...
THEY'RE VERY EAGER TO PREPARE FOR THE SCHOOL FESTIVAL.
THEY WANT TO LEARN THE BEST WAYS TO ENTERTAIN BEFORE THE BIG DAY.
SO I SET THE STAGE AND SELECT RANDOM GUESTS—
YOU ABDUCTED THEM, HUH?
THEY HAD A CHOICE.
I DIDN'T FORCE THEM TO DO ANYTHING.
...
YOU'VE GOT TO BE KIDDING ME.
WOBBLE...
I WENT THROUGH ALL THAT FOR *THIS?*
NOW THAT I KNOW WHAT IT IS...

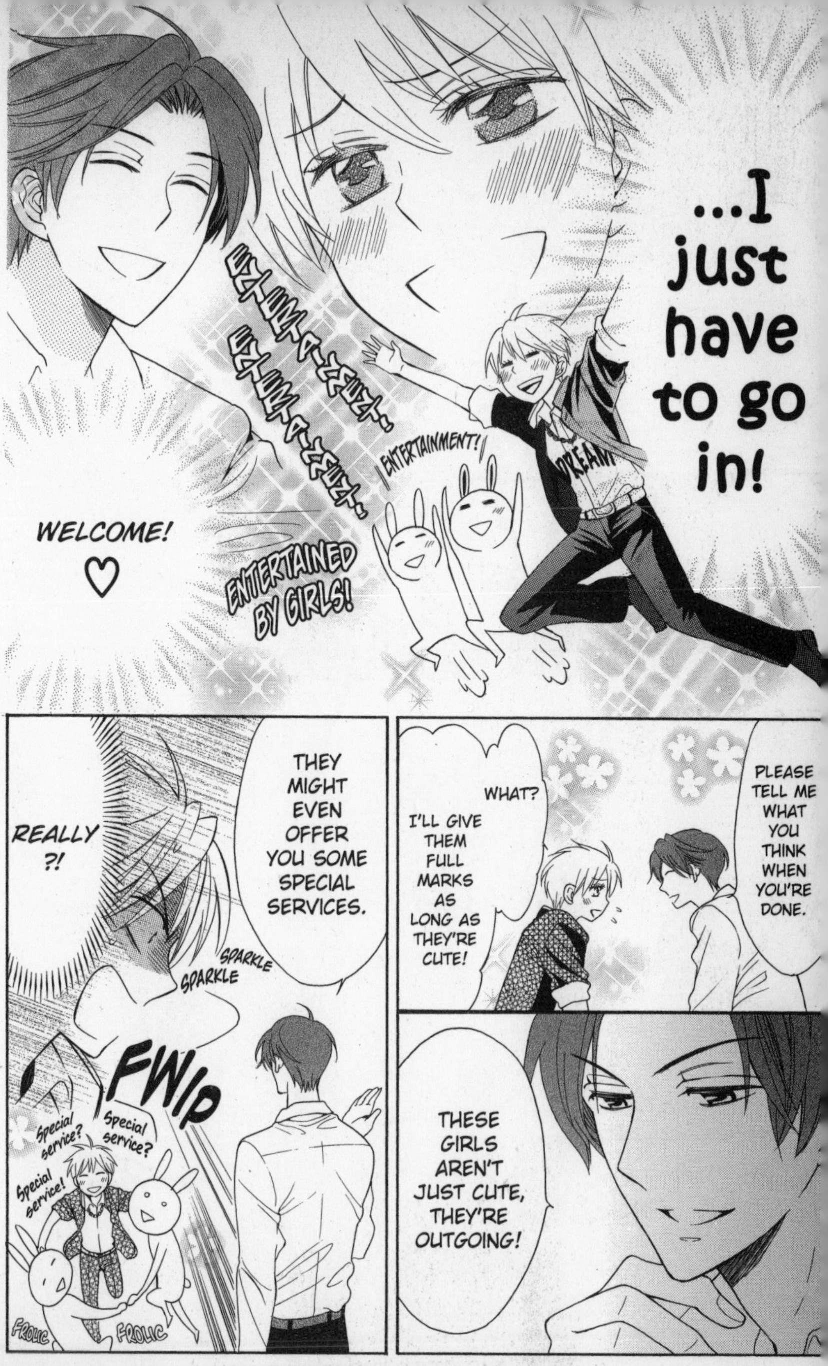
...I just have to go in!
ENTERTAINMENT!
ENTERTAINED BY GIRLS!
WELCOME! ♡
PLEASE TELL ME WHAT YOU THINK WHEN YOU'RE DONE.
WHAT?
I'LL GIVE THEM FULL MARKS AS LONG AS THEY'RE CUTE!
THESE GIRLS AREN'T JUST CUTE, THEY'RE OUTGOING!
THEY MIGHT EVEN OFFER YOU SOME SPECIAL SERVICES.
REALLY?!
SPARKLE
SPARKLE
FWIP
Special service?
Special service?
Special service!
FROLIC
FROLIC

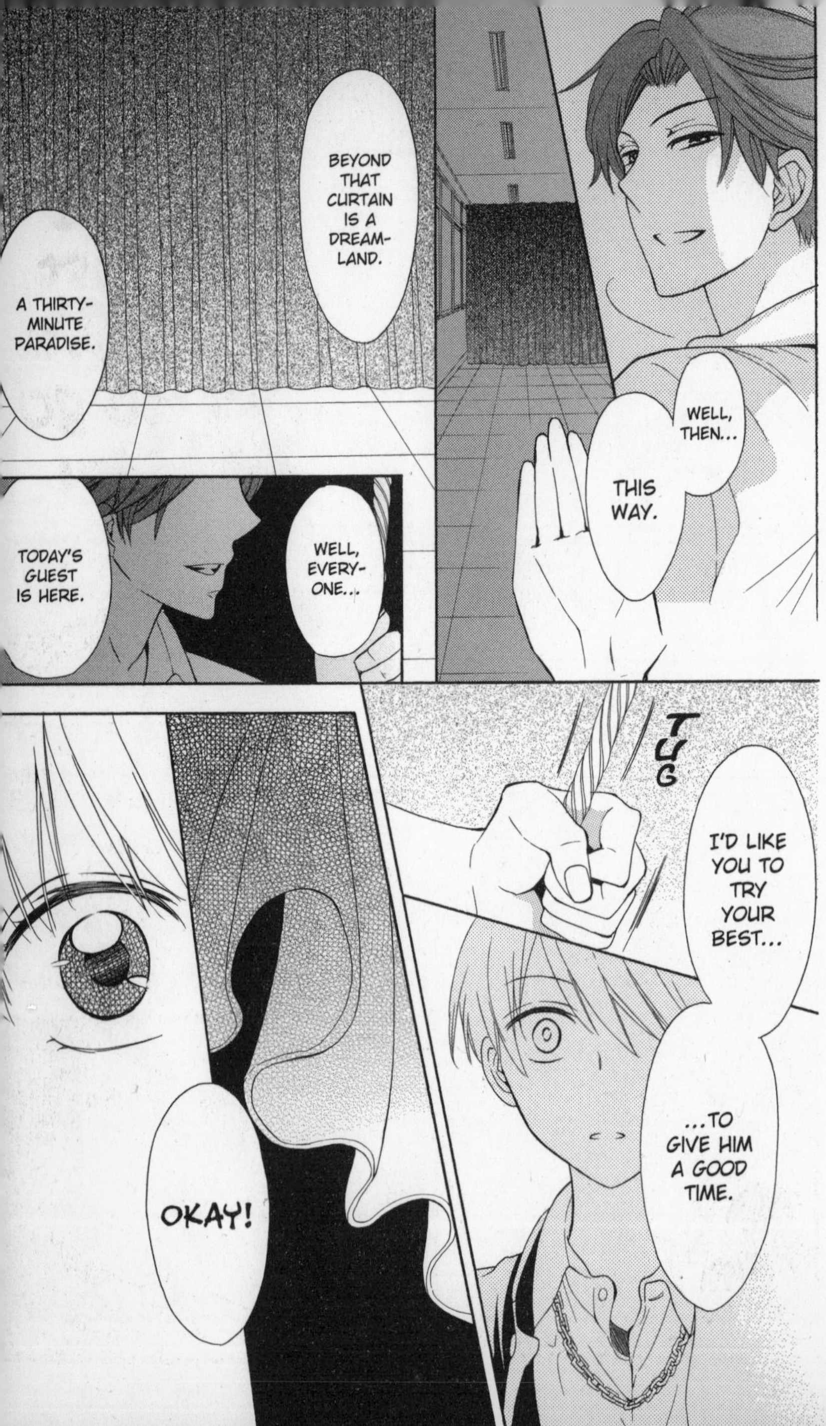

WELL, THEN...
THIS WAY.
BEYOND THAT CURTAIN IS A DREAM-LAND.
A THIRTY-MINUTE PARADISE.
WELL, EVERYONE...
TODAY'S GUEST IS HERE.
TUG
I'D LIKE YOU TO TRY YOUR BEST...
...TO GIVE HIM A GOOD TIME.
OKAY!

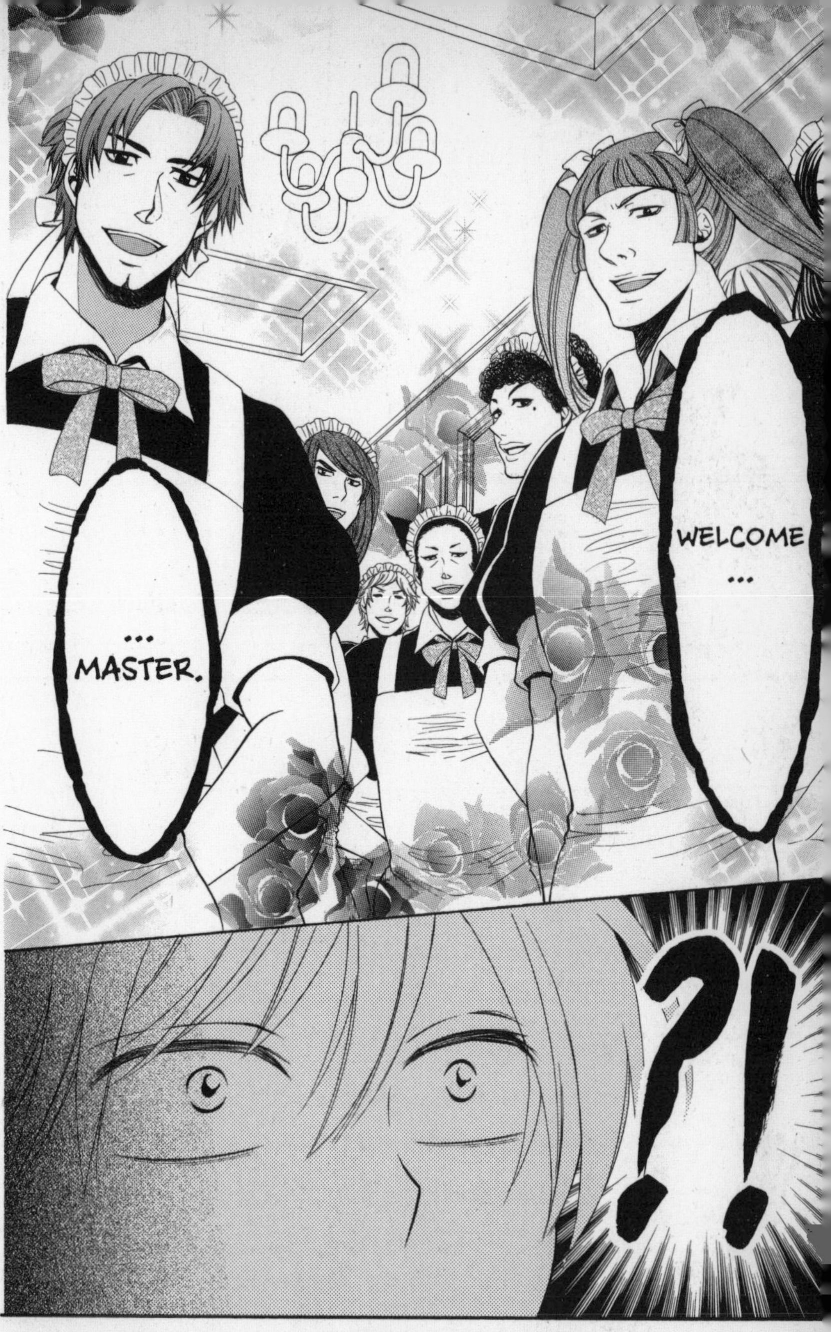
WELCOME ...
... MASTER.
?!

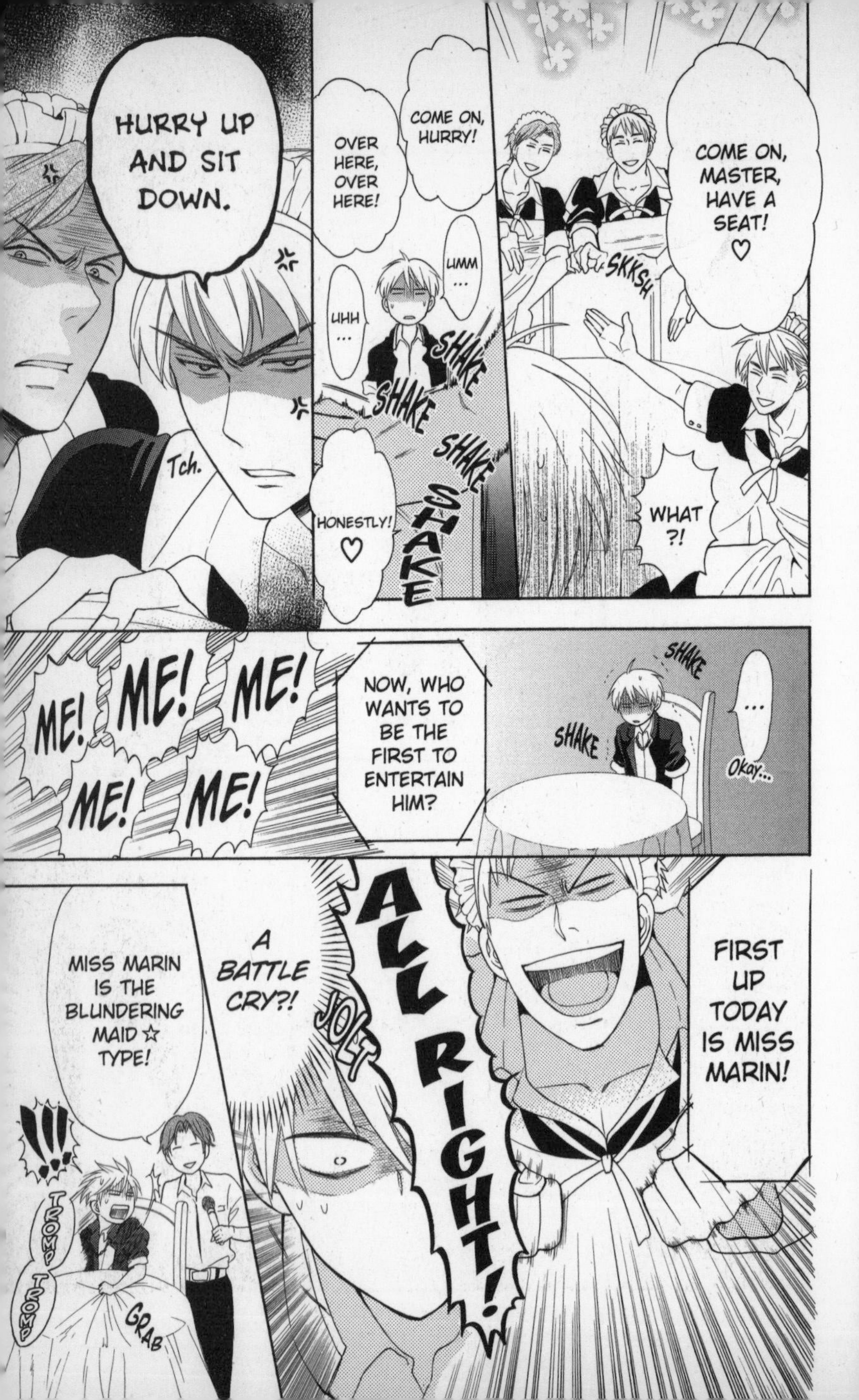
COME ON, MASTER, HAVE A SEAT! ♡
SKKSH
WHAT?!
COME ON, HURRY!
OVER HERE, OVER HERE!
UMM ...
UHH ...
SHAKE
SHAKE
SHAKE
SHAKE
HONESTLY! ♡
HURRY UP AND SIT DOWN.
Tch.
SHAKE
...
SHAKE
Okay...
NOW, WHO WANTS TO BE THE FIRST TO ENTERTAIN HIM?
ME!
ME!
ME!
ME!
ME!
FIRST UP TODAY IS MISS MARIN!
ALL RIGHT!
JOLT
A BATTLE CRY?!
MISS MARIN IS THE BLUNDERING MAID☆ TYPE!
!!!
TROMP
TROMP
GRAB

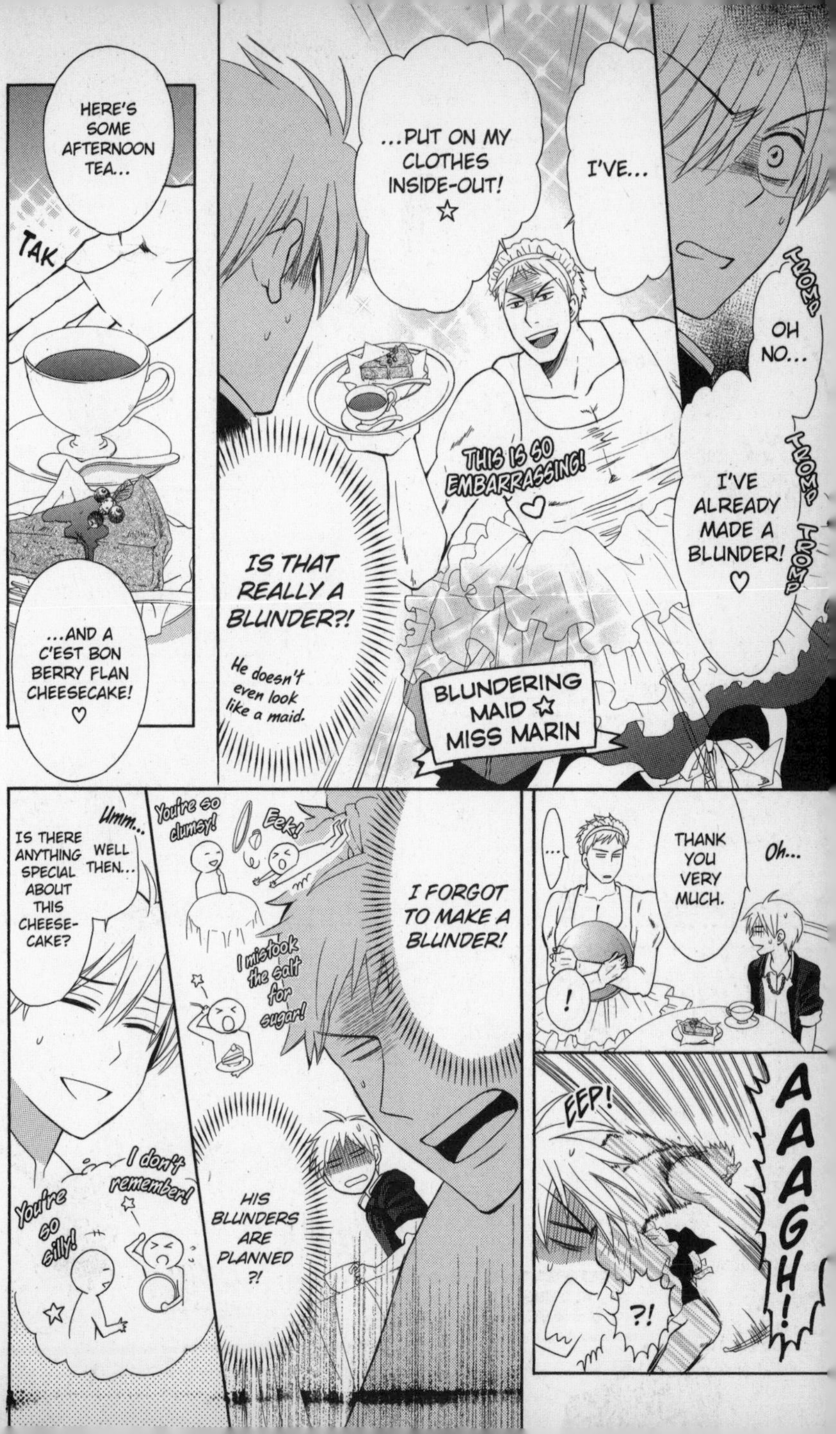
TROMP
OH NO...
TROMP
I'VE ALREADY MADE A BLUNDER! ♡
TROMP
I'VE...
...PUT ON MY CLOTHES INSIDE-OUT! ☆
THIS IS SO EMBARRASSING! ♡
BLUNDERING MAID ☆ MISS MARIN
IS THAT REALLY A BLUNDER?!
He doesn't even look like a maid.
HERE'S SOME AFTERNOON TEA...
TAK
...AND A C'EST BON BERRY FLAN CHEESECAKE! ♡
Oh...
THANK YOU VERY MUCH.
...
!
AAAAGH!
EEP!
?!
I FORGOT TO MAKE A BLUNDER!
Eek!
You're so clumsy!
I mistook the salt for sugar!
HIS BLUNDERS ARE PLANNED?!
Umm...
WELL THEN...
IS THERE ANYTHING SPECIAL ABOUT THIS CHEESECAKE?
I don't remember!
You're so silly!

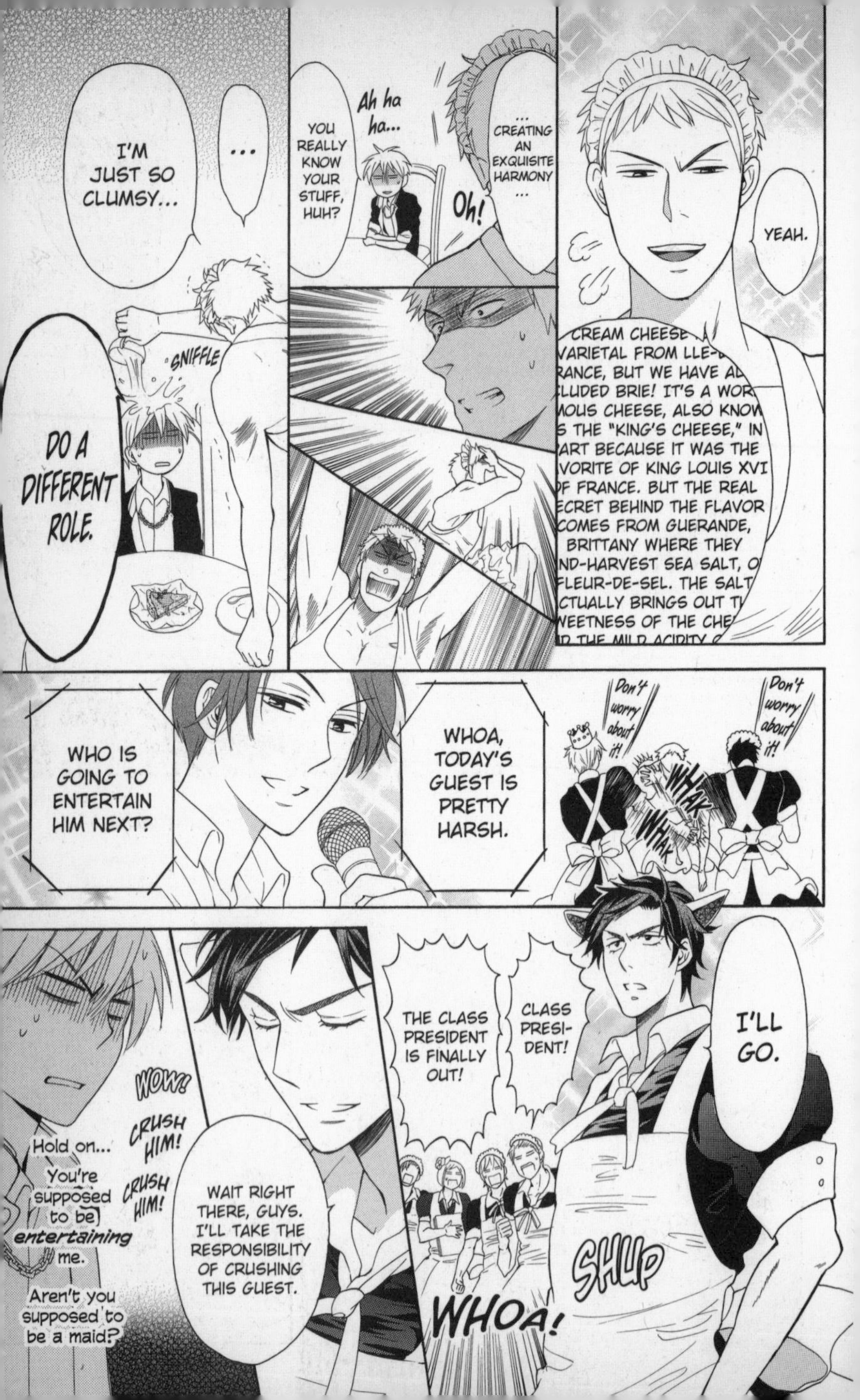
YEAH.
CREAM CHEESE
VARIETAL FROM LLE-
RANCE, BUT WE HAVE AL
CLUDED BRIE! IT'S A WOR
MOUS CHEESE, ALSO KNOW
S THE "KING'S CHEESE," IN
PART BECAUSE IT WAS THE
AVORITE OF KING LOUIS XVI
OF FRANCE. BUT THE REAL
ECRET BEHIND THE FLAVOR
COMES FROM GUERANDE,
BRITTANY WHERE THEY
ND-HARVEST SEA SALT, O
FLEUR-DE-SEL. THE SALT
CTUALLY BRINGS OUT T
WEETNESS OF THE CHE
... CREATING AN EXQUISITE HARMONY ...
Oh!
Ah ha ha...
YOU REALLY KNOW YOUR STUFF, HUH?
...
I'M JUST SO CLUMSY...
SNIFFLE
DO A DIFFERENT ROLE.
Don't worry about it!
Don't worry about it!
WHAK
WHAK
WHOA, TODAY'S GUEST IS PRETTY HARSH.
WHO IS GOING TO ENTERTAIN HIM NEXT?
I'LL GO.
CLASS PRESIDENT!
THE CLASS PRESIDENT IS FINALLY OUT!
SHUP
WHOA!
WAIT RIGHT THERE, GUYS. I'LL TAKE THE RESPONSIBILITY OF CRUSHING THIS GUEST.
WOW!
CRUSH HIM!
CRUSH HIM!
Hold on... You're supposed to be *entertaining* me.
Aren't you supposed to be a maid?

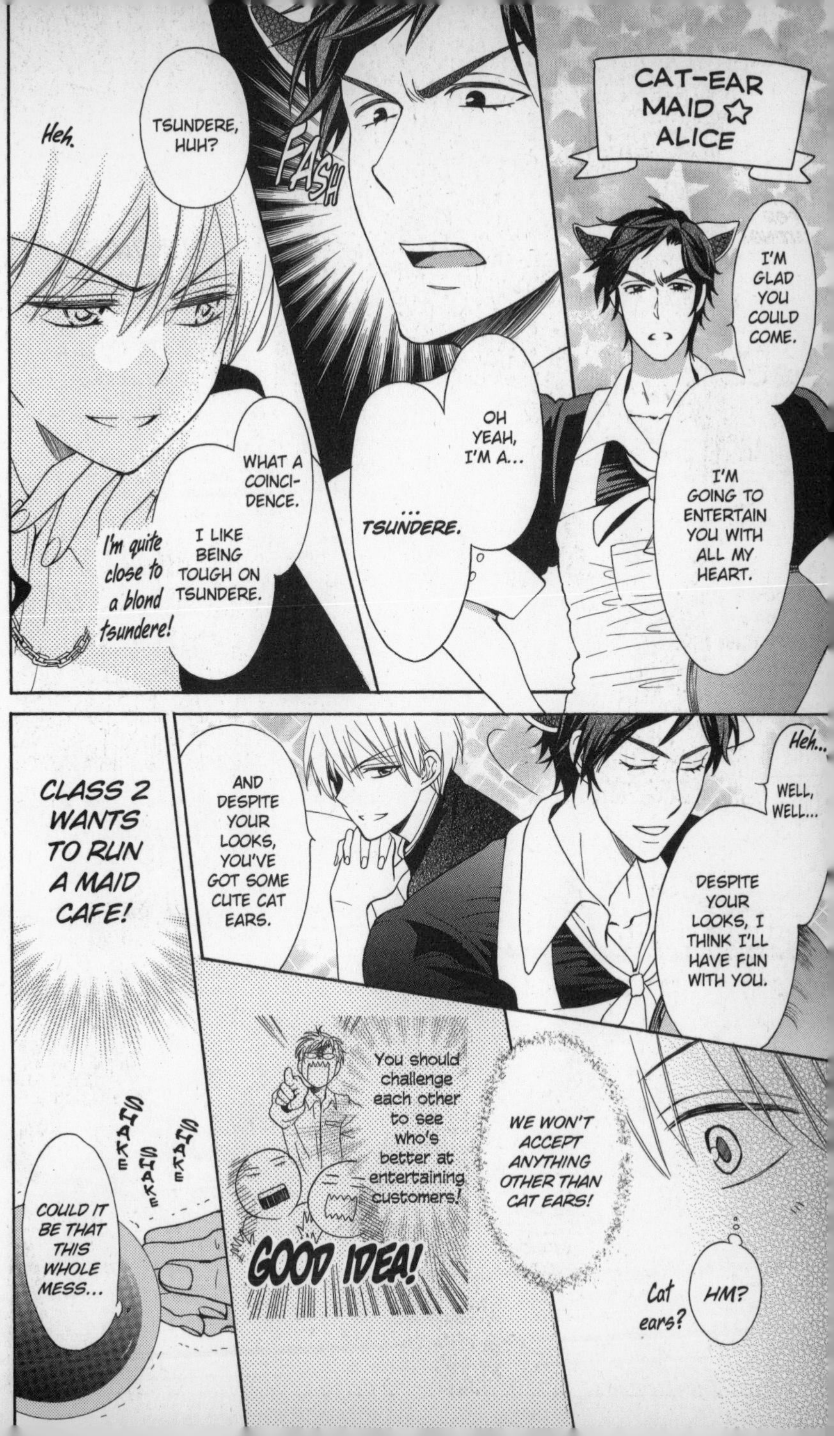
CAT-EAR MAID ☆ ALICE
I'M GLAD YOU COULD COME.
I'M GOING TO ENTERTAIN YOU WITH ALL MY HEART.
FASH
OH YEAH, I'M A...
...TSUNDERE.
TSUNDERE, HUH?
Heh.
WHAT A COINCIDENCE.
I LIKE BEING TOUGH ON TSUNDERE.
I'm quite close to a blond tsundere!
Heh...
WELL, WELL...
DESPITE YOUR LOOKS, I THINK I'LL HAVE FUN WITH YOU.
AND DESPITE YOUR LOOKS, YOU'VE GOT SOME CUTE CAT EARS.
CLASS 2 WANTS TO RUN A MAID CAFE!
HM?
Cat ears?
WE WON'T ACCEPT ANYTHING OTHER THAN CAT EARS!
You should challenge each other to see who's better at entertaining customers!
GOOD IDEA!
SHAKE
SHAKE
SHAKE
COULD IT BE THAT THIS WHOLE MESS...

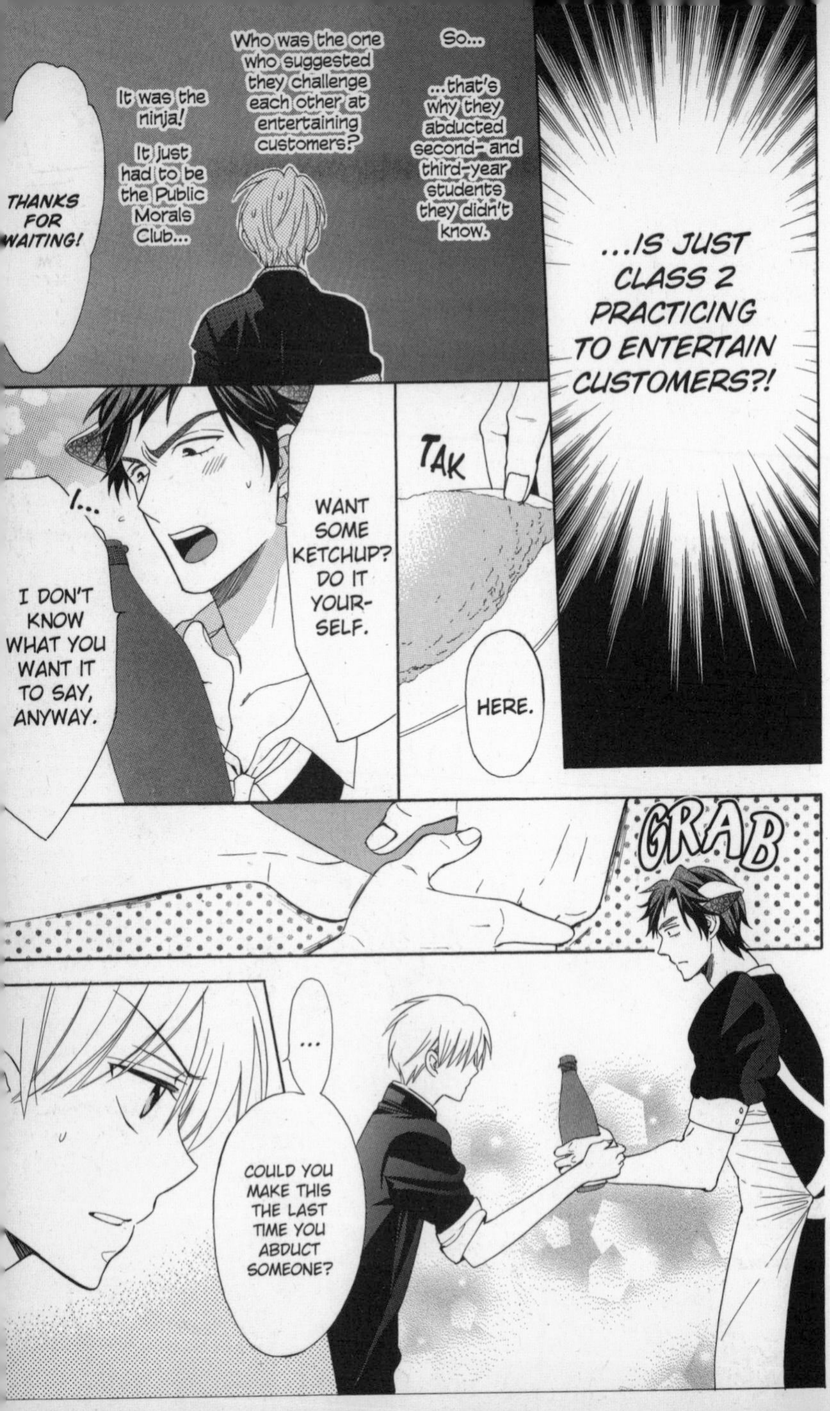
...IS JUST CLASS 2 PRACTICING TO ENTERTAIN CUSTOMERS?!
So...
...that's why they abducted second- and third-year students they didn't know.
Who was the one who suggested they challenge each other at entertaining customers?
It was the ninja!
It just had to be the Public Morals Club...
THANKS FOR WAITING!
TAK
HERE.
WANT SOME KETCHUP? DO IT YOURSELF.
I...
I DON'T KNOW WHAT YOU WANT IT TO SAY, ANYWAY.
GRAB
...
COULD YOU MAKE THIS THE LAST TIME YOU ABDUCT SOMEONE?

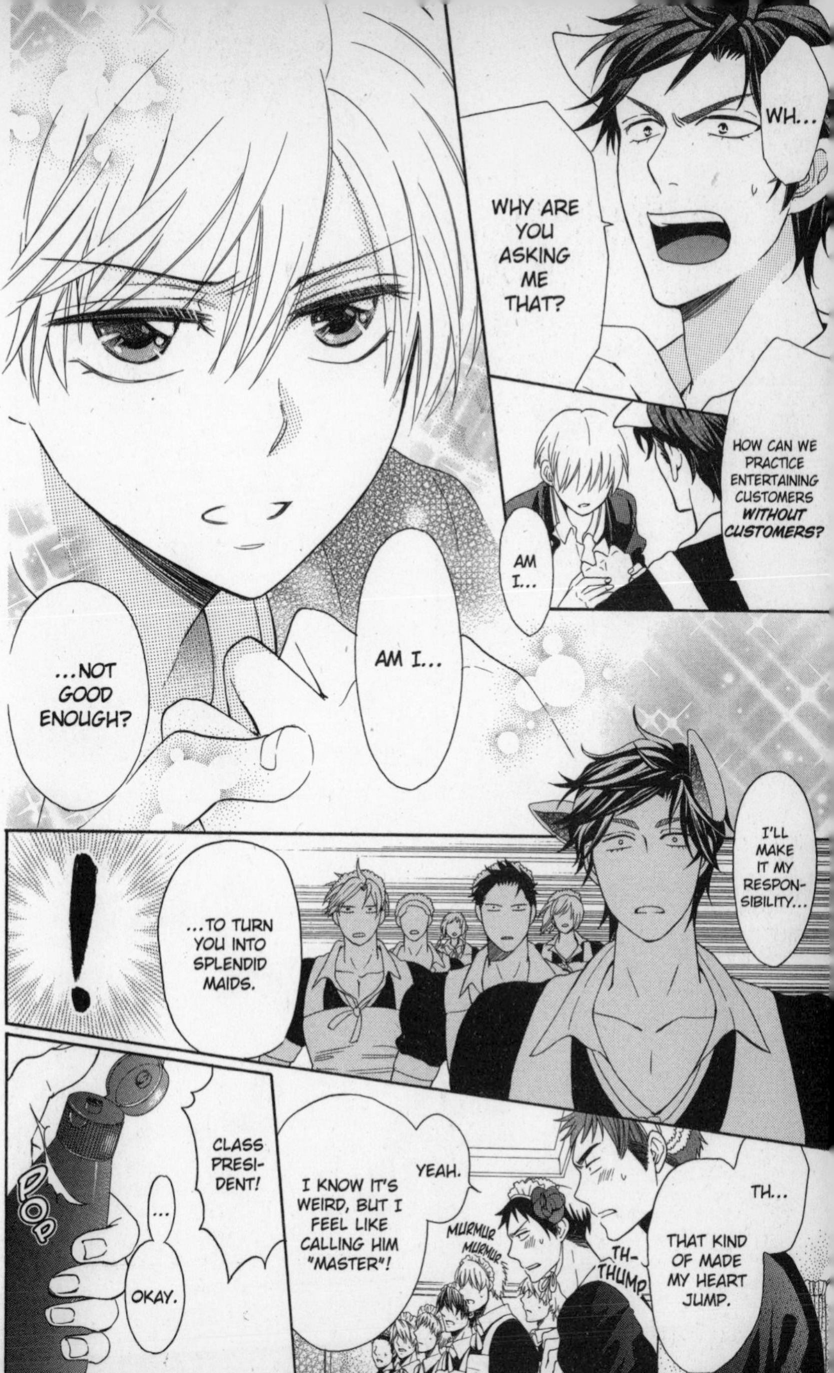
WH...
WHY ARE YOU ASKING ME THAT?
HOW CAN WE PRACTICE ENTERTAINING CUSTOMERS *WITHOUT CUSTOMERS?*
AM I...
AM I...
...NOT GOOD ENOUGH?
I'LL MAKE IT MY RESPONSIBILITY...
...TO TURN YOU INTO SPLENDID MAIDS.
!
TH...
THAT KIND OF MADE MY HEART JUMP.
TH-THUMP
MURMUR MURMUR
YEAH.
I KNOW IT'S WEIRD, BUT I FEEL LIKE CALLING HIM "MASTER"!
CLASS PRESIDENT!
...
OKAY.
POP

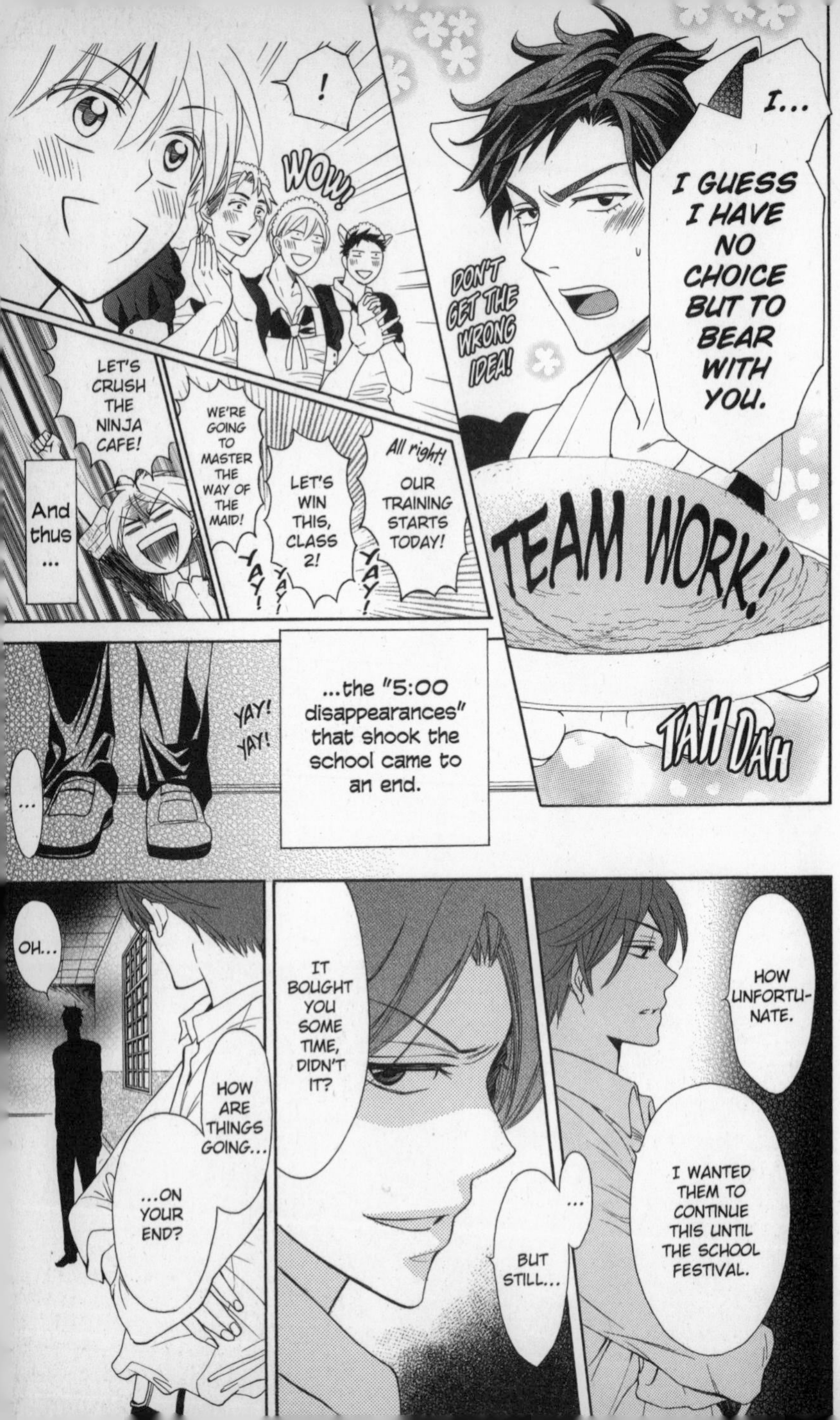
I...
I GUESS I HAVE NO CHOICE BUT TO BEAR WITH YOU.
DON'T GET THE WRONG IDEA!
TEAM WORK!
TAH DAH
!
WOW!
All right!
OUR TRAINING STARTS TODAY!
YAY!
LET'S WIN THIS, CLASS 2!
YAY!
YAY!
WE'RE GOING TO MASTER THE WAY OF THE MAID!
LET'S CRUSH THE NINJA CAFE!
And thus ...
...the "5:00 disappearances" that shook the school came to an end.
YAY! YAY!
...
HOW UNFORTU-NATE.
I WANTED THEM TO CONTINUE THIS UNTIL THE SCHOOL FESTIVAL.
...
BUT STILL...
IT BOUGHT YOU SOME TIME, DIDN'T IT?
OH...
HOW ARE THINGS GOING...
...ON YOUR END?

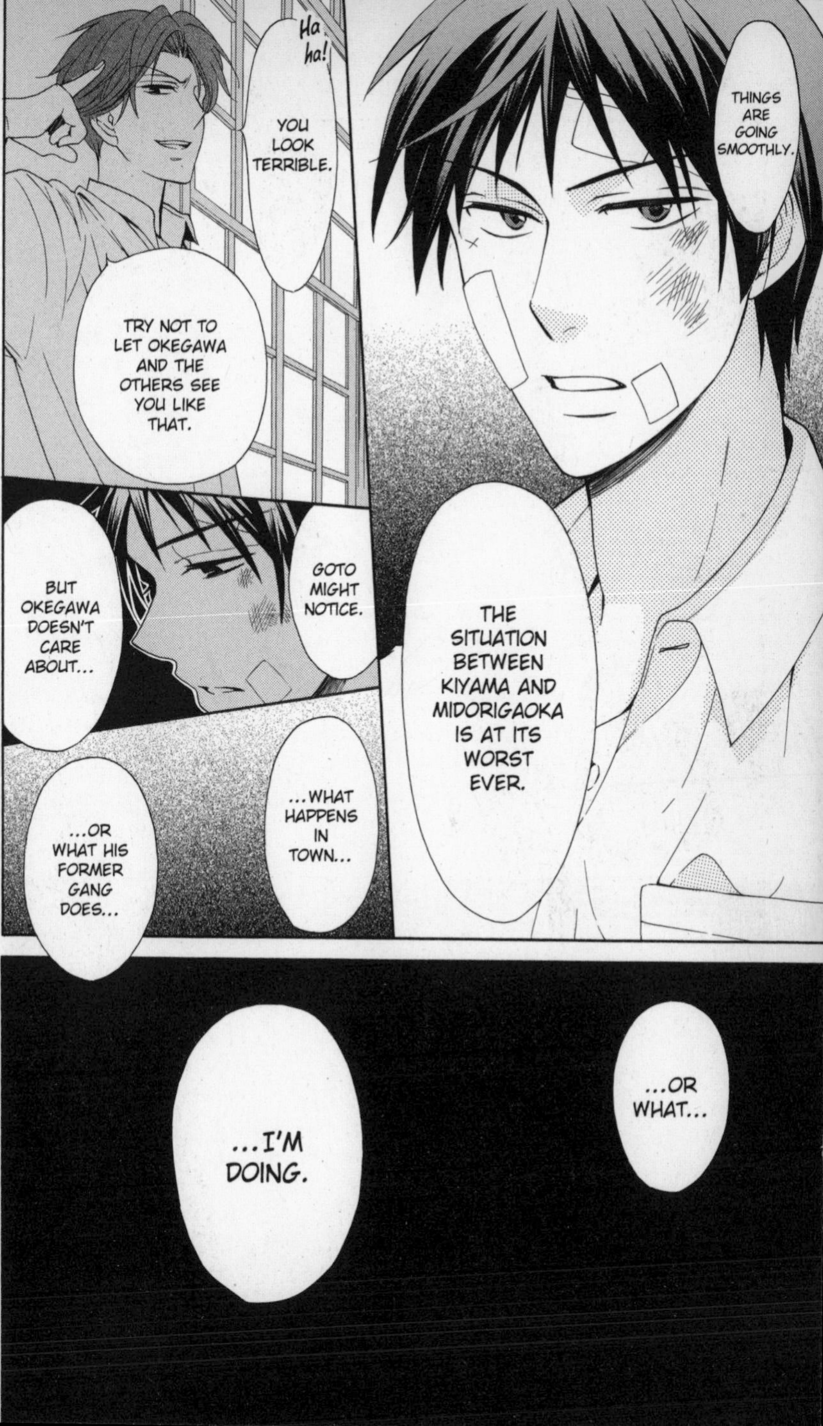
THINGS ARE GOING SMOOTHLY.
THE SITUATION BETWEEN KIYAMA AND MIDORIGAOKA IS AT ITS WORST EVER.
Ha ha!
YOU LOOK TERRIBLE.
TRY NOT TO LET OKEGAWA AND THE OTHERS SEE YOU LIKE THAT.
GOTO MIGHT NOTICE.
BUT OKEGAWA DOESN'T CARE ABOUT...
...WHAT HAPPENS IN TOWN...
...OR WHAT HIS FORMER GANG DOES...
...OR WHAT...
...I'M DOING.

Chapter 47

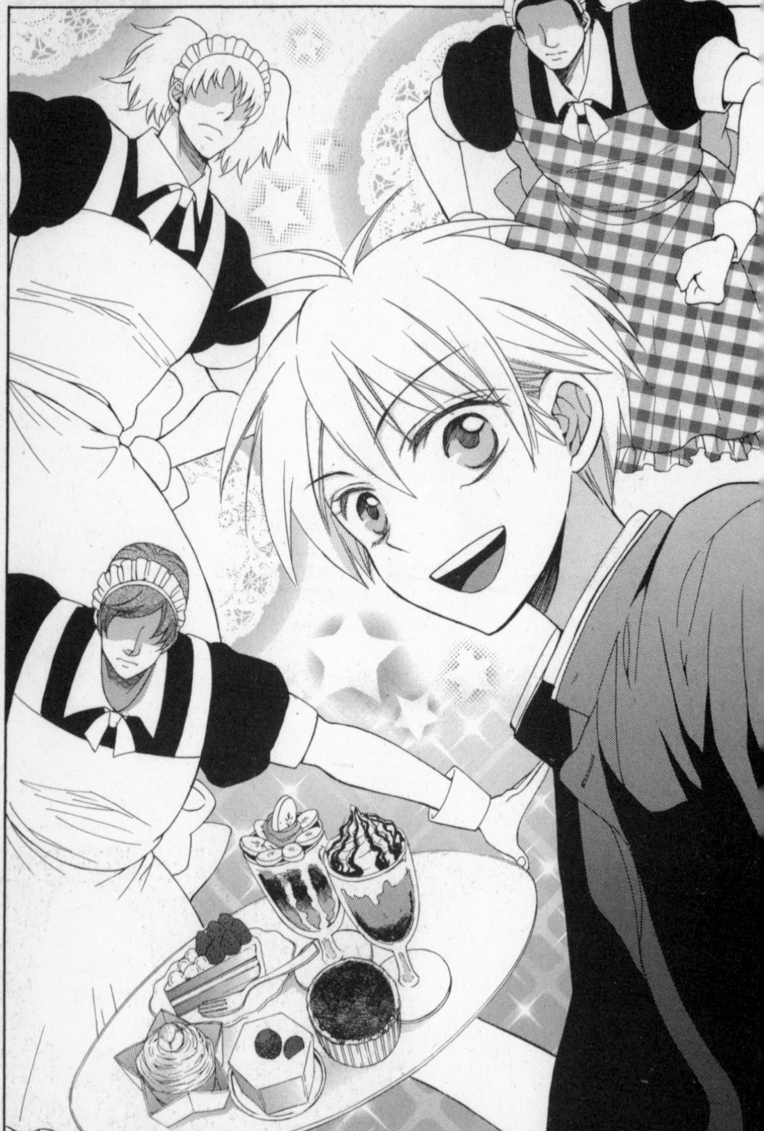

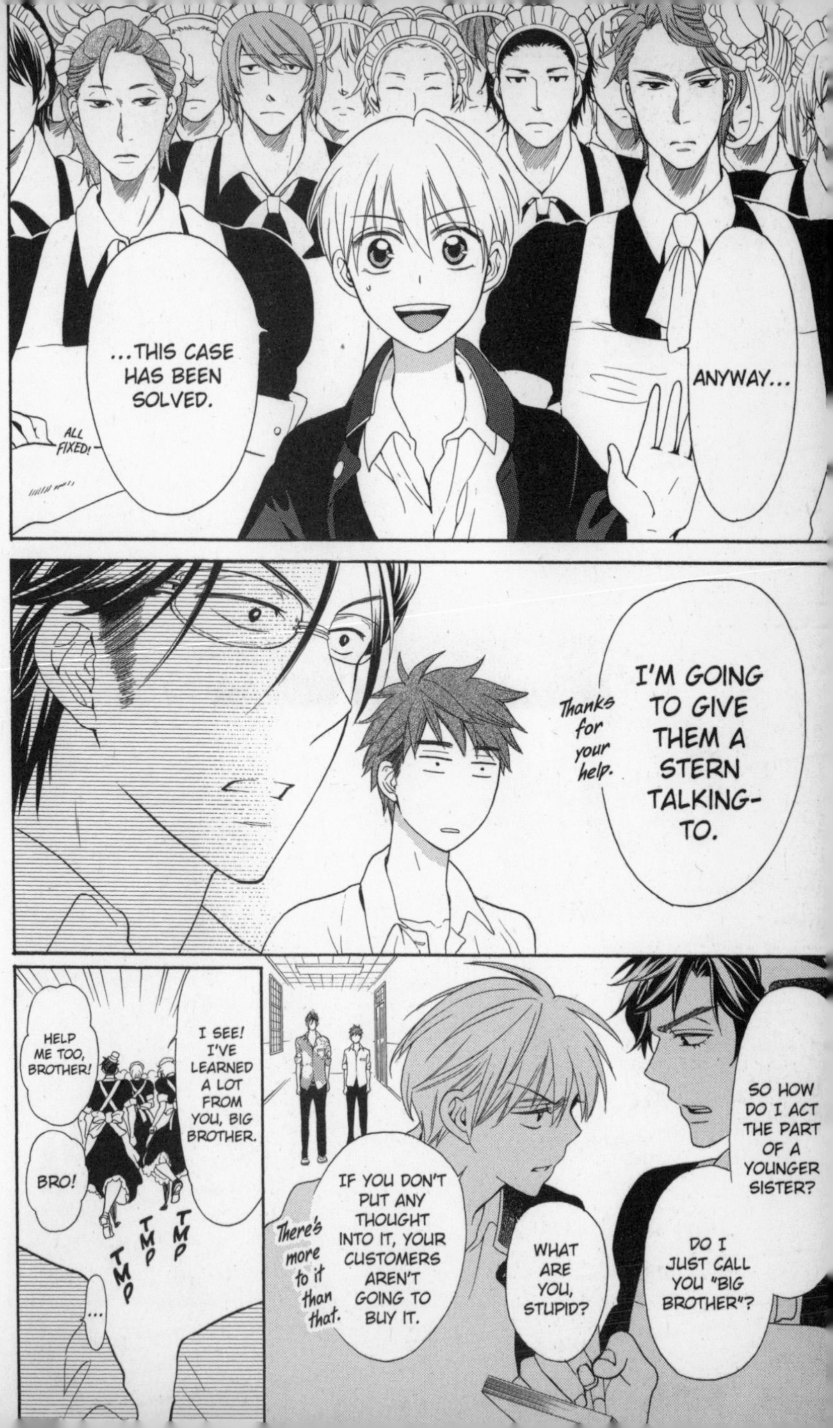
ANYWAY...
...THIS CASE HAS BEEN SOLVED.
ALL FIXED!
I'M GOING TO GIVE THEM A STERN TALKING-TO.
Thanks for your help.
SO HOW DO I ACT THE PART OF A YOUNGER SISTER?
DO I JUST CALL YOU "BIG BROTHER"?
WHAT ARE YOU, STUPID?
IF YOU DON'T PUT ANY THOUGHT INTO IT, YOUR CUSTOMERS AREN'T GOING TO BUY IT.
There's more to it than that.
I SEE! I'VE LEARNED A LOT FROM YOU, BIG BROTHER.
HELP ME TOO, BROTHER!
BRO!
TMP TMP TMP
...

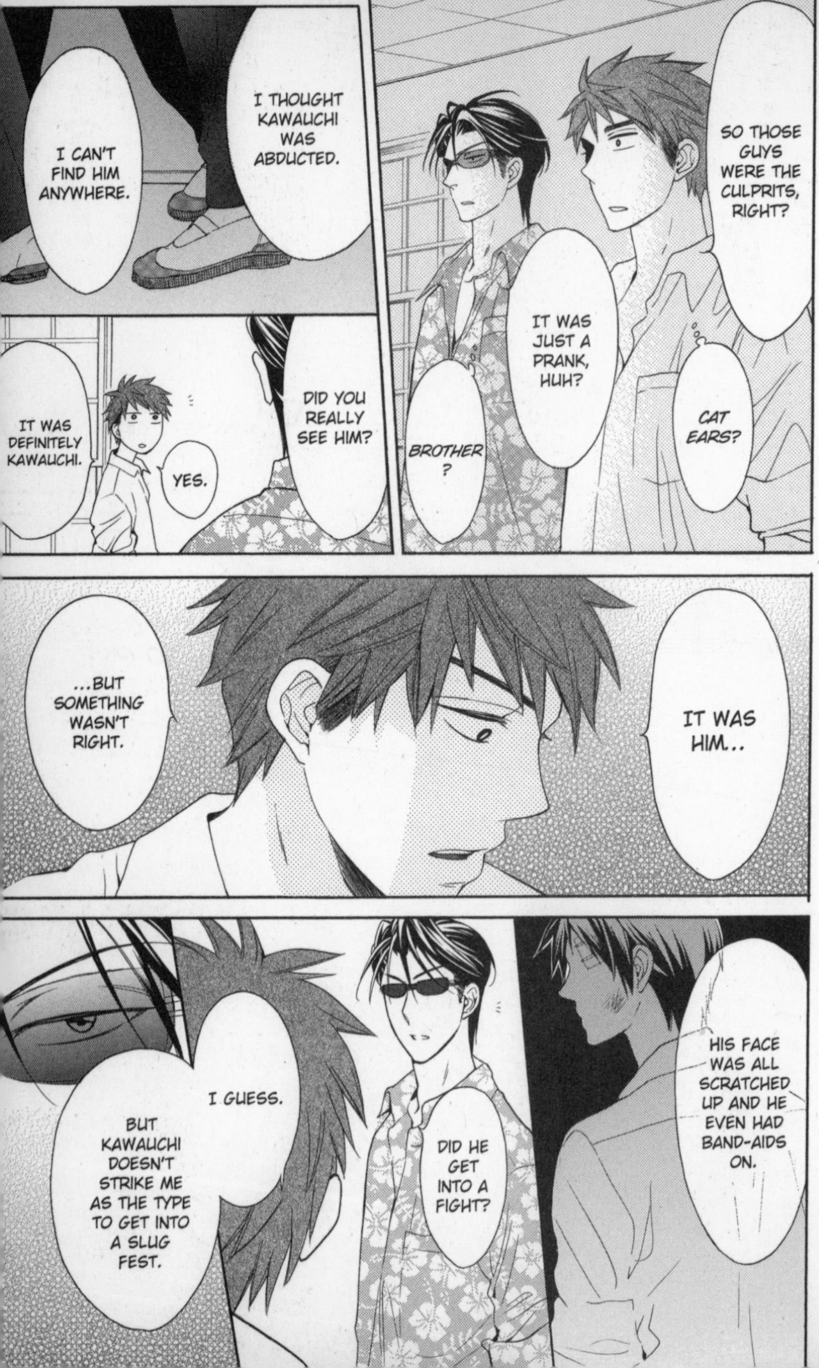
SO THOSE GUYS WERE THE CULPRITS, RIGHT?
CAT EARS?
IT WAS JUST A PRANK, HUH?
BROTHER?
I THOUGHT KAWAUCHI WAS ABDUCTED.
I CAN'T FIND HIM ANYWHERE.
DID YOU REALLY SEE HIM?
YES.
IT WAS DEFINITELY KAWAUCHI.
IT WAS HIM...
...BUT SOMETHING WASN'T RIGHT.
HIS FACE WAS ALL SCRATCHED UP AND HE EVEN HAD BAND-AIDS ON.
DID HE GET INTO A FIGHT?
I GUESS.
BUT KAWAUCHI DOESN'T STRIKE ME AS THE TYPE TO GET INTO A SLUG FEST.

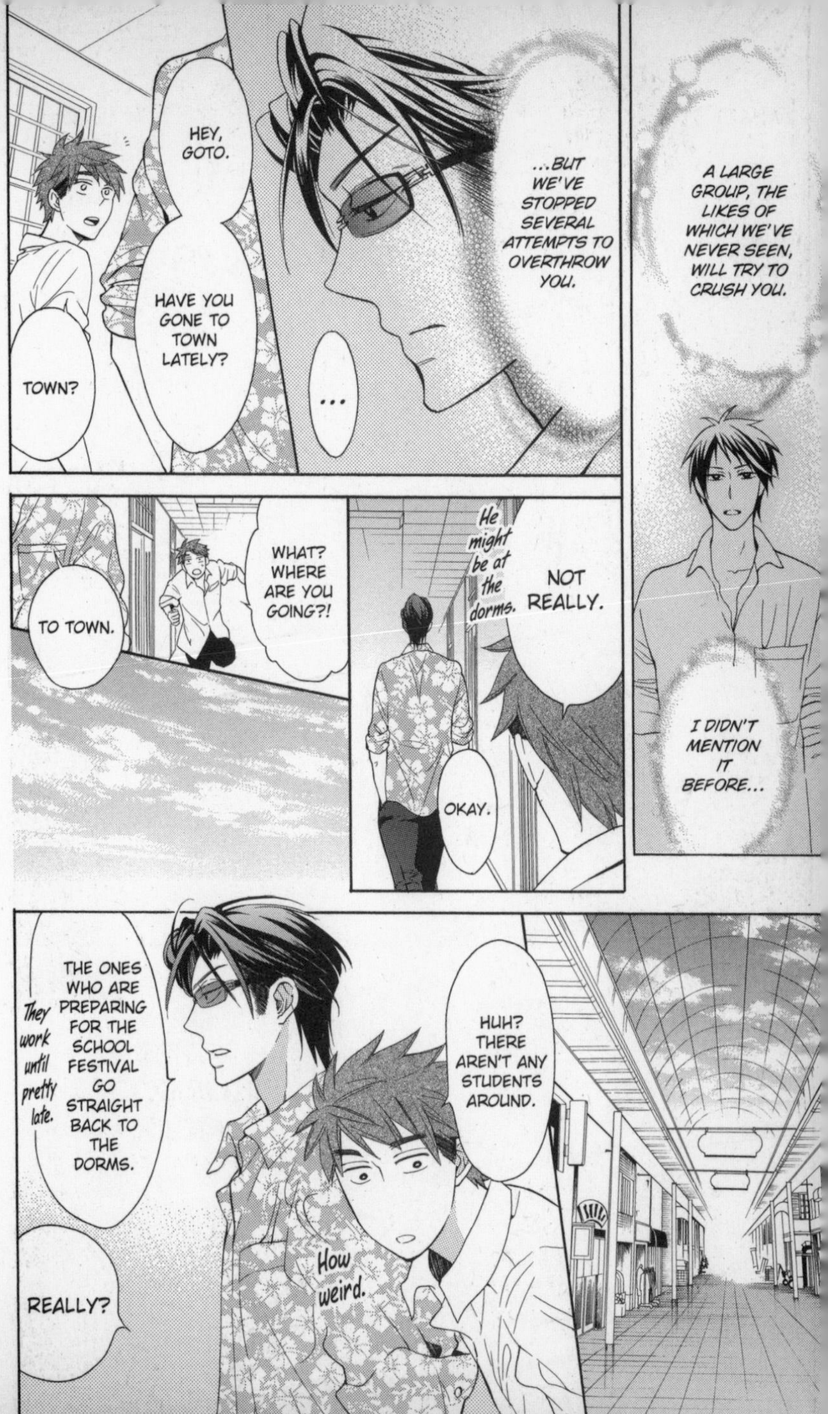
A LARGE GROUP, THE LIKES OF WHICH WE'VE NEVER SEEN, WILL TRY TO CRUSH YOU.
I DIDN'T MENTION IT BEFORE...
...BUT WE'VE STOPPED SEVERAL ATTEMPTS TO OVERTHROW YOU.
...
HEY, GOTO.
HAVE YOU GONE TO TOWN LATELY?
TOWN?
He might be at the dorms.
NOT REALLY.
OKAY.
WHAT? WHERE ARE YOU GOING?!
TO TOWN.
HUH? THERE AREN'T ANY STUDENTS AROUND.
How weird.
THE ONES WHO ARE PREPARING FOR THE SCHOOL FESTIVAL GO STRAIGHT BACK TO THE DORMS.
They work until pretty late.
REALLY?

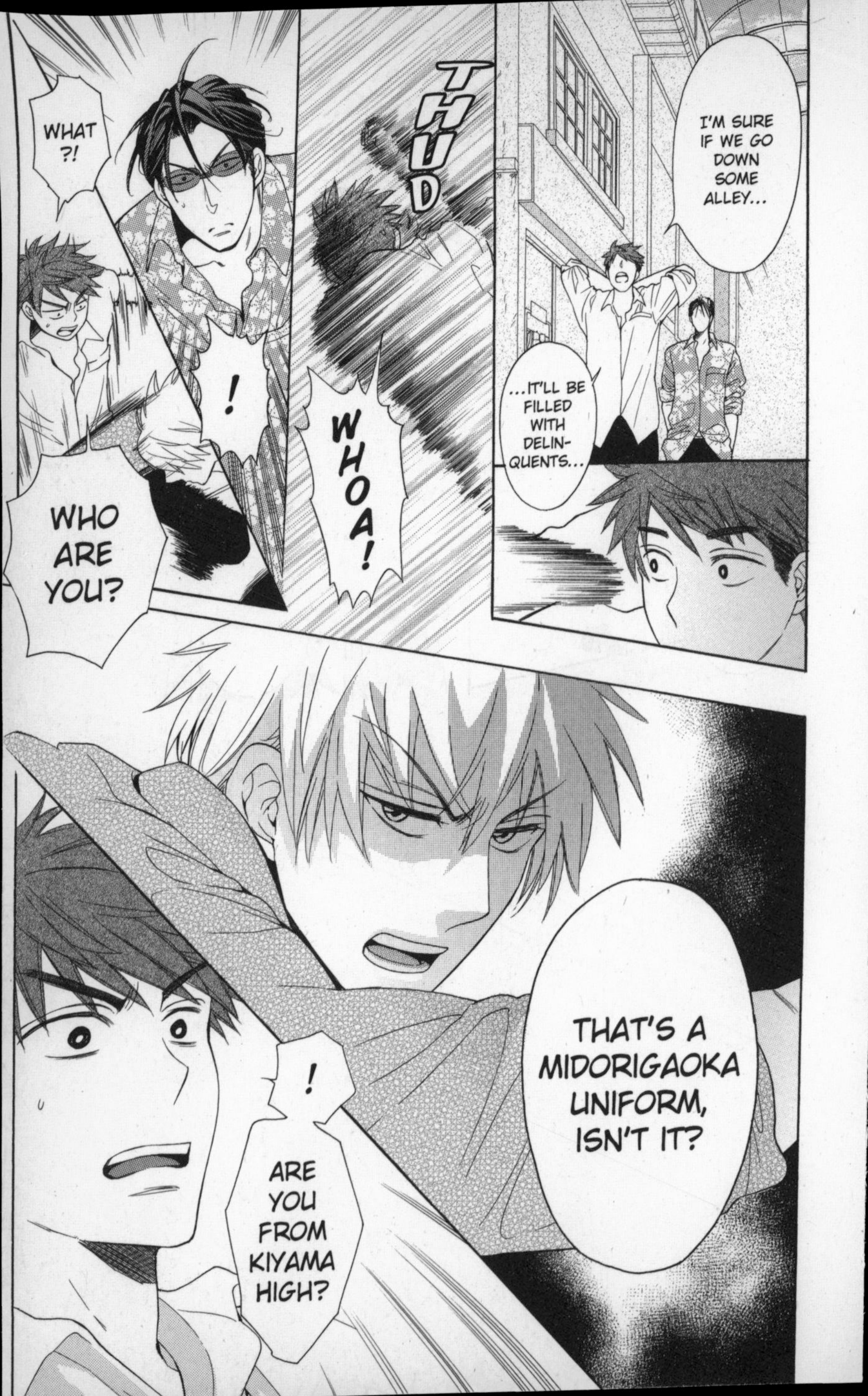
I'M SURE IF WE GO DOWN SOME ALLEY...
...IT'LL BE FILLED WITH DELIN-QUENTS...
THUD
WHOA!
WHAT?!
!
WHO ARE YOU?
THAT'S A MIDORIGAOKA UNIFORM, ISN'T IT?
!
ARE YOU FROM KIYAMA HIGH?

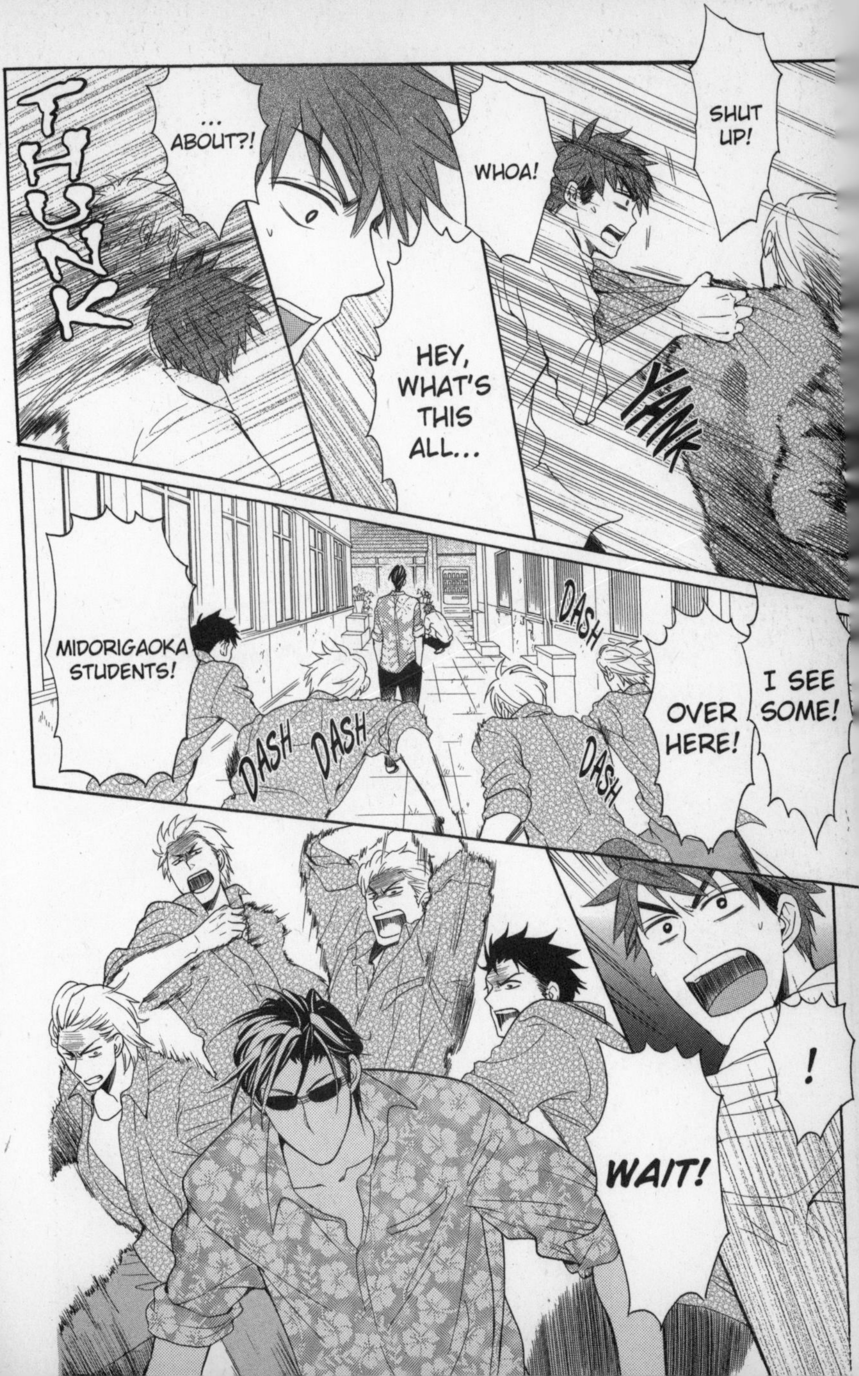
SHUT UP!
WHOA!
YANK
HEY, WHAT'S THIS ALL...
... ABOUT?!
THUNK
I SEE SOME!
OVER HERE!
DASH
DASH
DASH
DASH
DASH
MIDORIGAOKA STUDENTS!
!
WAIT!

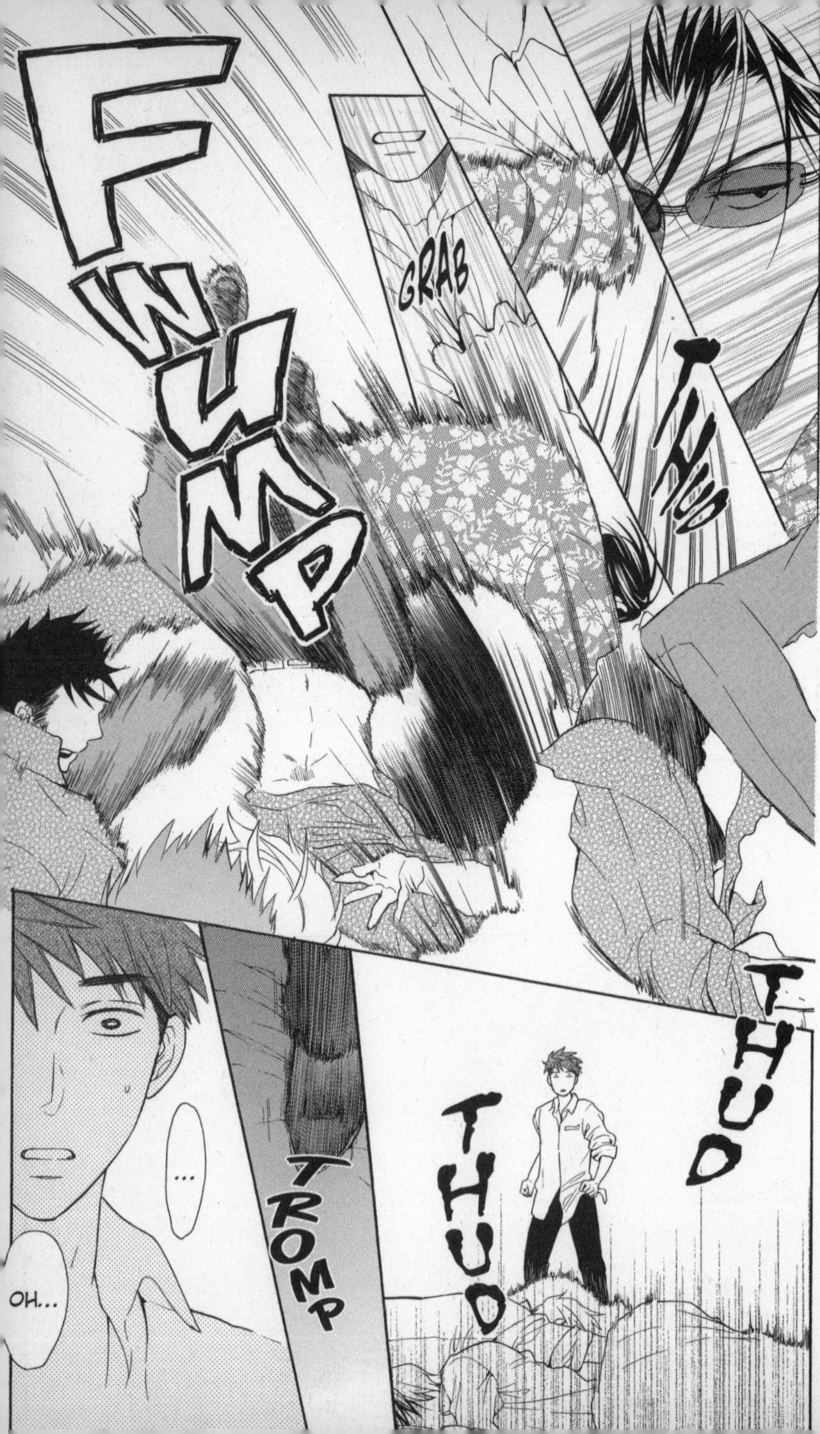
THUD
GRAB
FWUMP
THUD
THUD
TROMP
...
OH...

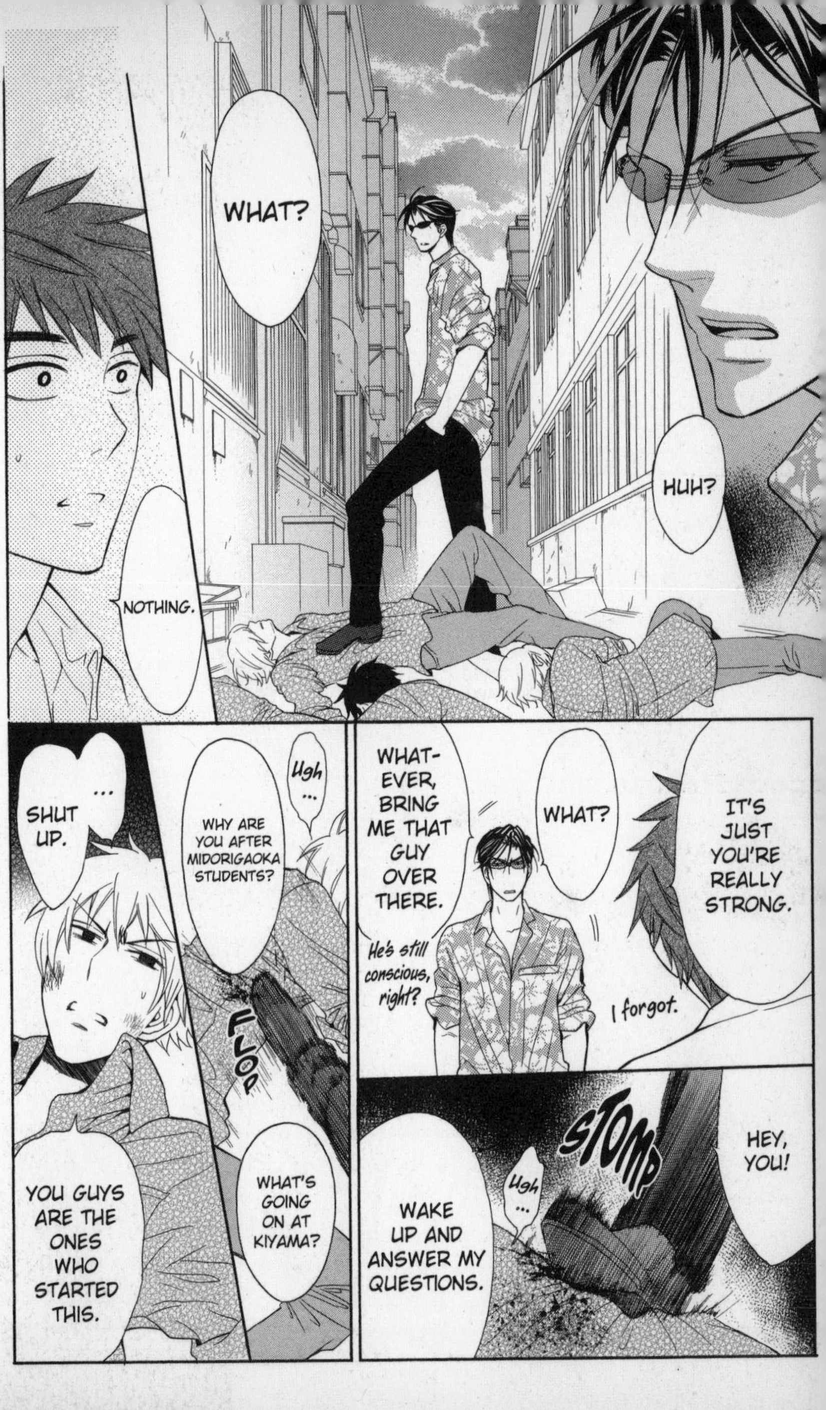
HUH?
WHAT?
NOTHING.
IT'S JUST YOU'RE REALLY STRONG.
I forgot.
WHAT?
WHAT-EVER, BRING ME THAT GUY OVER THERE.
He's still conscious, right?
HEY, YOU!
STOMP
Ugh ...
WAKE UP AND ANSWER MY QUESTIONS.
Ugh ...
WHY ARE YOU AFTER MIDORIGAOKA STUDENTS?
... SHUT UP.
FLOP
WHAT'S GOING ON AT KIYAMA?
YOU GUYS ARE THE ONES WHO STARTED THIS.

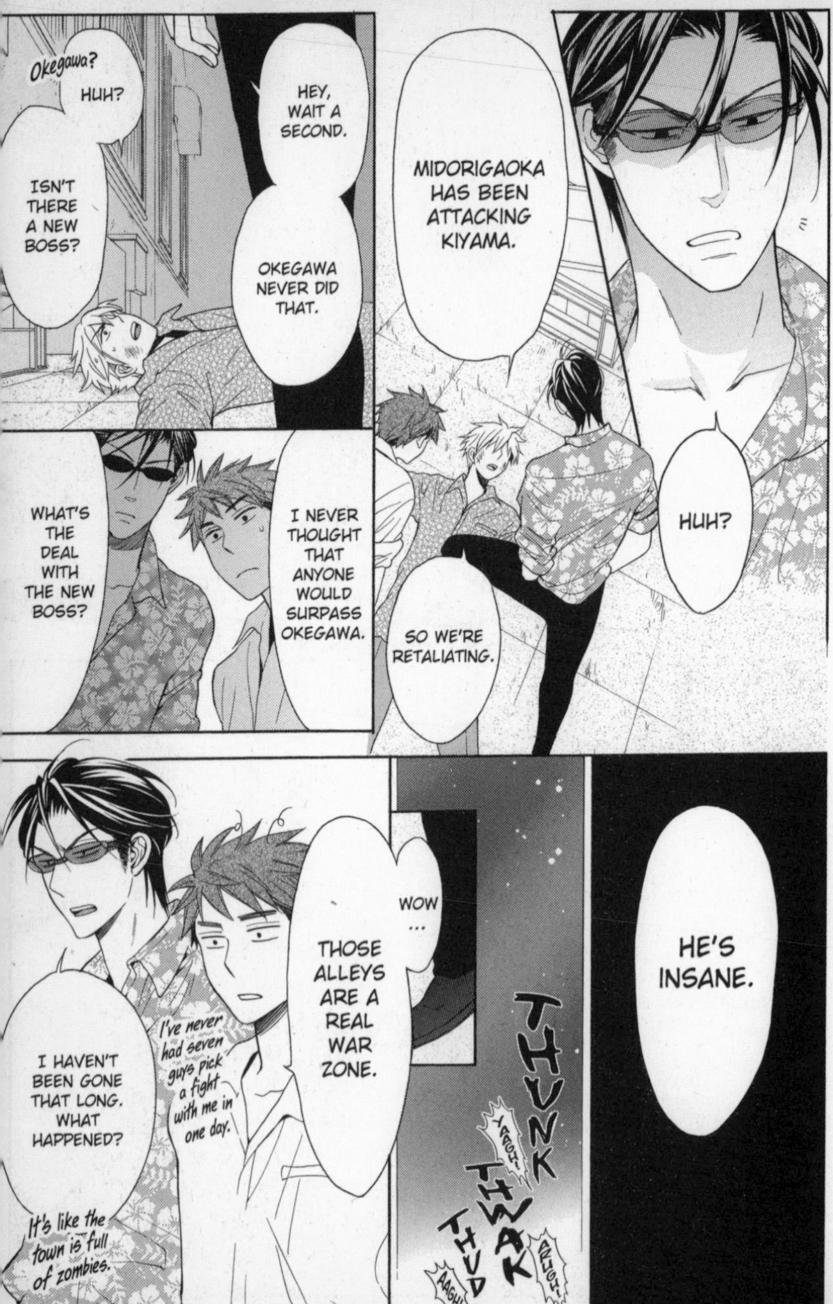
MIDORIGAOKA HAS BEEN ATTACKING KIYAMA.
SO WE'RE RETALIATING.
HUH?
HEY, WAIT A SECOND.
OKEGAWA NEVER DID THAT.
Okegawa?
HUH?
ISN'T THERE A NEW BOSS?
I NEVER THOUGHT THAT ANYONE WOULD SURPASS OKEGAWA.
WHAT'S THE DEAL WITH THE NEW BOSS?
HE'S INSANE.
THUNK
YAAGH!
THWAK
ARUGH!
THUD
AAGH!
WOW...
THOSE ALLEYS ARE A REAL WAR ZONE.
I've never had seven guys pick a fight with me in one day.
I HAVEN'T BEEN GONE THAT LONG. WHAT HAPPENED?
It's like the town is full of zombies.

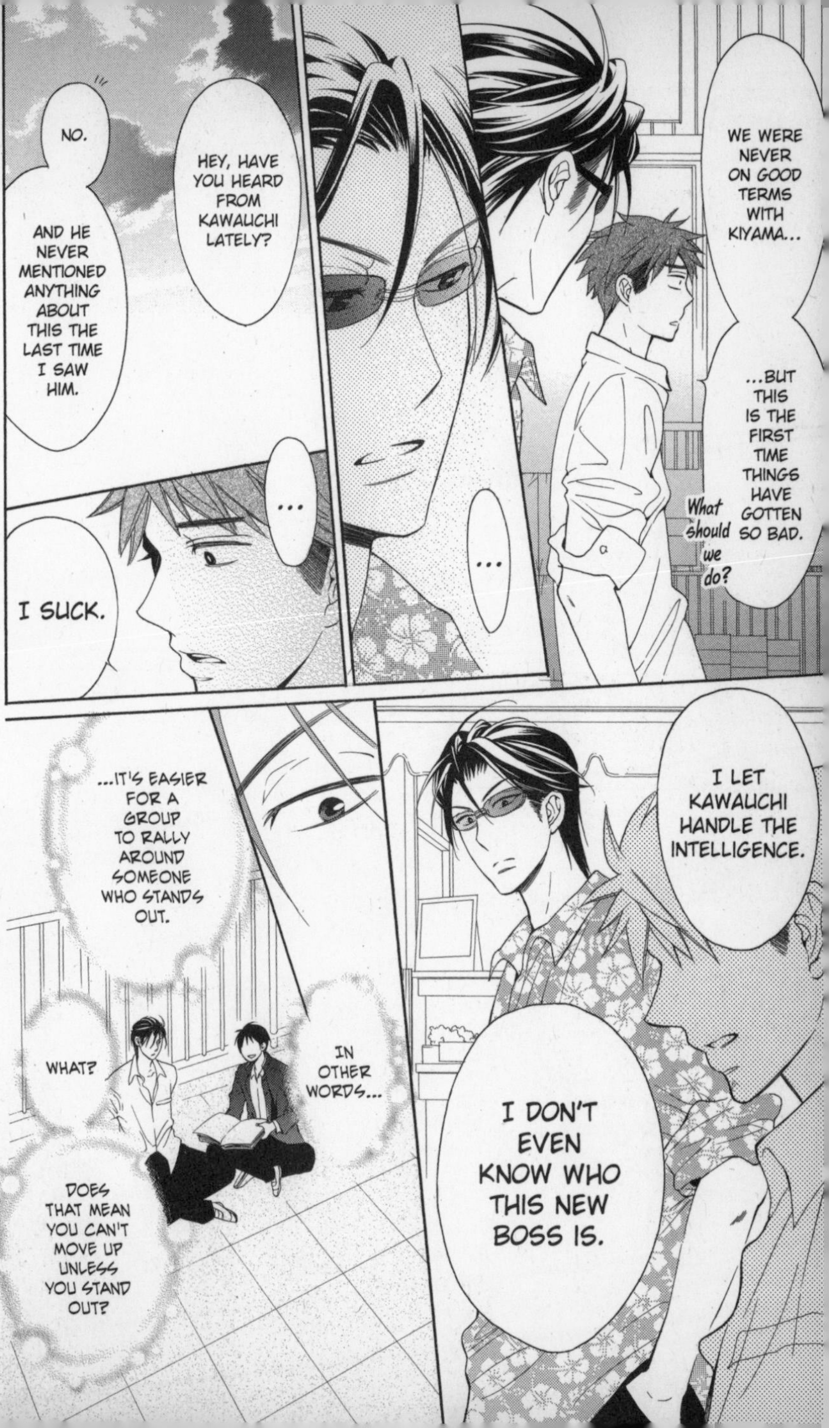
WE WERE NEVER ON GOOD TERMS WITH KIYAMA...
...BUT THIS IS THE FIRST TIME THINGS HAVE GOTTEN SO BAD.
What should we do?
HEY, HAVE YOU HEARD FROM KAWAUCHI LATELY?
...
NO.
AND HE NEVER MENTIONED ANYTHING ABOUT THIS THE LAST TIME I SAW HIM.
...
I SUCK.
I LET KAWAUCHI HANDLE THE INTELLIGENCE.
I DON'T EVEN KNOW WHO THIS NEW BOSS IS.
...IT'S EASIER FOR A GROUP TO RALLY AROUND SOMEONE WHO STANDS OUT.
IN OTHER WORDS...
WHAT?
DOES THAT MEAN YOU CAN'T MOVE UP UNLESS YOU STAND OUT?

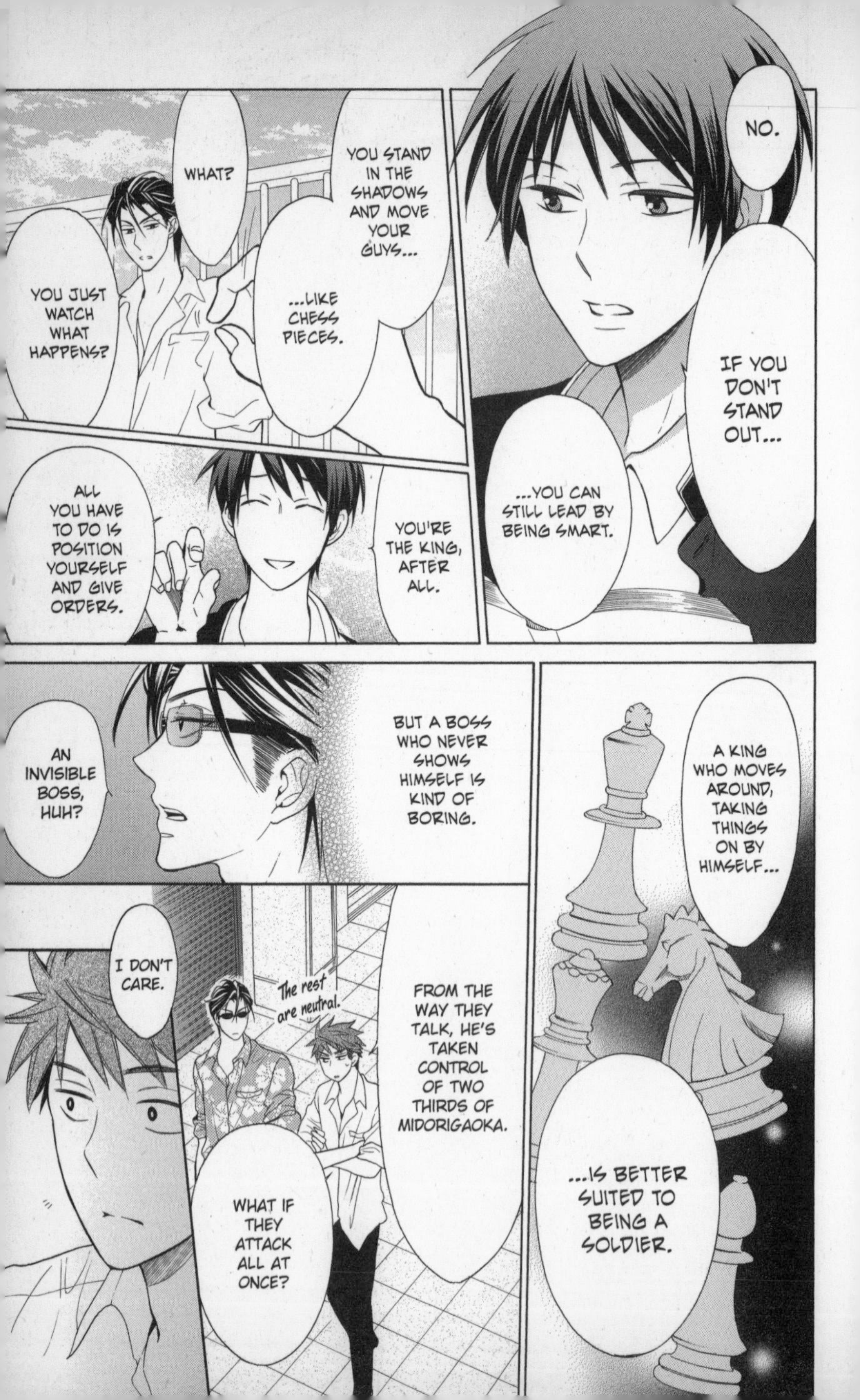
NO.
IF YOU DON'T STAND OUT...
...YOU CAN STILL LEAD BY BEING SMART.
YOU STAND IN THE SHADOWS AND MOVE YOUR GUYS...
...LIKE CHESS PIECES.
WHAT?
YOU JUST WATCH WHAT HAPPENS?
YOU'RE THE KING, AFTER ALL.
ALL YOU HAVE TO DO IS POSITION YOURSELF AND GIVE ORDERS.
A KING WHO MOVES AROUND, TAKING THINGS ON BY HIMSELF...
...IS BETTER SUITED TO BEING A SOLDIER.
BUT A BOSS WHO NEVER SHOWS HIMSELF IS KIND OF BORING.
AN INVISIBLE BOSS, HUH?
FROM THE WAY THEY TALK, HE'S TAKEN CONTROL OF TWO THIRDS OF MIDORIGAOKA.
WHAT IF THEY ATTACK ALL AT ONCE?
The rest are neutral.
I DON'T CARE.

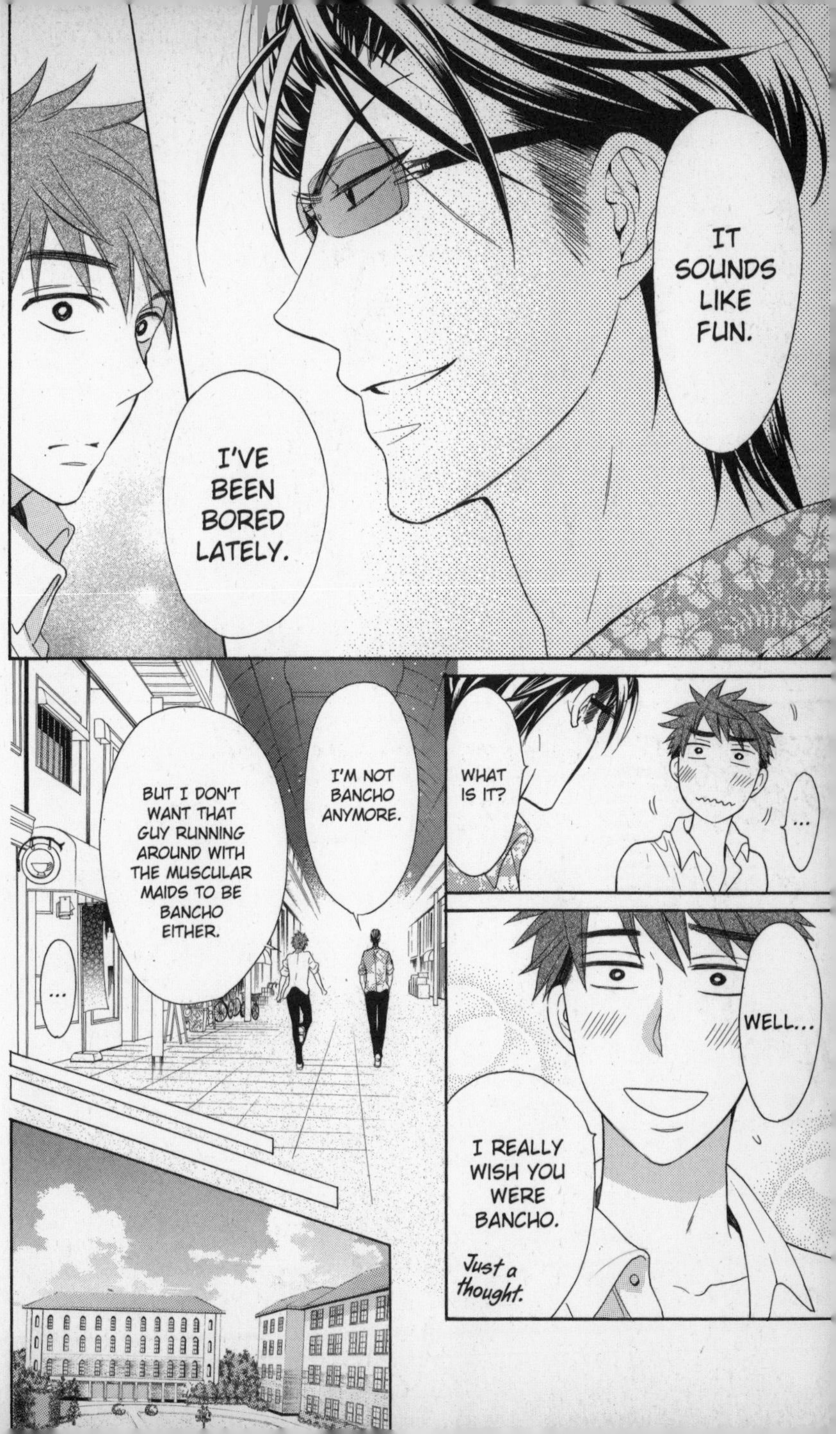
IT SOUNDS LIKE FUN.
I'VE BEEN BORED LATELY.
...
WHAT IS IT?
WELL...
I REALLY WISH YOU WERE BANCHO.
Just a thought.
I'M NOT BANCHO ANYMORE.
BUT I DON'T WANT THAT GUY RUNNING AROUND WITH THE MUSCULAR MAIDS TO BE BANCHO EITHER.
...

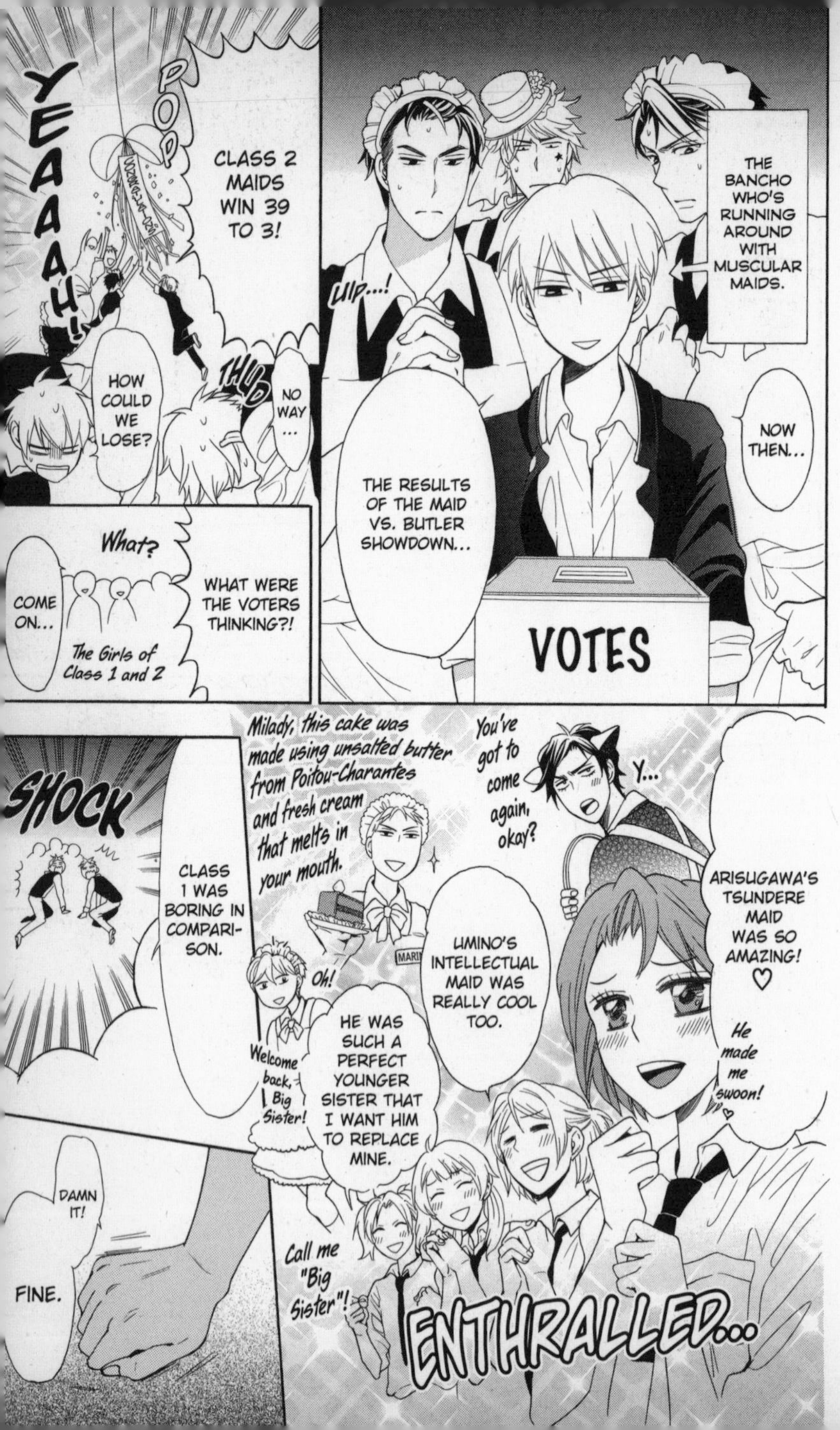
THE BANCHO WHO'S RUNNING AROUND WITH MUSCULAR MAIDS.
NOW THEN...
ULP...!
THE RESULTS OF THE MAID VS. BUTLER SHOWDOWN...
VOTES
POP
YEAAAAH!
CLASS 2 MAIDS WIN 39 TO 3!
NO WAY...
THUD
HOW COULD WE LOSE?
WHAT WERE THE VOTERS THINKING?!
What?
COME ON...
The Girls of Class 1 and 2
ARISUGAWA'S TSUNDERE MAID WAS SO AMAZING! ♡
He made me swoon! ♡
Y...
You've got to come again, okay?
Milady, this cake was made using unsalted butter from Poitou-Charantes and fresh cream that melts in your mouth.
UMINO'S INTELLECTUAL MAID WAS REALLY COOL TOO.
Oh!
HE WAS SUCH A PERFECT YOUNGER SISTER THAT I WANT HIM TO REPLACE MINE.
Welcome back, Big Sister!
Call me "Big Sister"!
ENTHRALLED...
SHOCK
CLASS 1 WAS BORING IN COMPARI-SON.
DAMN IT!
FINE.

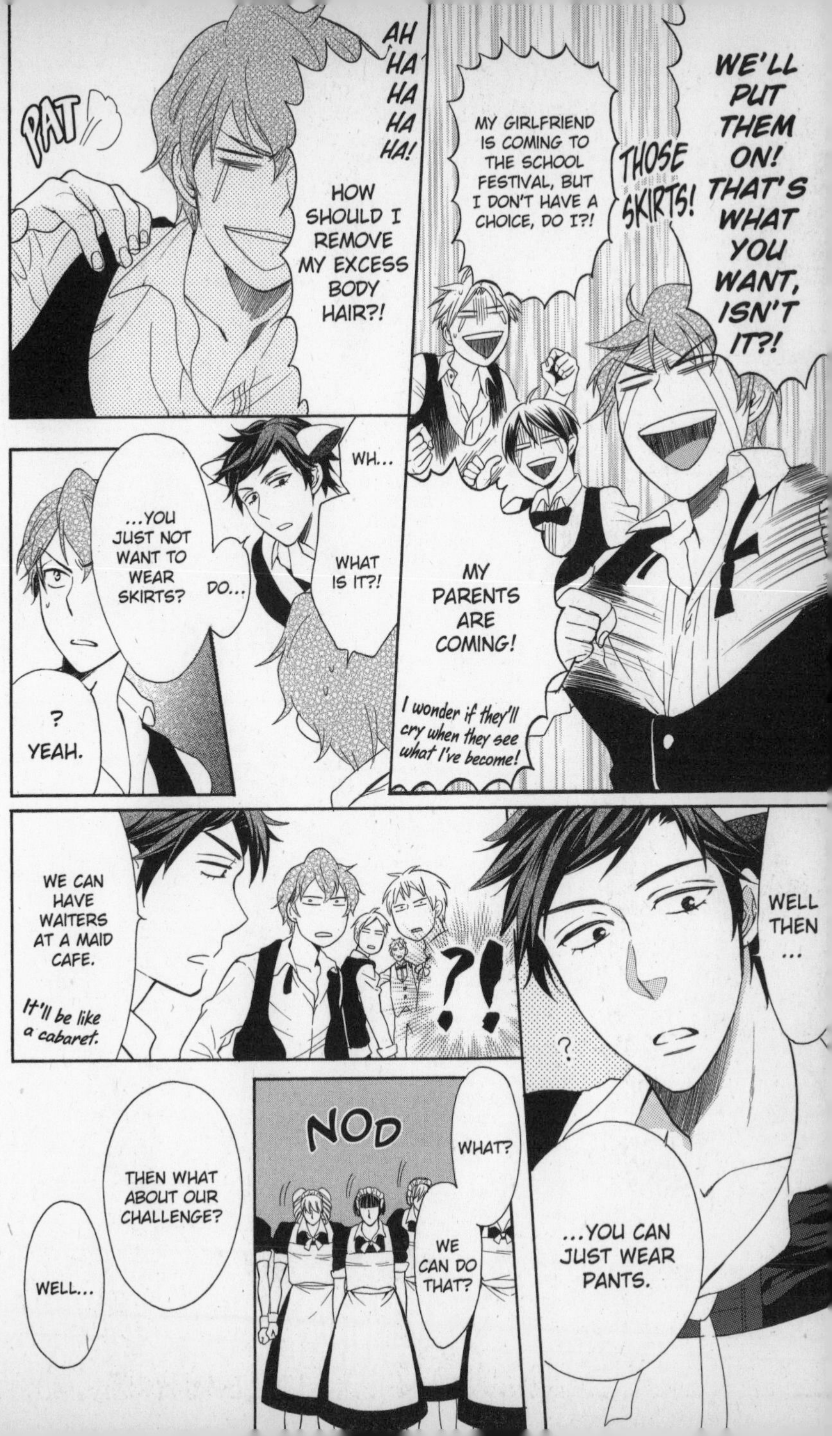
WE'LL PUT THEM ON! THAT'S WHAT YOU WANT, ISN'T IT?!
THOSE SKIRTS!
MY GIRLFRIEND IS COMING TO THE SCHOOL FESTIVAL, BUT I DON'T HAVE A CHOICE, DO I?!
MY PARENTS ARE COMING!
I wonder if they'll cry when they see what I've become!
AH HA HA HA HA!
PAT
HOW SHOULD I REMOVE MY EXCESS BODY HAIR?!
WH...
WHAT IS IT?!
DO...
...YOU JUST NOT WANT TO WEAR SKIRTS?
? YEAH.
WELL THEN ...
?
...YOU CAN JUST WEAR PANTS.
?!
WE CAN HAVE WAITERS AT A MAID CAFE.
It'll be like a cabaret.
WHAT?
NOD
WE CAN DO THAT?
THEN WHAT ABOUT OUR CHALLENGE?
WELL...

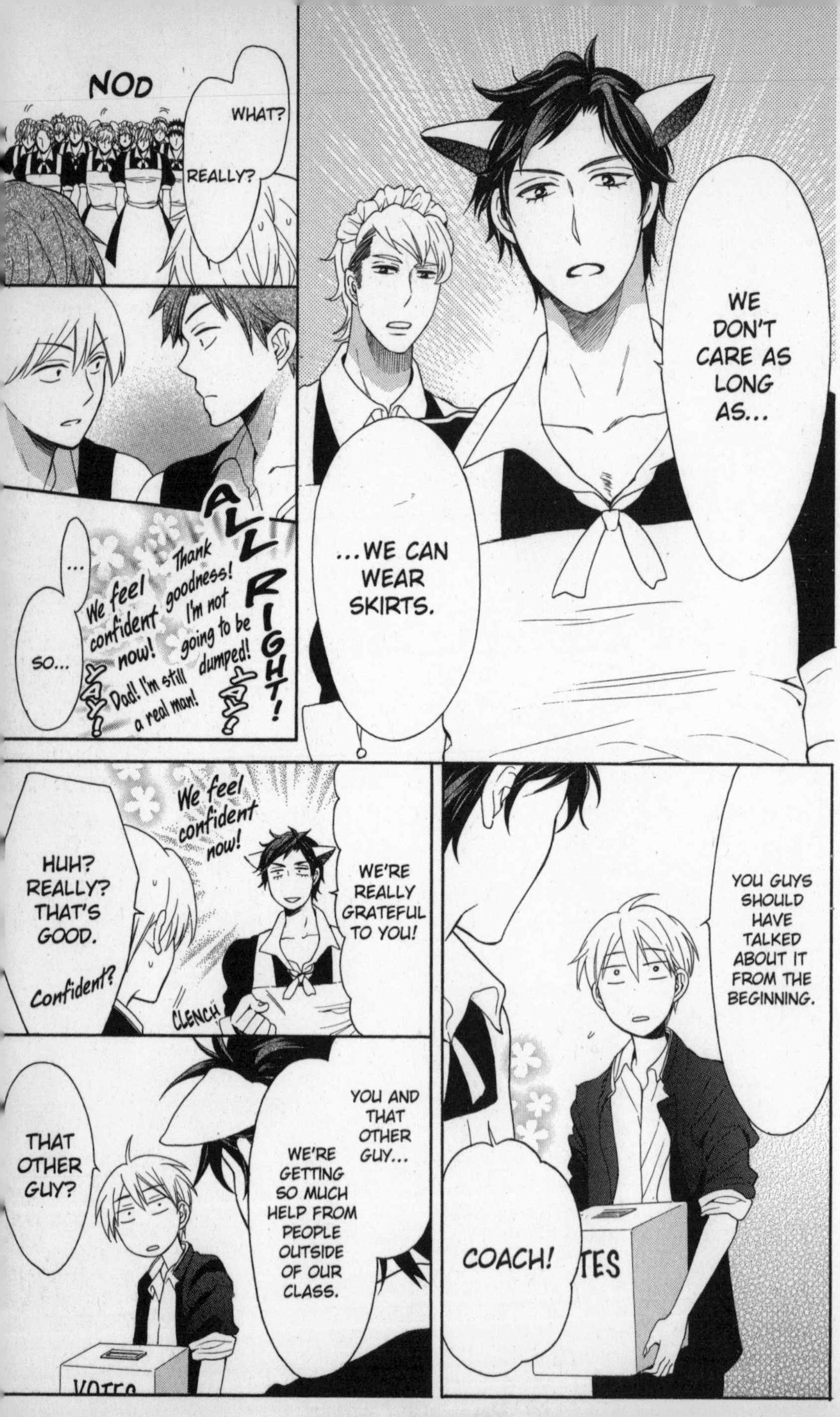
WE DON'T CARE AS LONG AS...
...WE CAN WEAR SKIRTS.
NOD
WHAT?
REALLY?
ALL RIGHT!
Thank goodness! I'm not going to be dumped!
YAY!
We feel confident now!
Dad! I'm still a real man!
YAY!
...
SO...
YOU GUYS SHOULD HAVE TALKED ABOUT IT FROM THE BEGINNING.
COACH!
TES
We feel confident now!
WE'RE REALLY GRATEFUL TO YOU!
CLENCH
HUH? REALLY? THAT'S GOOD.
Confident?
YOU AND THAT OTHER GUY...
WE'RE GETTING SO MUCH HELP FROM PEOPLE OUTSIDE OF OUR CLASS.
THAT OTHER GUY?

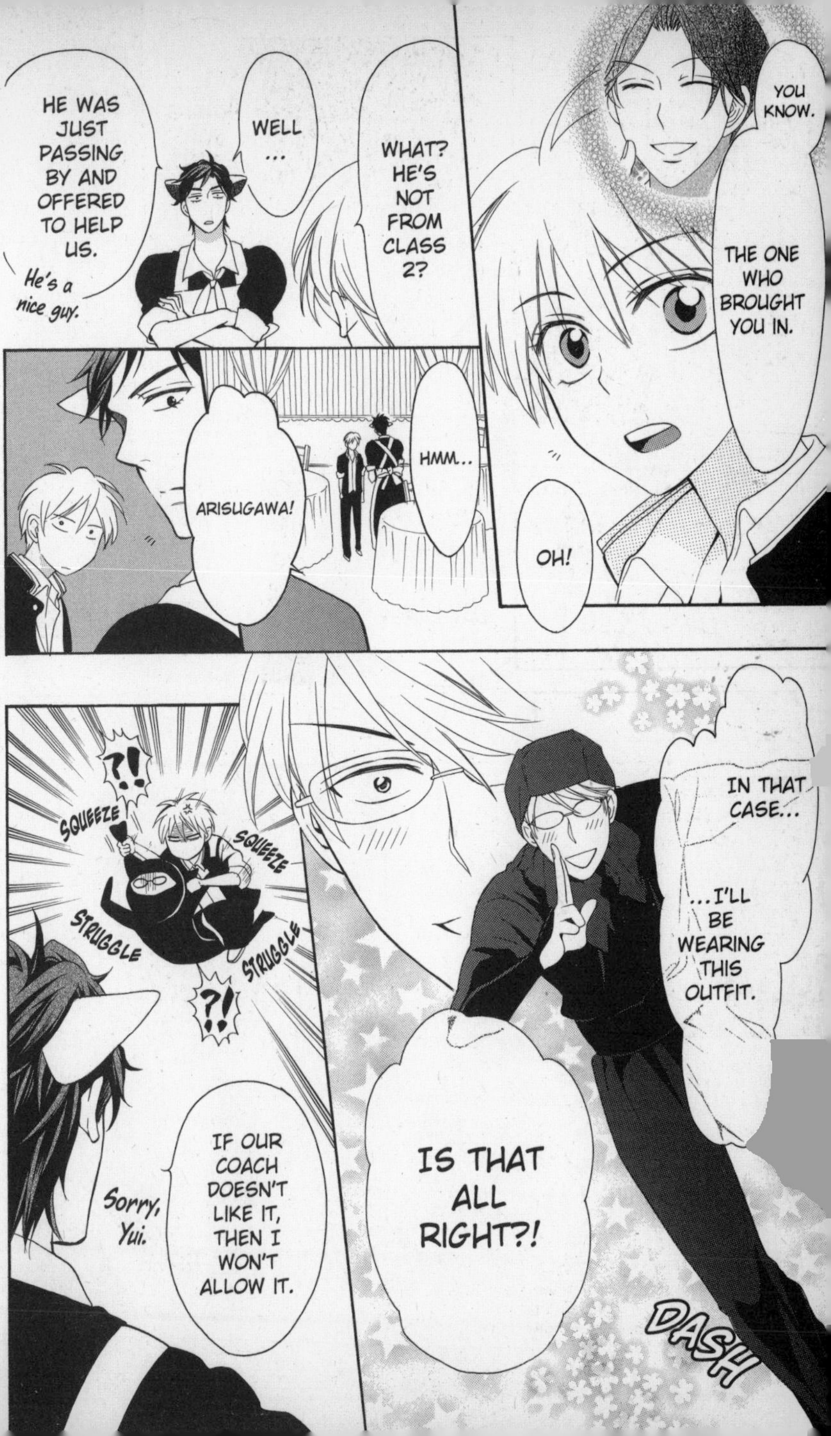
YOU KNOW.
THE ONE WHO BROUGHT YOU IN.
OH!
WHAT? HE'S NOT FROM CLASS 2?
WELL...
HE WAS JUST PASSING BY AND OFFERED TO HELP US.
He's a nice guy.
HMM..
ARISUGAWA!
IN THAT CASE...
...I'LL BE WEARING THIS OUTFIT.
IS THAT ALL RIGHT?!
DASH
?!
SQUEEZE
SQUEEZE
STRUGGLE
STRUGGLE
?!
IF OUR COACH DOESN'T LIKE IT, THEN I WON'T ALLOW IT.
Sorry, Yui.

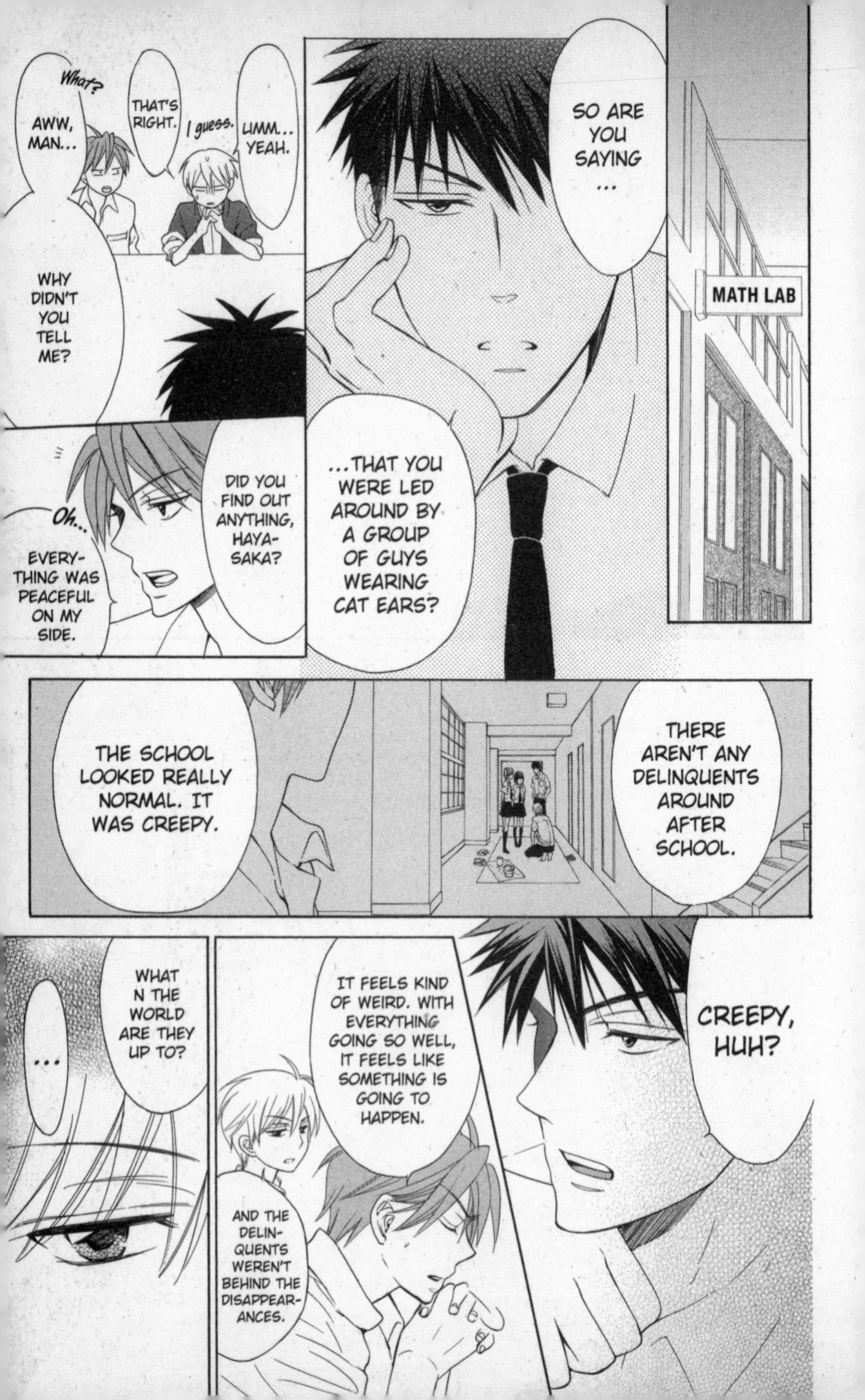
MATH LAB
SO ARE YOU SAYING ...
...THAT YOU WERE LED AROUND BY A GROUP OF GUYS WEARING CAT EARS?
UMM... YEAH.
I guess.
THAT'S RIGHT.
What?
AWW, MAN...
WHY DIDN'T YOU TELL ME?
DID YOU FIND OUT ANYTHING, HAYA-SAKA?
Oh...
EVERY-THING WAS PEACEFUL ON MY SIDE.
THERE AREN'T ANY DELINQUENTS AROUND AFTER SCHOOL.
THE SCHOOL LOOKED REALLY NORMAL. IT WAS CREEPY.
CREEPY, HUH?
IT FEELS KIND OF WEIRD. WITH EVERYTHING GOING SO WELL, IT FEELS LIKE SOMETHING IS GOING TO HAPPEN.
AND THE DELIN-QUENTS WEREN'T BEHIND THE DISAPPEAR-ANCES.
WHAT N THE WORLD ARE THEY UP TO?
...

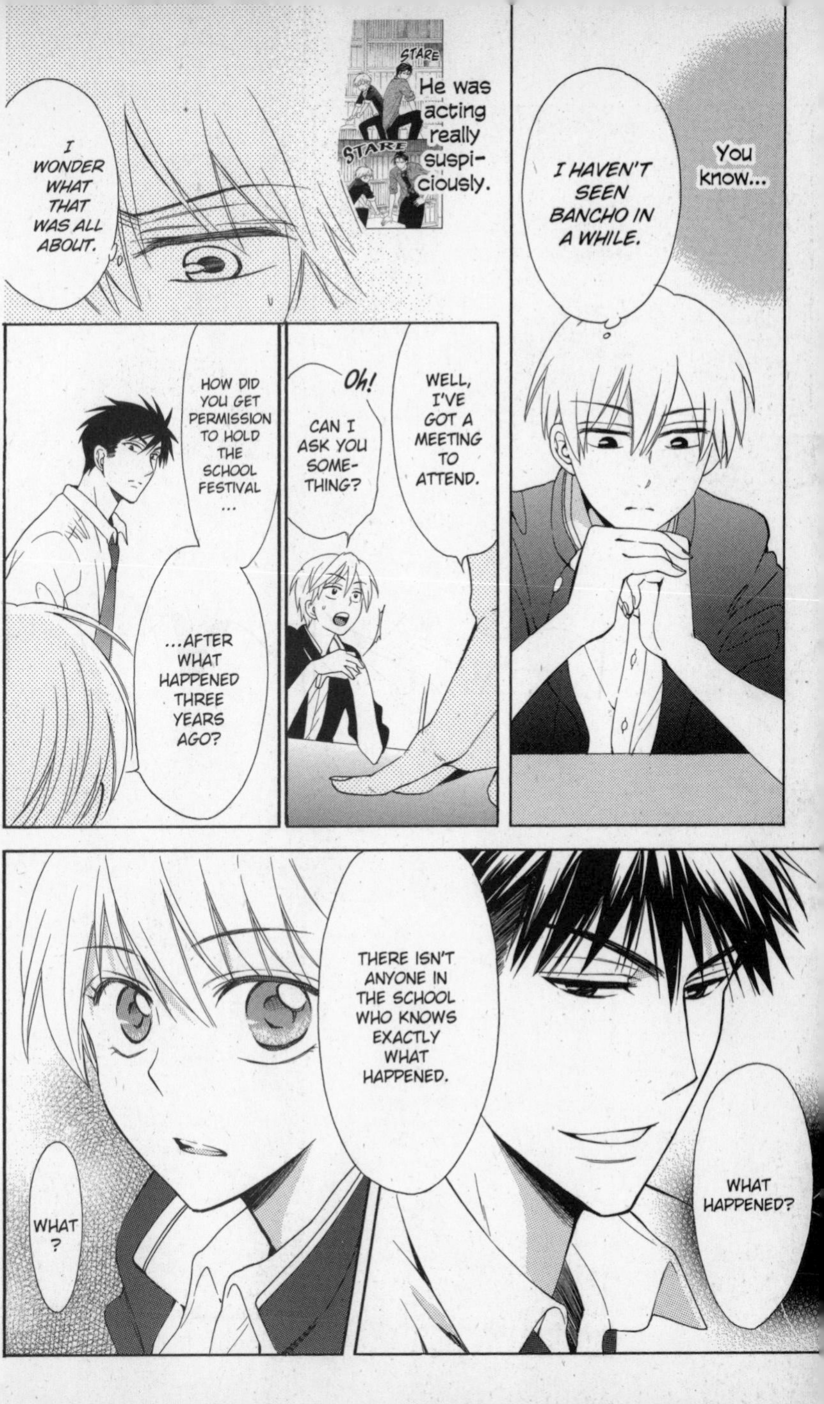
You know...
I HAVEN'T SEEN BANCHO IN A WHILE.
STARE
STARE
He was acting really suspiciously.
I WONDER WHAT THAT WAS ALL ABOUT.
WELL, I'VE GOT A MEETING TO ATTEND.
Oh!
CAN I ASK YOU SOME-THING?
HOW DID YOU GET PERMISSION TO HOLD THE SCHOOL FESTIVAL ...
...AFTER WHAT HAPPENED THREE YEARS AGO?
WHAT HAPPENED?
THERE ISN'T ANYONE IN THE SCHOOL WHO KNOWS EXACTLY WHAT HAPPENED.
WHAT?

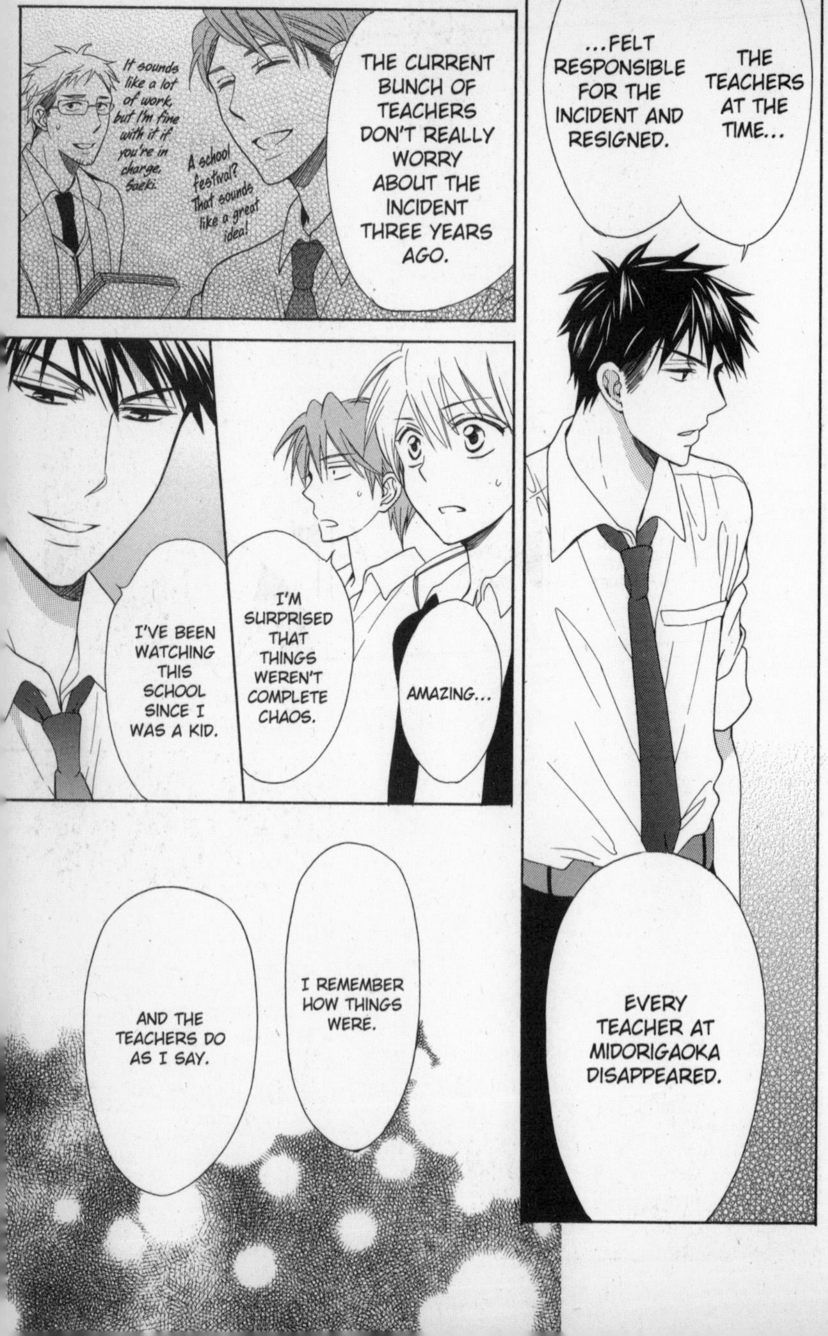
THE TEACHERS AT THE TIME...
...FELT RESPONSIBLE FOR THE INCIDENT AND RESIGNED.
EVERY TEACHER AT MIDORIGAOKA DISAPPEARED.
THE CURRENT BUNCH OF TEACHERS DON'T REALLY WORRY ABOUT THE INCIDENT THREE YEARS AGO.
A school festival? That sounds like a great idea!
It sounds like a lot of work, but I'm fine with it if you're in charge, Saeki.
AMAZING...
I'M SURPRISED THAT THINGS WEREN'T COMPLETE CHAOS.
I'VE BEEN WATCHING THIS SCHOOL SINCE I WAS A KID.
I REMEMBER HOW THINGS WERE.
AND THE TEACHERS DO AS I SAY.

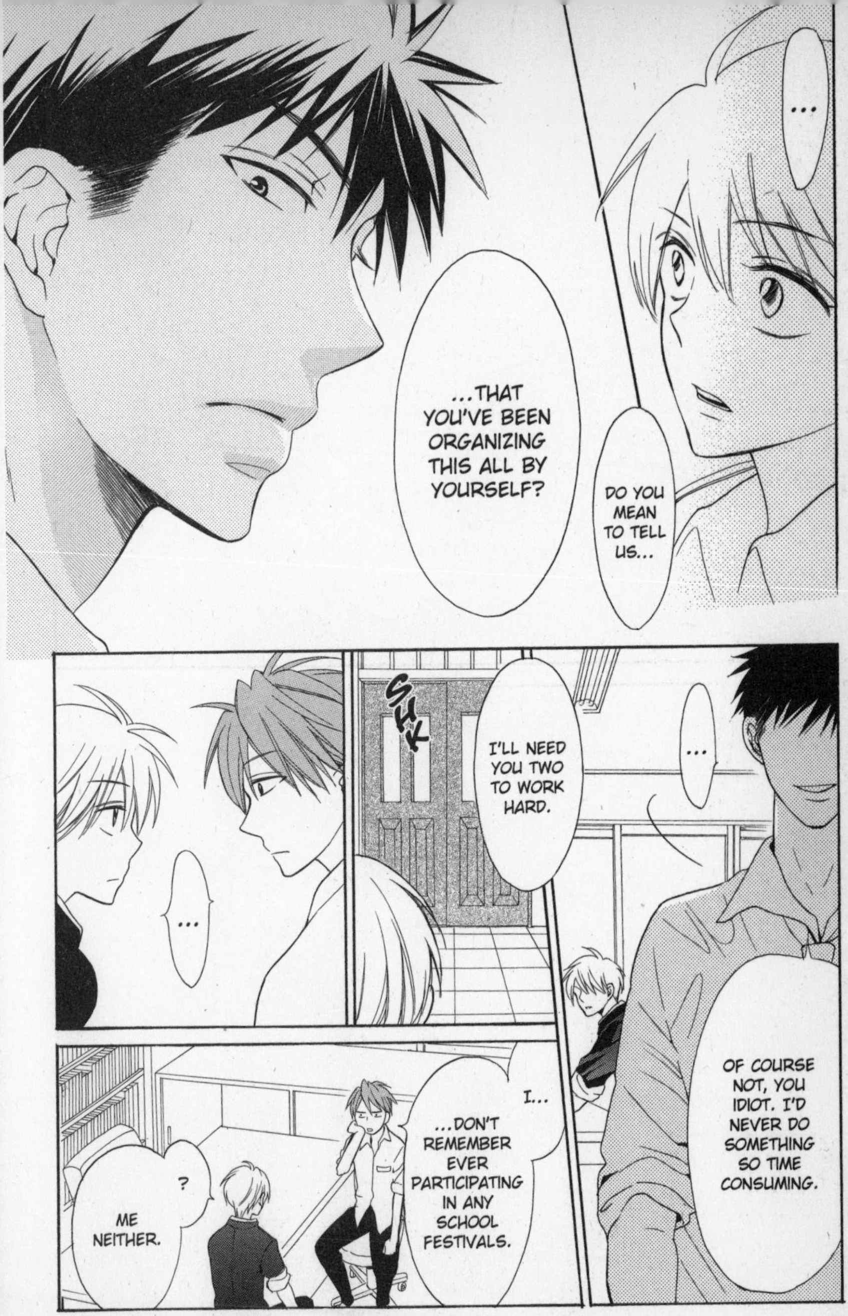
...
DO YOU MEAN TO TELL US...
...THAT YOU'VE BEEN ORGANIZING THIS ALL BY YOURSELF?
...
OF COURSE NOT, YOU IDIOT. I'D NEVER DO SOMETHING SO TIME CONSUMING.
SHK
I'LL NEED YOU TWO TO WORK HARD.
...
I...
...DON'T REMEMBER EVER PARTICIPATING IN ANY SCHOOL FESTIVALS.
?
ME NEITHER.

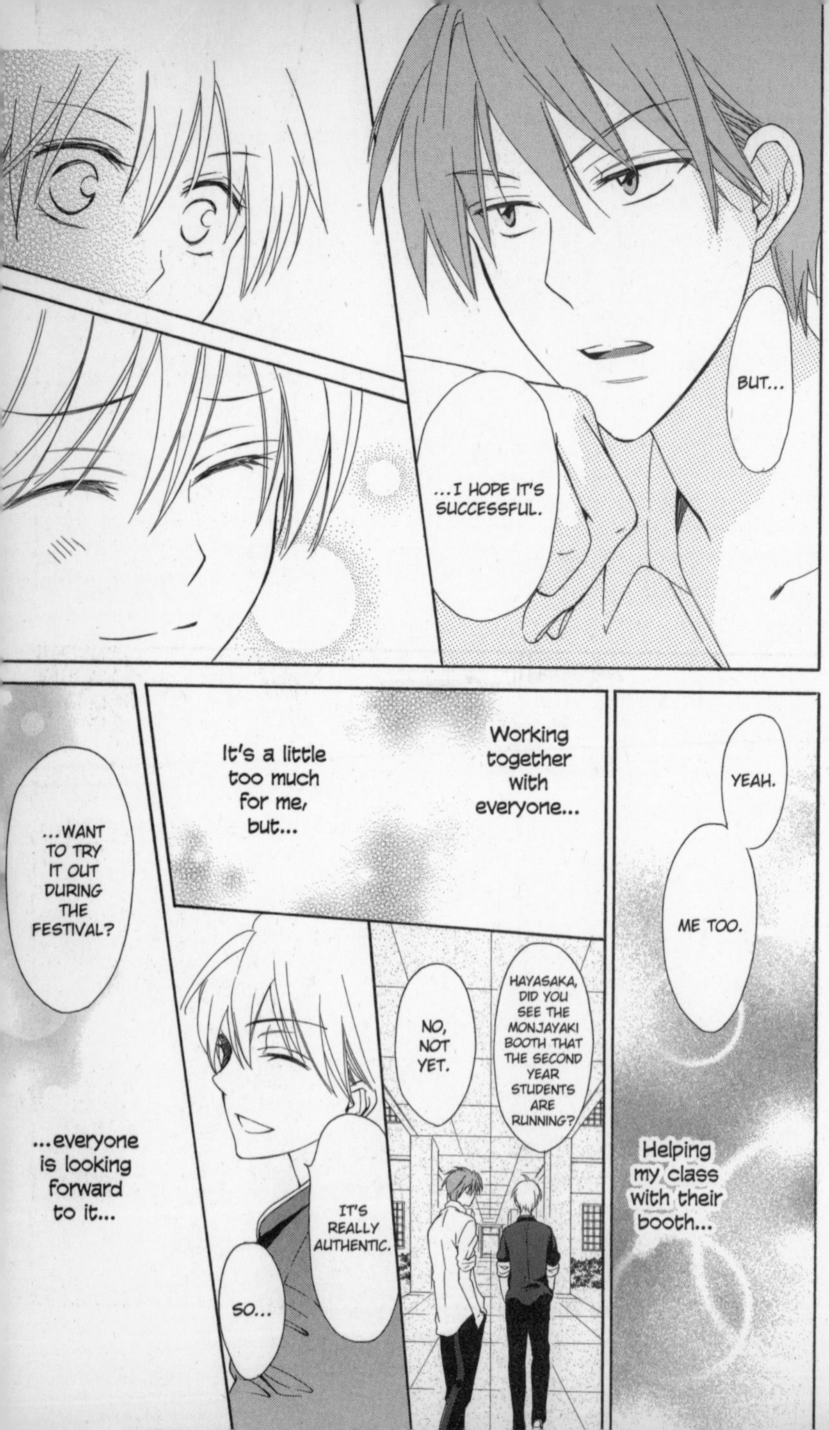
BUT...
...I HOPE IT'S SUCCESSFUL.
YEAH.
ME TOO.
Helping my class with their booth...
Working together with everyone...
It's a little too much for me, but...
HAYASAKA, DID YOU SEE THE MONJAYAKI BOOTH THAT THE SECOND YEAR STUDENTS ARE RUNNING?
NO, NOT YET.
IT'S REALLY AUTHENTIC.
SO...
...WANT TO TRY IT OUT DURING THE FESTIVAL?
...everyone is looking forward to it...

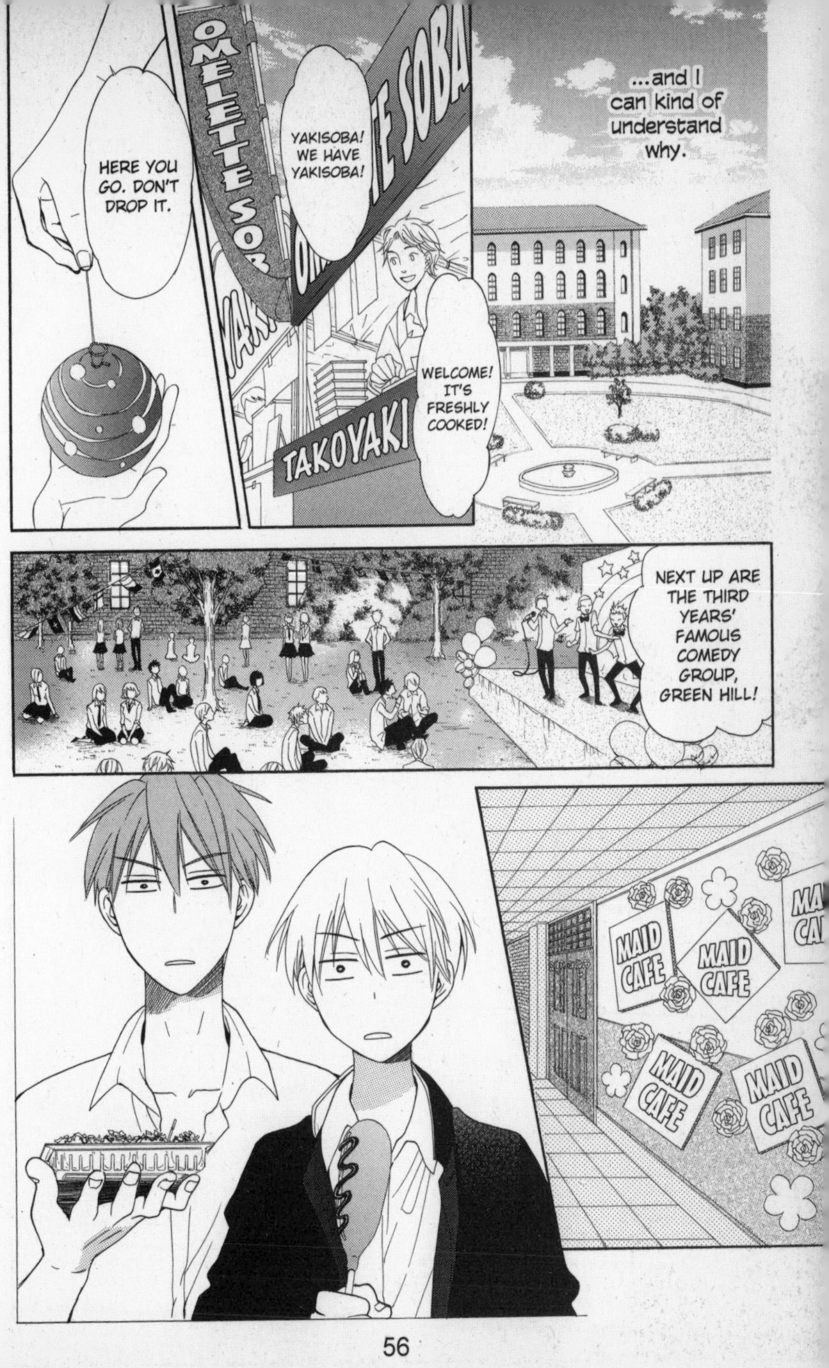
...and I can kind of understand why.
OMELETTE SOBA
YAKISOBA! WE HAVE YAKISOBA!
WELCOME! IT'S FRESHLY COOKED!
TAKOYAKI
HERE YOU GO. DON'T DROP IT.
NEXT UP ARE THE THIRD YEARS' FAMOUS COMEDY GROUP, GREEN HILL!
MAID CAFE
MAID CAFE
MAID CAFE
MAID CAFE

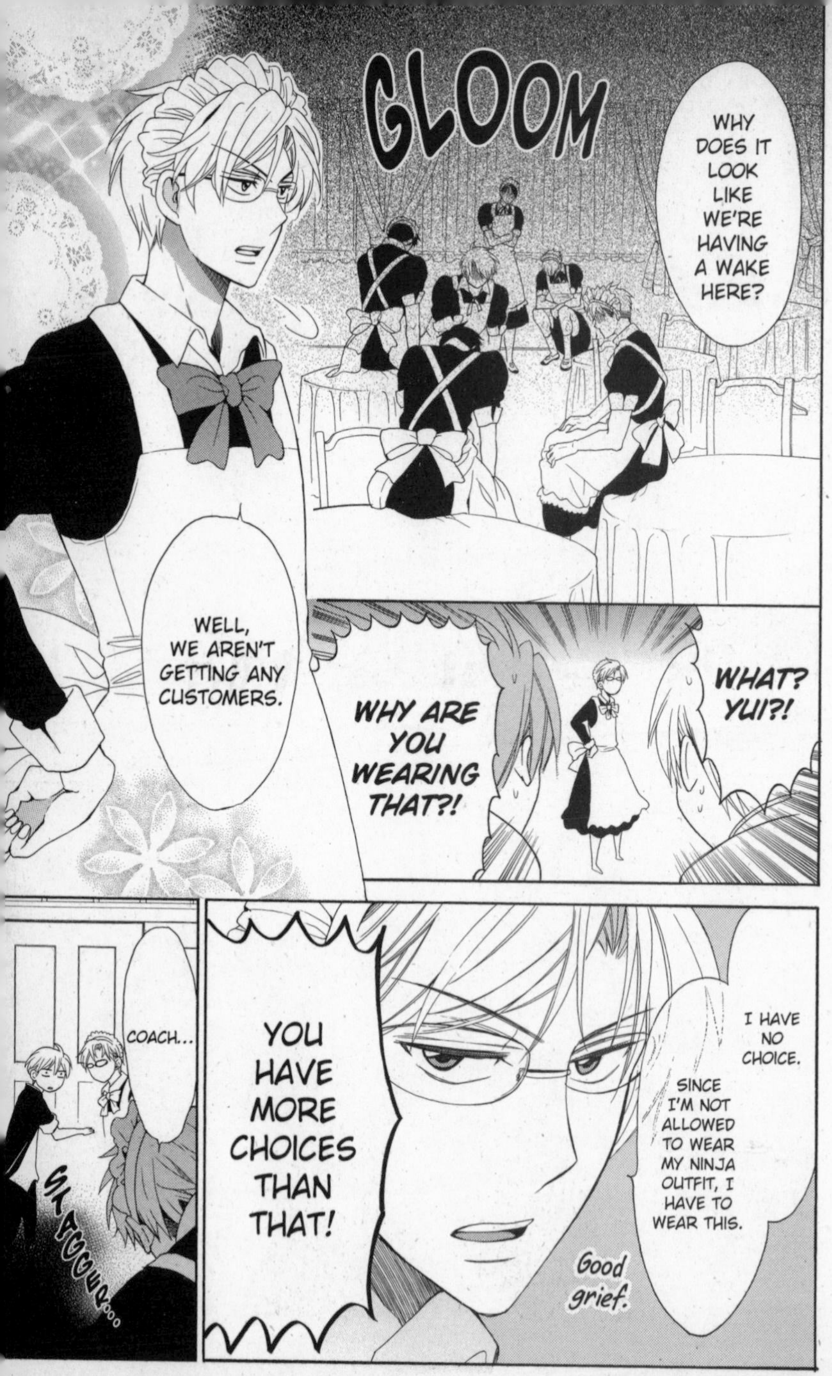
GLOOM
WHY DOES IT LOOK LIKE WE'RE HAVING A WAKE HERE?
WELL, WE AREN'T GETTING ANY CUSTOMERS.
WHAT? YUI?!
WHY ARE YOU WEARING THAT?!
I HAVE NO CHOICE.
SINCE I'M NOT ALLOWED TO WEAR MY NINJA OUTFIT, I HAVE TO WEAR THIS.
Good grief.
YOU HAVE MORE CHOICES THAN THAT!
COACH...
STAGGER...

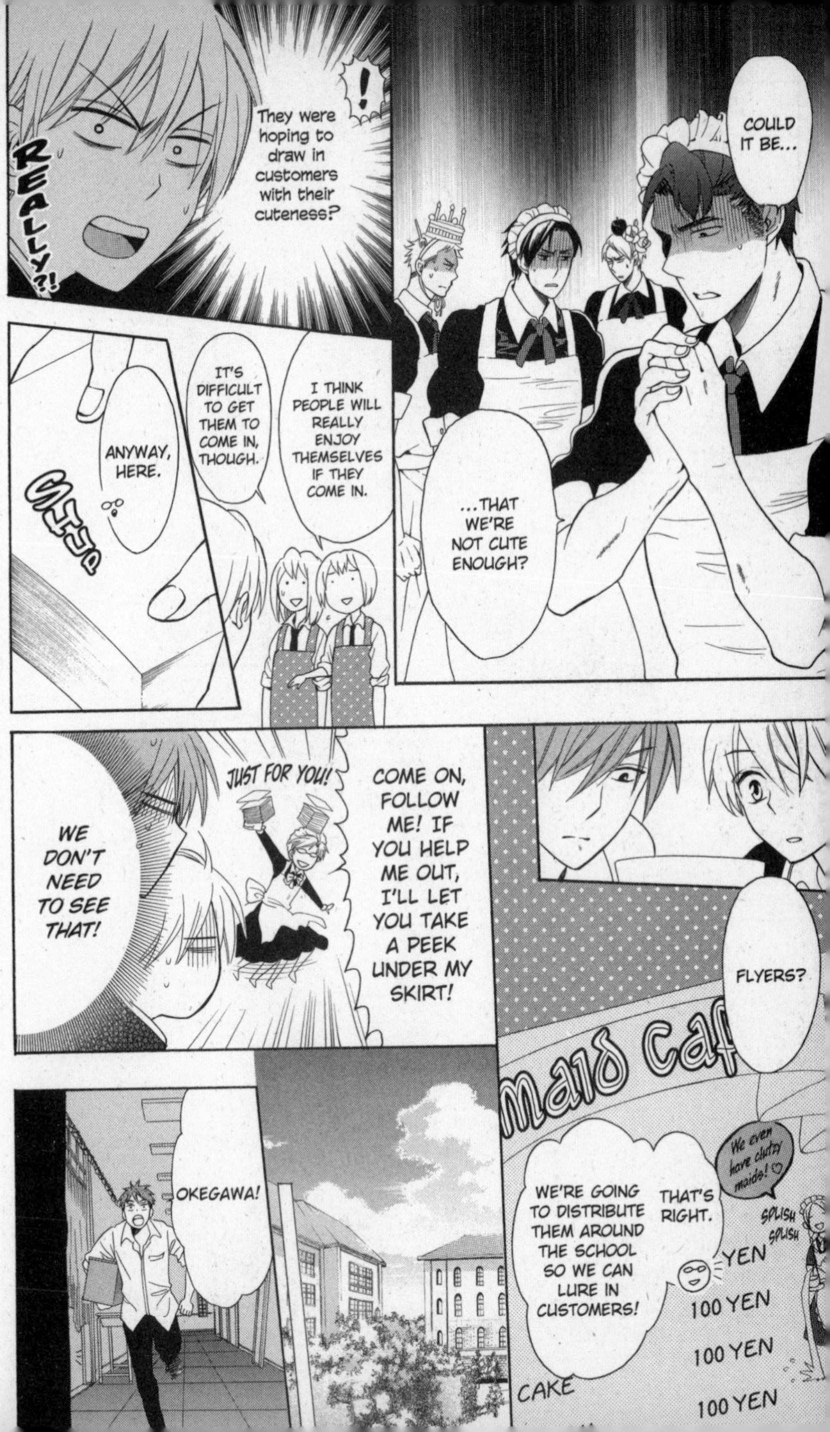

COULD IT BE...
...THAT WE'RE NOT CUTE ENOUGH?
!
They were hoping to draw in customers with their cuteness?
REALLY?!
I THINK PEOPLE WILL REALLY ENJOY THEMSELVES IF THEY COME IN.
IT'S DIFFICULT TO GET THEM TO COME IN, THOUGH.
ANYWAY, HERE.
FLYERS?
THAT'S RIGHT.
WE'RE GOING TO DISTRIBUTE THEM AROUND THE SCHOOL SO WE CAN LURE IN CUSTOMERS!
maid caf
We even have clutzy maids! ♡
SPLISH SPLISH
YEN
100 YEN
100 YEN
100 YEN
CAKE
COME ON, FOLLOW ME! IF YOU HELP ME OUT, I'LL LET YOU TAKE A PEEK UNDER MY SKIRT!
JUST FOR YOU!
WE DON'T NEED TO SEE THAT!
OKEGAWA!

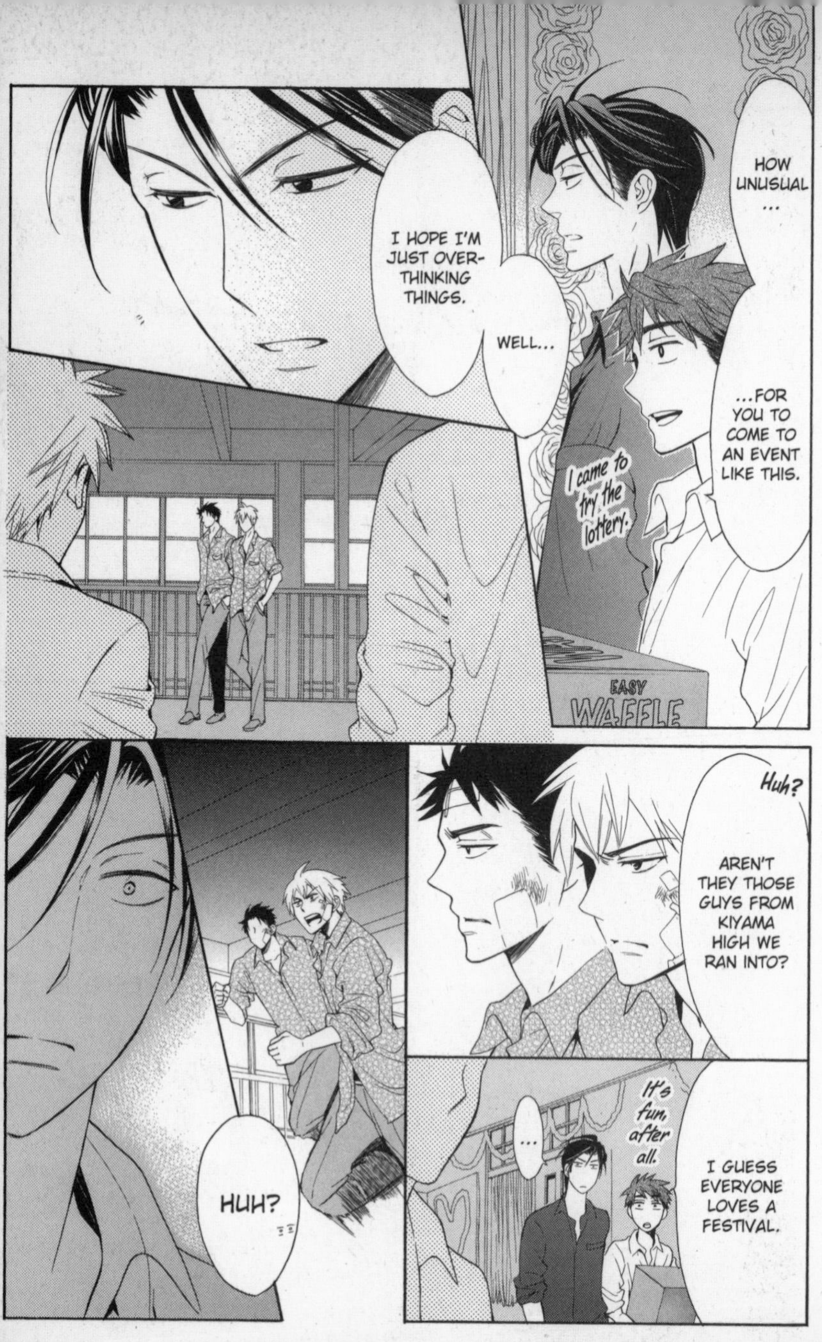
HOW UNUSUAL...
...FOR YOU TO COME TO AN EVENT LIKE THIS.
I came to try the lottery.
EASY WAFFLE
WELL...
I HOPE I'M JUST OVER-THINKING THINGS.
Huh?
AREN'T THEY THOSE GUYS FROM KIYAMA HIGH WE RAN INTO?
I GUESS EVERYONE LOVES A FESTIVAL.
It's fun, after all.
...
HUH?

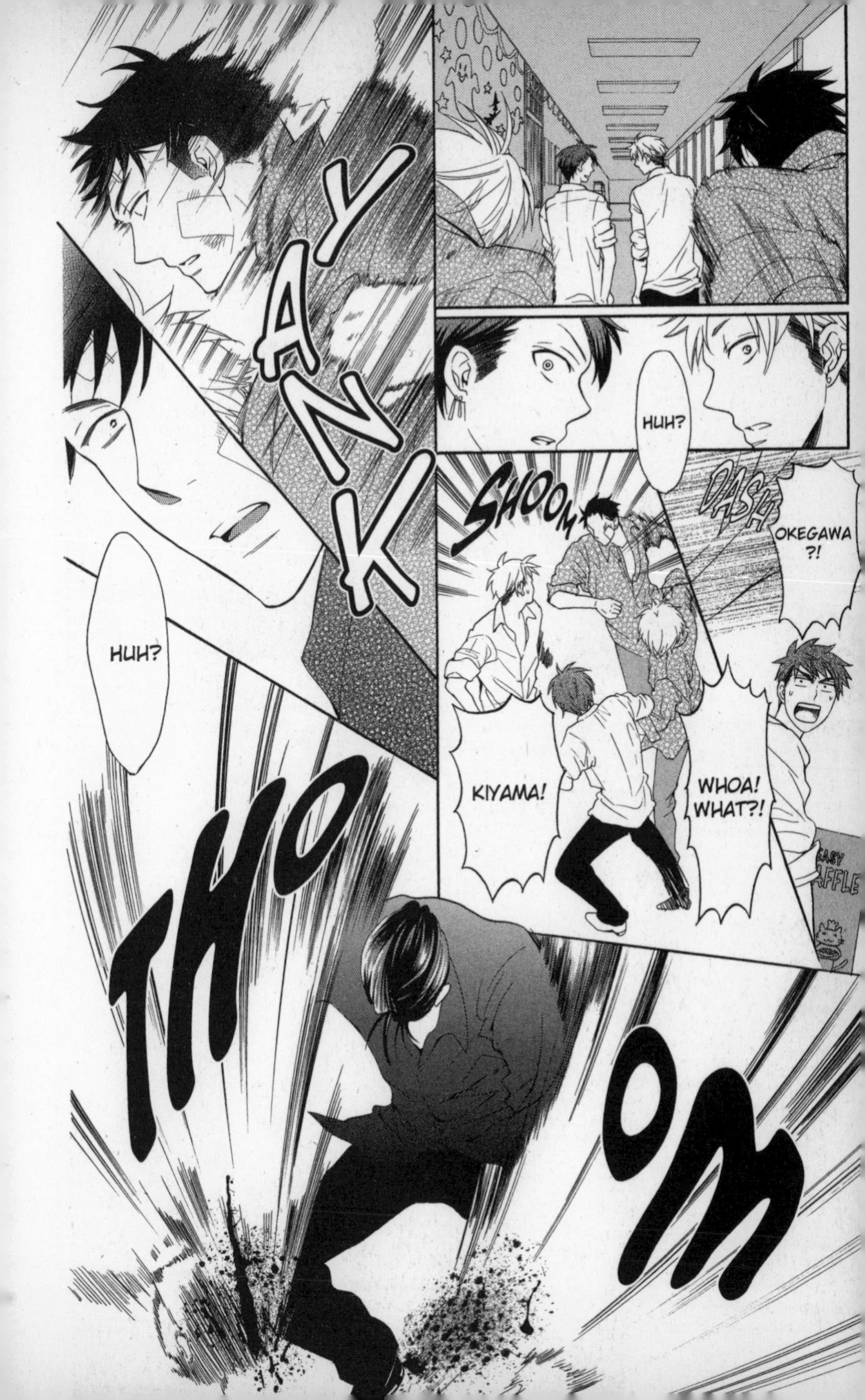

HUH?
DASH
OKEGAWA ?!
SHOOM
WHOA! WHAT?!
KIYAMA!
YANK
HUH?
THOOM

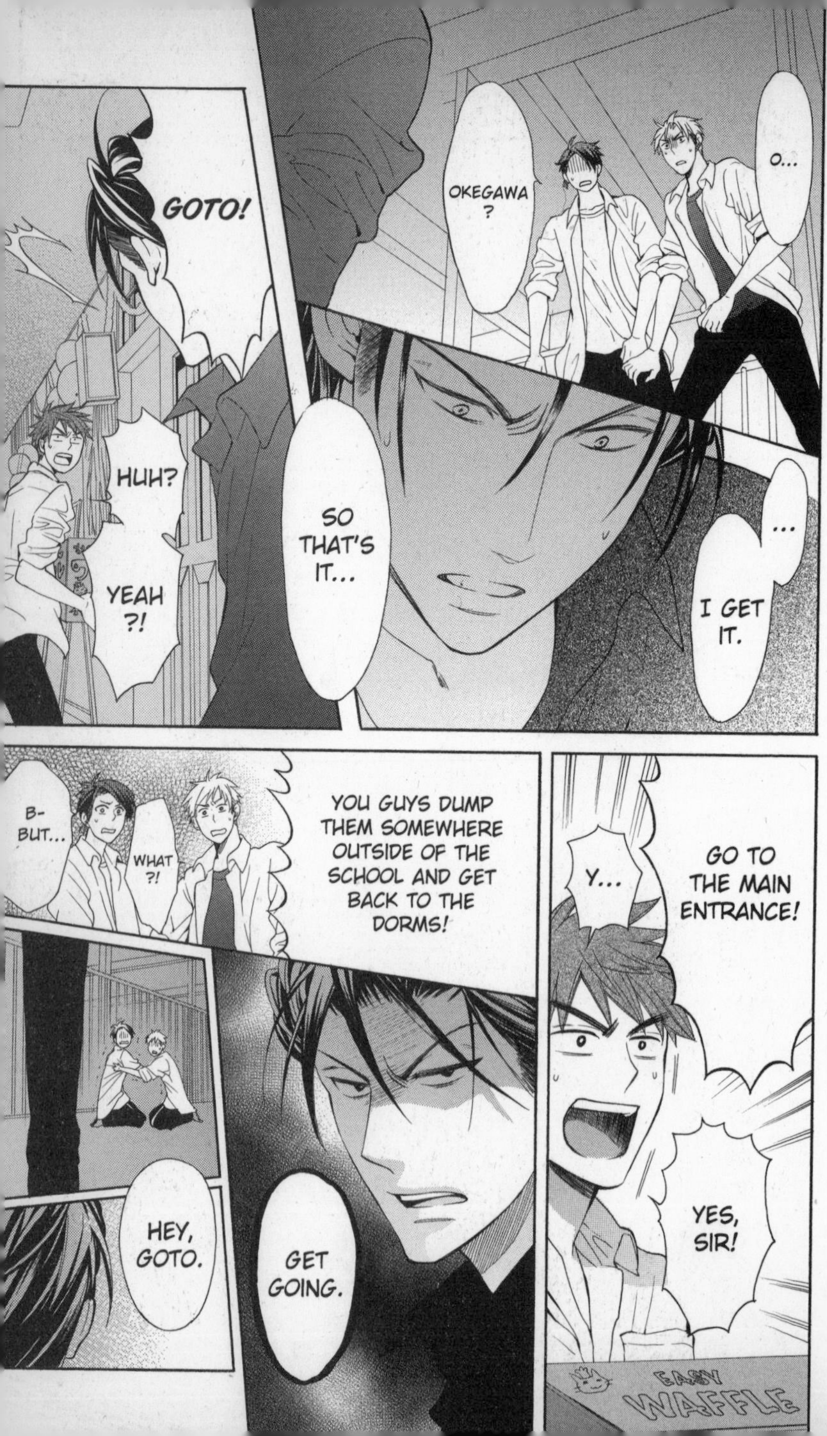
O...
OKEGAWA?
...
I GET IT.
SO THAT'S IT...
GOTO!
HUH?
YEAH?!
GO TO THE MAIN ENTRANCE!
Y...
YES, SIR!
YOU GUYS DUMP THEM SOMEWHERE OUTSIDE OF THE SCHOOL AND GET BACK TO THE DORMS!
WHAT?!
B-BUT...
GET GOING.
HEY, GOTO.
EASY WAFFLE

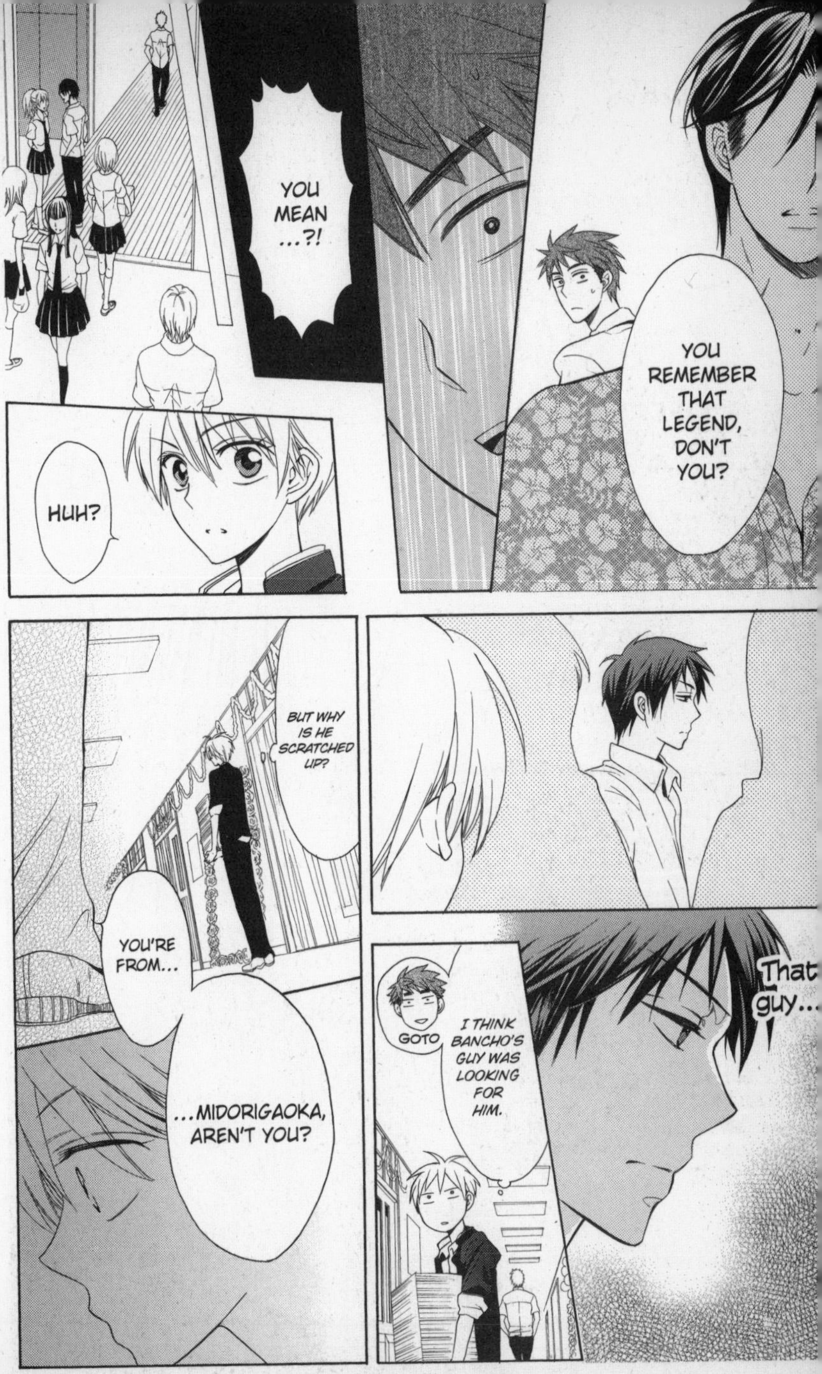
YOU REMEMBER THAT LEGEND, DON'T YOU?
YOU MEAN ...?!
HUH?
That guy...
I THINK BANCHO'S GUY WAS LOOKING FOR HIM.
GOTO
BUT WHY IS HE SCRATCHED UP?
YOU'RE FROM...
...MIDORIGAOKA, AREN'T YOU?

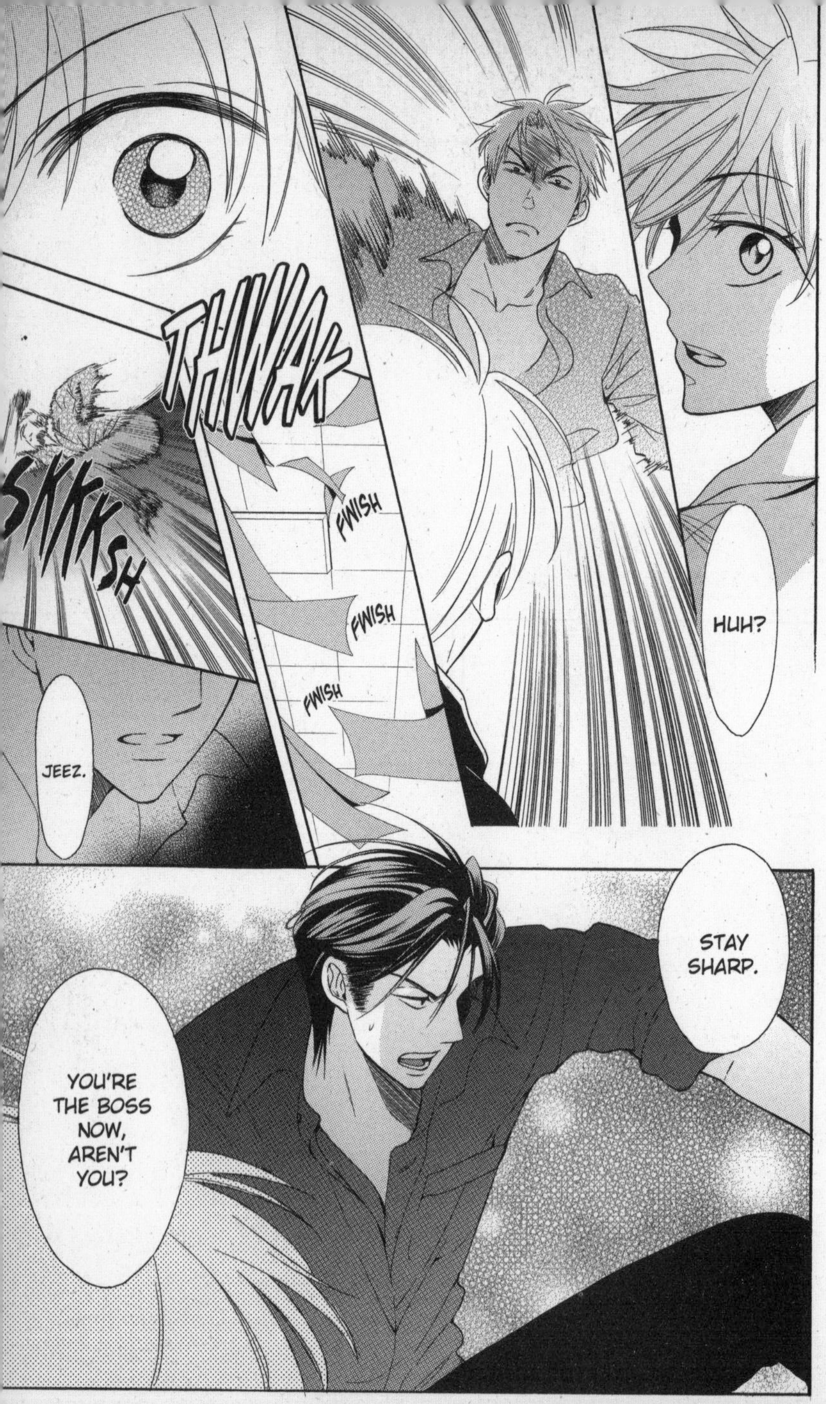
HUH?
FWISH
FWISH
FWISH
THWAK
SKKKSH
JEEZ.
STAY SHARP.
YOU'RE THE BOSS NOW, AREN'T YOU?

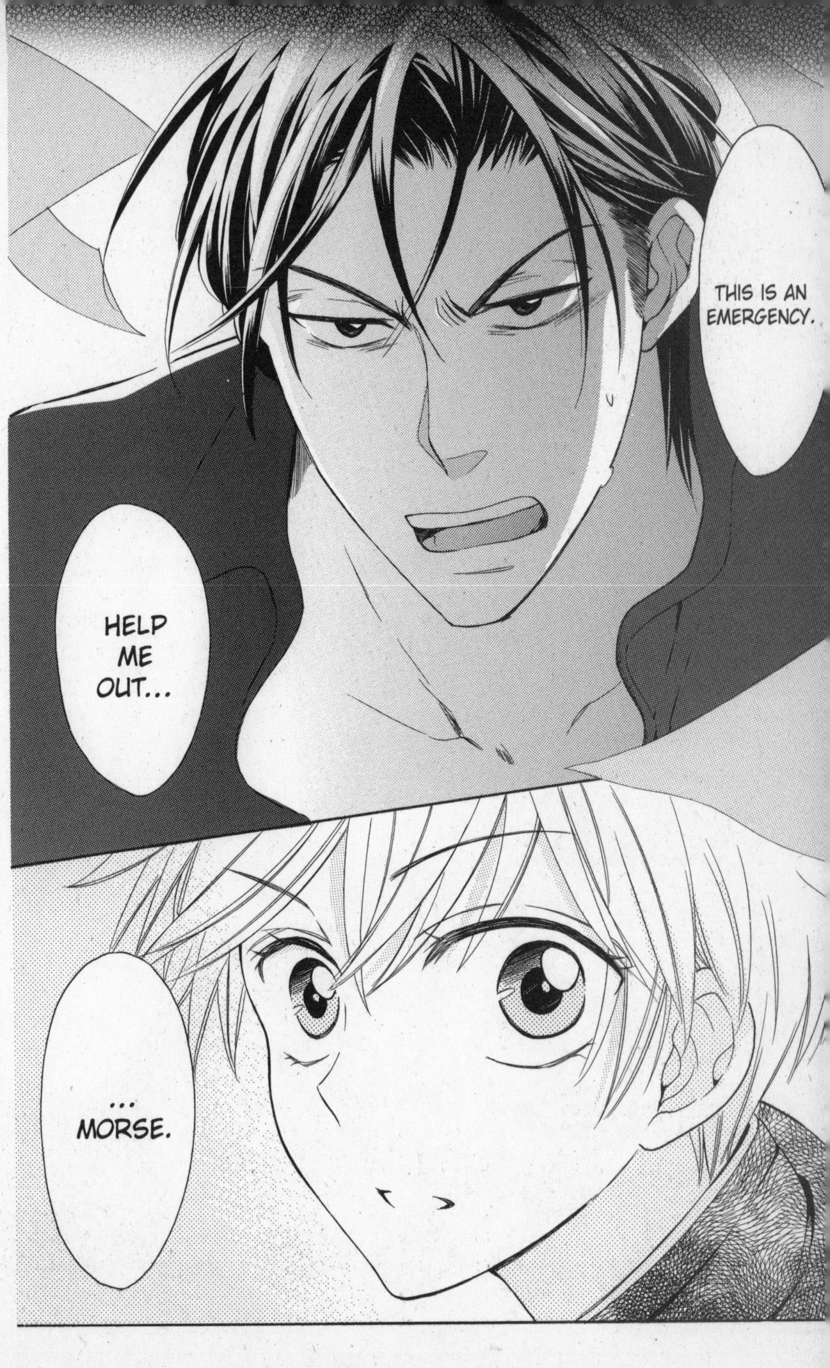
THIS IS AN EMERGENCY.
HELP ME OUT...
... MORSE.

Chapter 48

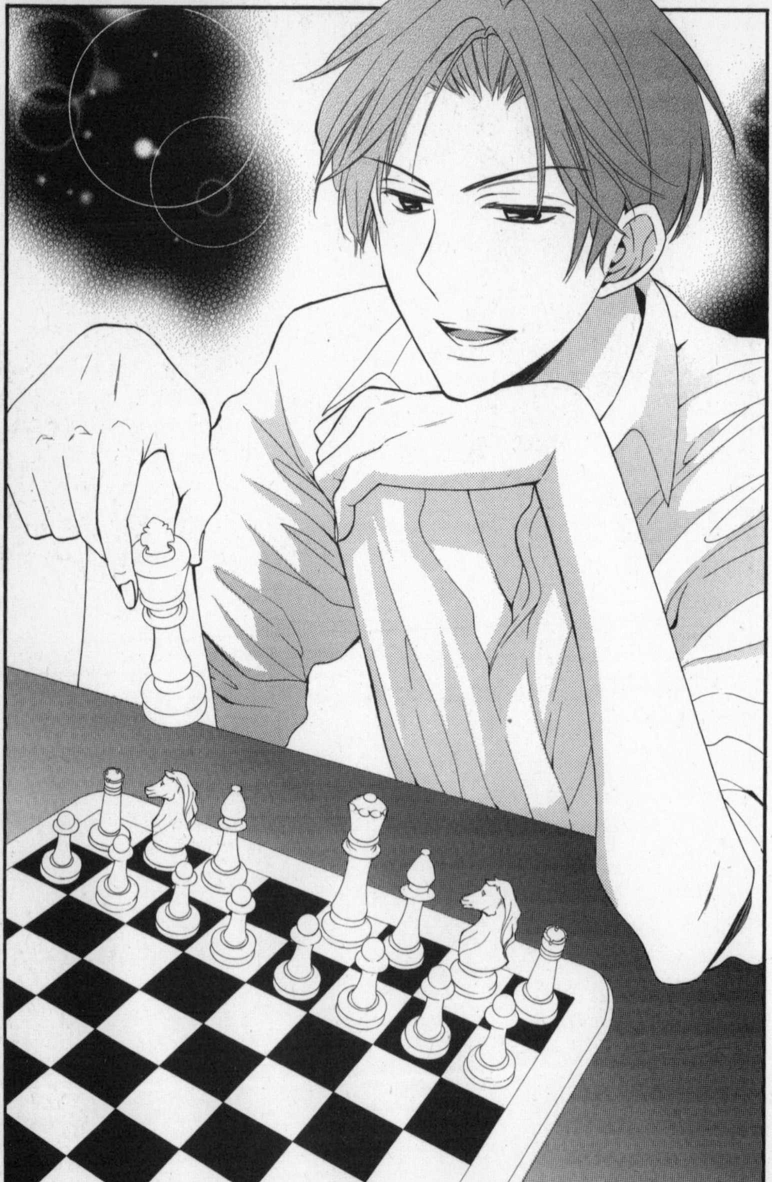

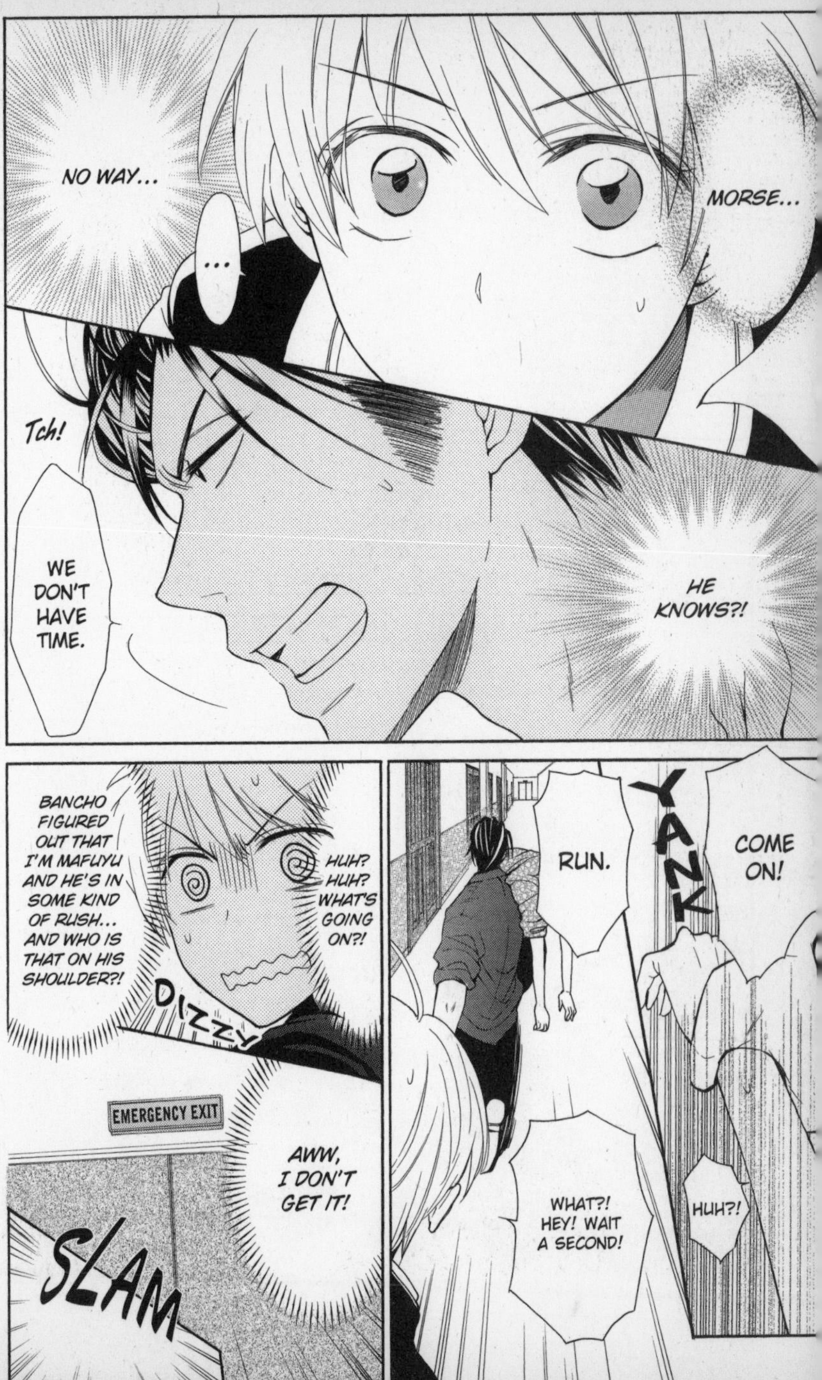
MORSE...
NO WAY...
...
HE KNOWS?!
Tch!
WE DON'T HAVE TIME.
COME ON!
YANK
RUN.
HUH?!
WHAT?! HEY! WAIT A SECOND!
HUH? HUH? WHAT'S GOING ON?!
BANCHO FIGURED OUT THAT I'M MAFUYU AND HE'S IN SOME KIND OF RUSH... AND WHO IS THAT ON HIS SHOULDER?!
DIZZY
AWW, I DON'T GET IT!
EMERGENCY EXIT
SLAM

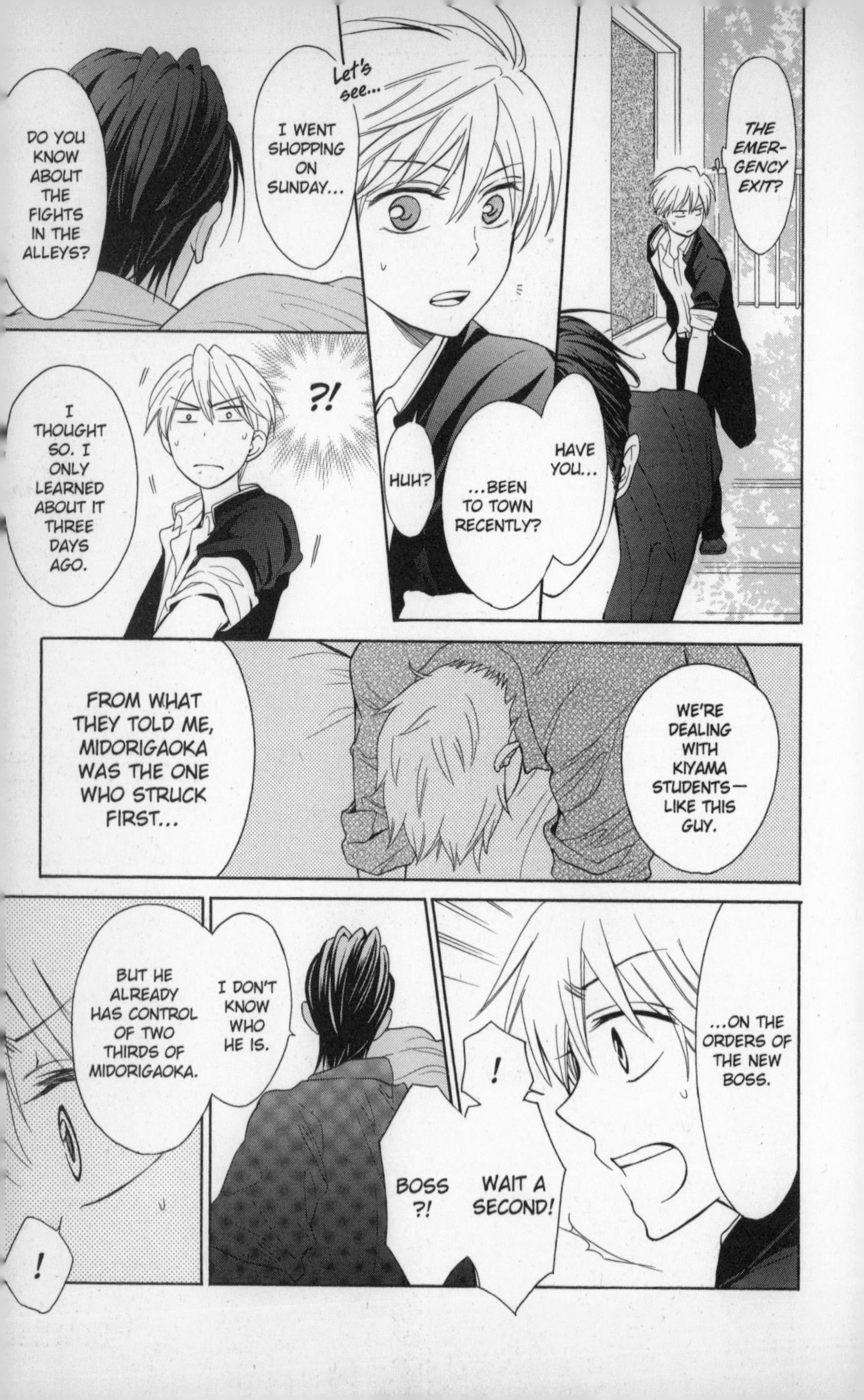
THE EMERGENCY EXIT?
HAVE YOU...
...BEEN TO TOWN RECENTLY?
HUH?
Let's see...
I WENT SHOPPING ON SUNDAY...
DO YOU KNOW ABOUT THE FIGHTS IN THE ALLEYS?
?!
I THOUGHT SO. I ONLY LEARNED ABOUT IT THREE DAYS AGO.
WE'RE DEALING WITH KIYAMA STUDENTS—LIKE THIS GUY.
FROM WHAT THEY TOLD ME, MIDORIGAOKA WAS THE ONE WHO STRUCK FIRST...
...ON THE ORDERS OF THE NEW BOSS.
WAIT A SECOND!
BOSS ?!
!
I DON'T KNOW WHO HE IS.
BUT HE ALREADY HAS CONTROL OF TWO THIRDS OF MIDORIGAOKA.
!

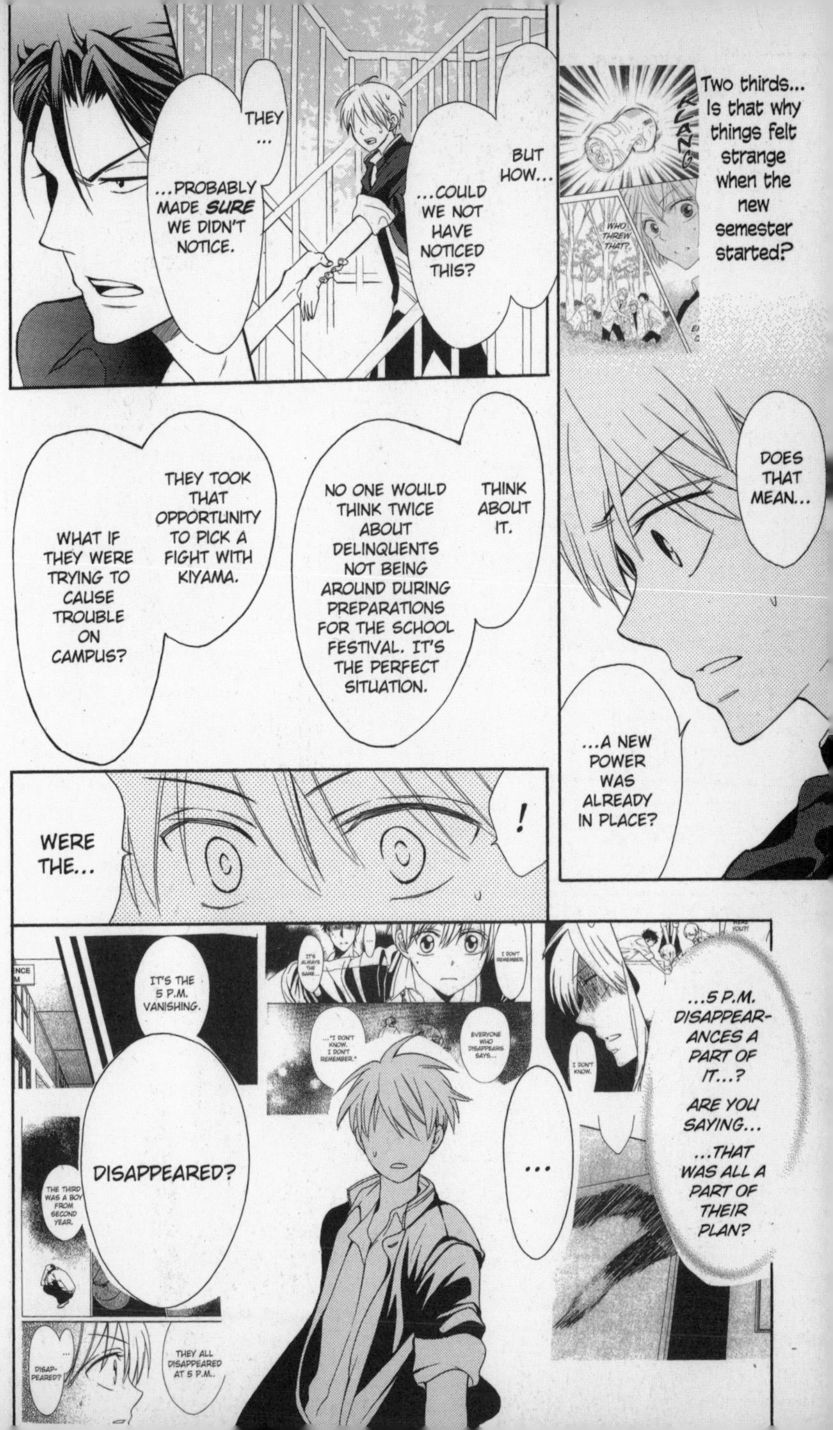
Two thirds... Is that why things felt strange when the new semester started?
KLANG
WHO THREW THAT?
BUT HOW...
...COULD WE NOT HAVE NOTICED THIS?
THEY...
...PROBABLY MADE SURE WE DIDN'T NOTICE.
THINK ABOUT IT.
NO ONE WOULD THINK TWICE ABOUT DELINQUENTS NOT BEING AROUND DURING PREPARATIONS FOR THE SCHOOL FESTIVAL. IT'S THE PERFECT SITUATION.
THEY TOOK THAT OPPORTUNITY TO PICK A FIGHT WITH KIYAMA.
WHAT IF THEY WERE TRYING TO CAUSE TROUBLE ON CAMPUS?
DOES THAT MEAN...
...A NEW POWER WAS ALREADY IN PLACE?
!
WERE THE...
...5 P.M. DISAPPEARANCES A PART OF IT...?
ARE YOU SAYING...
...THAT WAS ALL A PART OF THEIR PLAN?
I DON'T KNOW.
I DON'T REMEMBER.
...
IT'S ALWAYS THE SAME...
EVERYONE WHO DISAPPEARS SAYS...
..."I DON'T KNOW. I DON'T REMEMBER."
IT'S THE 5 P.M. VANISHING.
...
DISAPPEARED?
THE THIRD WAS A BOY FROM SECOND YEAR.
THEY ALL DISAPPEARED AT 5 P.M..
... DISAPPEARED?

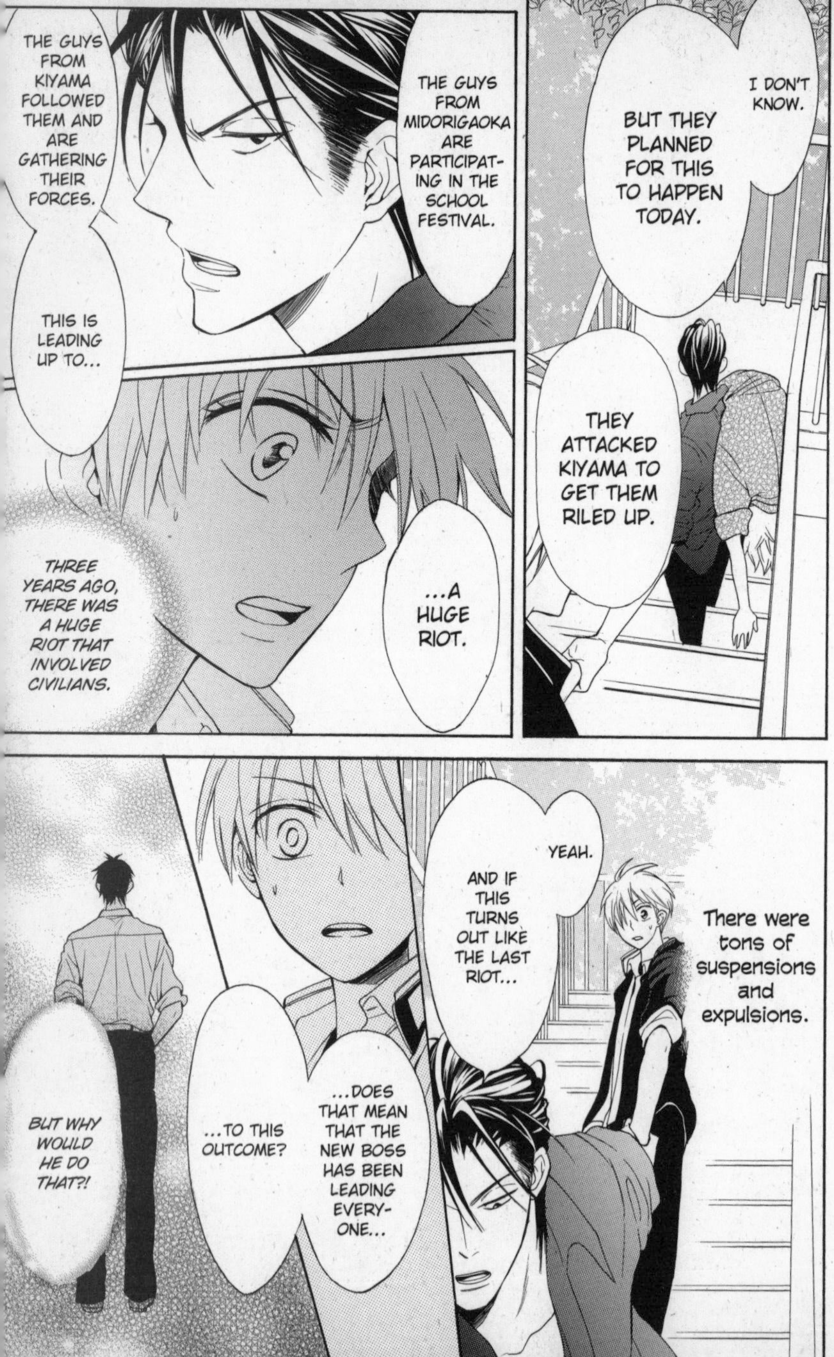
I DON'T KNOW.
BUT THEY PLANNED FOR THIS TO HAPPEN TODAY.
THEY ATTACKED KIYAMA TO GET THEM RILED UP.
THE GUYS FROM MIDORIGAOKA ARE PARTICIPATING IN THE SCHOOL FESTIVAL.
THE GUYS FROM KIYAMA FOLLOWED THEM AND ARE GATHERING THEIR FORCES.
THIS IS LEADING UP TO...
...A HUGE RIOT.
THREE YEARS AGO, THERE WAS A HUGE RIOT THAT INVOLVED CIVILIANS.
YEAH.
AND IF THIS TURNS OUT LIKE THE LAST RIOT...
There were tons of suspensions and expulsions.
...DOES THAT MEAN THAT THE NEW BOSS HAS BEEN LEADING EVERYONE...
...TO THIS OUTCOME?
BUT WHY WOULD HE DO THAT?!

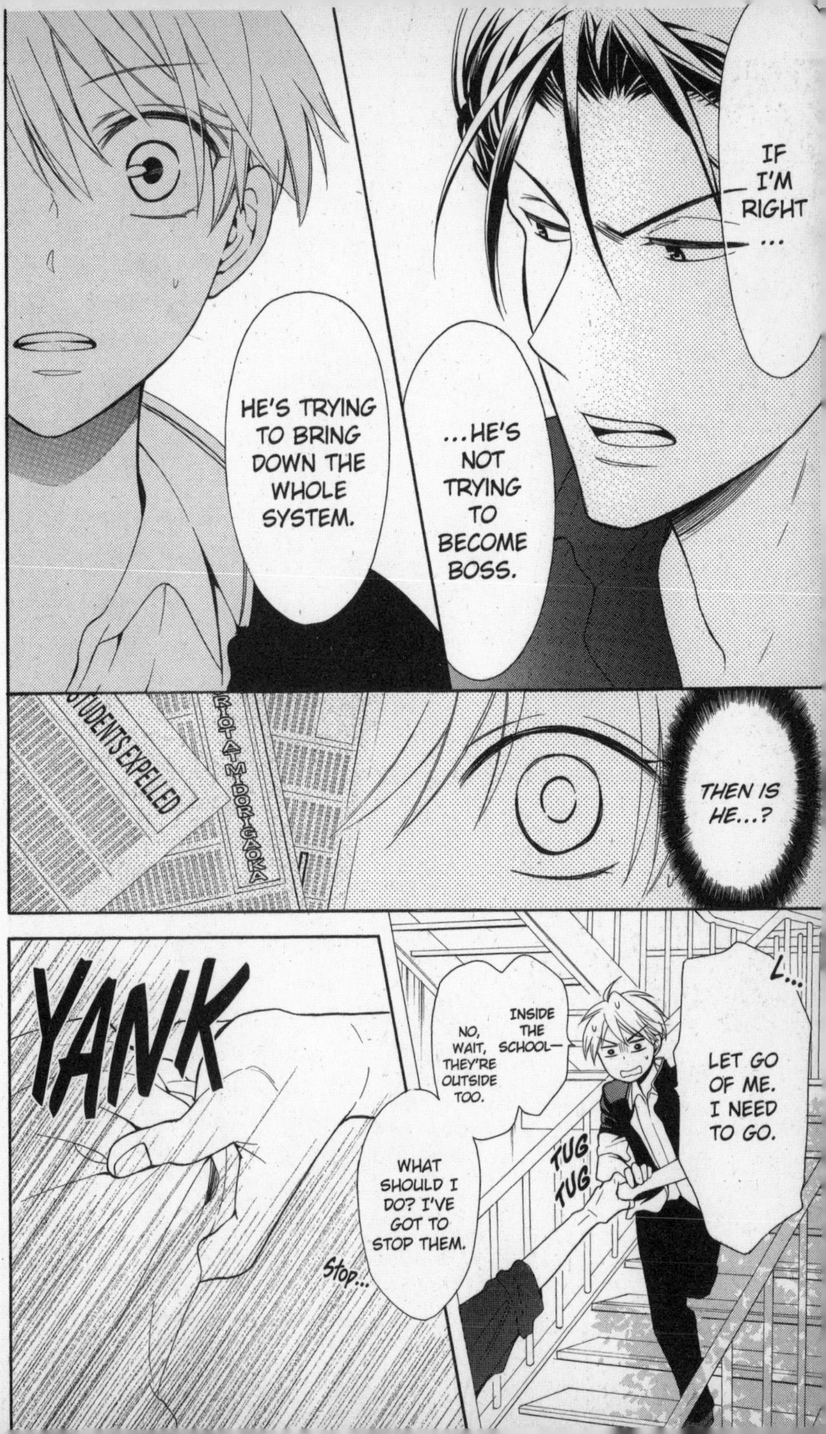
IF I'M RIGHT ...
...HE'S NOT TRYING TO BECOME BOSS.
HE'S TRYING TO BRING DOWN THE WHOLE SYSTEM.
THEN IS HE...?
RIOT AT MIDORIGAOKA
STUDENTS EXPELLED
L...
LET GO OF ME. I NEED TO GO.
TUG TUG
INSIDE THE SCHOOL—
NO, WAIT, THEY'RE OUTSIDE TOO.
WHAT SHOULD I DO? I'VE GOT TO STOP THEM.
Stop...
YANK

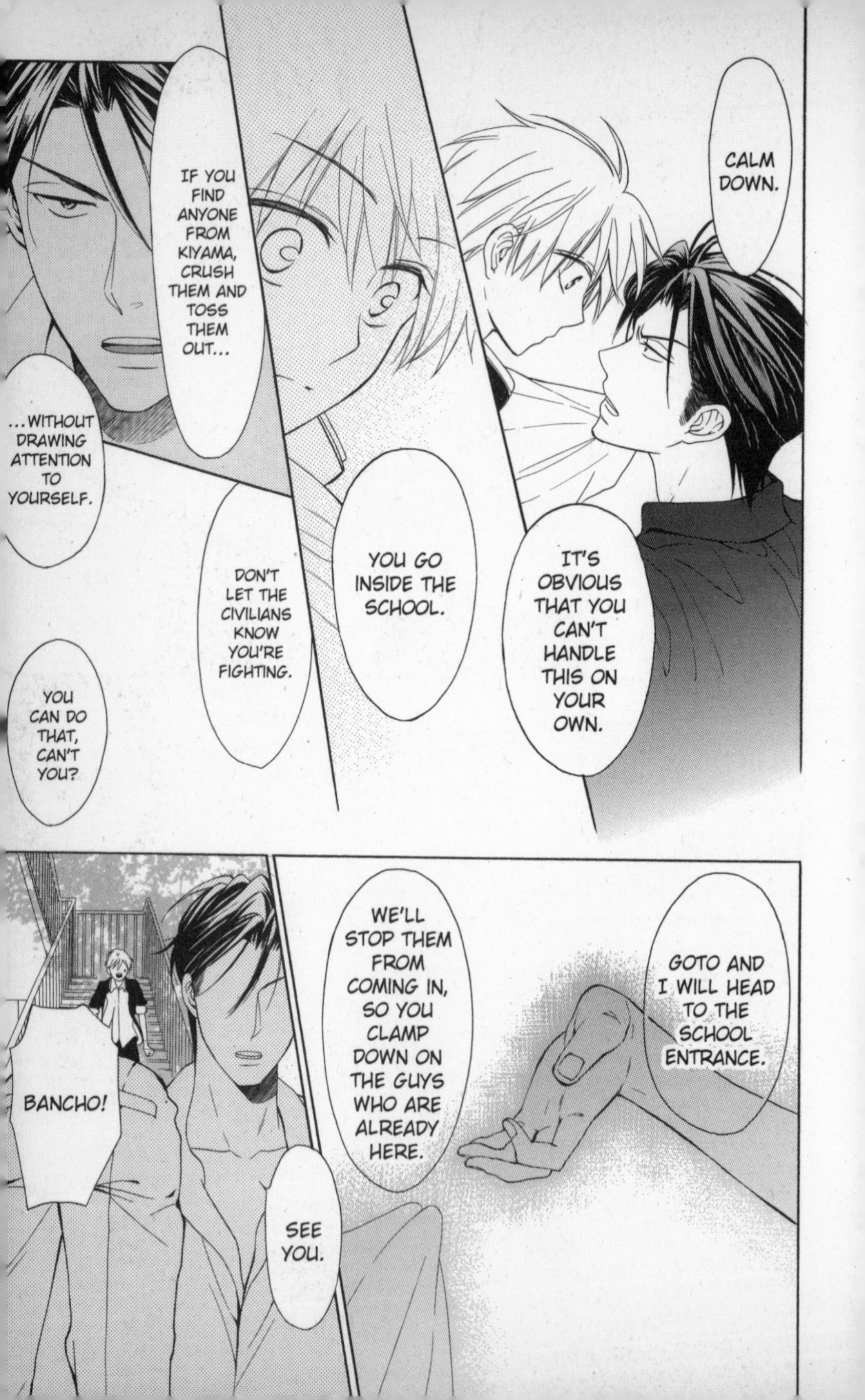
CALM DOWN.
IT'S OBVIOUS THAT YOU CAN'T HANDLE THIS ON YOUR OWN.
YOU GO INSIDE THE SCHOOL.
IF YOU FIND ANYONE FROM KIYAMA, CRUSH THEM AND TOSS THEM OUT...
...WITHOUT DRAWING ATTENTION TO YOURSELF.
DON'T LET THE CIVILIANS KNOW YOU'RE FIGHTING.
YOU CAN DO THAT, CAN'T YOU?
GOTO AND I WILL HEAD TO THE SCHOOL ENTRANCE.
WE'LL STOP THEM FROM COMING IN, SO YOU CLAMP DOWN ON THE GUYS WHO ARE ALREADY HERE.
SEE YOU.
BANCHO!

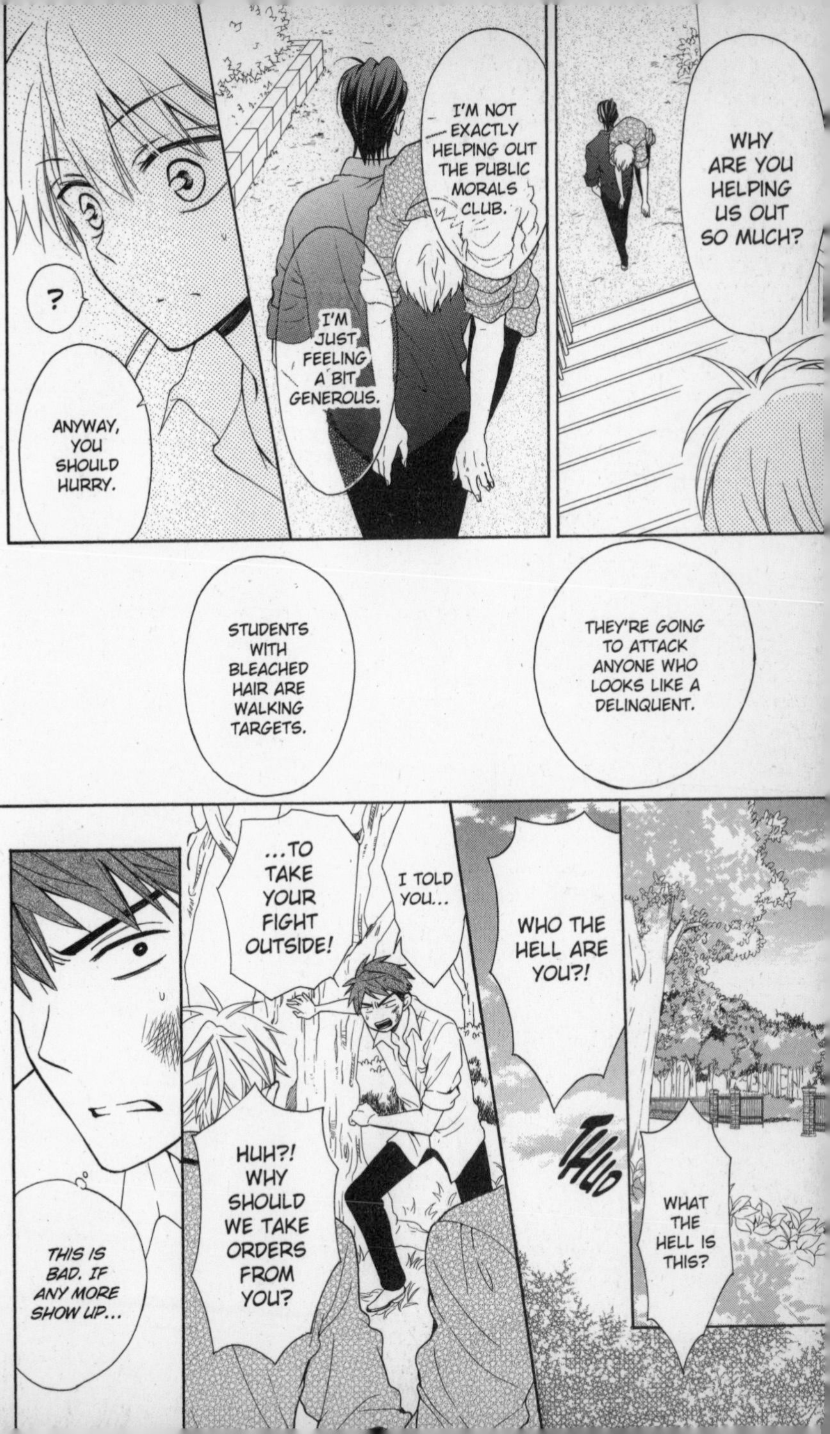
WHY ARE YOU HELPING US OUT SO MUCH?
I'M NOT EXACTLY HELPING OUT THE PUBLIC MORALS CLUB.
I'M JUST FEELING A BIT GENEROUS.
?
ANYWAY, YOU SHOULD HURRY.
THEY'RE GOING TO ATTACK ANYONE WHO LOOKS LIKE A DELINQUENT.
STUDENTS WITH BLEACHED HAIR ARE WALKING TARGETS.
WHAT THE HELL IS THIS?
WHO THE HELL ARE YOU?!
THUD
I TOLD YOU...
...TO TAKE YOUR FIGHT OUTSIDE!
HUH?! WHY SHOULD WE TAKE ORDERS FROM YOU?
THIS IS BAD. IF ANY MORE SHOW UP...

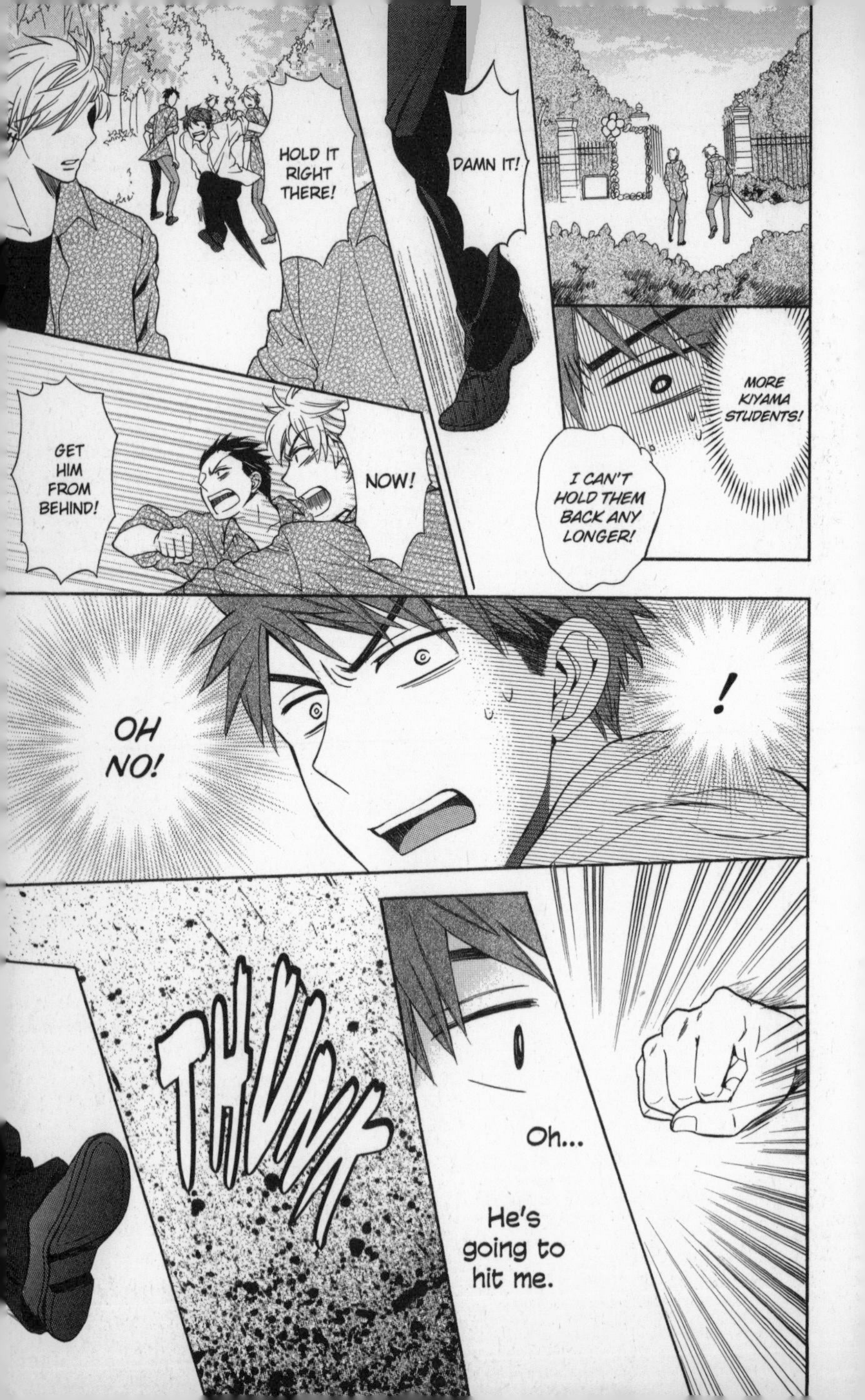
DAMN IT!
HOLD IT RIGHT THERE!
MORE KIYAMA STUDENTS!
I CAN'T HOLD THEM BACK ANY LONGER!
NOW!
GET HIM FROM BEHIND!
!
OH NO!
Oh...
He's going to hit me.
THUNK

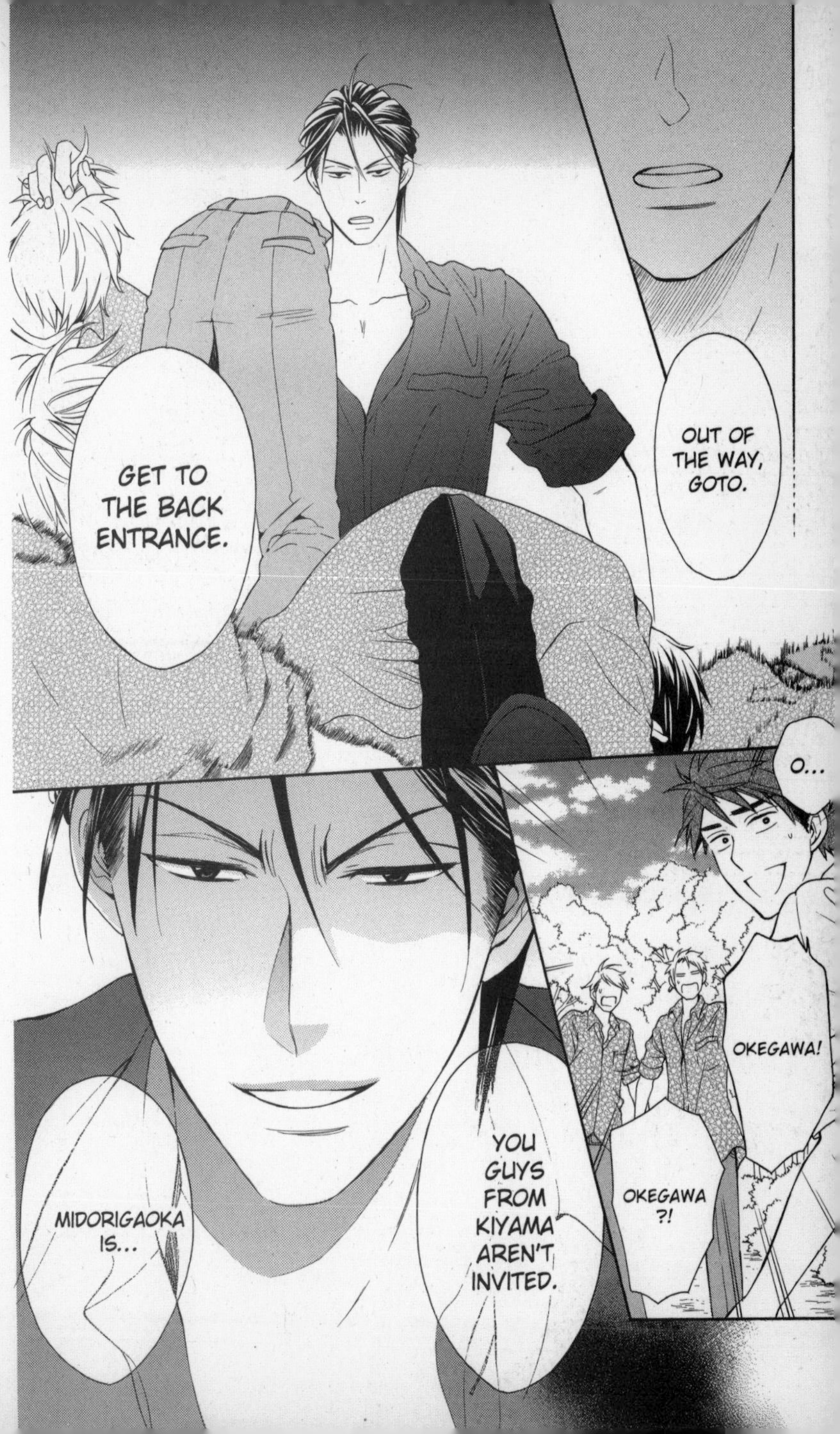
OUT OF THE WAY, GOTO.
GET TO THE BACK ENTRANCE.
O...
OKEGAWA!
OKEGAWA?!
YOU GUYS FROM KIYAMA AREN'T INVITED.
MIDORIGAOKA IS...

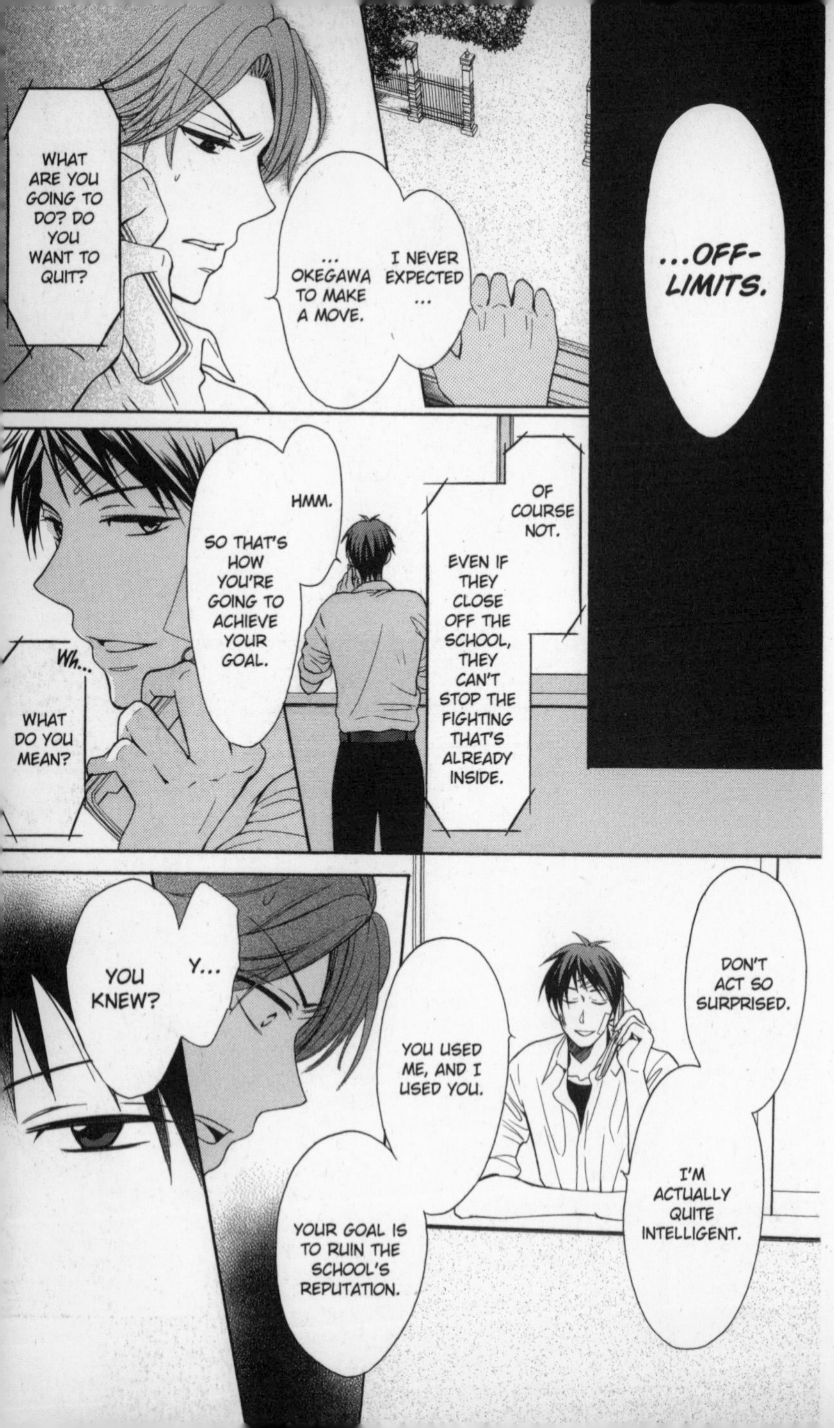
...OFF-LIMITS.
I NEVER EXPECTED ...
... OKEGAWA TO MAKE A MOVE.
WHAT ARE YOU GOING TO DO? DO YOU WANT TO QUIT?
OF COURSE NOT.
EVEN IF THEY CLOSE OFF THE SCHOOL, THEY CAN'T STOP THE FIGHTING THAT'S ALREADY INSIDE.
HMM.
SO THAT'S HOW YOU'RE GOING TO ACHIEVE YOUR GOAL.
Wh...
WHAT DO YOU MEAN?
DON'T ACT SO SURPRISED.
YOU USED ME, AND I USED YOU.
I'M ACTUALLY QUITE INTELLIGENT.
YOUR GOAL IS TO RUIN THE SCHOOL'S REPUTATION.
Y...
YOU KNEW?

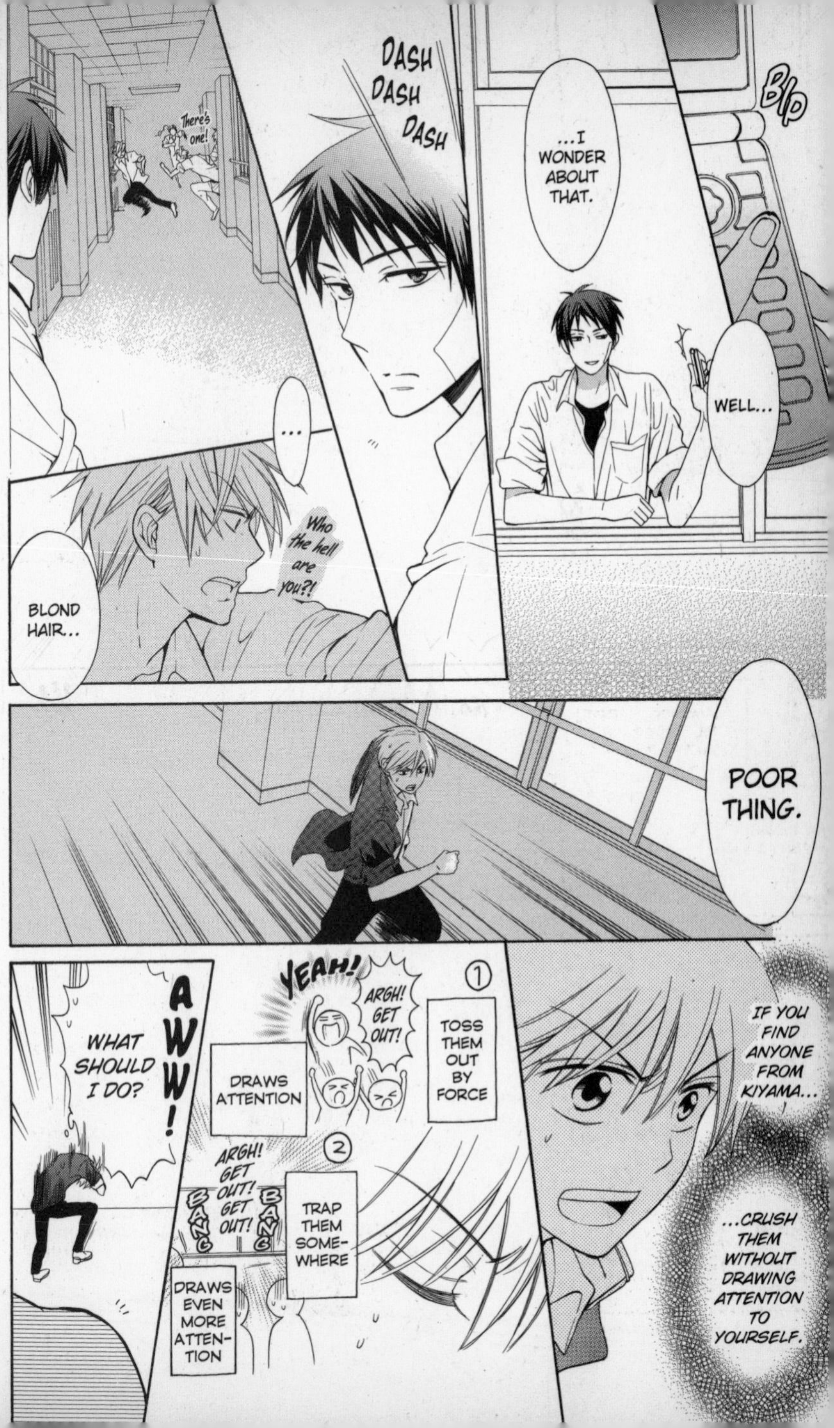
BIP
...I WONDER ABOUT THAT.
WELL...
DASH DASH DASH
There's one!
...
Who the hell are you?!
BLOND HAIR...
POOR THING.
IF YOU FIND ANYONE FROM KIYAMA...
...CRUSH THEM WITHOUT DRAWING ATTENTION TO YOURSELF.
①
TOSS THEM OUT BY FORCE
ARGH! GET OUT!
YEAH!
DRAWS ATTENTION
②
TRAP THEM SOMEWHERE
ARGH! GET OUT! GET OUT!
BANG
BANG
DRAWS EVEN MORE ATTENTION
AWW!
WHAT SHOULD I DO?

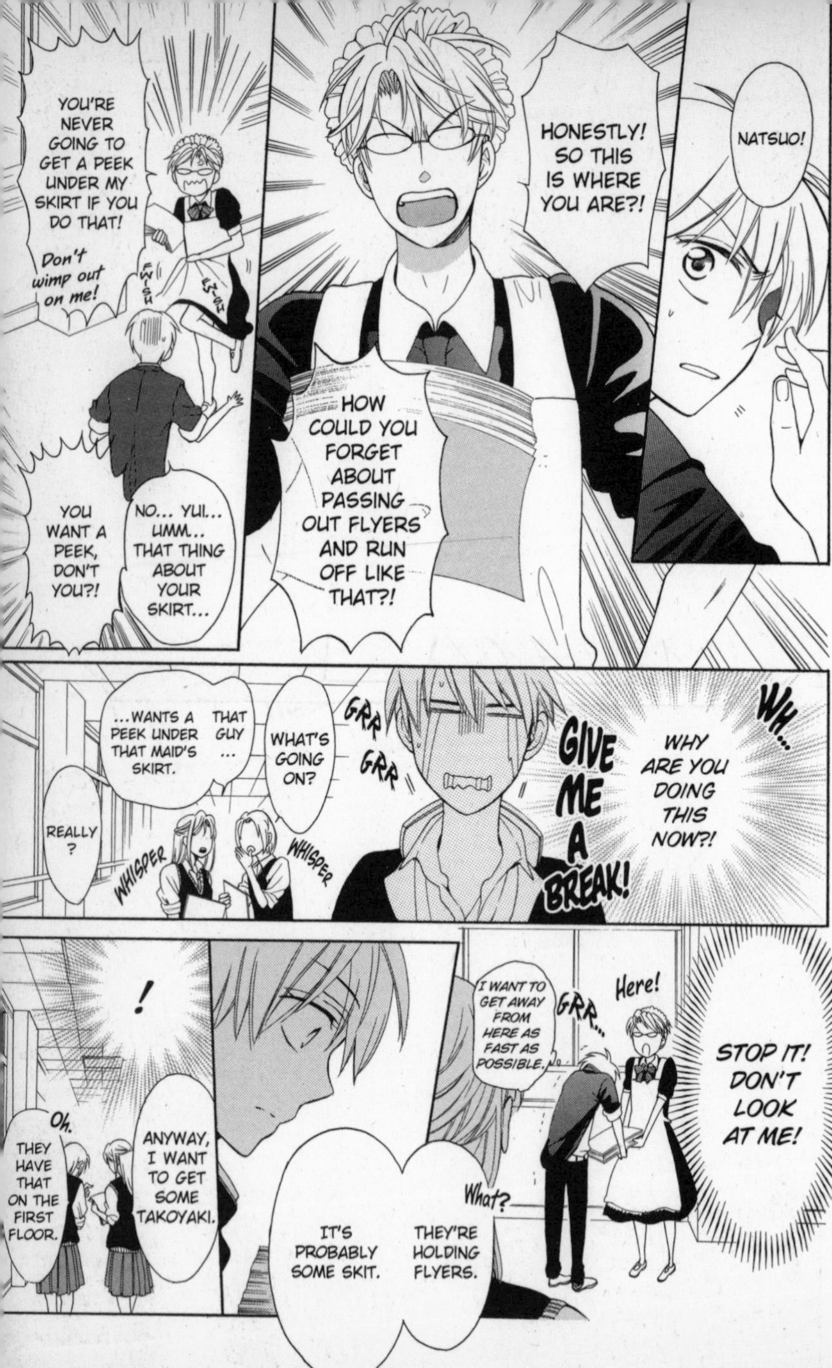
NATSUO!
HONESTLY! SO THIS IS WHERE YOU ARE?!
HOW COULD YOU FORGET ABOUT PASSING OUT FLYERS AND RUN OFF LIKE THAT?!
YOU'RE NEVER GOING TO GET A PEEK UNDER MY SKIRT IF YOU DO THAT!
FWISH
FWISH
Don't wimp out on me!
NO... YUI... UMM... THAT THING ABOUT YOUR SKIRT...
YOU WANT A PEEK, DON'T YOU?!
WH...
WHY ARE YOU DOING THIS NOW?!
GIVE ME A BREAK!
GRR
GRR
WHAT'S GOING ON?
THAT GUY...
...WANTS A PEEK UNDER THAT MAID'S SKIRT.
REALLY?
WHISPER
WHISPER
STOP IT! DON'T LOOK AT ME!
Here!
GRR...
I WANT TO GET AWAY FROM HERE AS FAST AS POSSIBLE.
What?
THEY'RE HOLDING FLYERS.
IT'S PROBABLY SOME SKIT.
!
ANYWAY, I WANT TO GET SOME TAKOYAKI.
Oh.
THEY HAVE THAT ON THE FIRST FLOOR.

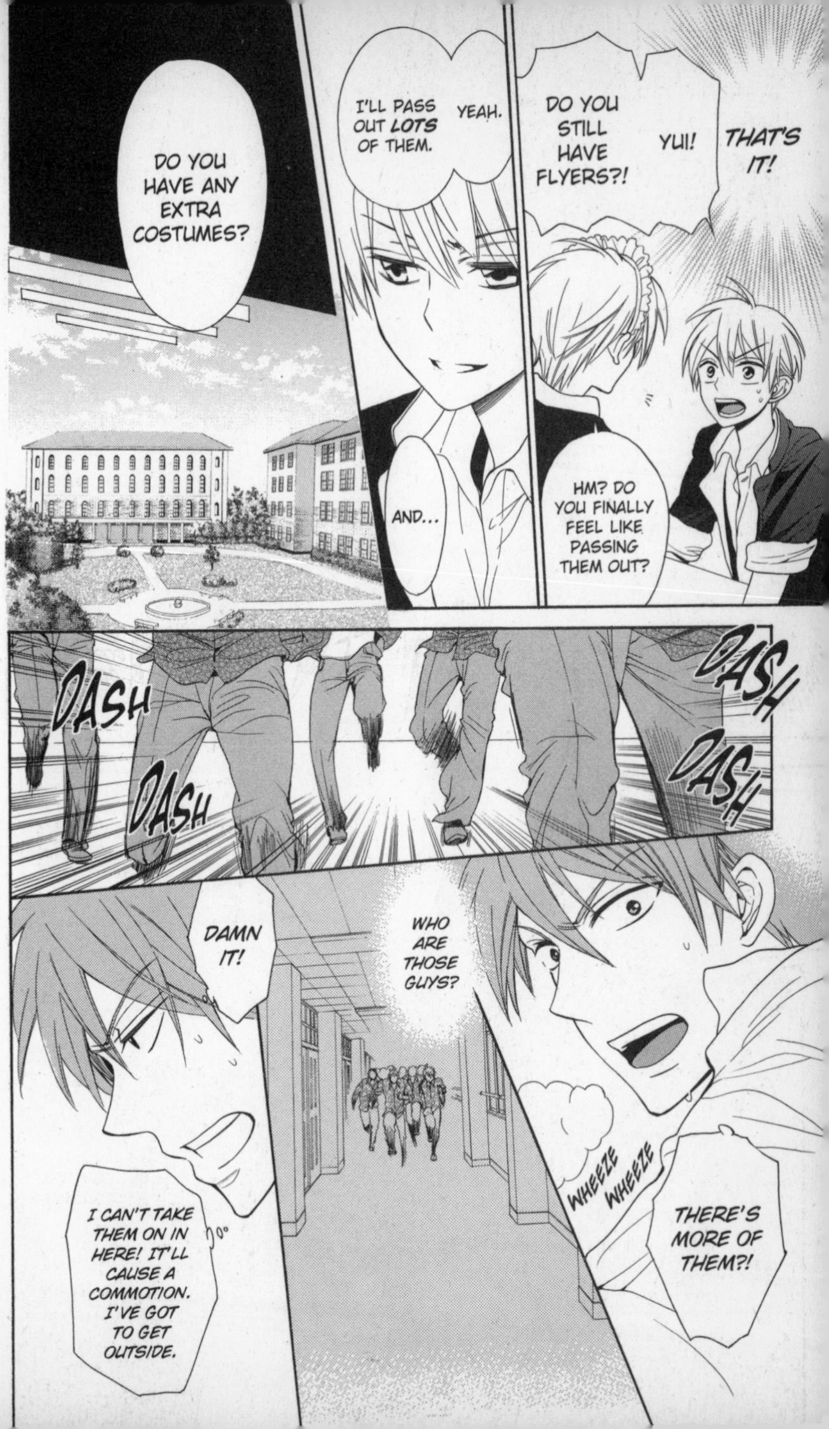
THAT'S IT!
YUI!
DO YOU STILL HAVE FLYERS?!
HM? DO YOU FINALLY FEEL LIKE PASSING THEM OUT?
YEAH.
I'LL PASS OUT LOTS OF THEM.
AND...
DO YOU HAVE ANY EXTRA COSTUMES?
DASH
DASH
DASH
DASH
WHO ARE THOSE GUYS?
WHEEZE WHEEZE
THERE'S MORE OF THEM?!
DAMN IT!
I CAN'T TAKE THEM ON IN HERE! IT'LL CAUSE A COMMOTION. I'VE GOT TO GET OUTSIDE.

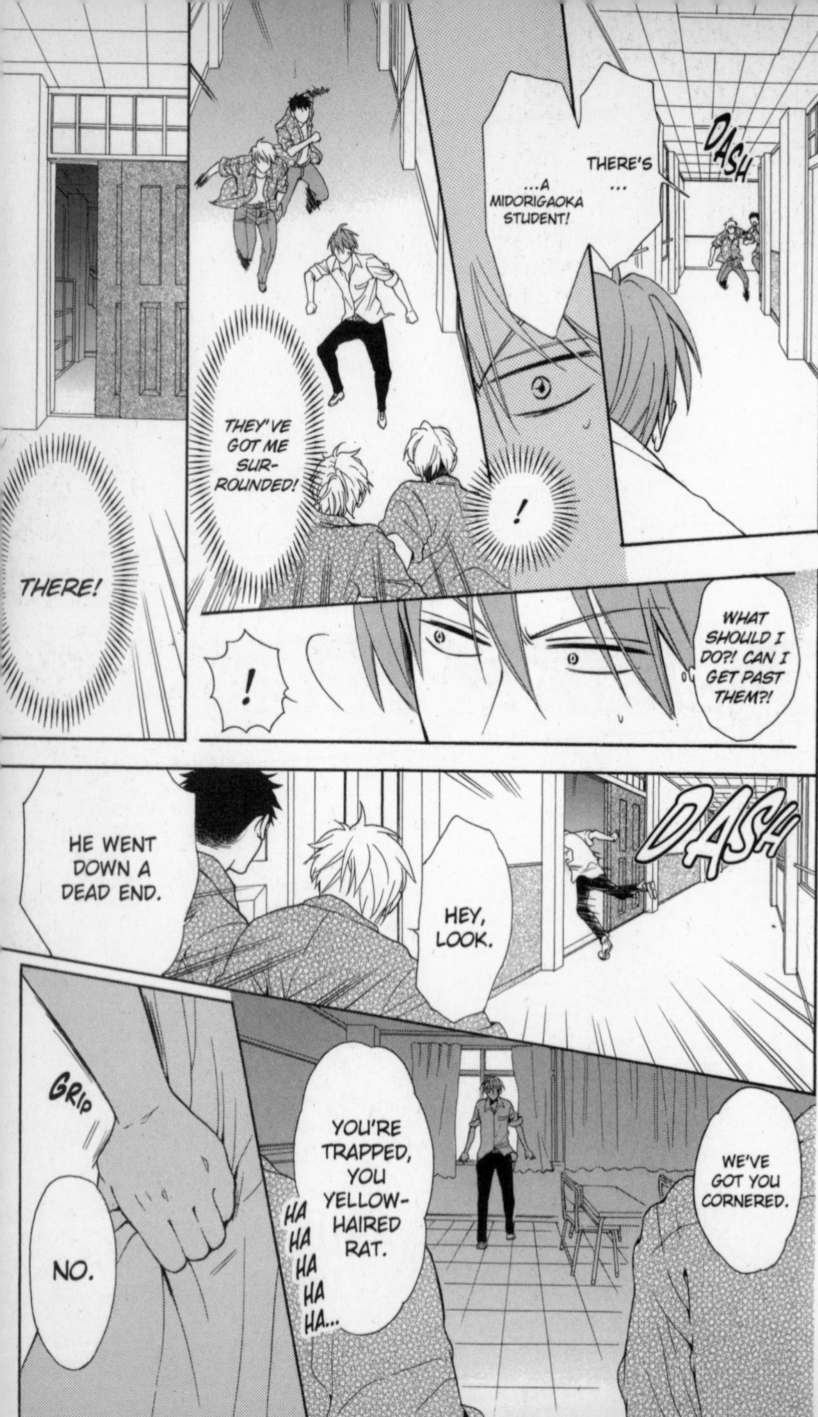
DASH
THERE'S ...
...A MIDORIGAOKA STUDENT!
!
THEY'VE GOT ME SUR-ROUNDED!
WHAT SHOULD I DO?! CAN I GET PAST THEM?!
!
THERE!
DASH
HEY, LOOK.
HE WENT DOWN A DEAD END.
WE'VE GOT YOU CORNERED.
YOU'RE TRAPPED, YOU YELLOW-HAIRED RAT.
HA HA HA HA HA...
GRIP
NO.

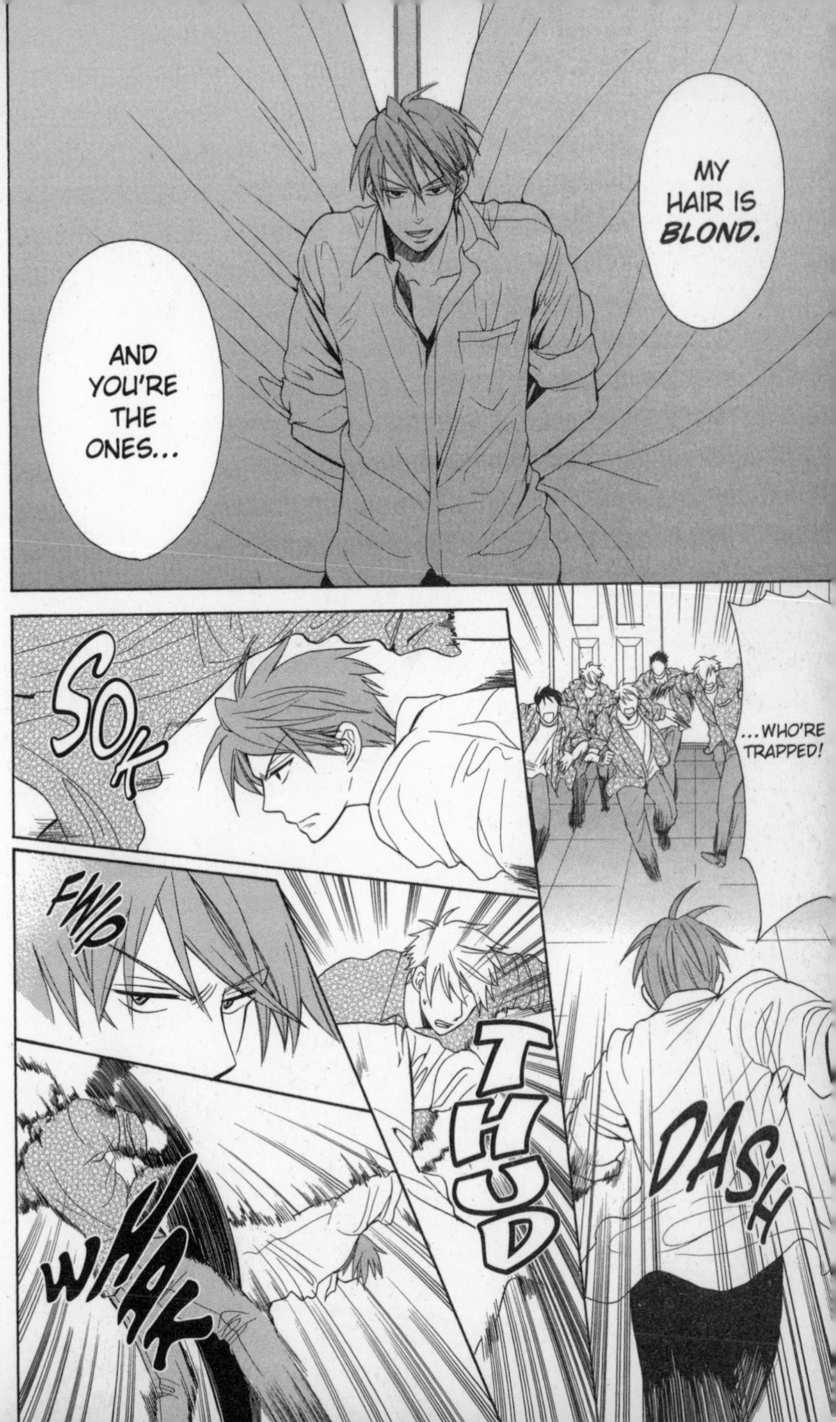
MY HAIR IS BLOND.
AND YOU'RE THE ONES...
...WHO'RE TRAPPED!
SOK
DASH
FWIP
THUD
WHAK

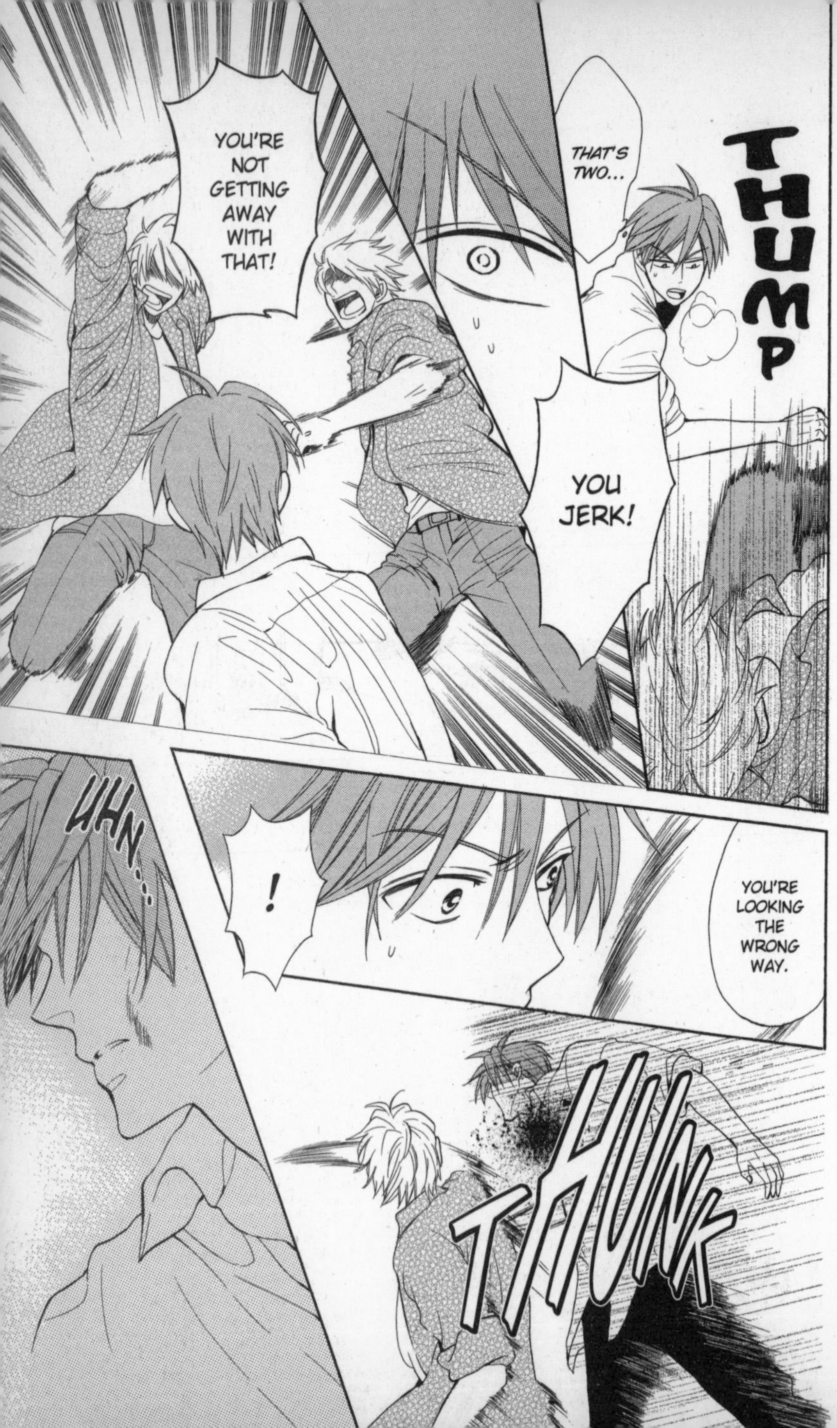
THUMP
THAT'S TWO...
YOU JERK!
YOU'RE NOT GETTING AWAY WITH THAT!
YOU'RE LOOKING THE WRONG WAY.
!
THUNK
UHN...

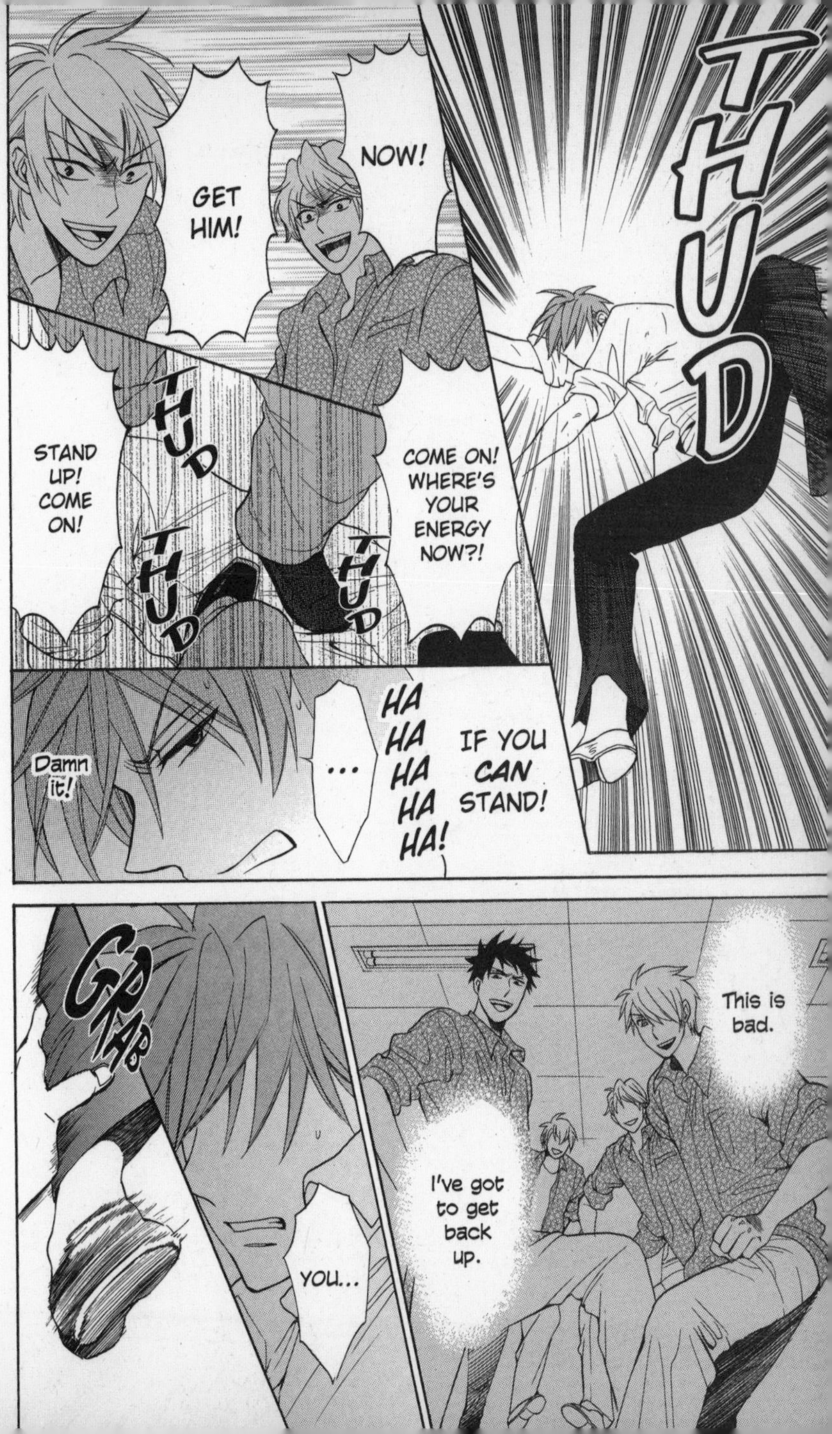
THUD
NOW!
GET HIM!
COME ON! WHERE'S YOUR ENERGY NOW?!
THUD
THUD
THUD
STAND UP! COME ON!
IF YOU CAN STAND!
HA HA HA HA HA!
...
Damn it!
This is bad.
I've got to get back up.
YOU...
GRAB

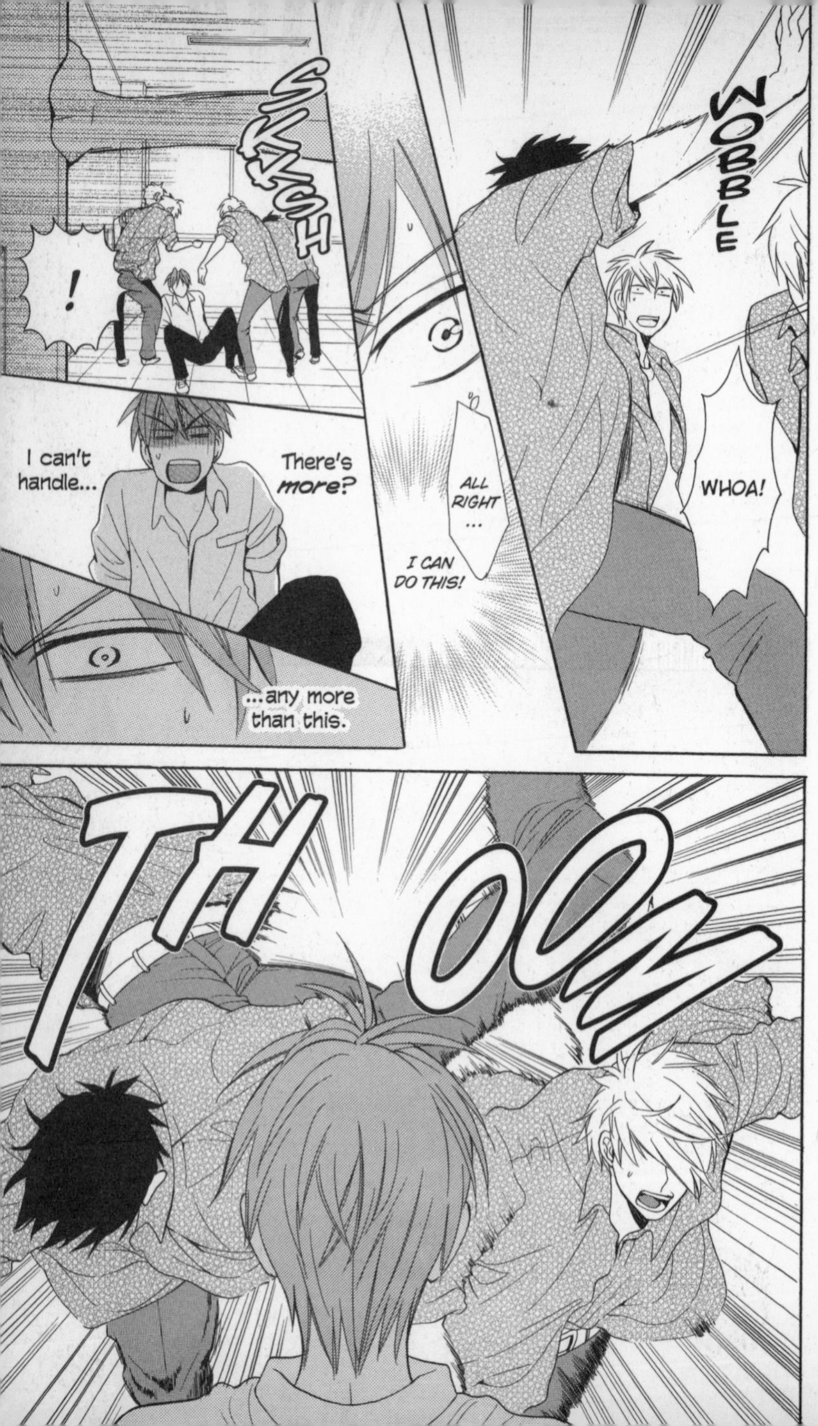
WOBBLE
WHOA!
ALL RIGHT ...
I CAN DO THIS!
SKKSH
!
There's *more*?
I can't handle...
...any more than this.
THOOM

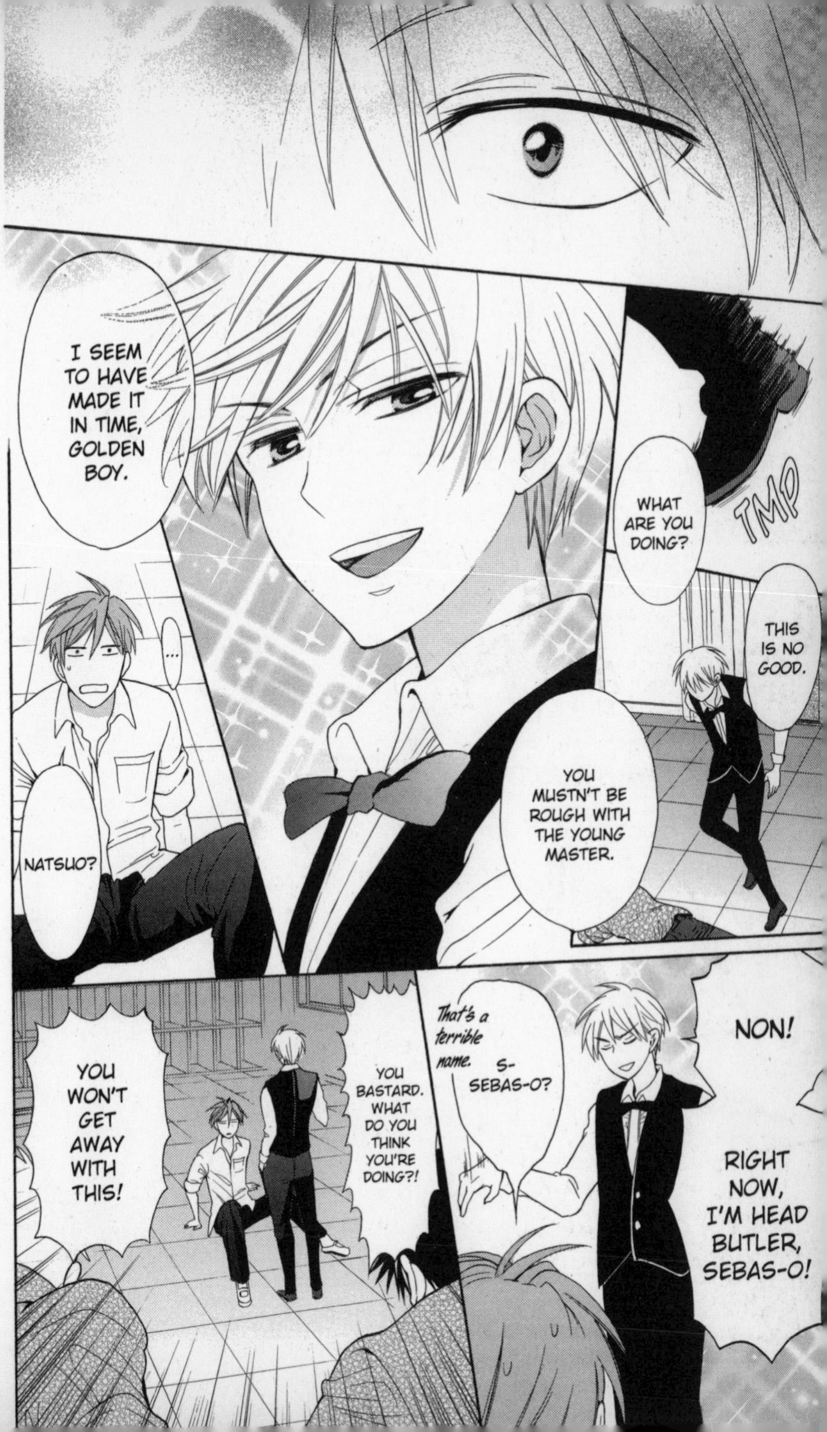
TMP
WHAT ARE YOU DOING?
THIS IS NO GOOD.
YOU MUSTN'T BE ROUGH WITH THE YOUNG MASTER.
I SEEM TO HAVE MADE IT IN TIME, GOLDEN BOY.
...
NATSUO?
NON!
RIGHT NOW, I'M HEAD BUTLER, SEBAS-O!
S-SEBAS-O?
That's a terrible name.
YOU BASTARD. WHAT DO YOU THINK YOU'RE DOING?!
YOU WON'T GET AWAY WITH THIS!

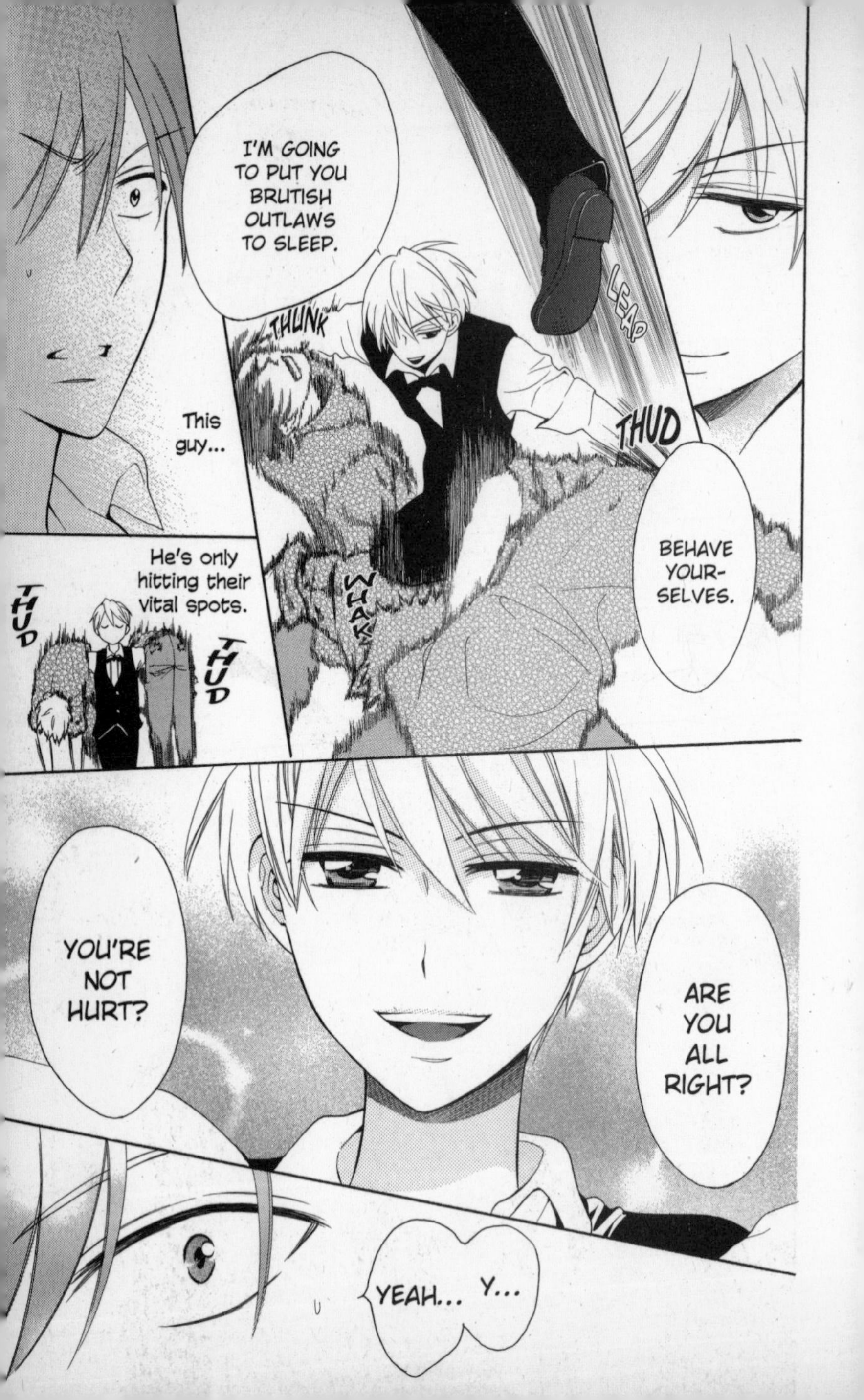
LEAP
THUD
BEHAVE YOURSELVES.
I'M GOING TO PUT YOU BRUTISH OUTLAWS TO SLEEP.
THUNK
WHAK
This guy...
He's only hitting their vital spots.
THUD
THUD
ARE YOU ALL RIGHT?
YOU'RE NOT HURT?
YEAH... Y...

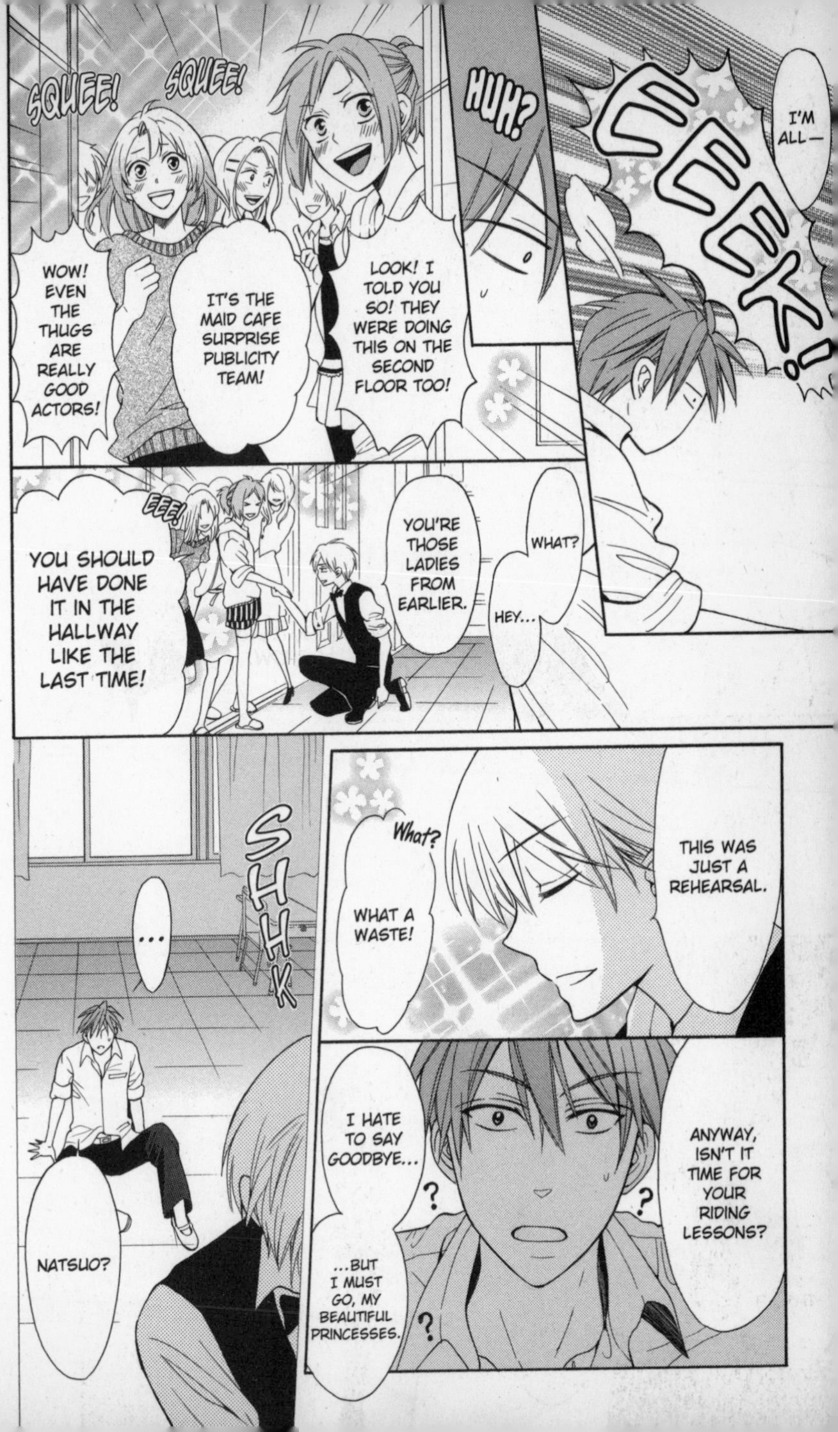
I'M ALL—
EEEK!
HUH?
SQUEE! SQUEE!
LOOK! I TOLD YOU SO! THEY WERE DOING THIS ON THE SECOND FLOOR TOO!
IT'S THE MAID CAFE SURPRISE PUBLICITY TEAM!
WOW! EVEN THE THUGS ARE REALLY GOOD ACTORS!
WHAT?
HEY...
YOU'RE THOSE LADIES FROM EARLIER.
EEE!
YOU SHOULD HAVE DONE IT IN THE HALLWAY LIKE THE LAST TIME!
THIS WAS JUST A REHEARSAL.
What?
WHAT A WASTE!
ANYWAY, ISN'T IT TIME FOR YOUR RIDING LESSONS?
I HATE TO SAY GOODBYE...
...BUT I MUST GO, MY BEAUTIFUL PRINCESSES.
SHHK
...
NATSUO?

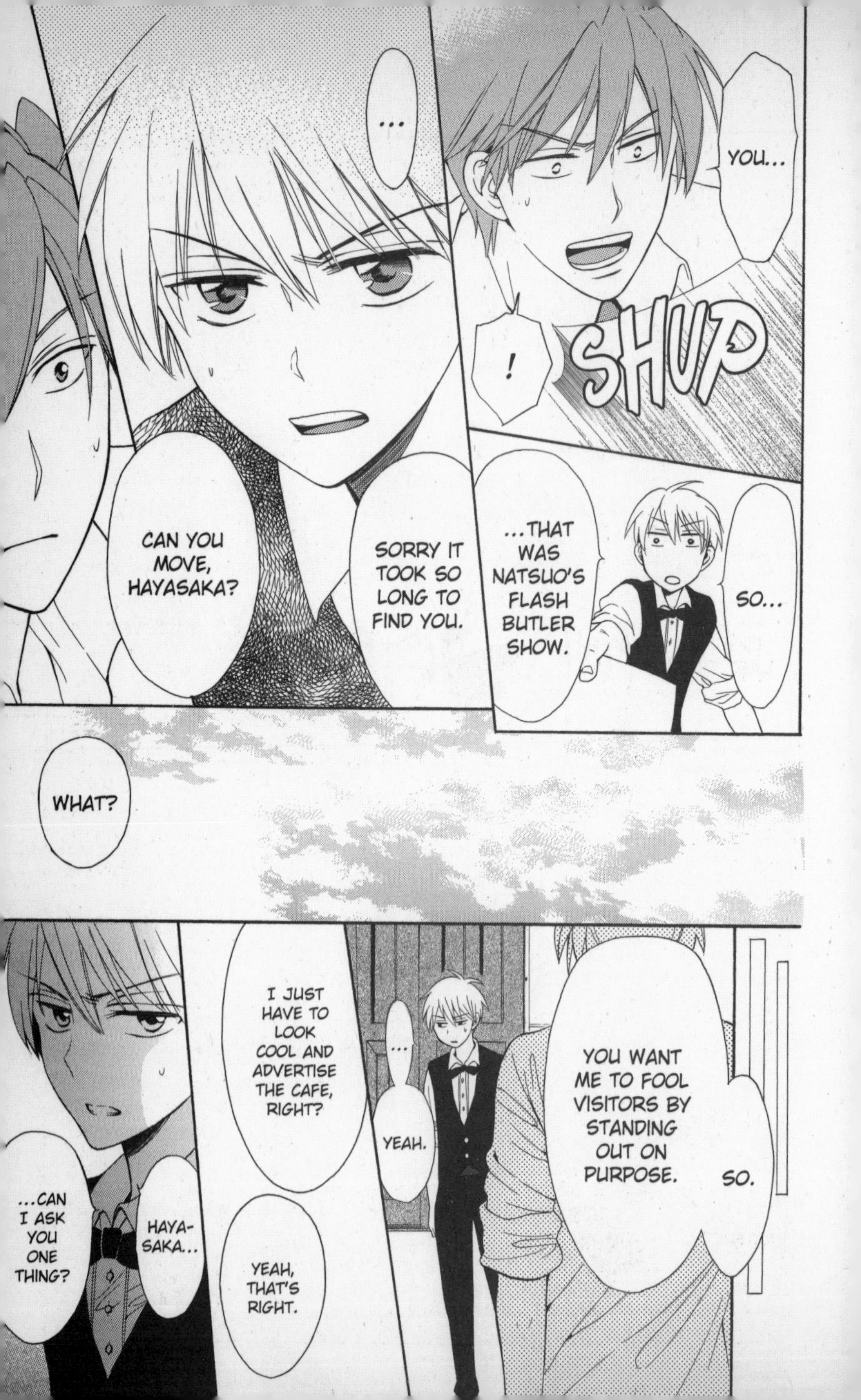
YOU...
SHUP
!
SO...
...THAT WAS NATSUO'S FLASH BUTLER SHOW.
...
SORRY IT TOOK SO LONG TO FIND YOU.
CAN YOU MOVE, HAYASAKA?
WHAT?
SO.
YOU WANT ME TO FOOL VISITORS BY STANDING OUT ON PURPOSE.
...
YEAH.
I JUST HAVE TO LOOK COOL AND ADVERTISE THE CAFE, RIGHT?
YEAH, THAT'S RIGHT.
HAYA-SAKA...
...CAN I ASK YOU ONE THING?

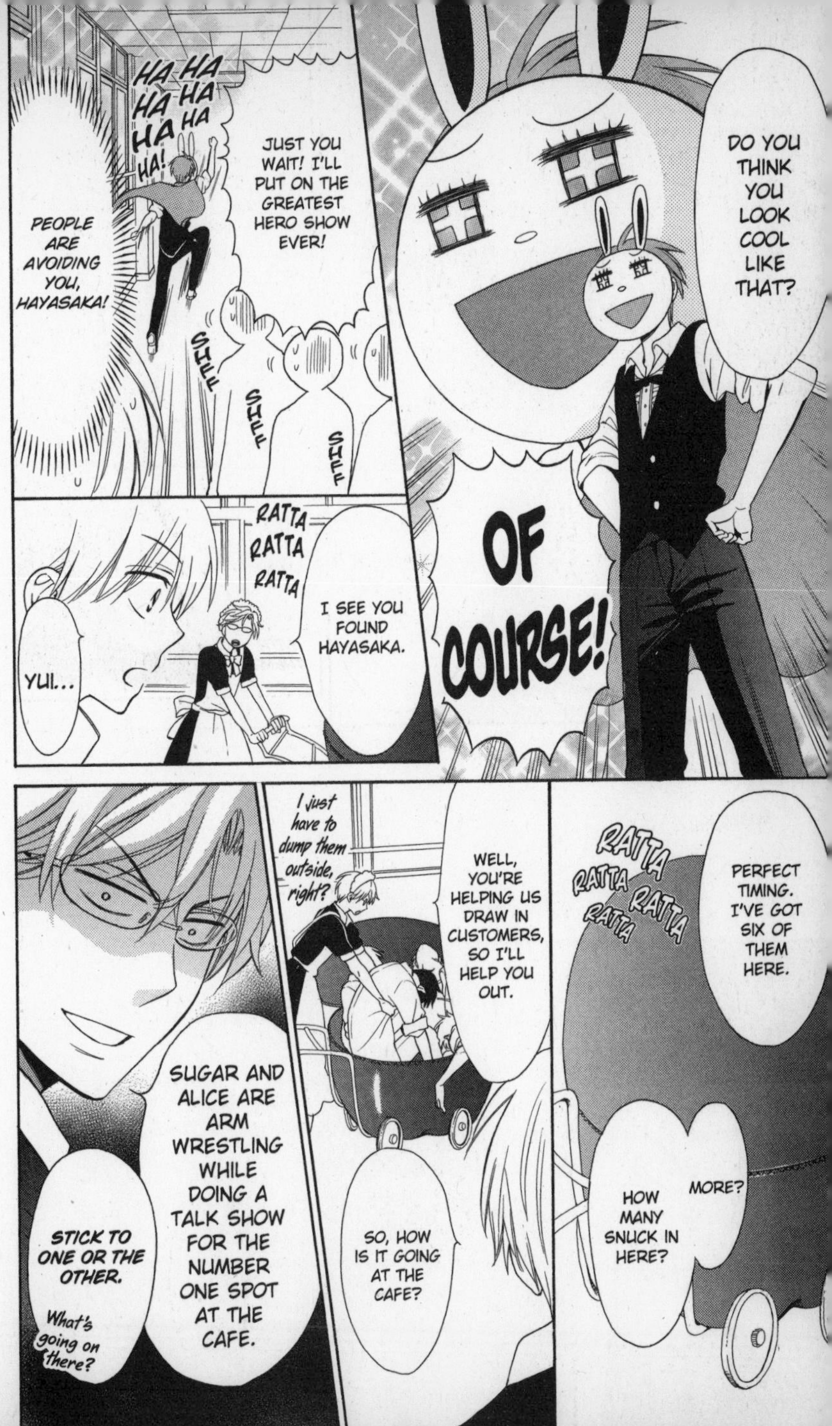
DO YOU THINK YOU LOOK COOL LIKE THAT?
OF COURSE!
HA-HA HA-HA HA-HA HA HA HA!
JUST YOU WAIT! I'LL PUT ON THE GREATEST HERO SHOW EVER!
PEOPLE ARE AVOIDING YOU, HAYASAKA!
SHFF
SHFF
SHFF
RATTA RATTA RATTA
I SEE YOU FOUND HAYASAKA.
YUI...
RATTA RATTA RATTA RATTA
PERFECT TIMING. I'VE GOT SIX OF THEM HERE.
MORE?
HOW MANY SNUCK IN HERE?
WELL, YOU'RE HELPING US DRAW IN CUSTOMERS, SO I'LL HELP YOU OUT.
I just have to dump them outside, right?
SO, HOW IS IT GOING AT THE CAFE?
SUGAR AND ALICE ARE ARM WRESTLING WHILE DOING A TALK SHOW FOR THE NUMBER ONE SPOT AT THE CAFE.
STICK TO ONE OR THE OTHER.
What's going on there?

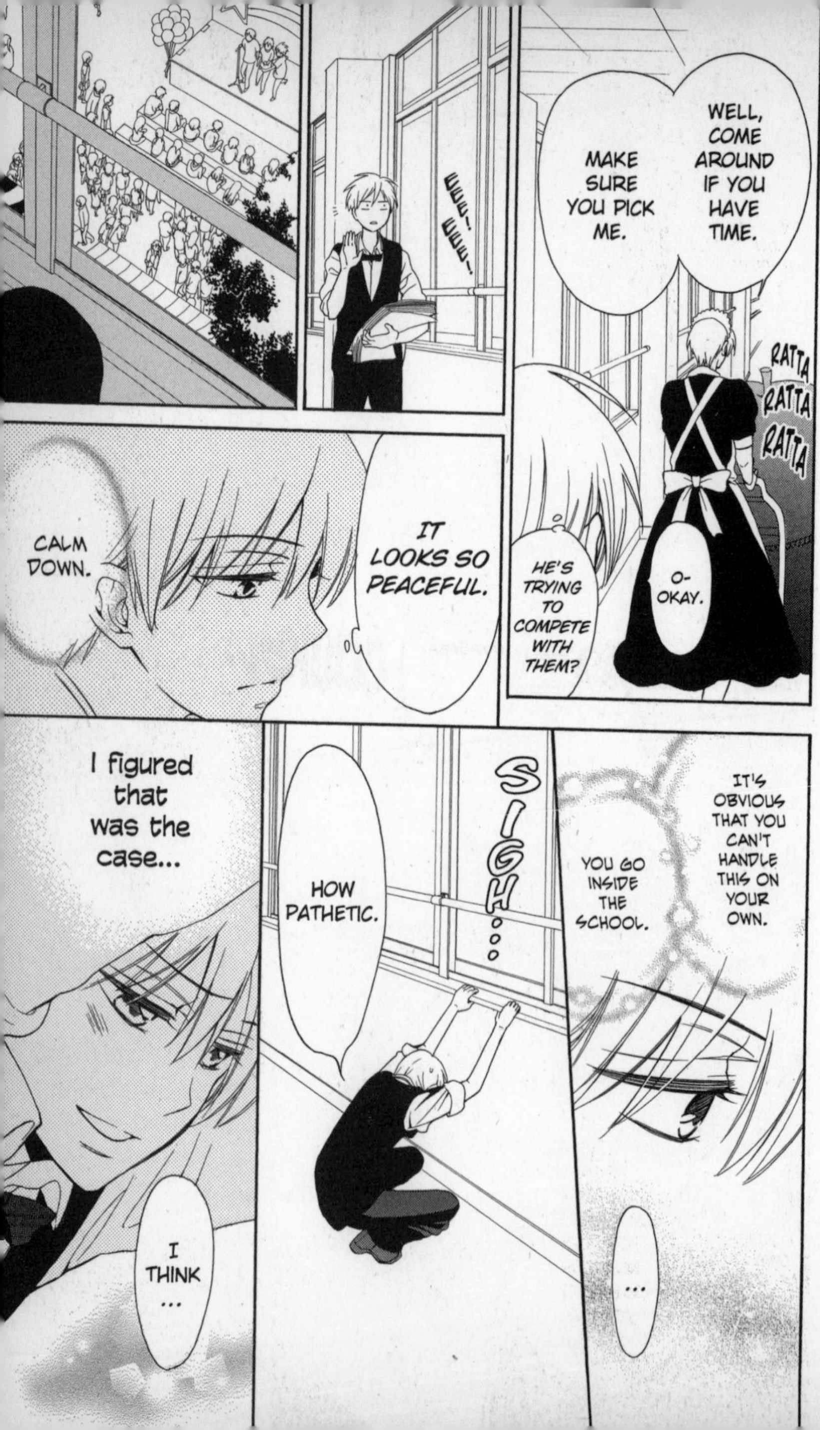
WELL, COME AROUND IF YOU HAVE TIME.
MAKE SURE YOU PICK ME.
RATTA RATTA RATTA
O-OKAY.
HE'S TRYING TO COMPETE WITH THEM?
EEE! EEE!
IT LOOKS SO PEACEFUL.
CALM DOWN.
IT'S OBVIOUS THAT YOU CAN'T HANDLE THIS ON YOUR OWN.
YOU GO INSIDE THE SCHOOL.
...
SIGH...
HOW PATHETIC.
I figured that was the case...
I THINK...

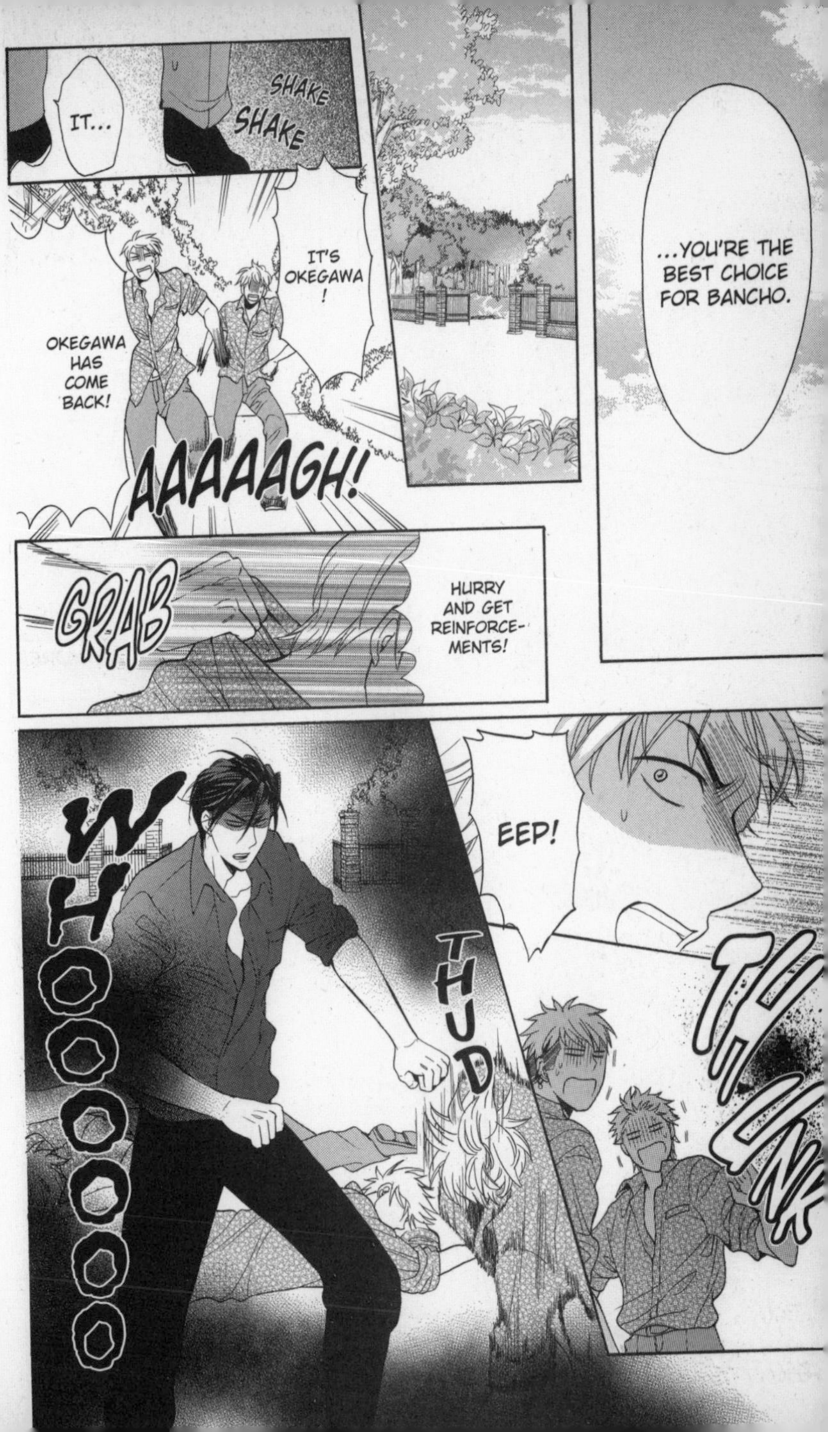
...YOU'RE THE BEST CHOICE FOR BANCHO.
IT...
SHAKE SHAKE
IT'S OKEGAWA!
OKEGAWA HAS COME BACK!
AAAAAGH!
HURRY AND GET REINFORCE-MENTS!
GRAB
EEP!
THUNK
THUD
WHOOOOOOO

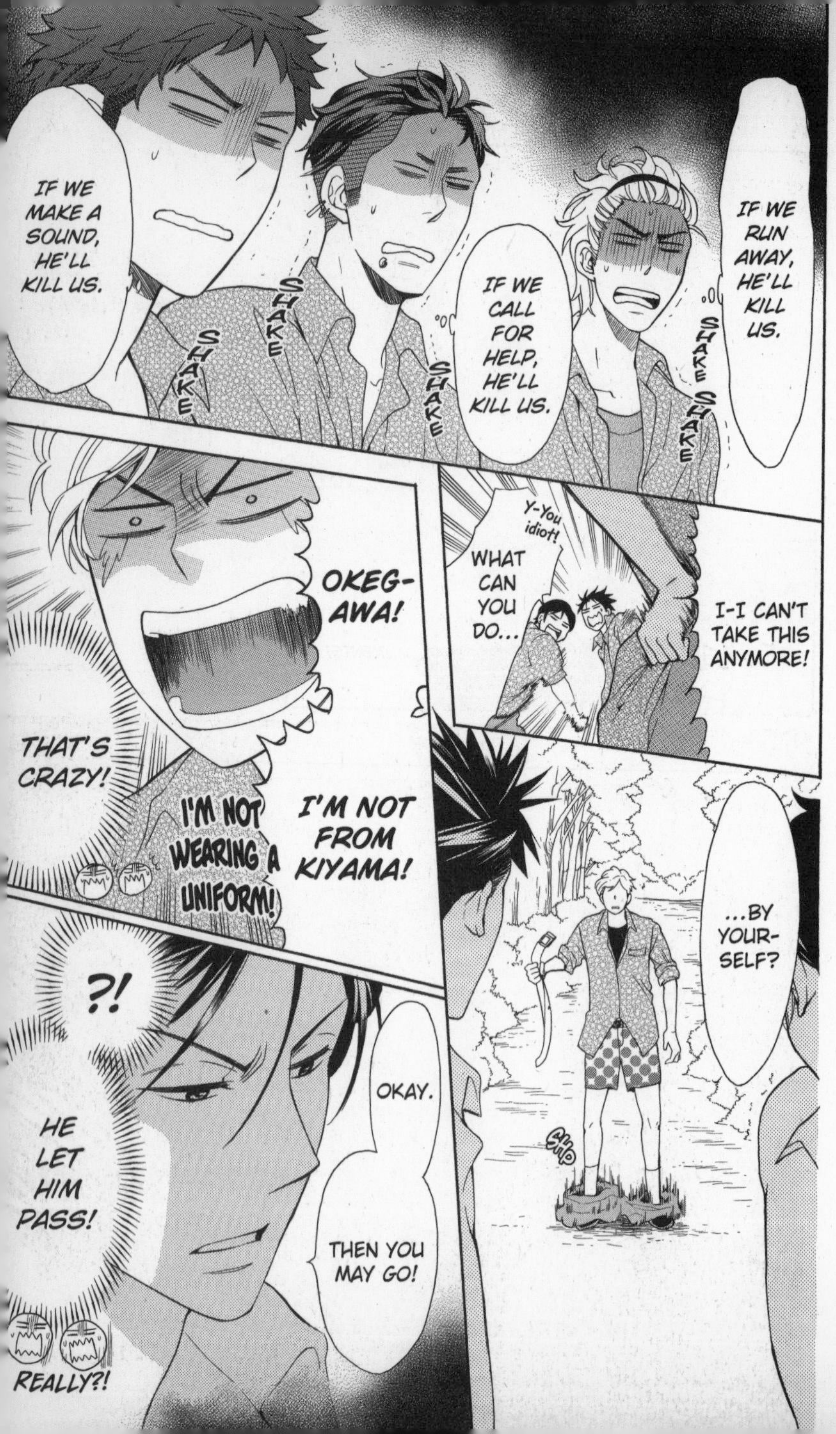
IF WE RUN AWAY, HE'LL KILL US.
SHAKE SHAKE
IF WE CALL FOR HELP, HE'LL KILL US.
SHAKE
SHAKE
IF WE MAKE A SOUND, HE'LL KILL US.
SHAKE
I-I CAN'T TAKE THIS ANYMORE!
Y-You idiot!
WHAT CAN YOU DO...
OKEG-AWA!
I'M NOT FROM KIYAMA!
I'M NOT WEARING A UNIFORM!
THAT'S CRAZY!
...BY YOURSELF?
OKAY.
THEN YOU MAY GO!
?!
HE LET HIM PASS!
REALLY?!

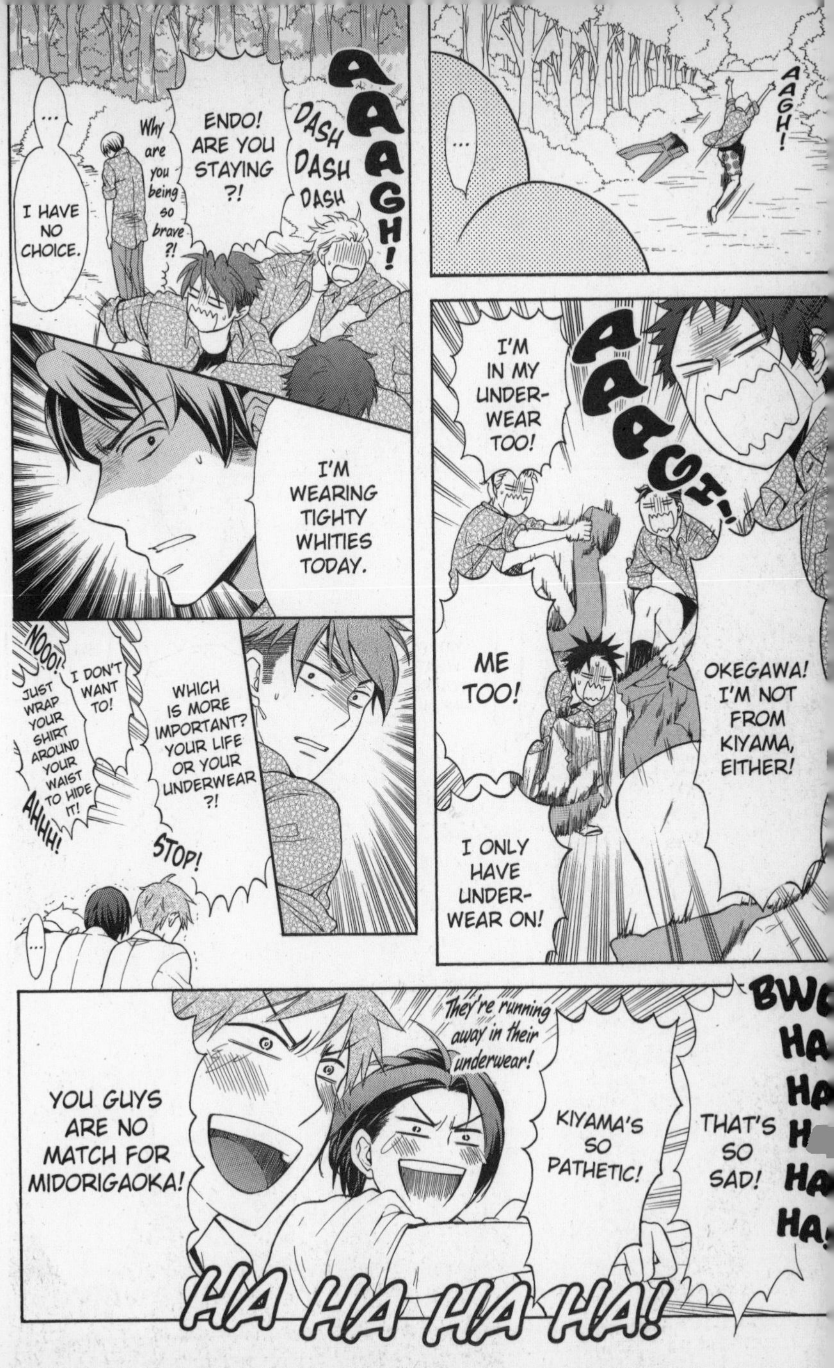
AAGH!
AAAAGH!
DASH DASH DASH
ENDO! ARE YOU STAYING?!
Why are you being so brave?!
...
I HAVE NO CHOICE.
...
AAAAGH!
I'M IN MY UNDERWEAR TOO!
OKEGAWA! I'M NOT FROM KIYAMA, EITHER!
ME TOO!
I ONLY HAVE UNDERWEAR ON!
I'M WEARING TIGHTY WHITIES TODAY.
WHICH IS MORE IMPORTANT? YOUR LIFE OR YOUR UNDERWEAR?!
I DON'T WANT TO!
NOOO!
JUST WRAP YOUR SHIRT AROUND YOUR WAIST TO HIDE IT!
AHHHH!
STOP!
...
THAT'S SO SAD!
KIYAMA'S SO PATHETIC!
They're running away in their underwear!
YOU GUYS ARE NO MATCH FOR MIDORIGAOKA!
HA HA HA HA HA!

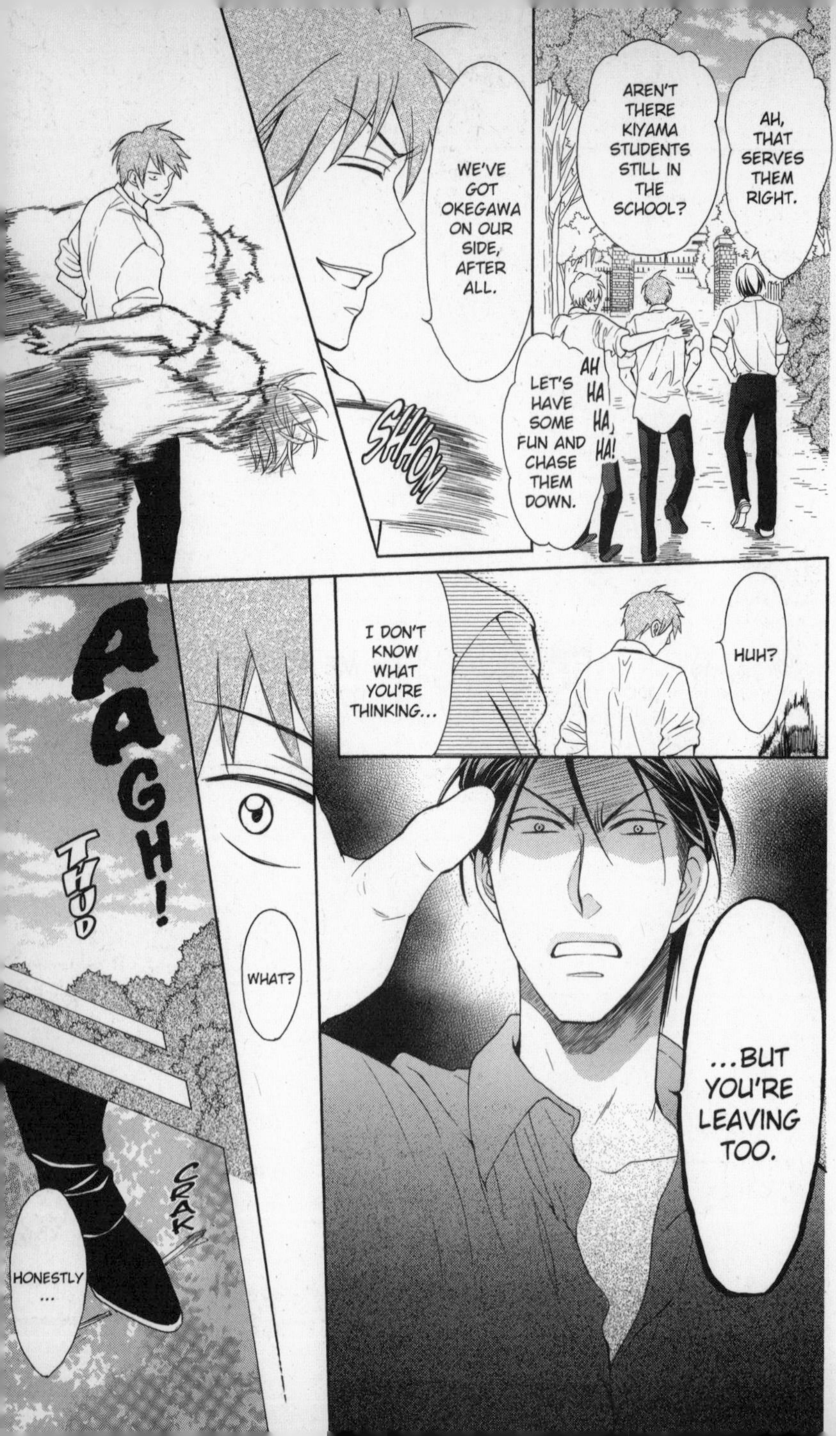
AH, THAT SERVES THEM RIGHT.
AREN'T THERE KIYAMA STUDENTS STILL IN THE SCHOOL?
AH HA HA, HA!
LET'S HAVE SOME FUN AND CHASE THEM DOWN.
WE'VE GOT OKEGAWA ON OUR SIDE, AFTER ALL.
SHHOM
HUH?
I DON'T KNOW WHAT YOU'RE THINKING...
...BUT YOU'RE LEAVING TOO.
WHAT?
AAGH!
THUD
CRAK
HONESTLY...

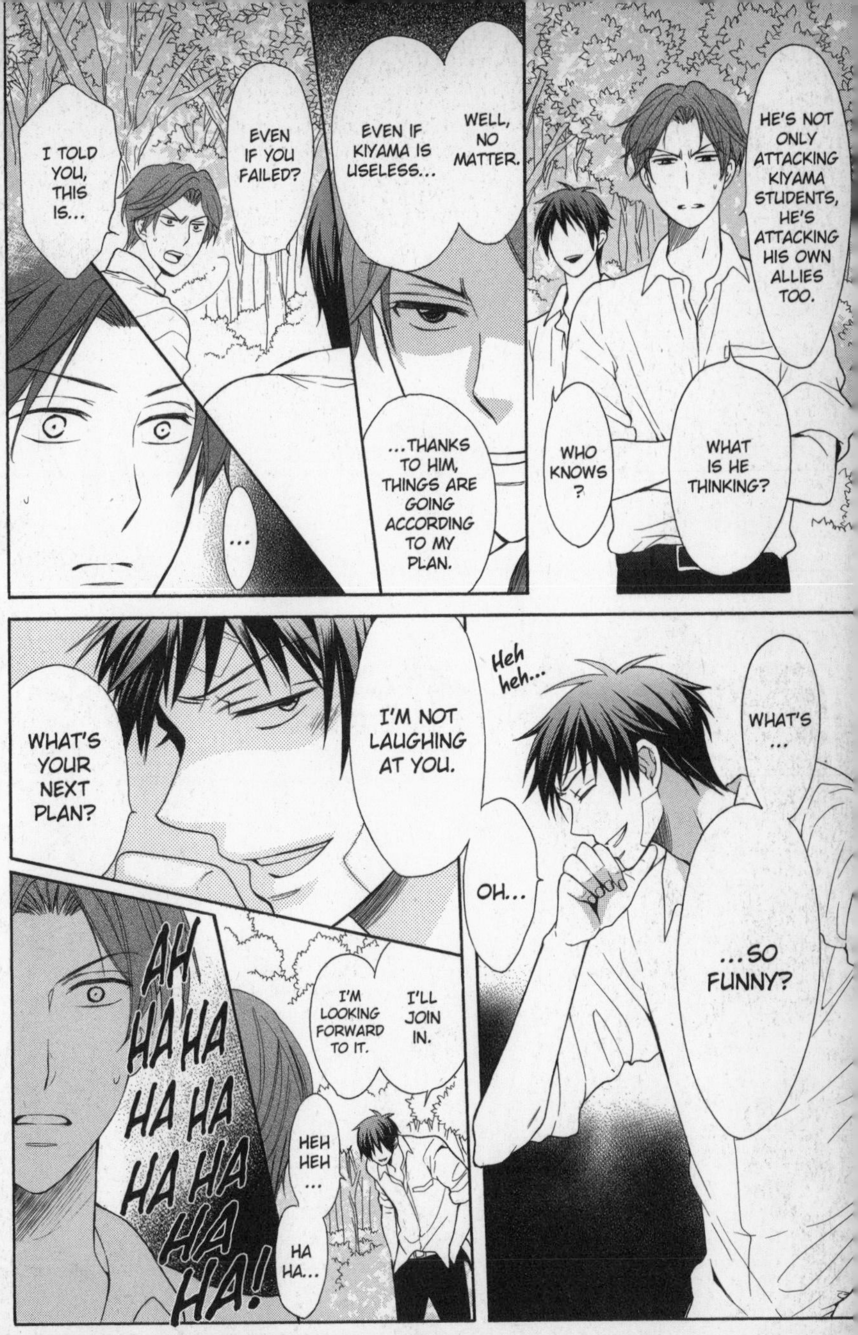
HE'S NOT ONLY ATTACKING KIYAMA STUDENTS, HE'S ATTACKING HIS OWN ALLIES TOO.
WHAT IS HE THINKING?
WHO KNOWS?
WELL, NO MATTER.
EVEN IF KIYAMA IS USELESS...
...THANKS TO HIM, THINGS ARE GOING ACCORDING TO MY PLAN.
EVEN IF YOU FAILED?
I TOLD YOU, THIS IS...
...
WHAT'S ...
...SO FUNNY?
Heh heh...
OH...
I'M NOT LAUGHING AT YOU.
WHAT'S YOUR NEXT PLAN?
I'LL JOIN IN.
I'M LOOKING FORWARD TO IT.
HEH HEH ...
HA HA...
AH HA HA HA HA HA HA HA HA HA HA!

Chapter 49

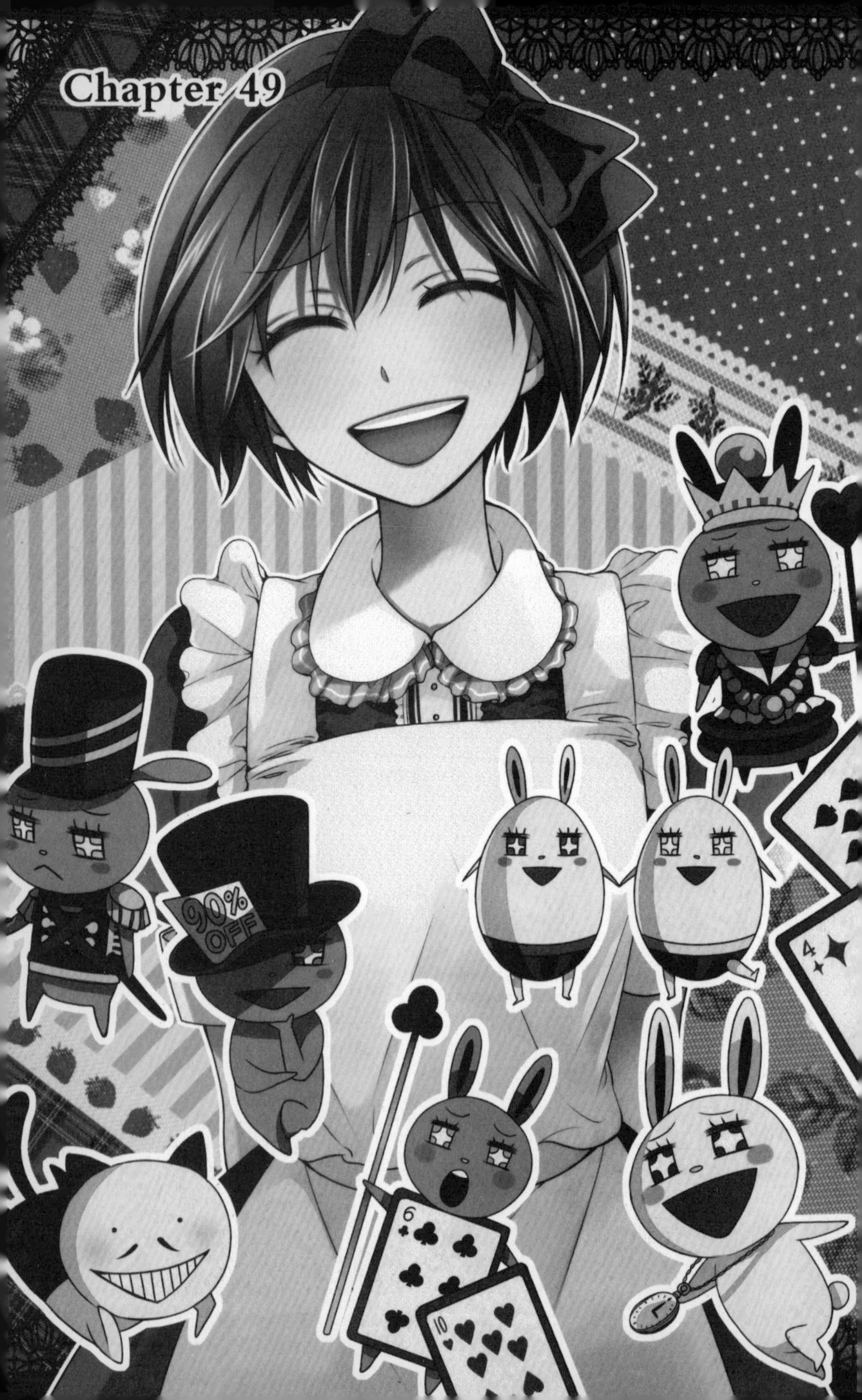
90% OFF

A DEAL

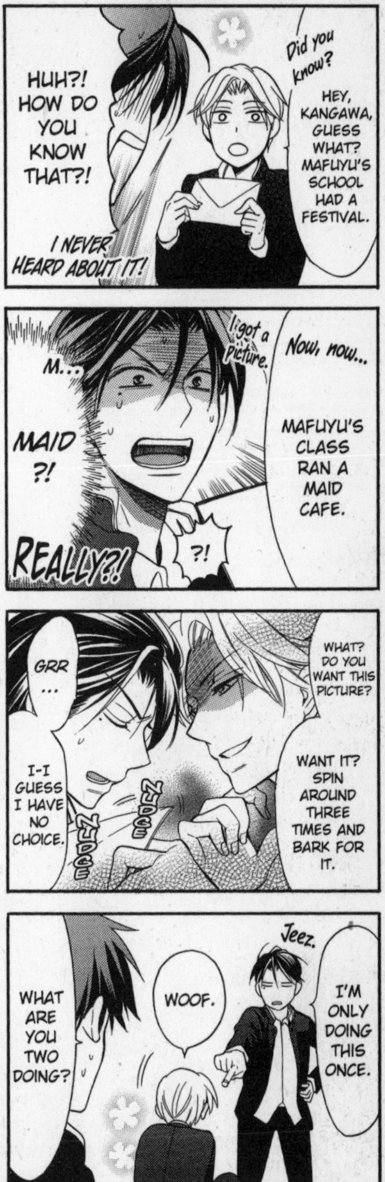
Did you know?
HEY, KANGAWA, GUESS WHAT? MAFUYU'S SCHOOL HAD A FESTIVAL.
HUH?! HOW DO YOU KNOW THAT?!
I NEVER HEARD ABOUT IT!
Now, now...
MAFUYU'S CLASS RAN A MAID CAFE.
I got a picture.
M...
MAID ?!
?!
REALLY?!
WHAT? DO YOU WANT THIS PICTURE?
WANT IT? SPIN AROUND THREE TIMES AND BARK FOR IT.
GRR ...
NUDGE
NUDGE
I-I GUESS I HAVE NO CHOICE.
Jeez.
I'M ONLY DOING THIS ONCE.
WOOF.
WHAT ARE YOU TWO DOING?

REWARD

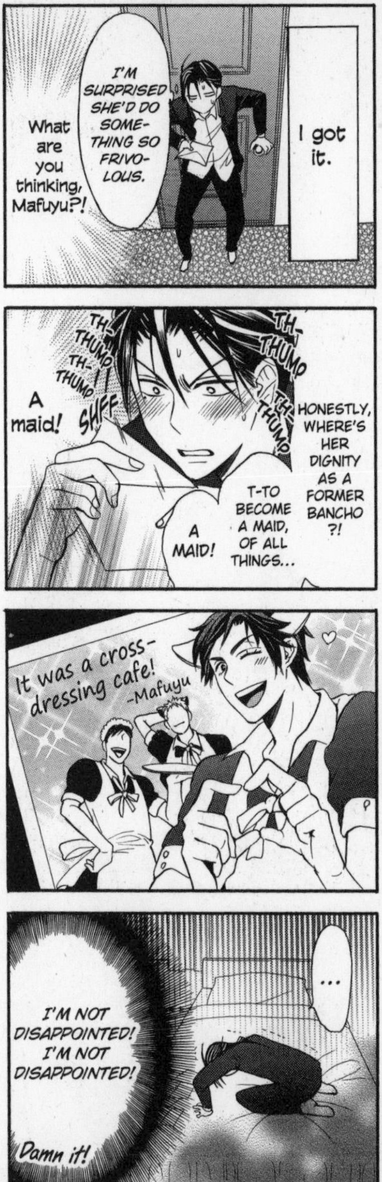
I got it.
I'M SURPRISED SHE'D DO SOME-THING SO FRIVO-LOUS.
What are you thinking, Mafuyu?!
TH-THUMP TH-THUMP
HONESTLY, WHERE'S HER DIGNITY AS A FORMER BANCHO ?!
T-TO BECOME A MAID, OF ALL THINGS...
A MAID!
TH-THUMP TH-THUMP
SHFF
A maid!
It was a cross-dressing cafe! -Mafuyu
...
I'M NOT DISAPPOINTED! I'M NOT DISAPPOINTED!
Damn it!

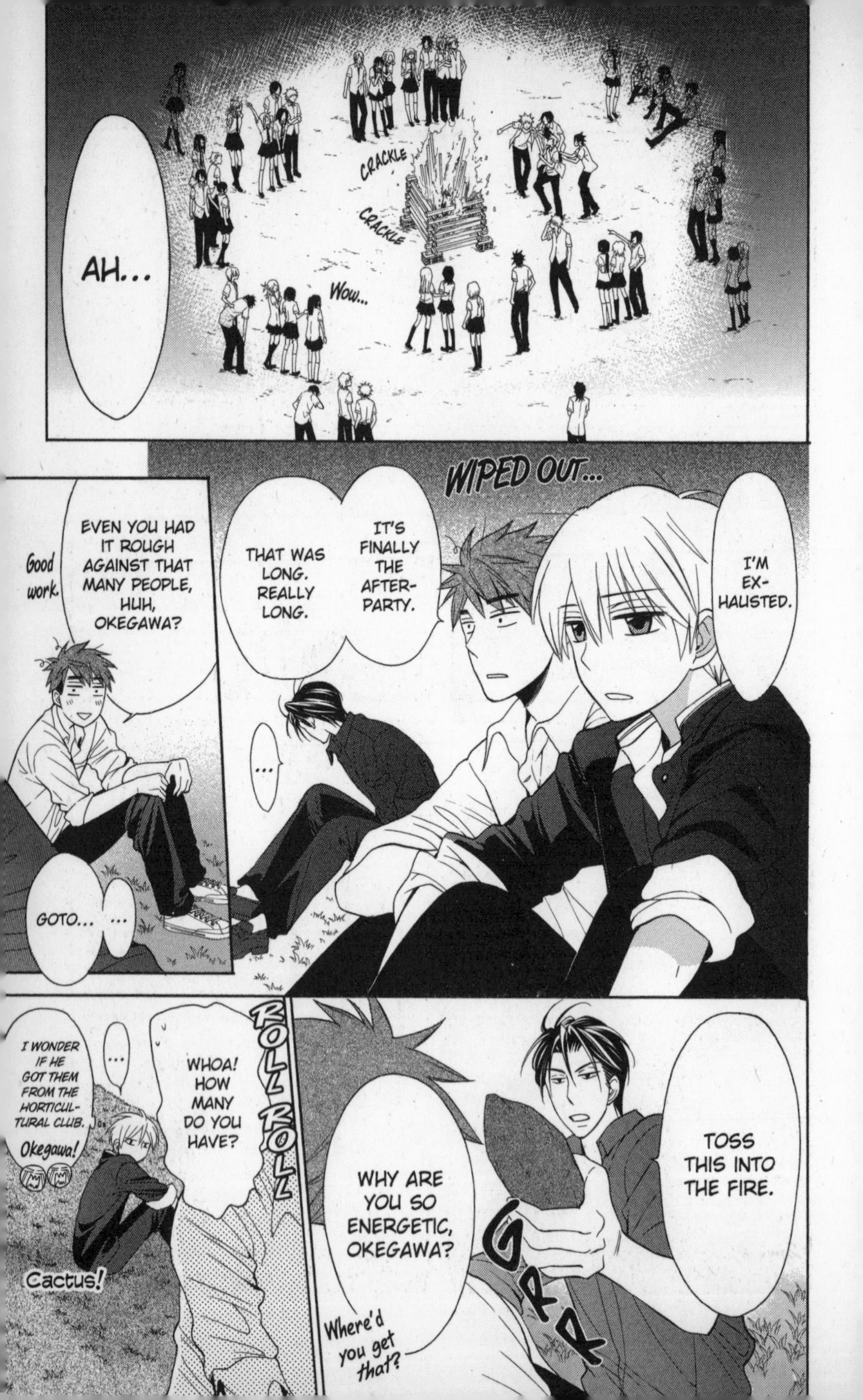
CRACKLE
CRACKLE
Wow...
AH...
WIPED OUT...
I'M EX-HAUSTED.
IT'S FINALLY THE AFTER-PARTY.
THAT WAS LONG. REALLY LONG.
...
EVEN YOU HAD IT ROUGH AGAINST THAT MANY PEOPLE, HUH, OKEGAWA?
Good work.
GOTO... ...
TOSS THIS INTO THE FIRE.
GRR
WHY ARE YOU SO ENERGETIC, OKEGAWA?
Where'd you get that?
ROLL ROLL
WHOA! HOW MANY DO YOU HAVE?
...
I WONDER IF HE GOT THEM FROM THE HORTICUL-TURAL CLUB.
Okegawa!
Cactus!

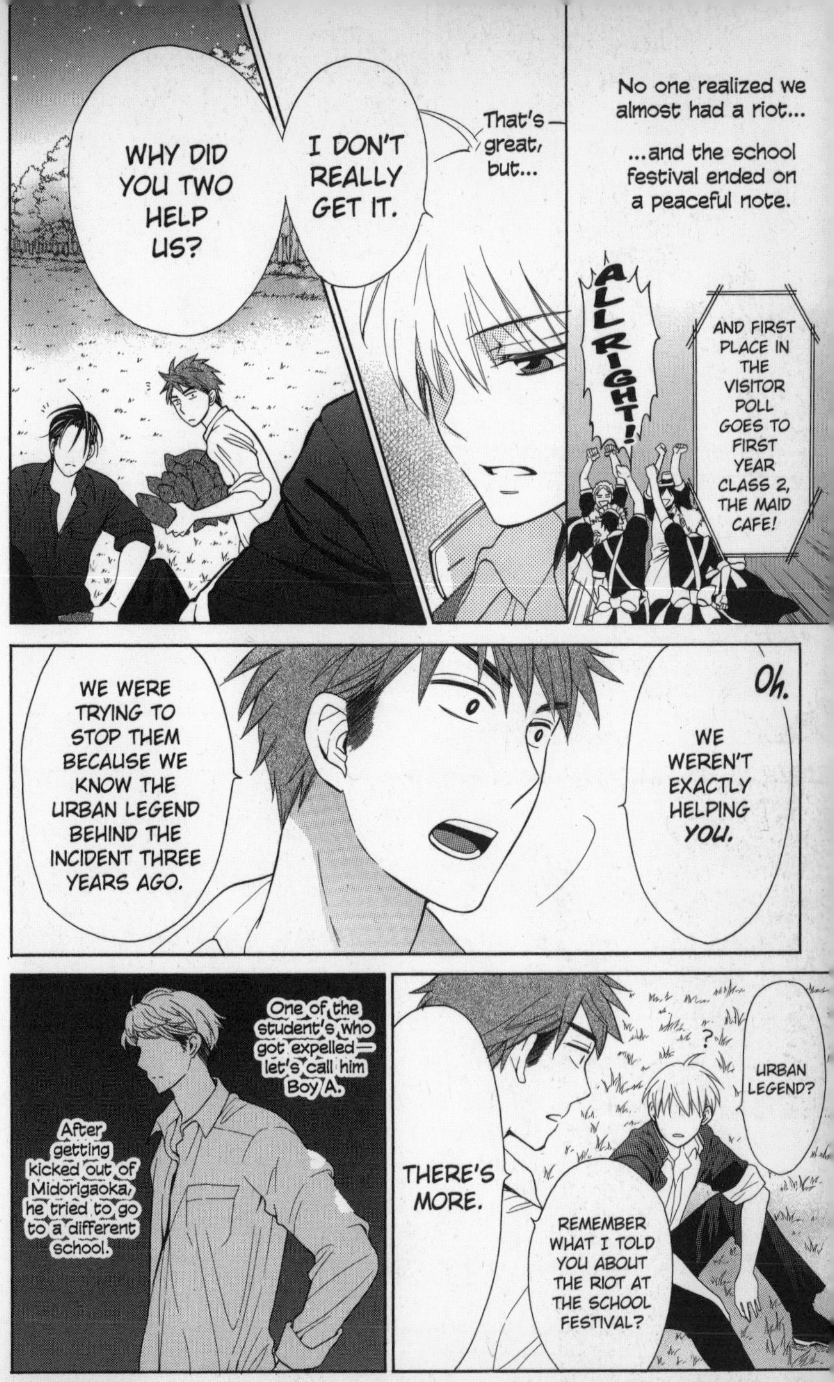
No one realized we almost had a riot...
...and the school festival ended on a peaceful note.
AND FIRST PLACE IN THE VISITOR POLL GOES TO FIRST YEAR CLASS 2, THE MAID CAFE!
ALL RIGHT!
That's great, but...
I DON'T REALLY GET IT.
WHY DID YOU TWO HELP US?
Oh.
WE WEREN'T EXACTLY HELPING YOU.
WE WERE TRYING TO STOP THEM BECAUSE WE KNOW THE URBAN LEGEND BEHIND THE INCIDENT THREE YEARS AGO.
?
URBAN LEGEND?
THERE'S MORE.
REMEMBER WHAT I TOLD YOU ABOUT THE RIOT AT THE SCHOOL FESTIVAL?
One of the student's who got expelled—let's call him Boy A.
After getting kicked out of Midorigaoka, he tried to go to a different school.

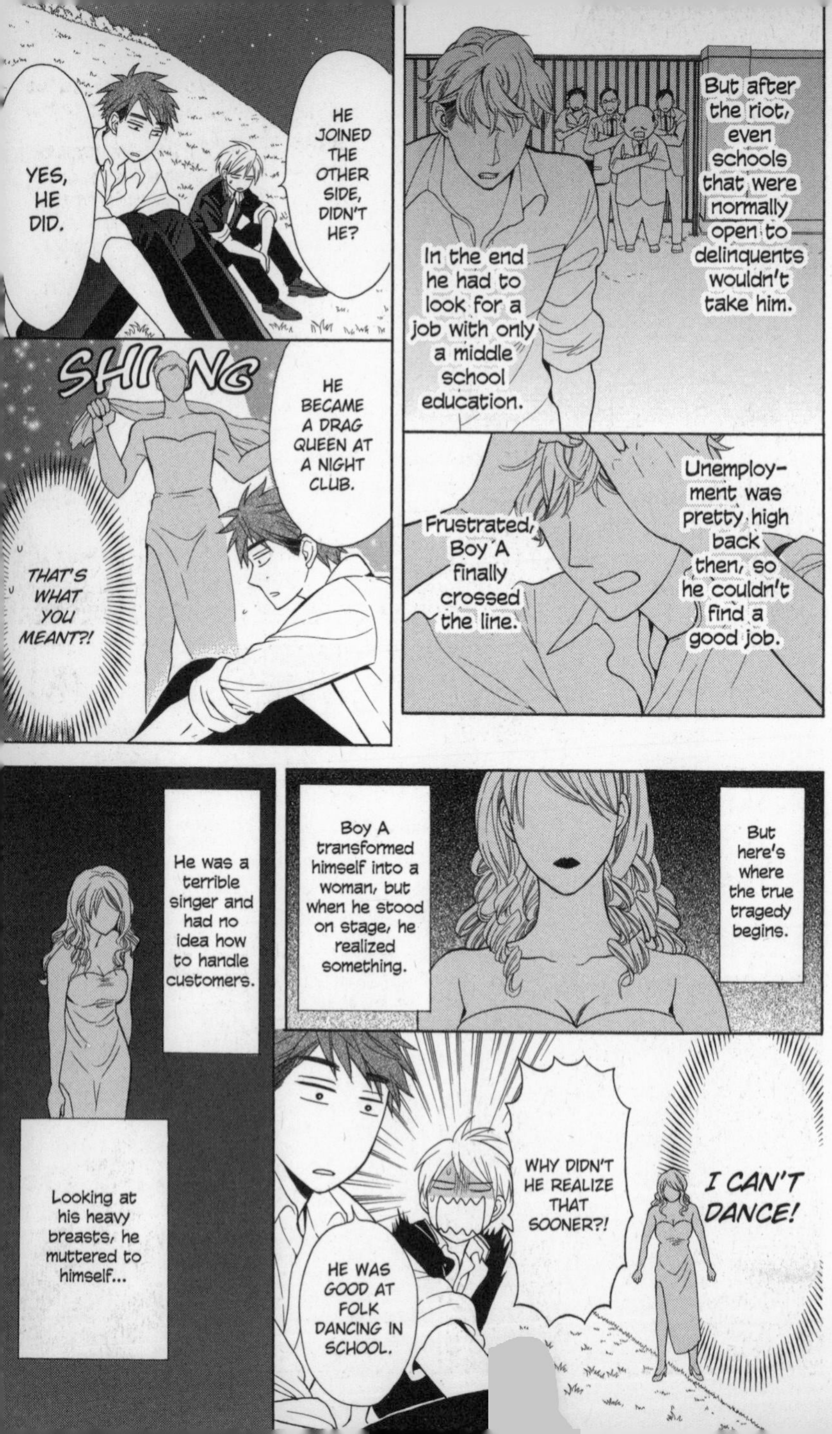

But after the riot, even schools that were normally open to delinquents wouldn't take him.
In the end he had to look for a job with only a middle school education.
Unemployment was pretty high back then, so he couldn't find a good job.
Frustrated, Boy A finally crossed the line.
HE JOINED THE OTHER SIDE, DIDN'T HE?
YES, HE DID.
SHING
HE BECAME A DRAG QUEEN AT A NIGHT CLUB.
THAT'S WHAT YOU MEANT?!
But here's where the true tragedy begins.
Boy A transformed himself into a woman, but when he stood on stage, he realized something.
I CAN'T DANCE!
WHY DIDN'T HE REALIZE THAT SOONER?!
HE WAS GOOD AT FOLK DANCING IN SCHOOL.
He was a terrible singer and had no idea how to handle customers.
Looking at his heavy breasts, he muttered to himself...

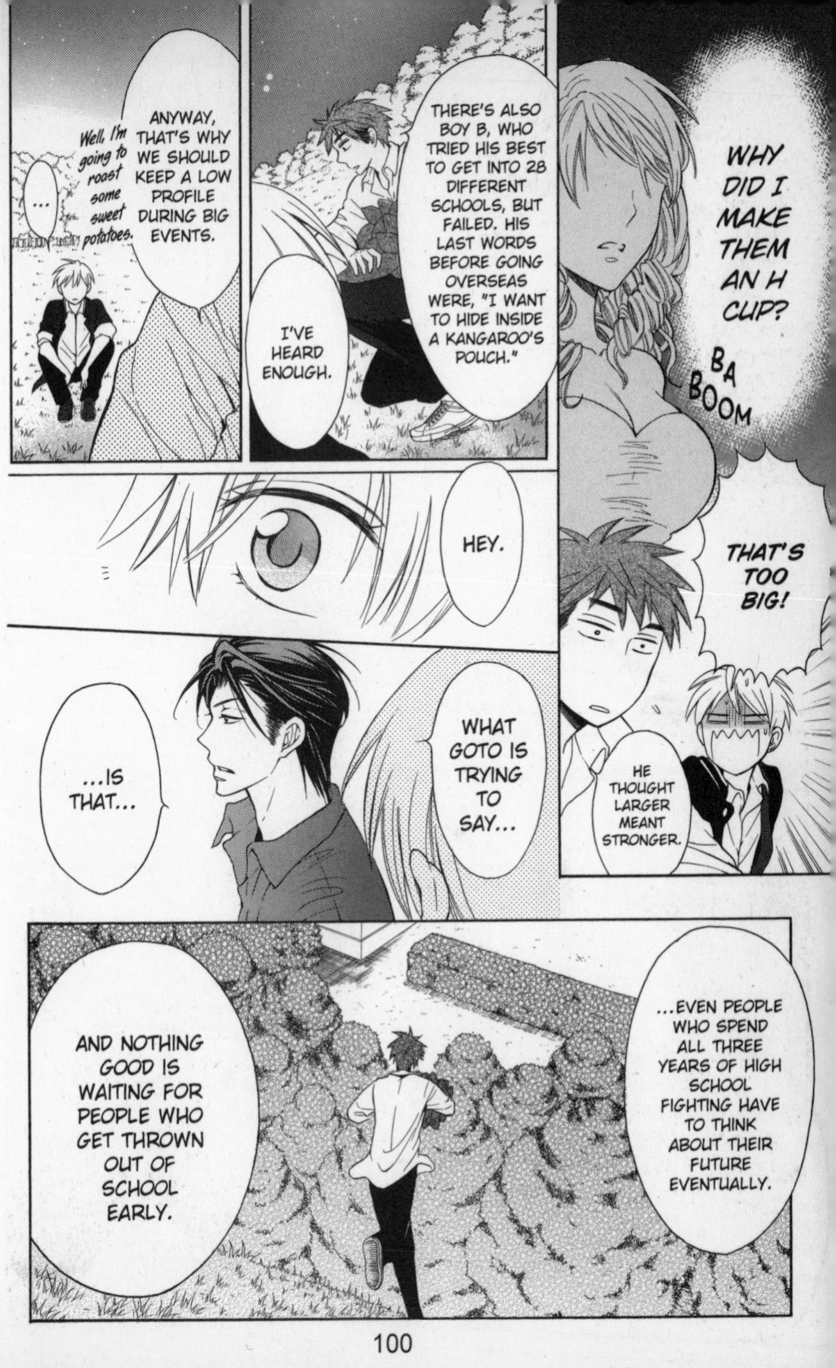
WHY DID I MAKE THEM AN H CUP?
BA BOOM
THAT'S TOO BIG!
HE THOUGHT LARGER MEANT STRONGER.
THERE'S ALSO BOY B, WHO TRIED HIS BEST TO GET INTO 28 DIFFERENT SCHOOLS, BUT FAILED. HIS LAST WORDS BEFORE GOING OVERSEAS WERE, "I WANT TO HIDE INSIDE A KANGAROO'S POUCH."
I'VE HEARD ENOUGH.
ANYWAY, THAT'S WHY WE SHOULD KEEP A LOW PROFILE DURING BIG EVENTS.
Well, I'm going to roast some sweet potatoes.
...
HEY.
WHAT GOTO IS TRYING TO SAY...
...IS THAT...
...EVEN PEOPLE WHO SPEND ALL THREE YEARS OF HIGH SCHOOL FIGHTING HAVE TO THINK ABOUT THEIR FUTURE EVENTUALLY.
AND NOTHING GOOD IS WAITING FOR PEOPLE WHO GET THROWN OUT OF SCHOOL EARLY.

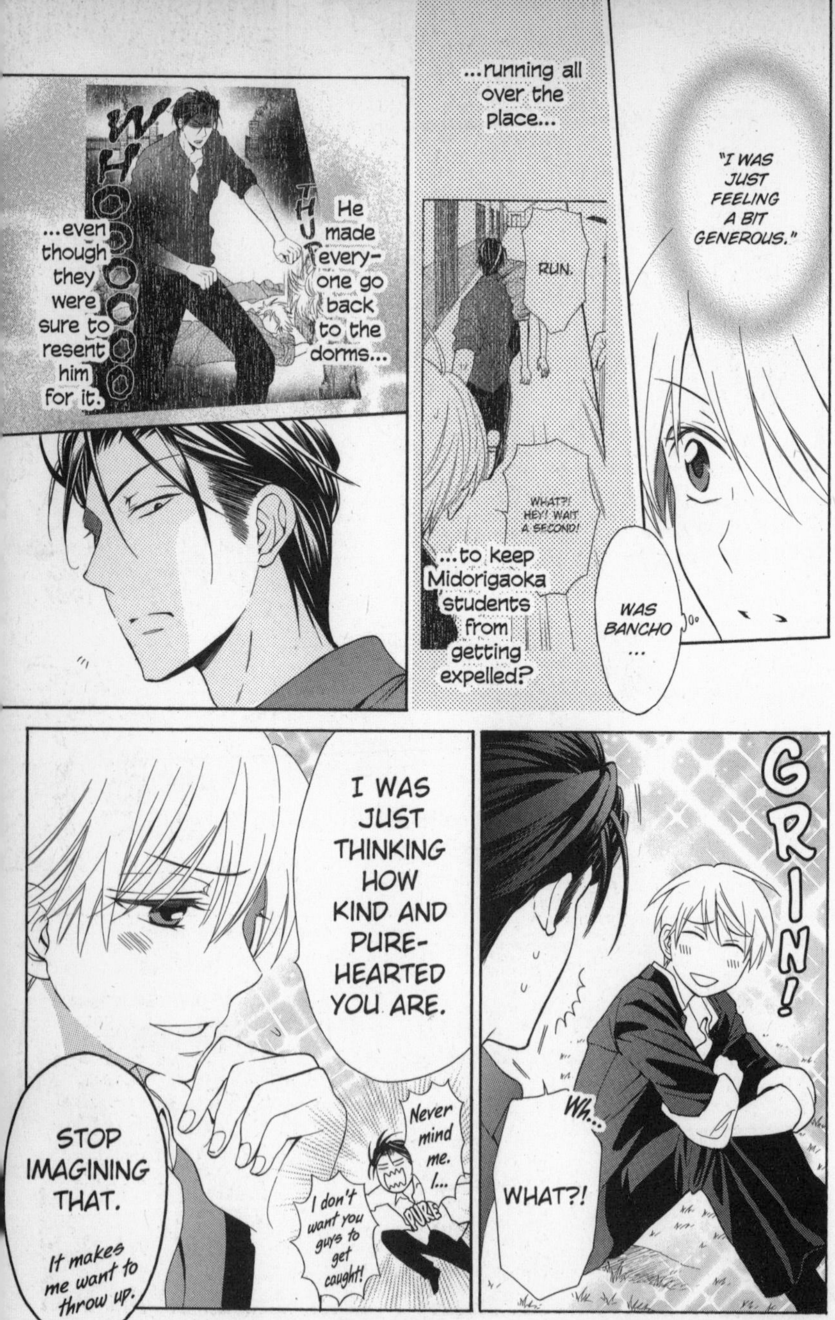
"I WAS JUST FEELING A BIT GENEROUS."
WAS BANCHO ...
...running all over the place...
RUN.
WHAT?! HEY! WAIT A SECOND!
...to keep Midorigaoka students from getting expelled?
He made every-one go back to the dorms...
...even though they were sure to resent him for it.
WHOOOOOO
GRIN!
Wh...
WHAT?!
I WAS JUST THINKING HOW KIND AND PURE-HEARTED YOU ARE.
Never mind me. I...
I don't want you guys to get caught!
STOP IMAGINING THAT.
It makes me want to throw up.

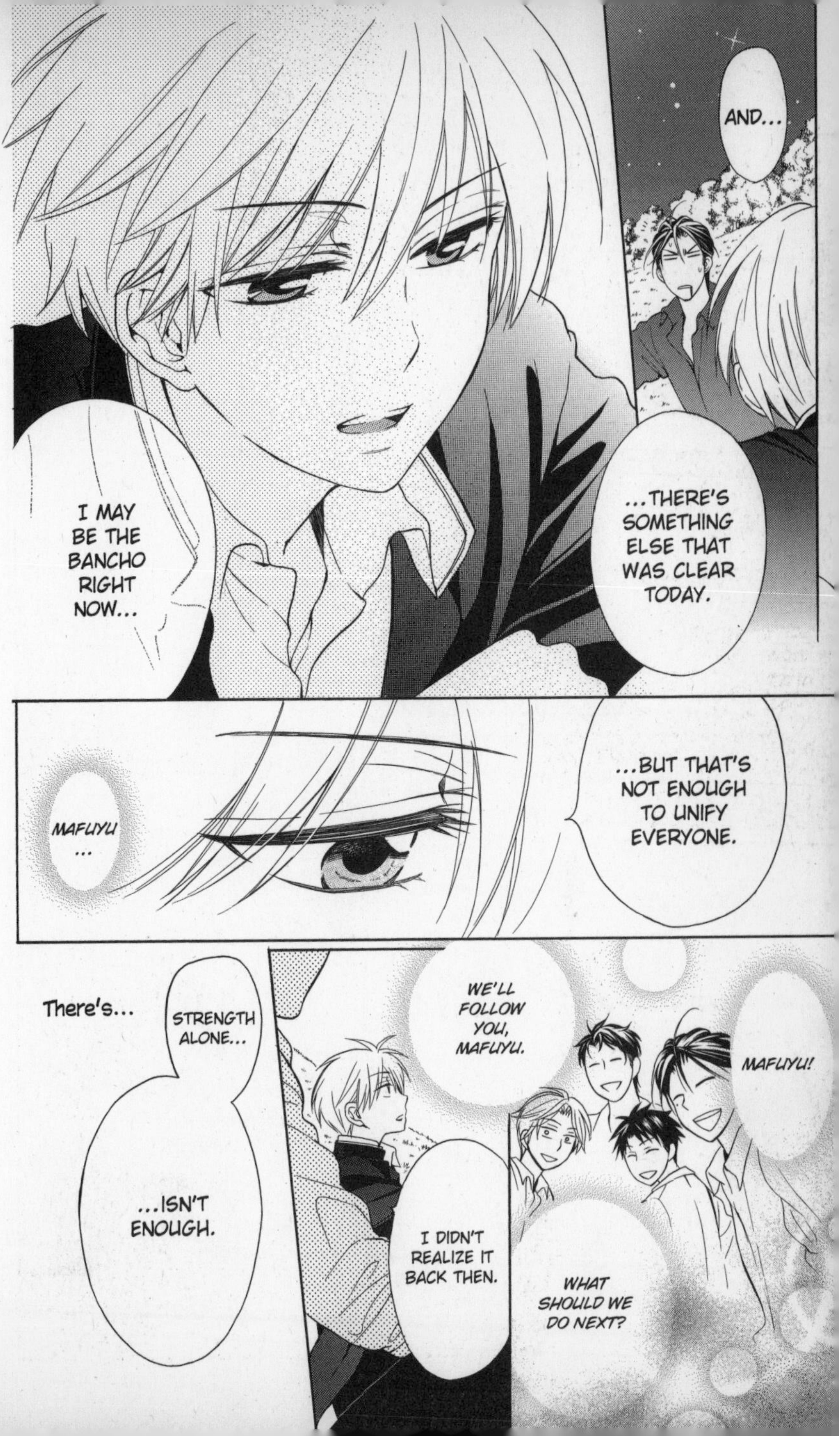
AND...
...THERE'S SOMETHING ELSE THAT WAS CLEAR TODAY.
I MAY BE THE BANCHO RIGHT NOW...
...BUT THAT'S NOT ENOUGH TO UNIFY EVERYONE.
MAFUYU ...
MAFUYU!
WE'LL FOLLOW YOU, MAFUYU.
WHAT SHOULD WE DO NEXT?
I DIDN'T REALIZE IT BACK THEN.
STRENGTH ALONE...
There's...
...ISN'T ENOUGH.

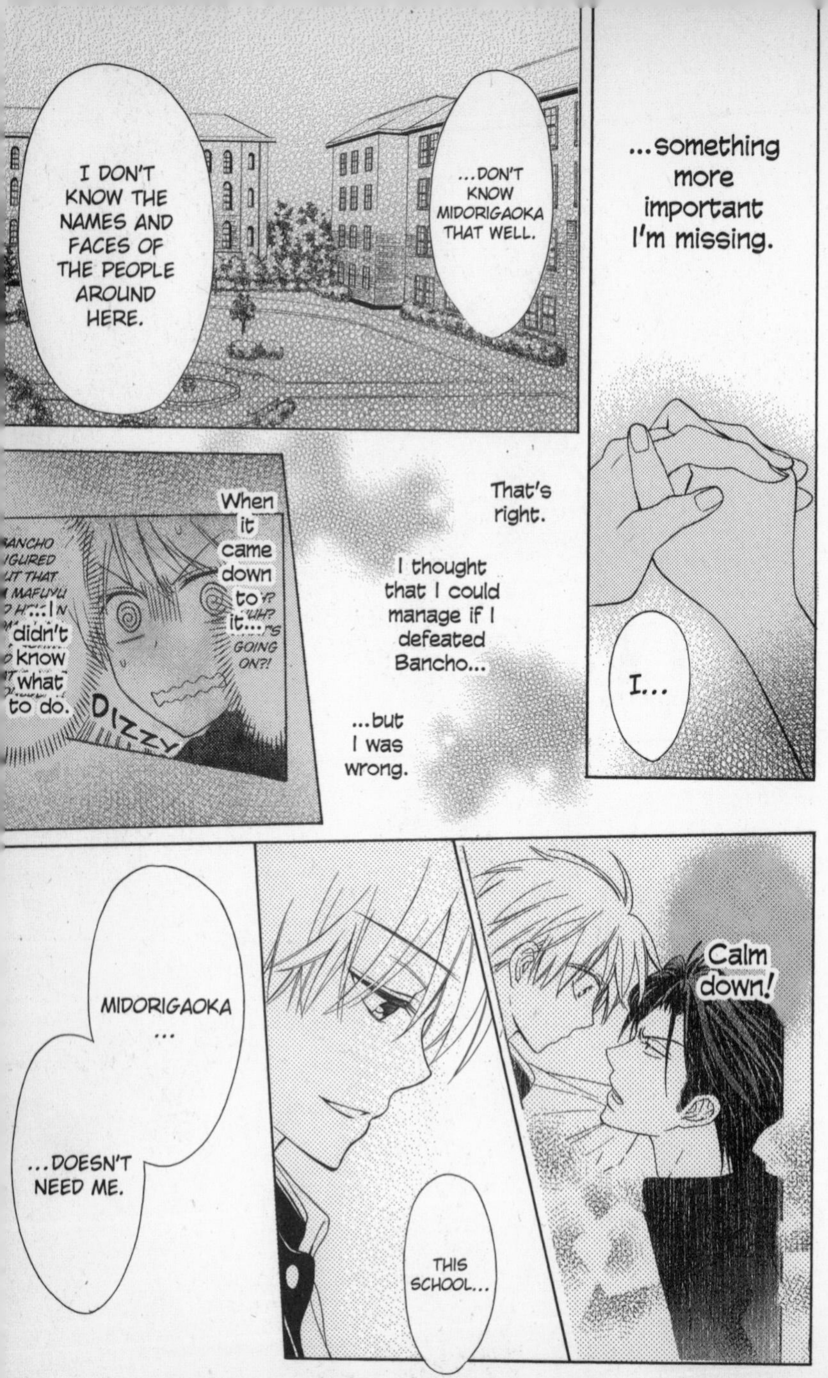
...something more important I'm missing.
I...
...DON'T KNOW MIDORIGAOKA THAT WELL.
I DON'T KNOW THE NAMES AND FACES OF THE PEOPLE AROUND HERE.
That's right.
I thought that I could manage if I defeated Bancho...
...but I was wrong.
When it came down to it...
...I didn't know what to do.
DIZZY
Calm down!
THIS SCHOOL...
MIDORIGAOKA...
...DOESN'T NEED ME.

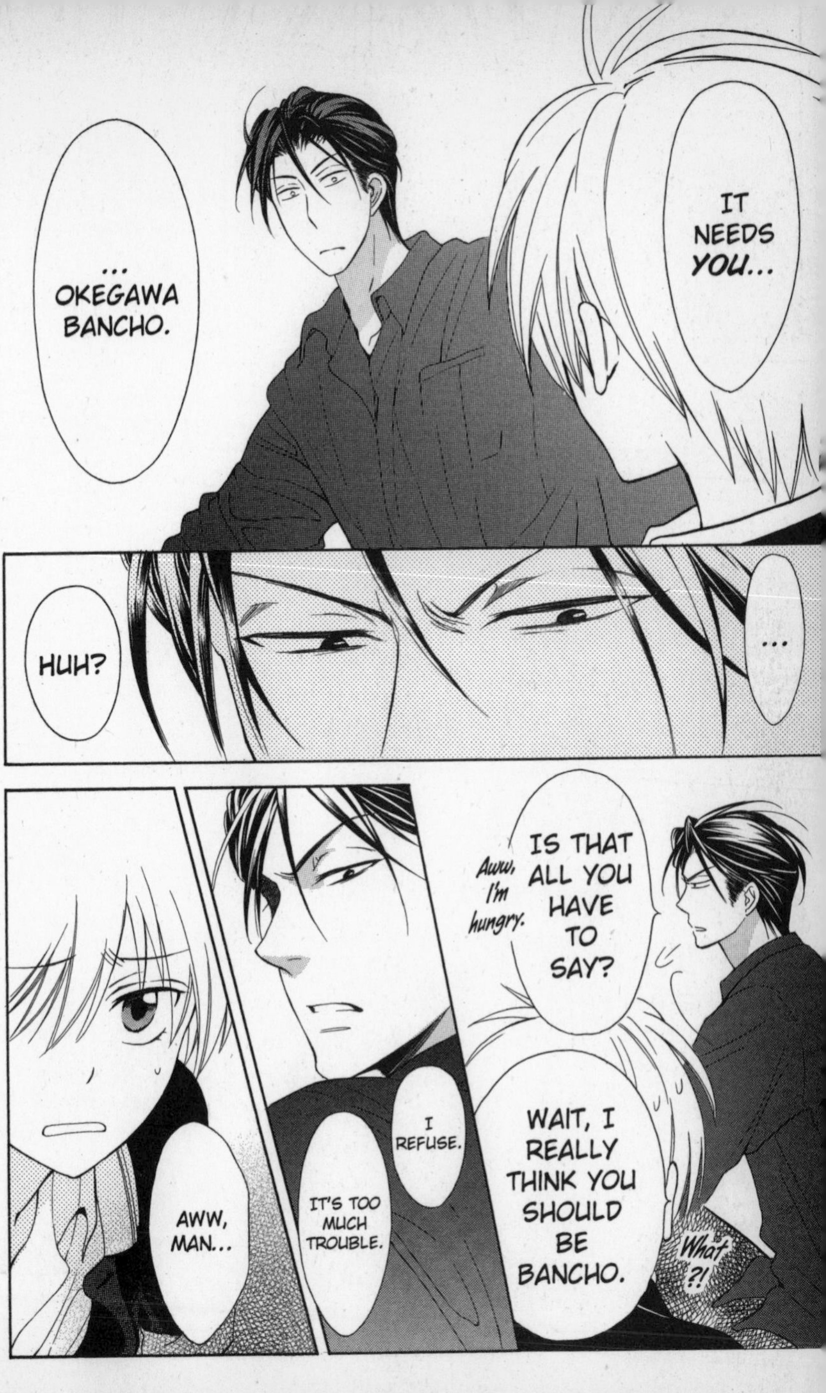
IT NEEDS YOU...
... OKEGAWA BANCHO.
...
HUH?
IS THAT ALL YOU HAVE TO SAY?
Aww, I'm hungry.
WAIT, I REALLY THINK YOU SHOULD BE BANCHO.
What?!
I REFUSE.
IT'S TOO MUCH TROUBLE.
AWW, MAN...

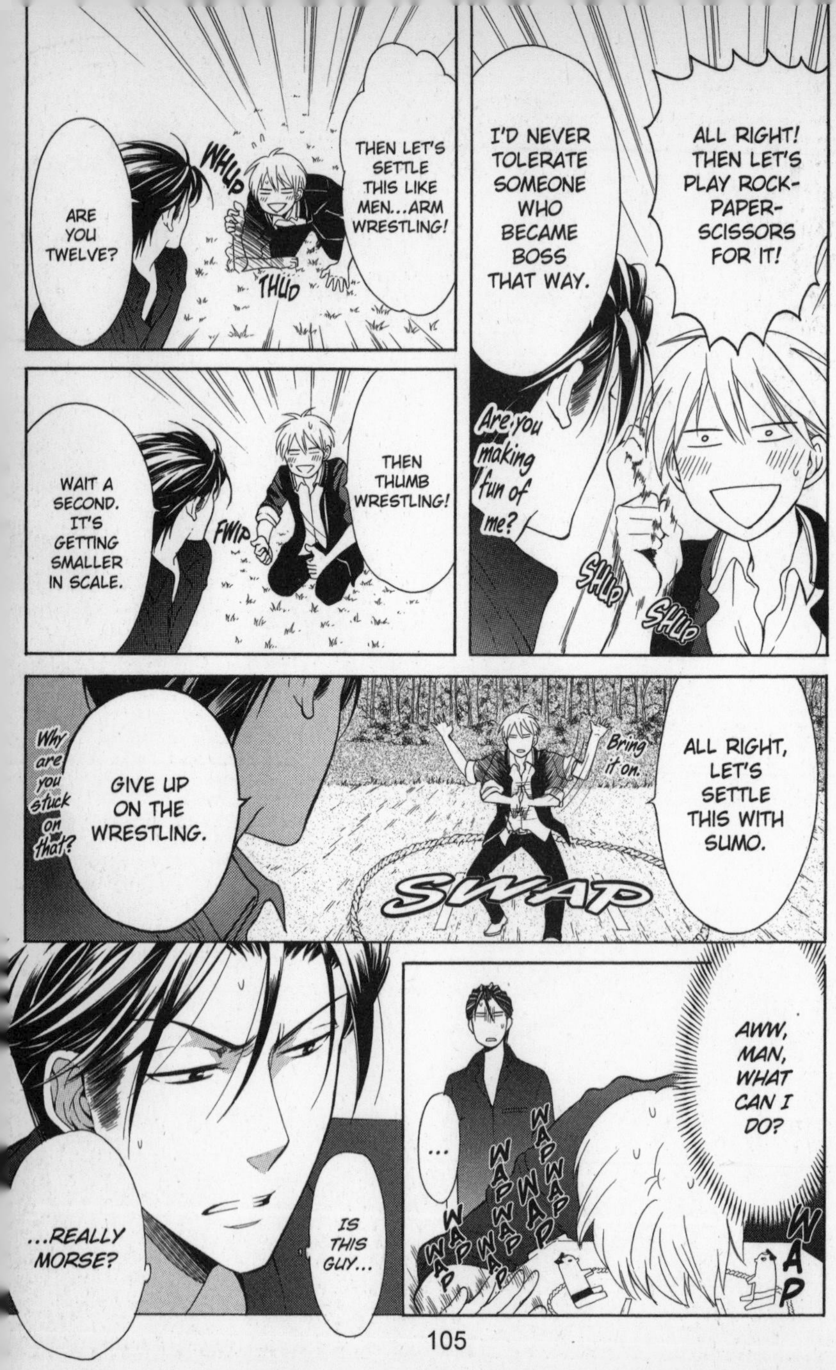
ALL RIGHT! THEN LET'S PLAY ROCK-PAPER-SCISSORS FOR IT!
I'D NEVER TOLERATE SOMEONE WHO BECAME BOSS THAT WAY.
Are you making fun of me?
SHUP
SHUP
THEN LET'S SETTLE THIS LIKE MEN...ARM WRESTLING!
WHUP
THUD
ARE YOU TWELVE?
THEN THUMB WRESTLING!
FWIP
WAIT A SECOND. IT'S GETTING SMALLER IN SCALE.
ALL RIGHT, LET'S SETTLE THIS WITH SUMO.
Bring it on.
SWAP
GIVE UP ON THE WRESTLING.
Why are you stuck on that?
AWW, MAN, WHAT CAN I DO?
WAP
WAP WAP WAP
WAP WAP WAP
WAP WAP
WAP WAP
...
IS THIS GUY...
...REALLY MORSE?

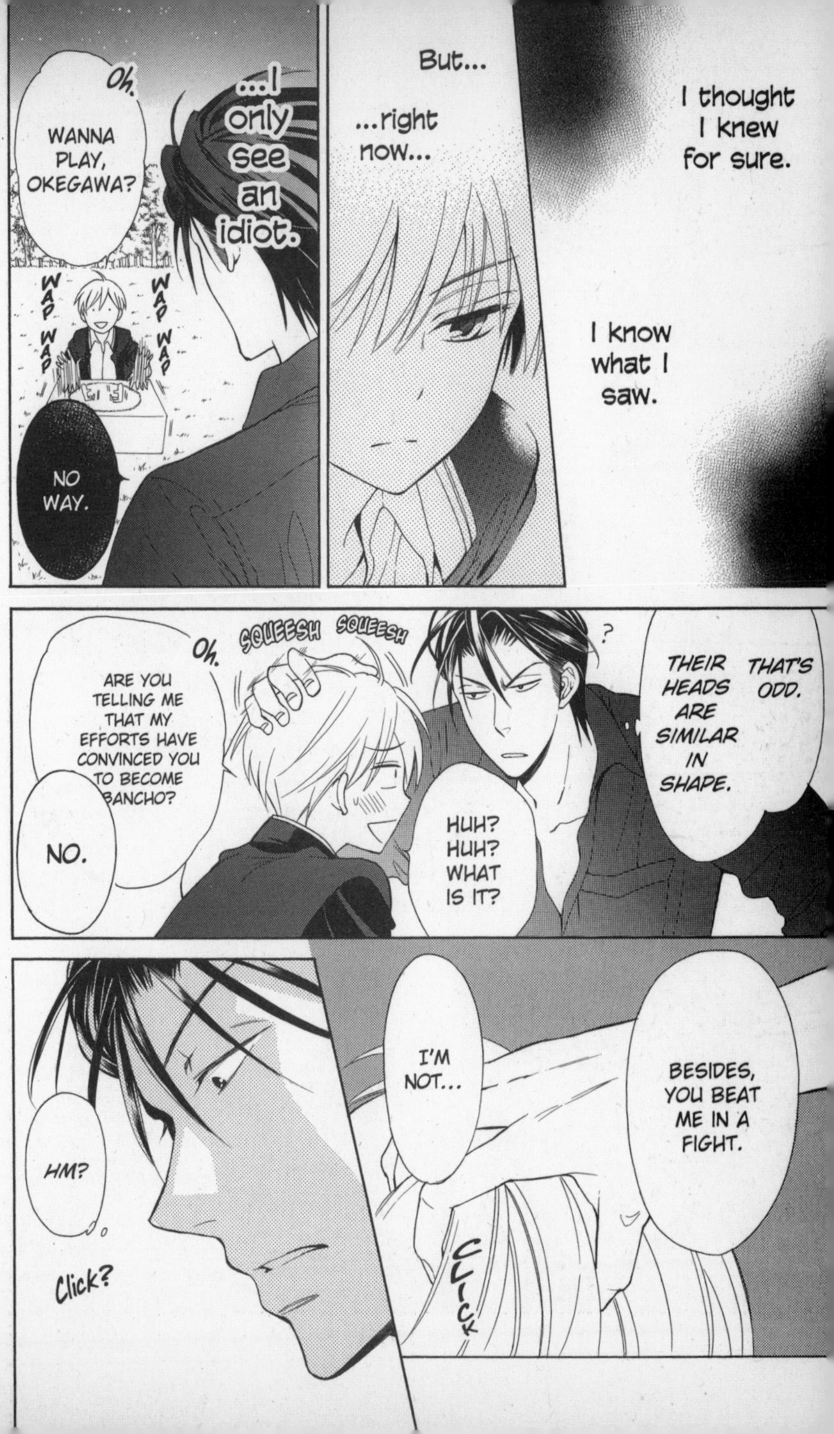
I thought I knew for sure.
I know what I saw.
But...
...right now...
...I only see an idiot.
Oh.
WANNA PLAY, OKEGAWA?
WAP WAP
WAP WAP
NO WAY.
THAT'S ODD.
THEIR HEADS ARE SIMILAR IN SHAPE.
?
SQUEESH SQUEESH
HUH? HUH? WHAT IS IT?
Oh.
ARE YOU TELLING ME THAT MY EFFORTS HAVE CONVINCED YOU TO BECOME BANCHO?
NO.
BESIDES, YOU BEAT ME IN A FIGHT.
I'M NOT...
CLICK CLICK
HM?
Click?

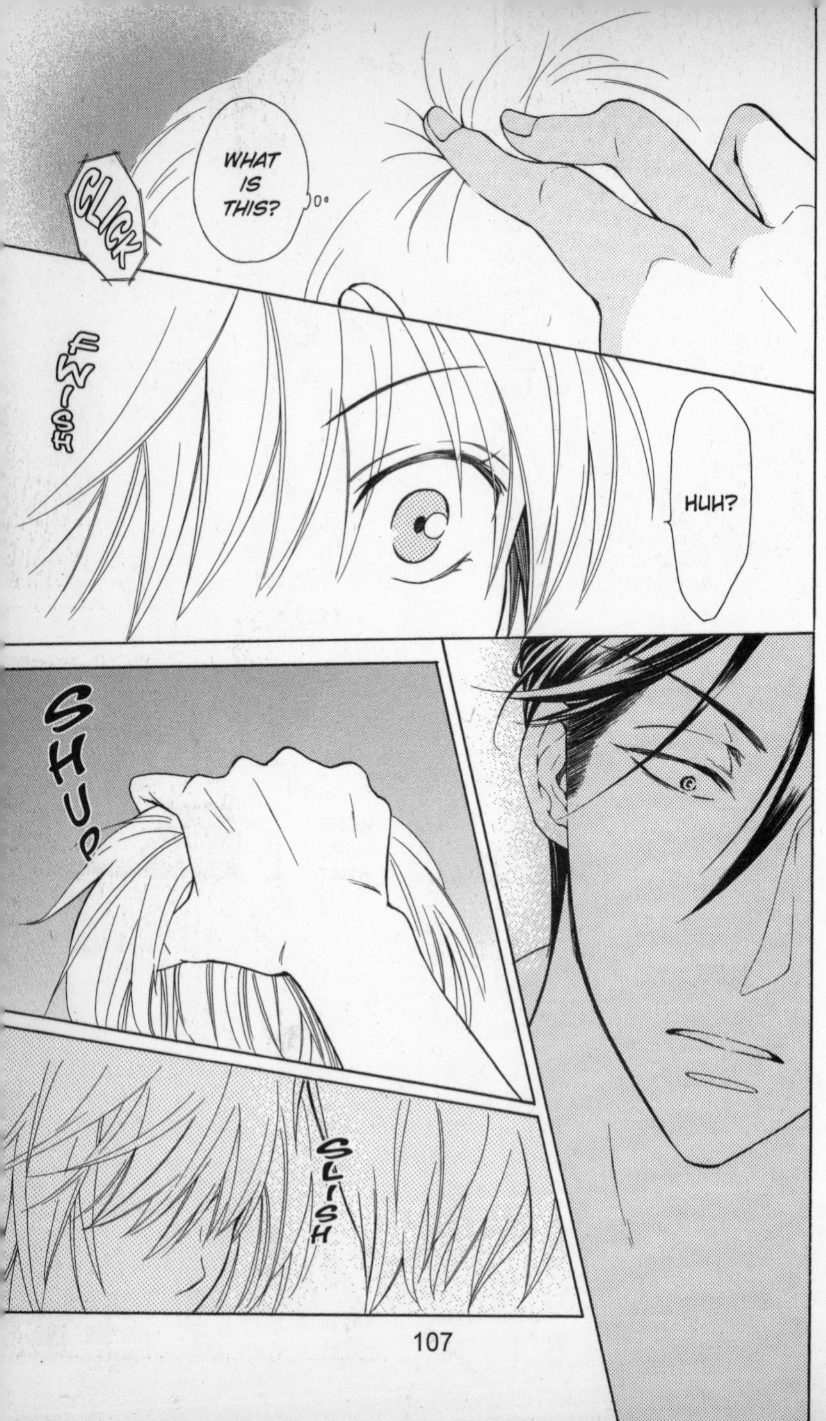
CLICK
WHAT IS THIS?
HUH?
FWISH
SHUP
SLISH

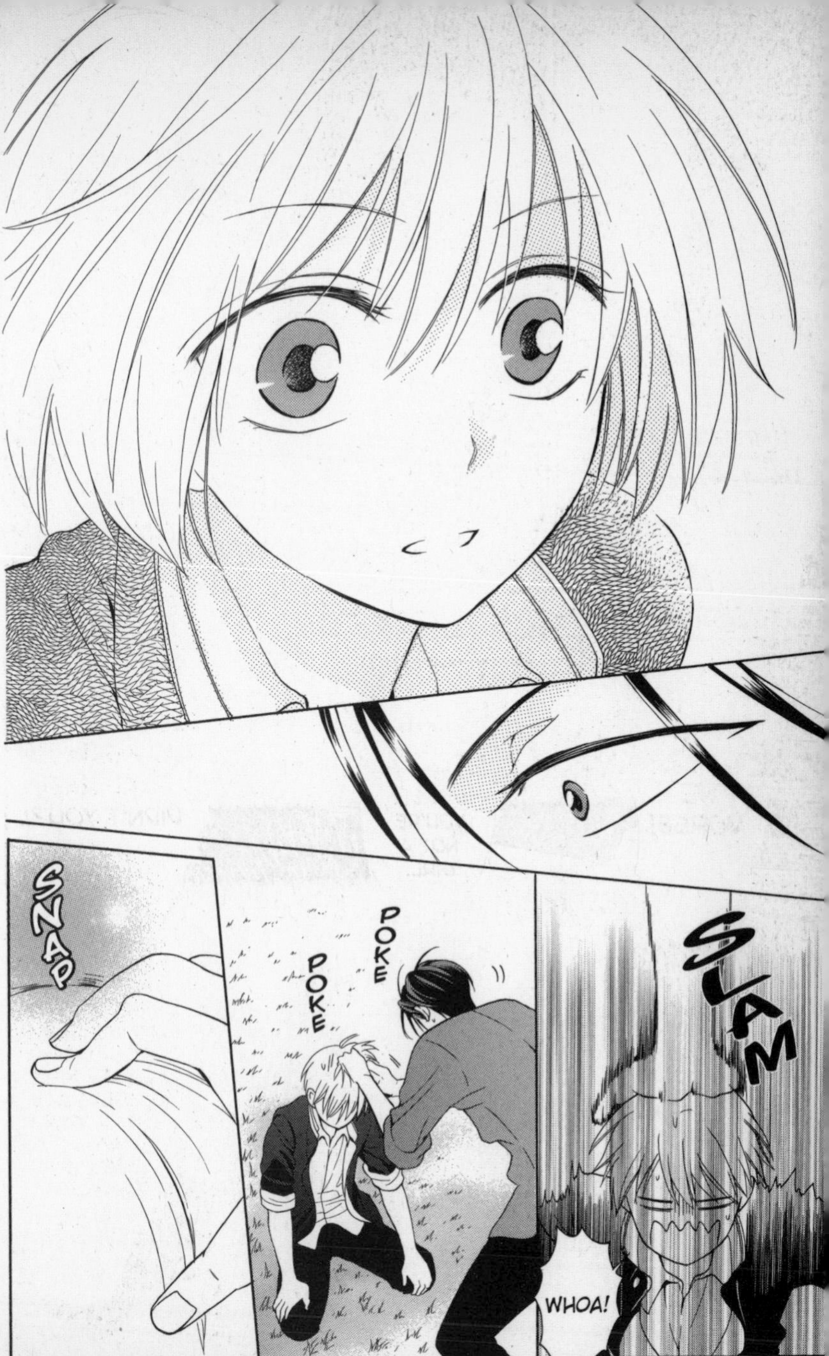
SLAM
WHOA!
POKE
POKE
SNAP

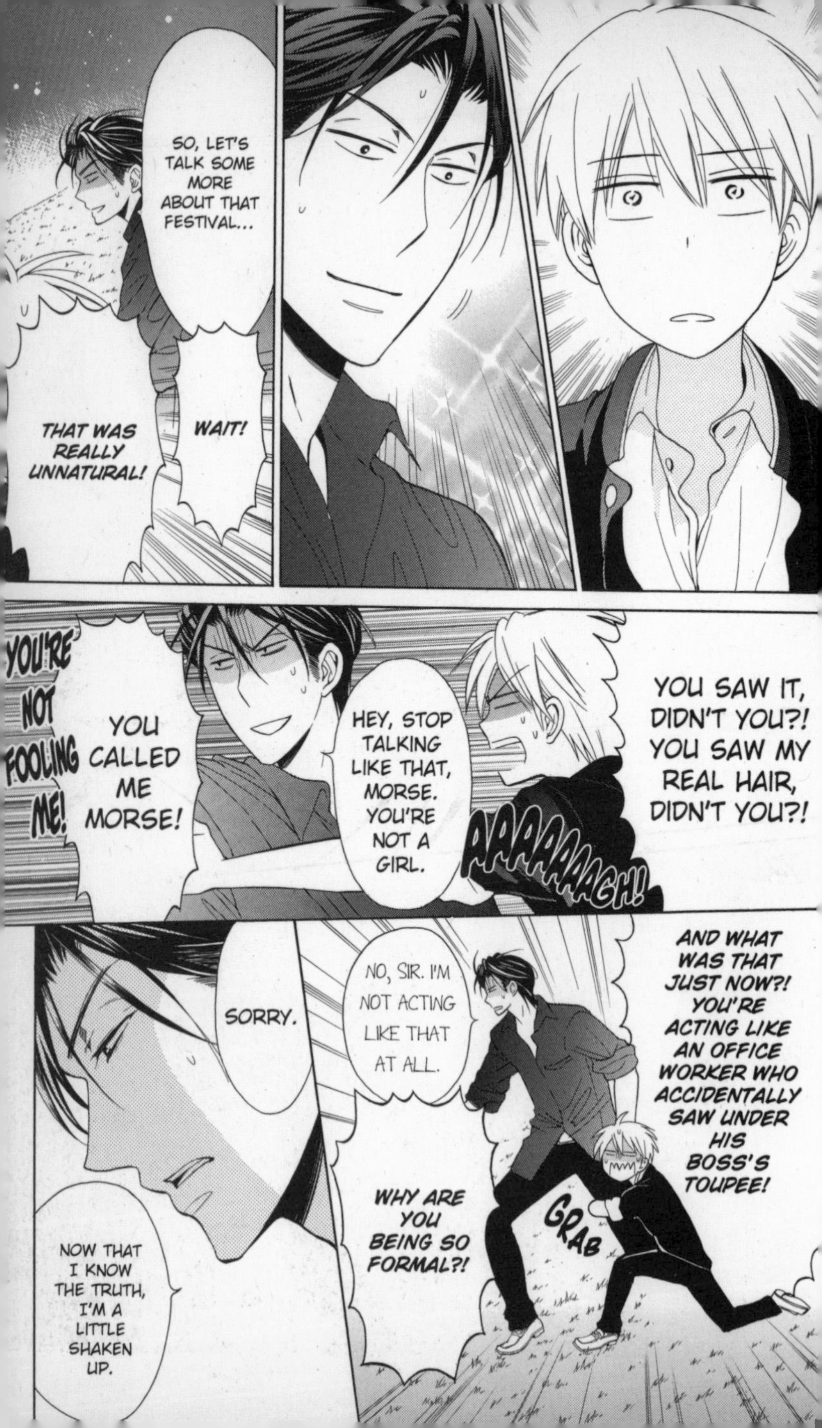
SO, LET'S TALK SOME MORE ABOUT THAT FESTIVAL...
WAIT!
THAT WAS REALLY UNNATURAL!
YOU SAW IT, DIDN'T YOU?! YOU SAW MY REAL HAIR, DIDN'T YOU?!
AAAAAAAGH!
HEY, STOP TALKING LIKE THAT, MORSE. YOU'RE NOT A GIRL.
YOU CALLED ME MORSE!
YOU'RE NOT FOOLING ME!
AND WHAT WAS THAT JUST NOW?! YOU'RE ACTING LIKE AN OFFICE WORKER WHO ACCIDENTALLY SAW UNDER HIS BOSS'S TOUPEE!
NO, SIR. I'M NOT ACTING LIKE THAT AT ALL.
WHY ARE YOU BEING SO FORMAL?!
GRAB
SORRY.
NOW THAT I KNOW THE TRUTH, I'M A LITTLE SHAKEN UP.

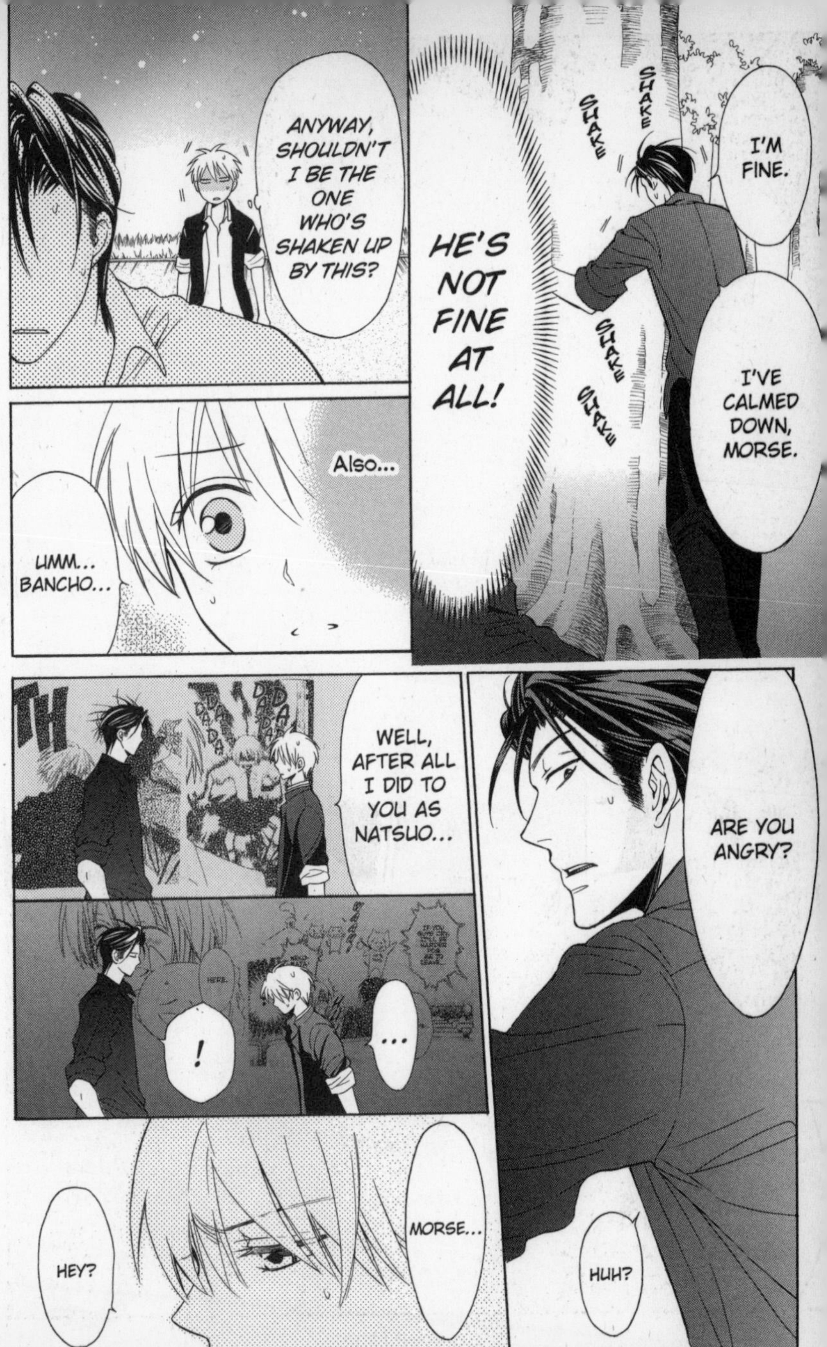
I'M FINE.
SHAKE
SHAKE
I'VE CALMED DOWN, MORSE.
SHAKE
SHAKE
HE'S NOT FINE AT ALL!
ANYWAY, SHOULDN'T I BE THE ONE WHO'S SHAKEN UP BY THIS?
Also...
UMM... BANCHO...
ARE YOU ANGRY?
HUH?
WELL, AFTER ALL I DID TO YOU AS NATSUO...
...
!
MORSE...
HEY?

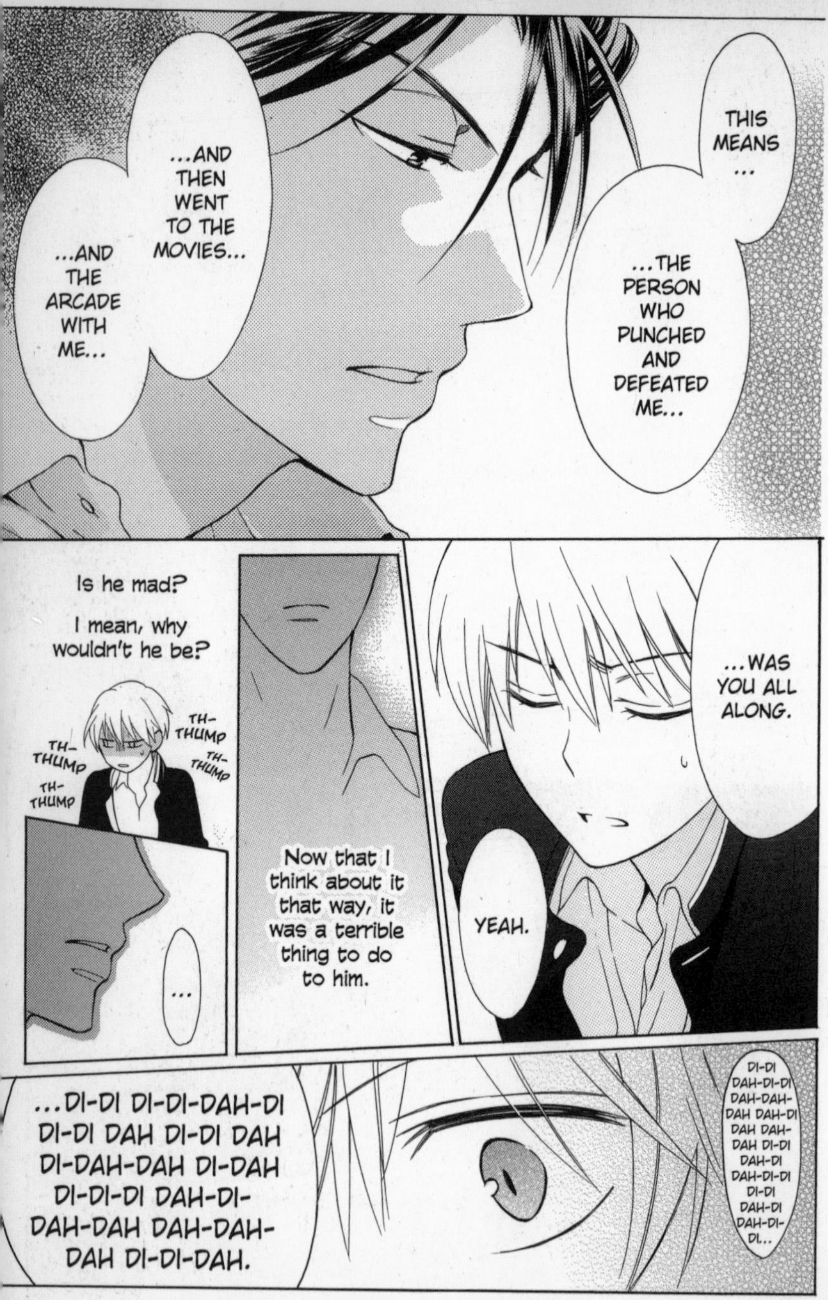
THIS MEANS ...
...THE PERSON WHO PUNCHED AND DEFEATED ME...
...AND THEN WENT TO THE MOVIES...
...AND THE ARCADE WITH ME...
...WAS YOU ALL ALONG.
YEAH.
Now that I think about it that way, it was a terrible thing to do to him.
Is he mad?
I mean, why wouldn't he be?
TH-THUMP
TH-THUMP
TH-THUMP
TH-THUMP
...
DI-DI DAH-DI-DI DAH-DAH-DAH DAH-DI DAH DAH-DAH DI-DI DAH-DI DAH-DI-DI DI-DI DAH-DI DAH-DI-DI...
...DI-DI DI-DI-DAH-DI DI-DI DAH DI-DI DAH DI-DAH-DAH DI-DAH DI-DI-DI DAH-DI-DAH-DAH DAH-DAH-DAH DI-DI-DAH.

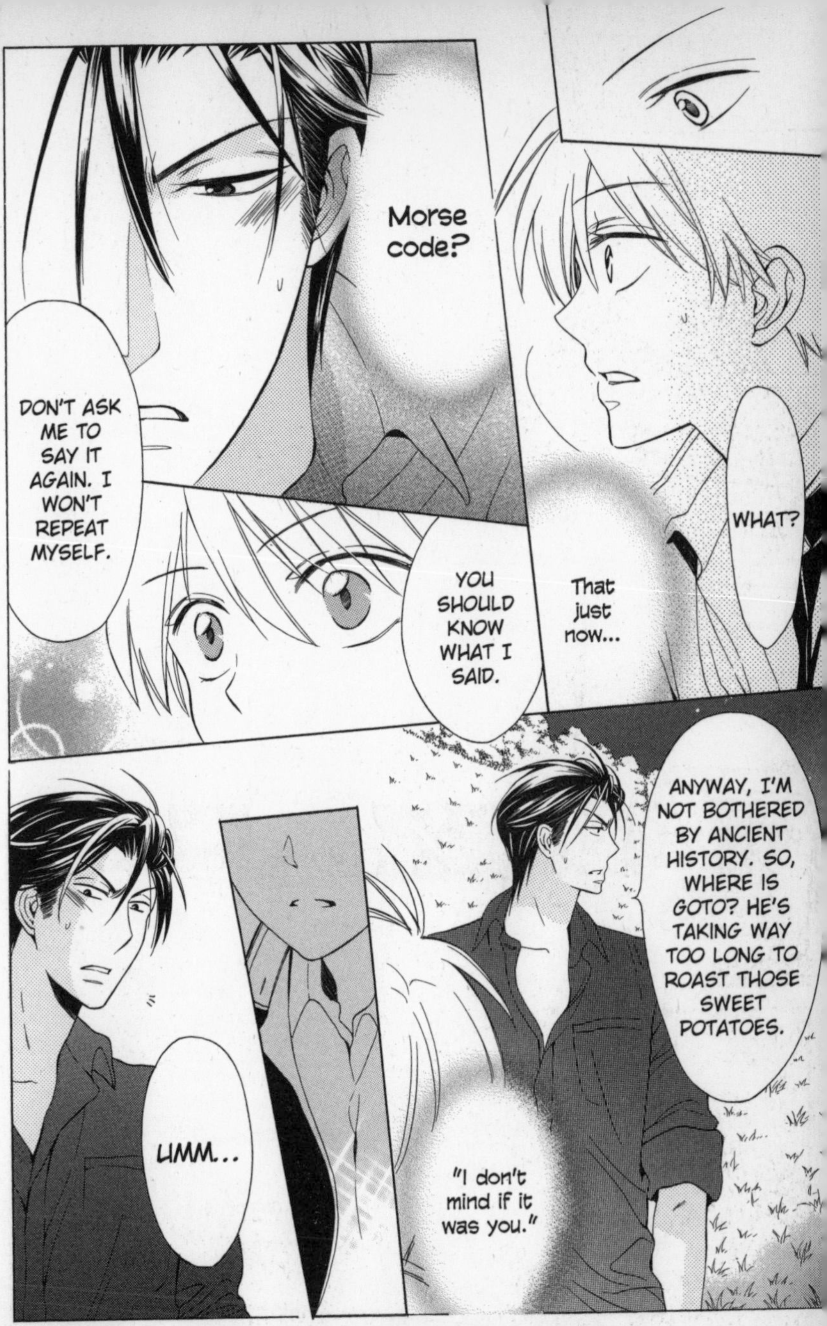

WHAT?
That just now...
Morse code?
DON'T ASK ME TO SAY IT AGAIN. I WON'T REPEAT MYSELF.
YOU SHOULD KNOW WHAT I SAID.
ANYWAY, I'M NOT BOTHERED BY ANCIENT HISTORY. SO, WHERE IS GOTO? HE'S TAKING WAY TOO LONG TO ROAST THOSE SWEET POTATOES.
"I don't mind if it was you."
UMM...

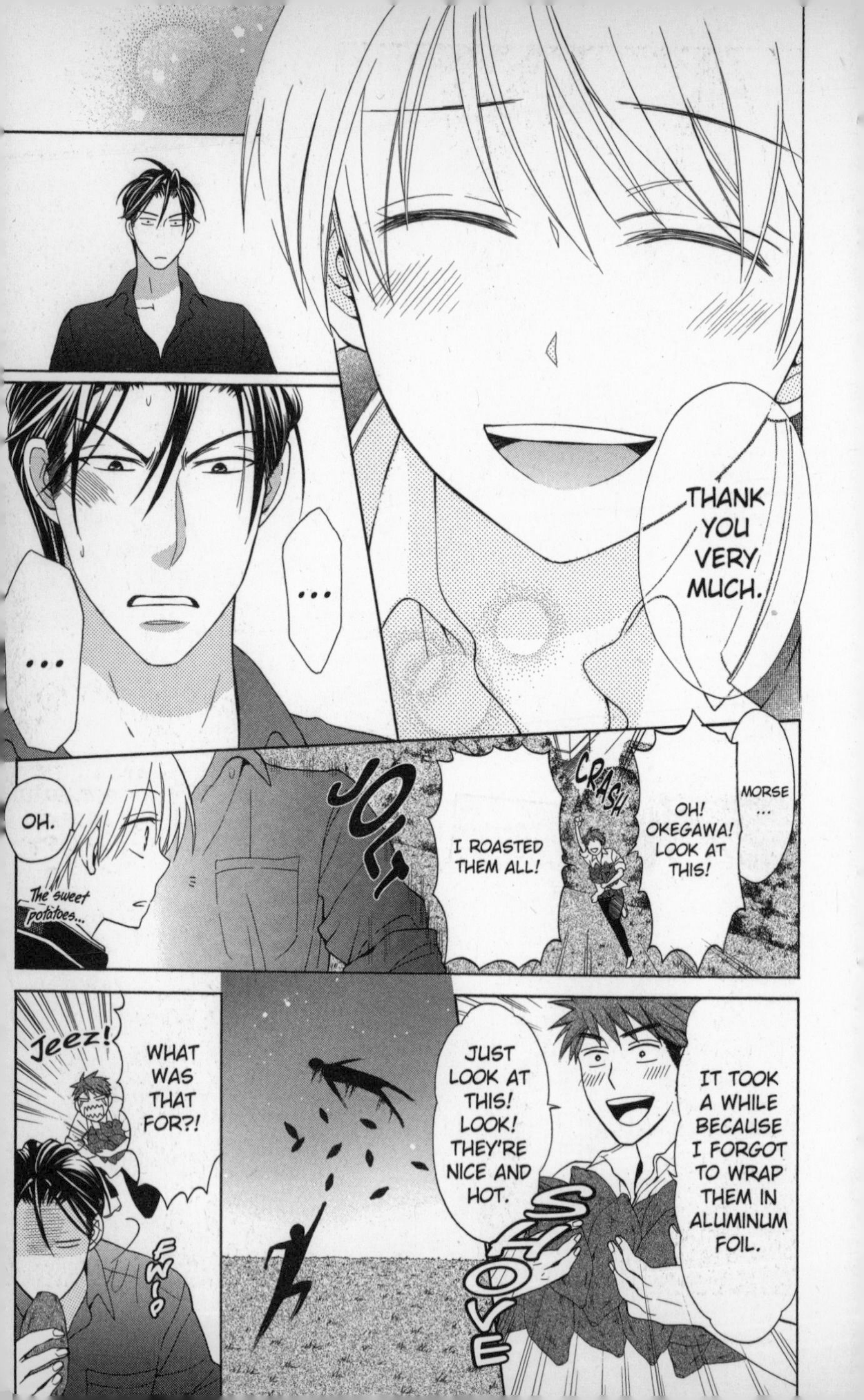
THANK YOU VERY MUCH.
...
...
MORSE ...
CRASH
OH! OKEGAWA! LOOK AT THIS!
I ROASTED THEM ALL!
JOLT
OH.
The sweet potatoes...
IT TOOK A WHILE BECAUSE I FORGOT TO WRAP THEM IN ALUMINUM FOIL.
JUST LOOK AT THIS! LOOK! THEY'RE NICE AND HOT.
SHOVE
WHAT WAS THAT FOR?!
Jeez!
FWIP

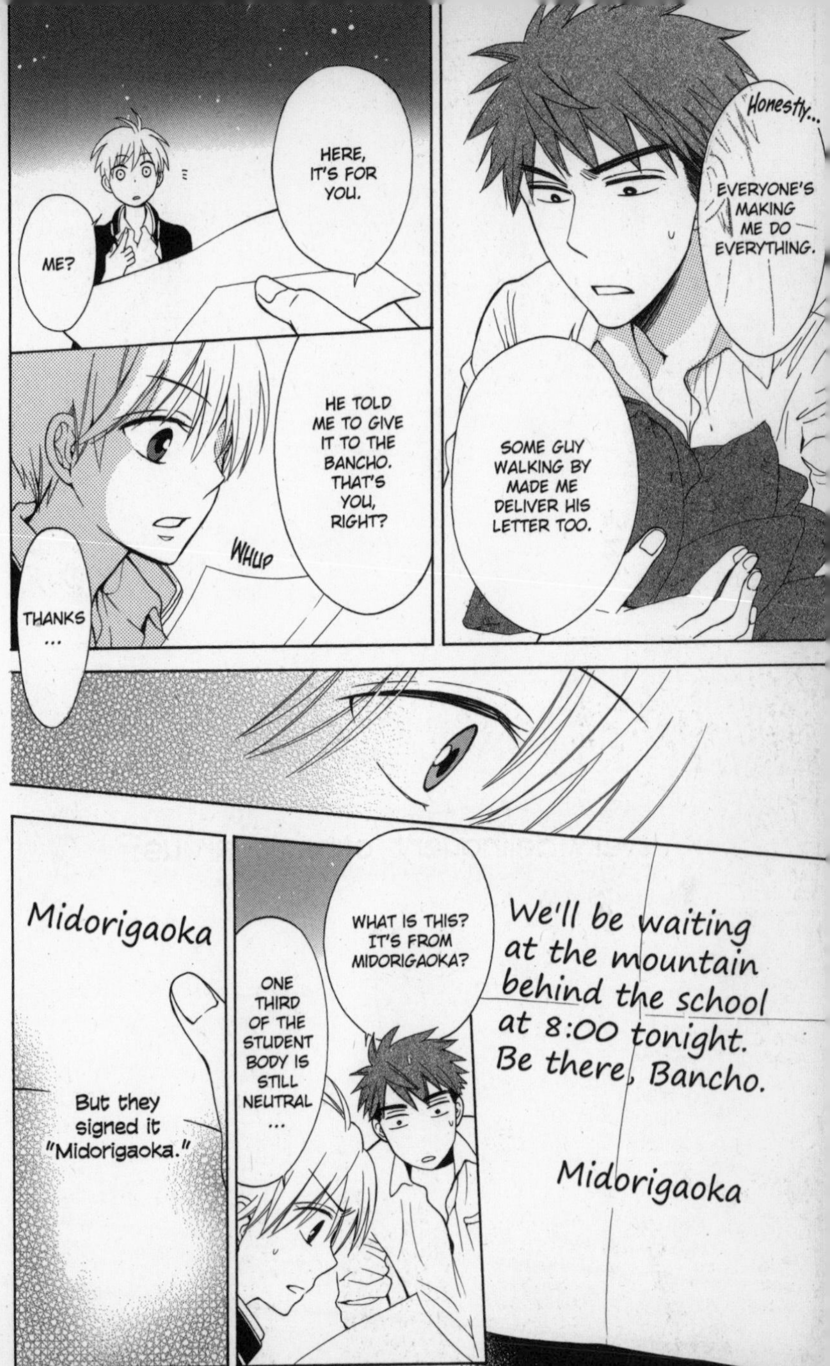
Honestly...
EVERYONE'S MAKING ME DO EVERYTHING.
SOME GUY WALKING BY MADE ME DELIVER HIS LETTER TOO.
HERE, IT'S FOR YOU.
ME?
HE TOLD ME TO GIVE IT TO THE BANCHO. THAT'S YOU, RIGHT?
WHUP
THANKS...
We'll be waiting at the mountain behind the school at 8:00 tonight. Be there, Bancho.
Midorigaoka
WHAT IS THIS? IT'S FROM MIDORIGAOKA?
ONE THIRD OF THE STUDENT BODY IS STILL NEUTRAL...
Midorigaoka
But they signed it "Midorigaoka."

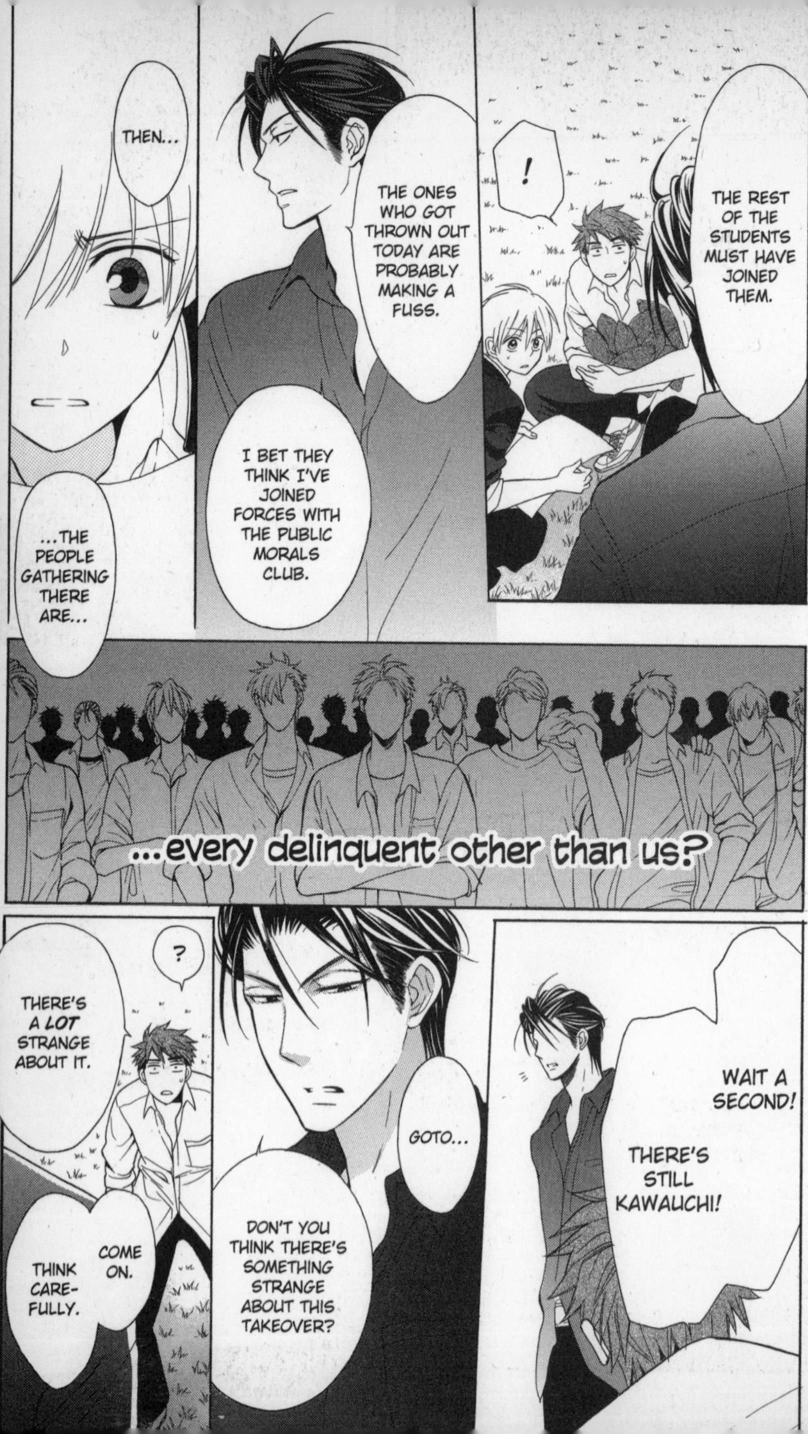
THE REST OF THE STUDENTS MUST HAVE JOINED THEM.
!
THE ONES WHO GOT THROWN OUT TODAY ARE PROBABLY MAKING A FUSS.
I BET THEY THINK I'VE JOINED FORCES WITH THE PUBLIC MORALS CLUB.
THEN...
...THE PEOPLE GATHERING THERE ARE...
...every delinquent other than us?
WAIT A SECOND!
THERE'S STILL KAWAUCHI!
GOTO...
DON'T YOU THINK THERE'S SOMETHING STRANGE ABOUT THIS TAKEOVER?
?
THERE'S A *LOT* STRANGE ABOUT IT.
COME ON.
THINK CAREFULLY.

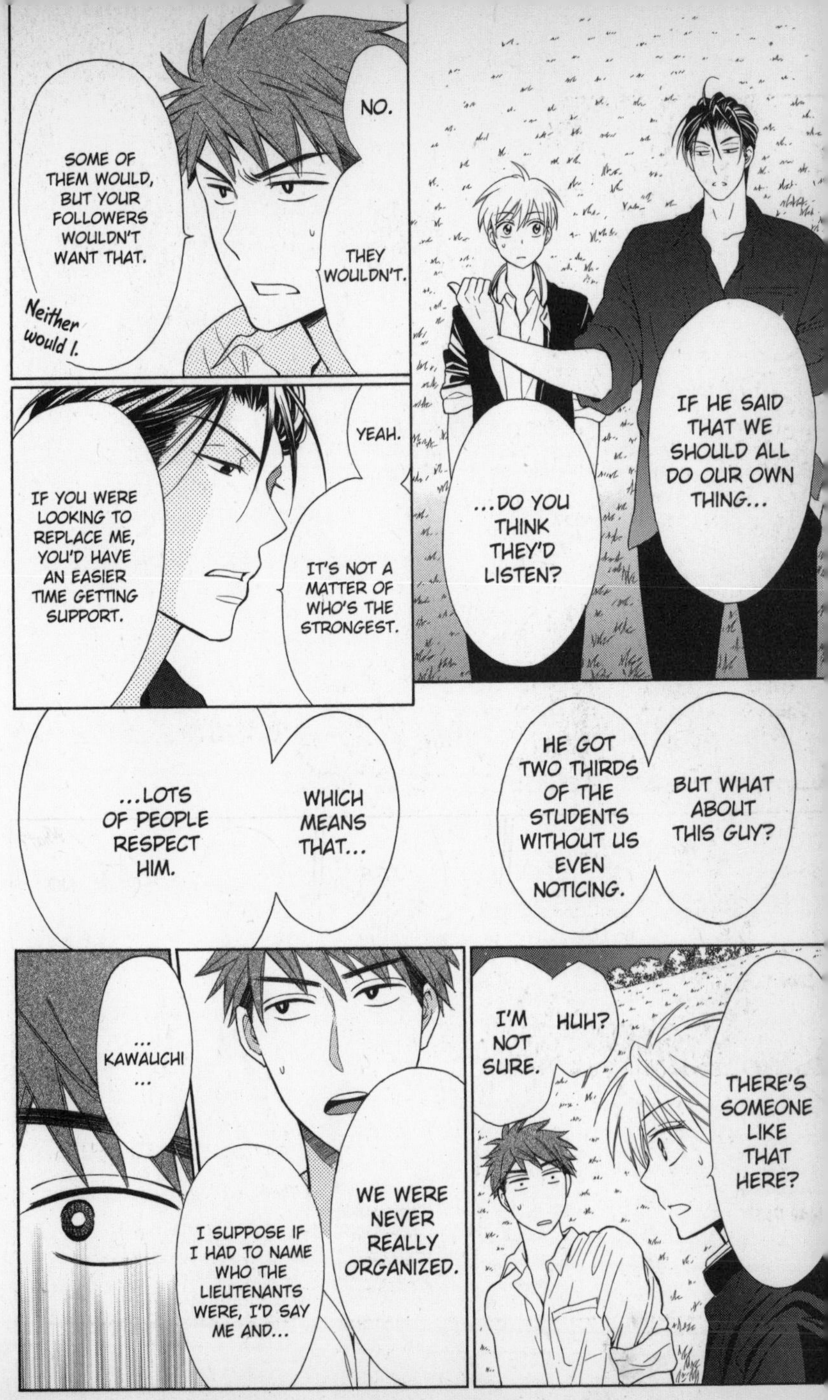
IF HE SAID THAT WE SHOULD ALL DO OUR OWN THING...
...DO YOU THINK THEY'D LISTEN?
NO.
THEY WOULDN'T.
SOME OF THEM WOULD, BUT YOUR FOLLOWERS WOULDN'T WANT THAT.
Neither would I.
YEAH.
IT'S NOT A MATTER OF WHO'S THE STRONGEST.
IF YOU WERE LOOKING TO REPLACE ME, YOU'D HAVE AN EASIER TIME GETTING SUPPORT.
BUT WHAT ABOUT THIS GUY?
HE GOT TWO THIRDS OF THE STUDENTS WITHOUT US EVEN NOTICING.
WHICH MEANS THAT...
...LOTS OF PEOPLE RESPECT HIM.
THERE'S SOMEONE LIKE THAT HERE?
HUH?
I'M NOT SURE.
WE WERE NEVER REALLY ORGANIZED.
I SUPPOSE IF I HAD TO NAME WHO THE LIEUTENANTS WERE, I'D SAY ME AND...
... KAWAUCHI ...

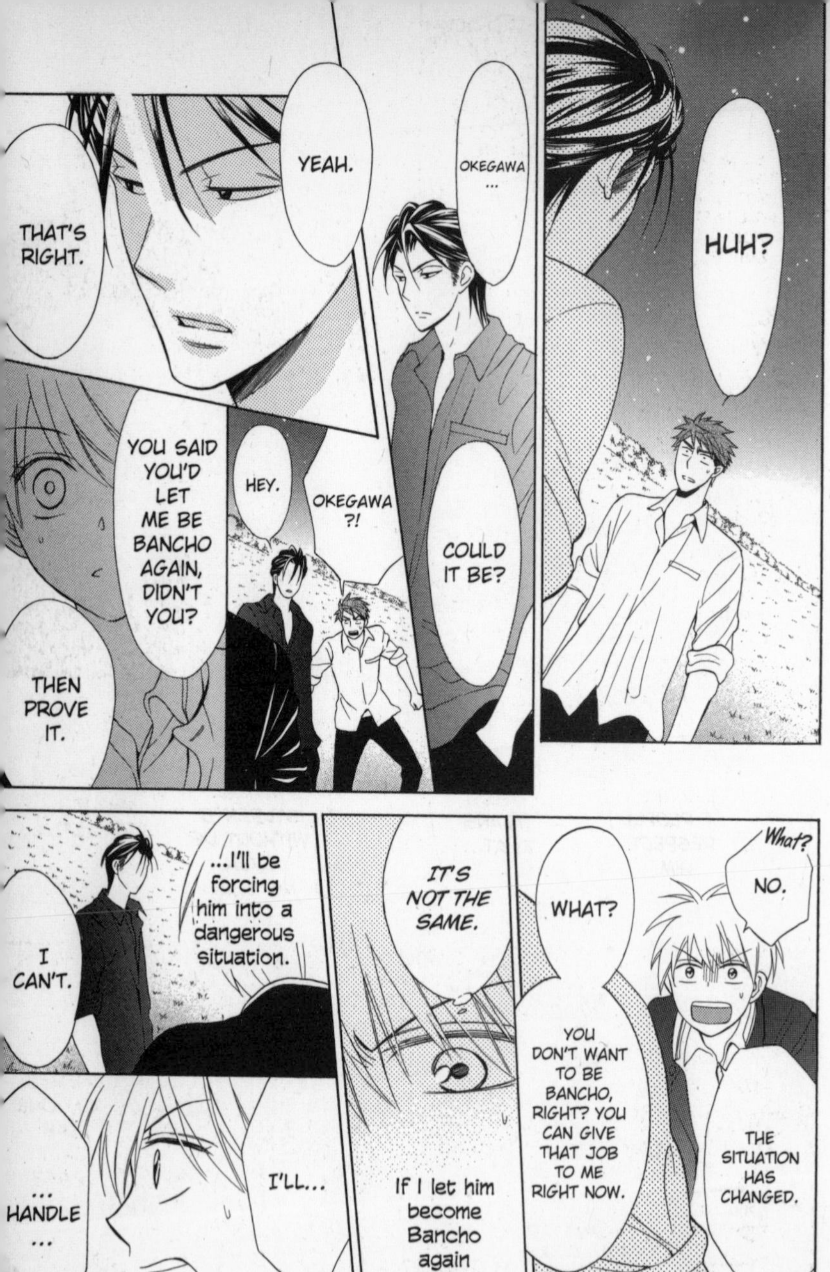
HUH?
OKEGAWA ...
COULD IT BE?
YEAH.
THAT'S RIGHT.
HEY.
OKEGAWA ?!
YOU SAID YOU'D LET ME BE BANCHO AGAIN, DIDN'T YOU?
THEN PROVE IT.
What?
NO.
WHAT?
YOU DON'T WANT TO BE BANCHO, RIGHT? YOU CAN GIVE THAT JOB TO ME RIGHT NOW.
THE SITUATION HAS CHANGED.
IT'S NOT THE SAME.
If I let him become Bancho again now...
...I'll be forcing him into a dangerous situation.
I CAN'T.
I'LL...
... HANDLE ...

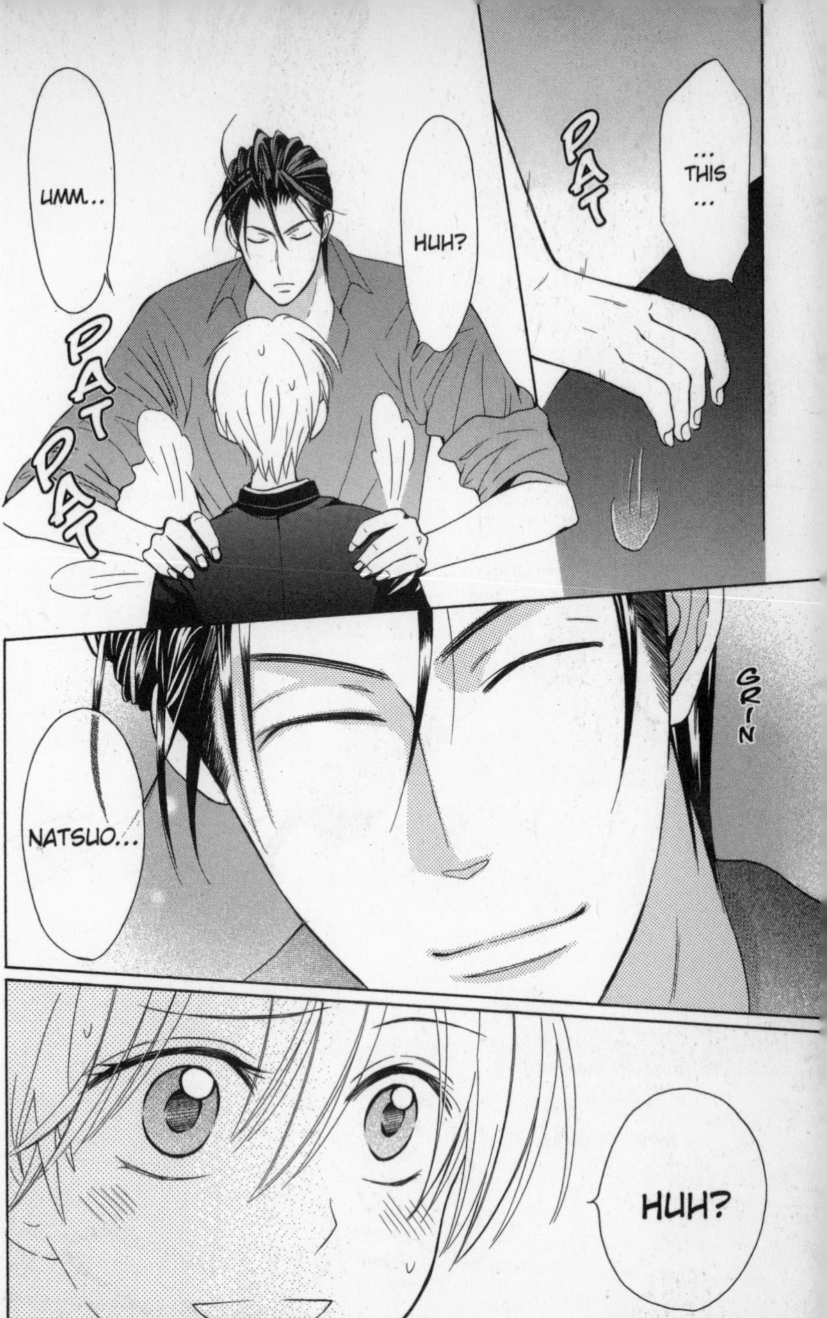
...THIS...
PAT
HUH?
UMM...
PAT PAT
GRIN
NATSUO...
HUH?

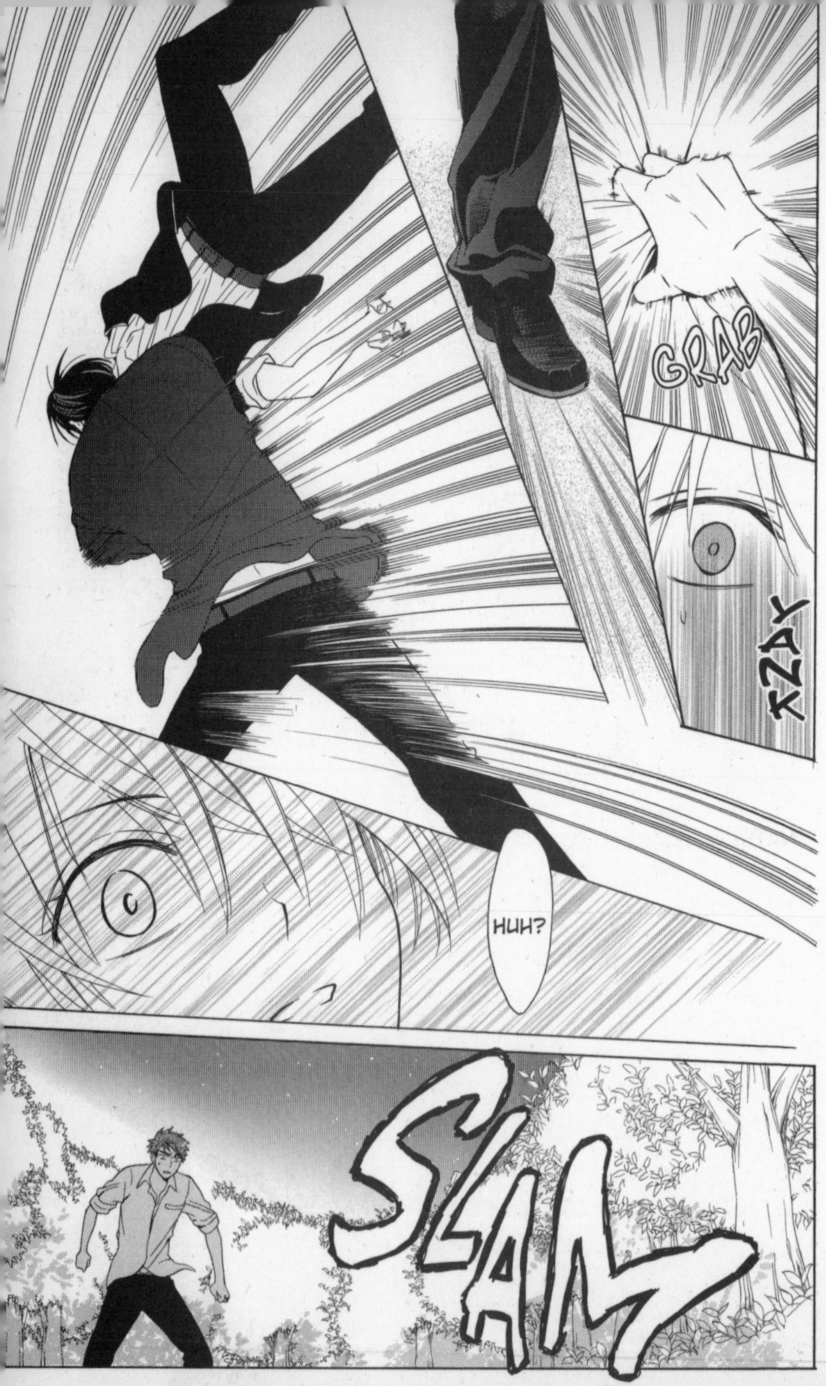
GRAB
YANK
HUH?
SLAM

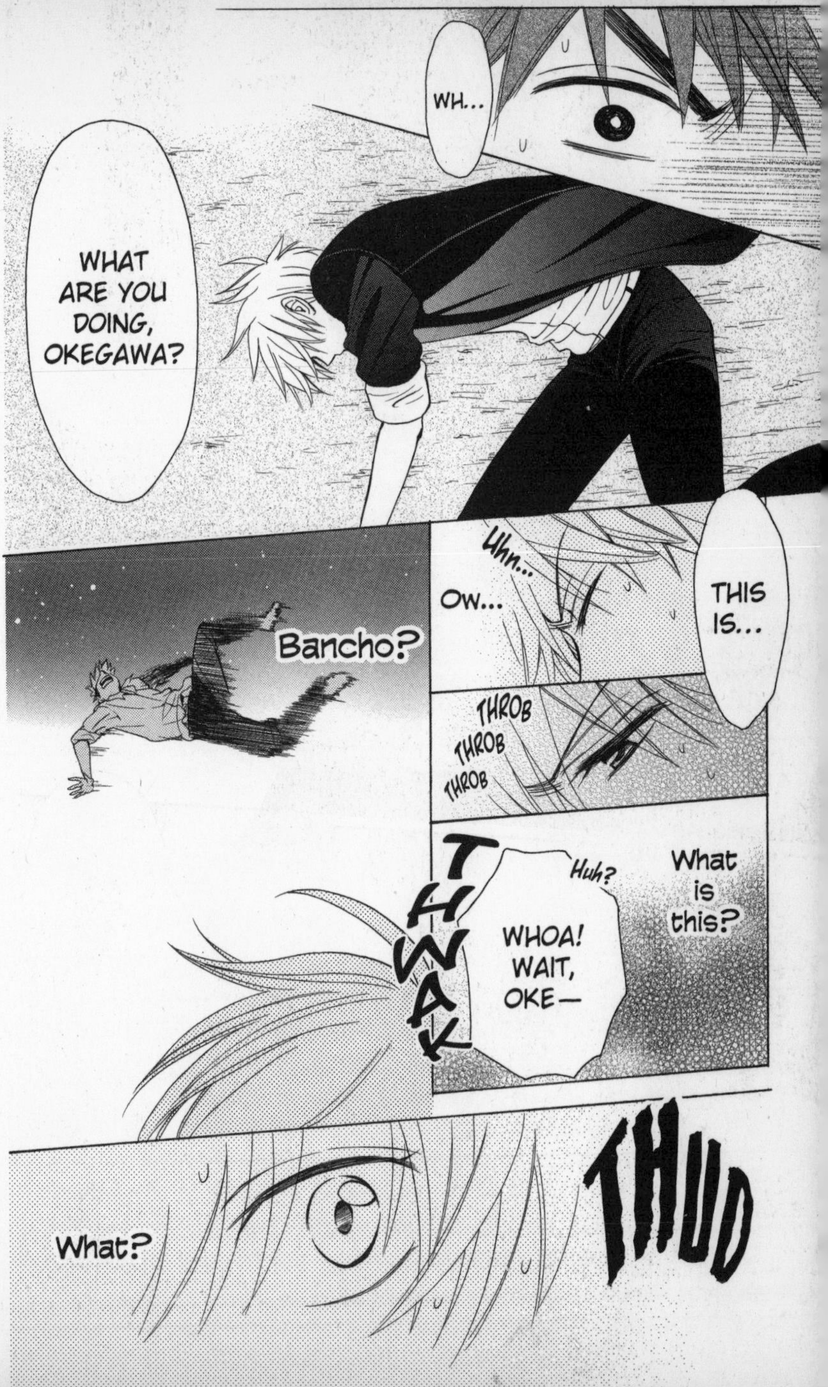
WH...
WHAT ARE YOU DOING, OKEGAWA?
THIS IS...
Uhn...
Ow...
THROB
THROB
THROB
What is this?
Huh?
WHOA! WAIT, OKE—
THWAK
Bancho?
THUD
What?

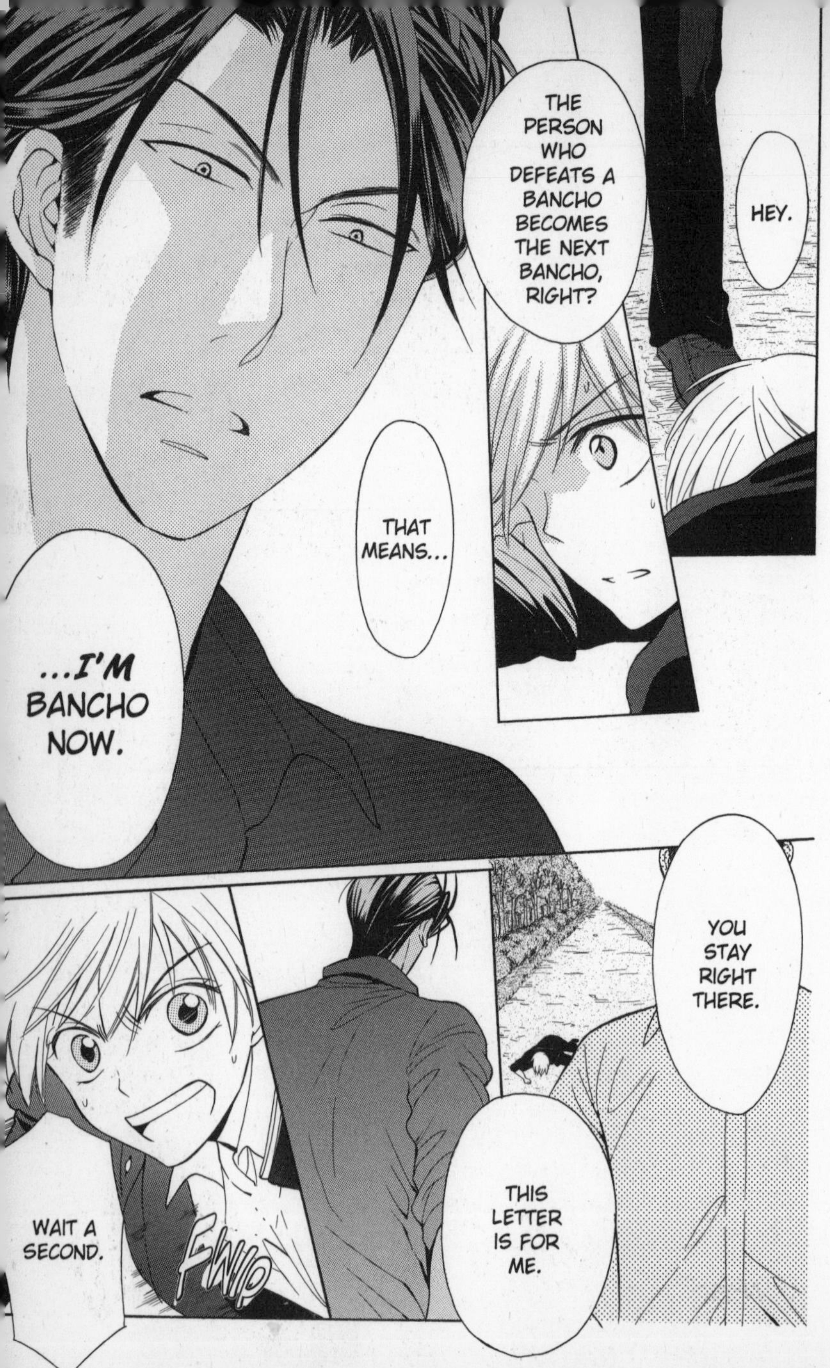
HEY.
THE PERSON WHO DEFEATS A BANCHO BECOMES THE NEXT BANCHO, RIGHT?
THAT MEANS...
...I'M BANCHO NOW.
YOU STAY RIGHT THERE.
THIS LETTER IS FOR ME.
FWIP
WAIT A SECOND.

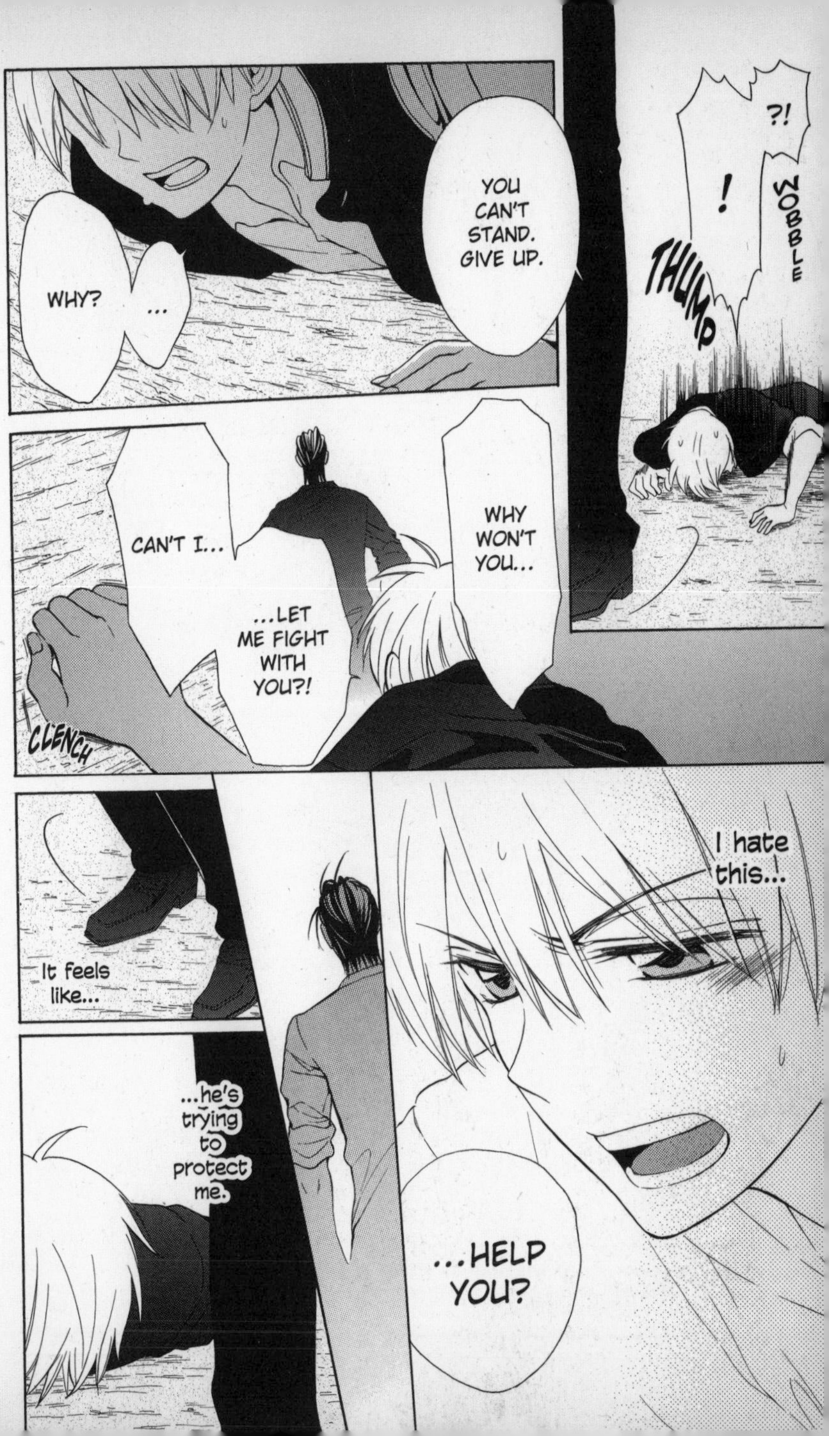
?!
WOBBLE
!
THUMP
YOU CAN'T STAND. GIVE UP.
...
WHY?
WHY WON'T YOU...
CAN'T I...
...LET ME FIGHT WITH YOU?!
CLENCH
I hate this...
...HELP YOU?
It feels like...
...he's trying to protect me.

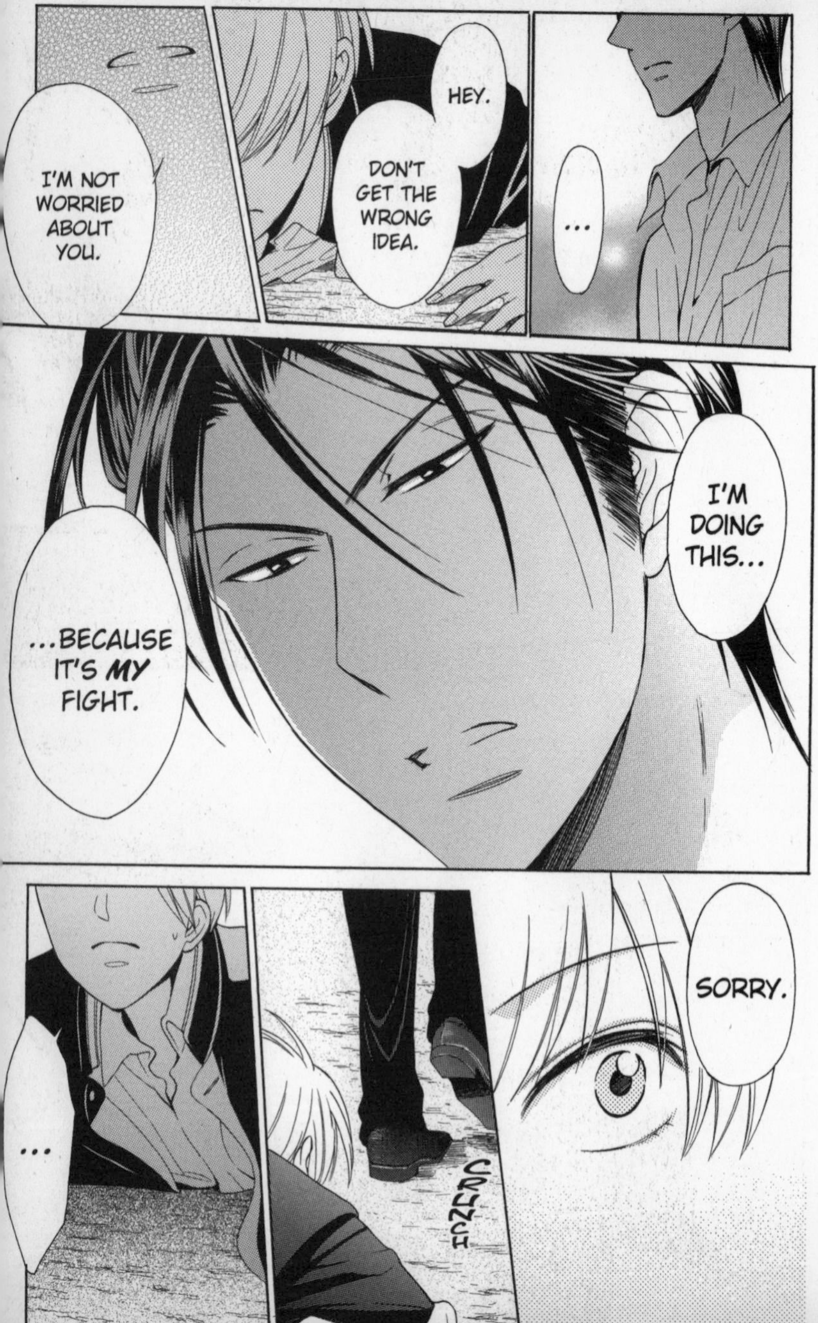
...
HEY.
DON'T GET THE WRONG IDEA.
I'M NOT WORRIED ABOUT YOU.
I'M DOING THIS...
...BECAUSE IT'S *MY* FIGHT.
SORRY.
CRUNCH
...

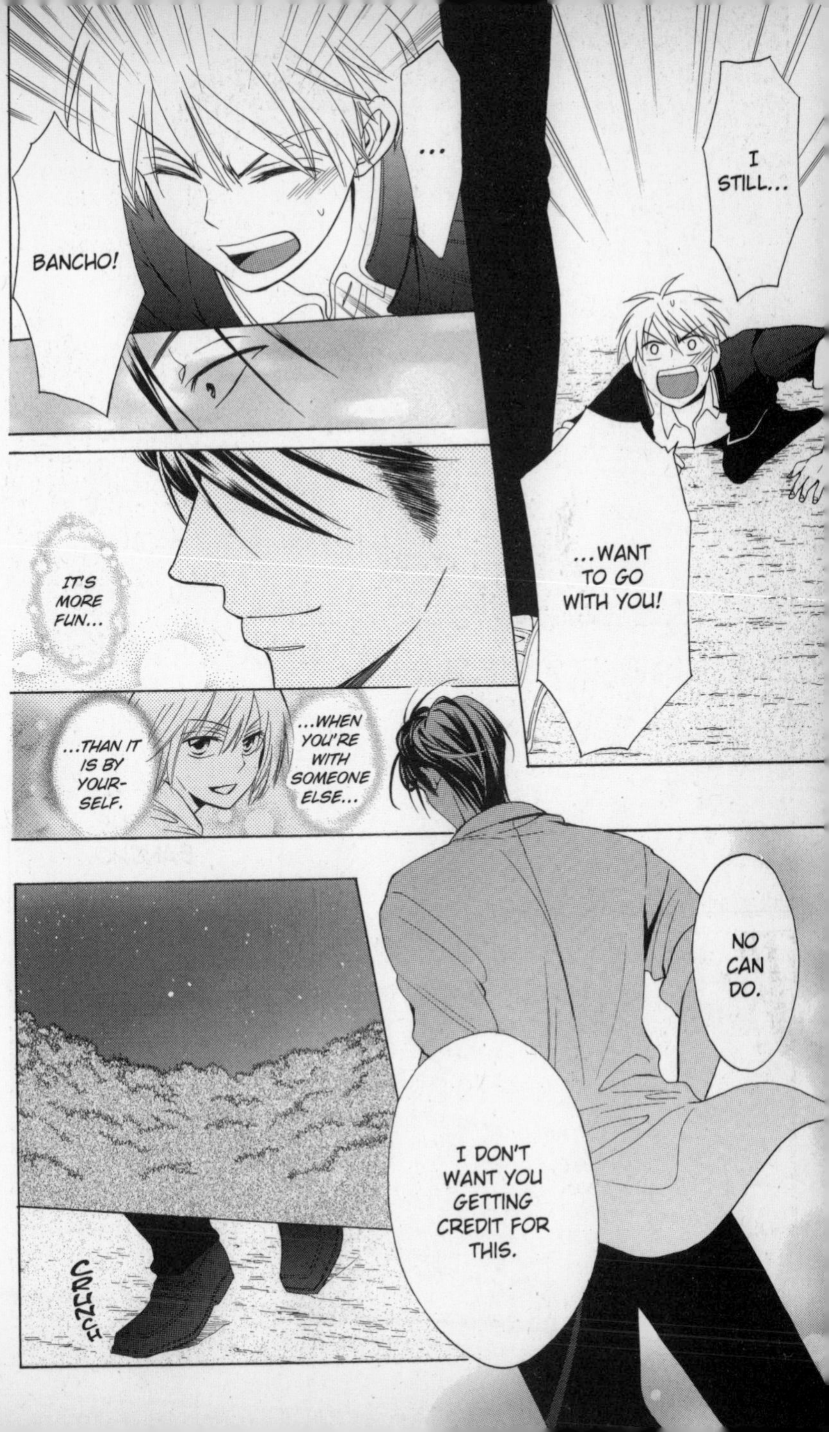
I STILL...
...WANT TO GO WITH YOU!
...
BANCHO!
IT'S MORE FUN...
...WHEN YOU'RE WITH SOMEONE ELSE...
...THAN IT IS BY YOURSELF.
NO CAN DO.
I DON'T WANT YOU GETTING CREDIT FOR THIS.
CRUNCH

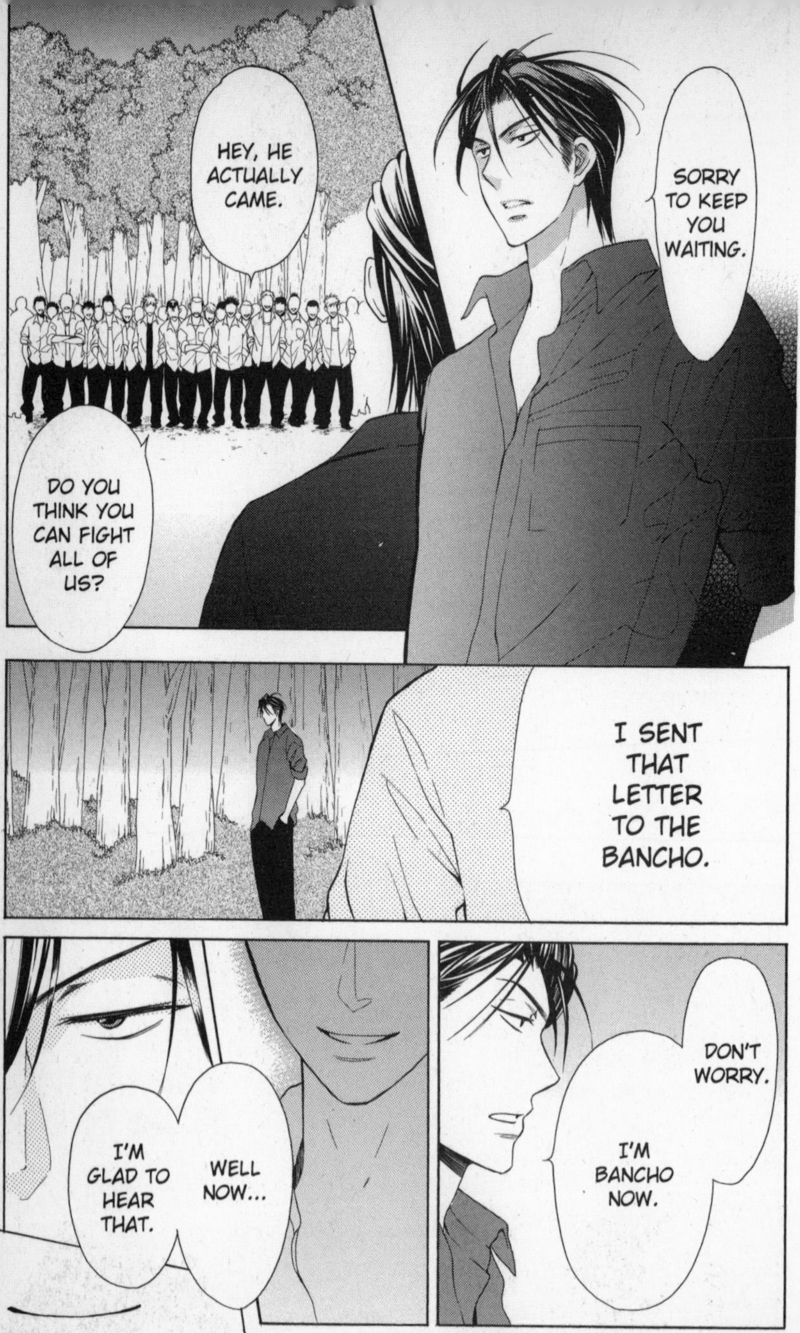
SORRY TO KEEP YOU WAITING.
HEY, HE ACTUALLY CAME.
DO YOU THINK YOU CAN FIGHT ALL OF US?
I SENT THAT LETTER TO THE BANCHO.
DON'T WORRY.
I'M BANCHO NOW.
WELL NOW...
I'M GLAD TO HEAR THAT.

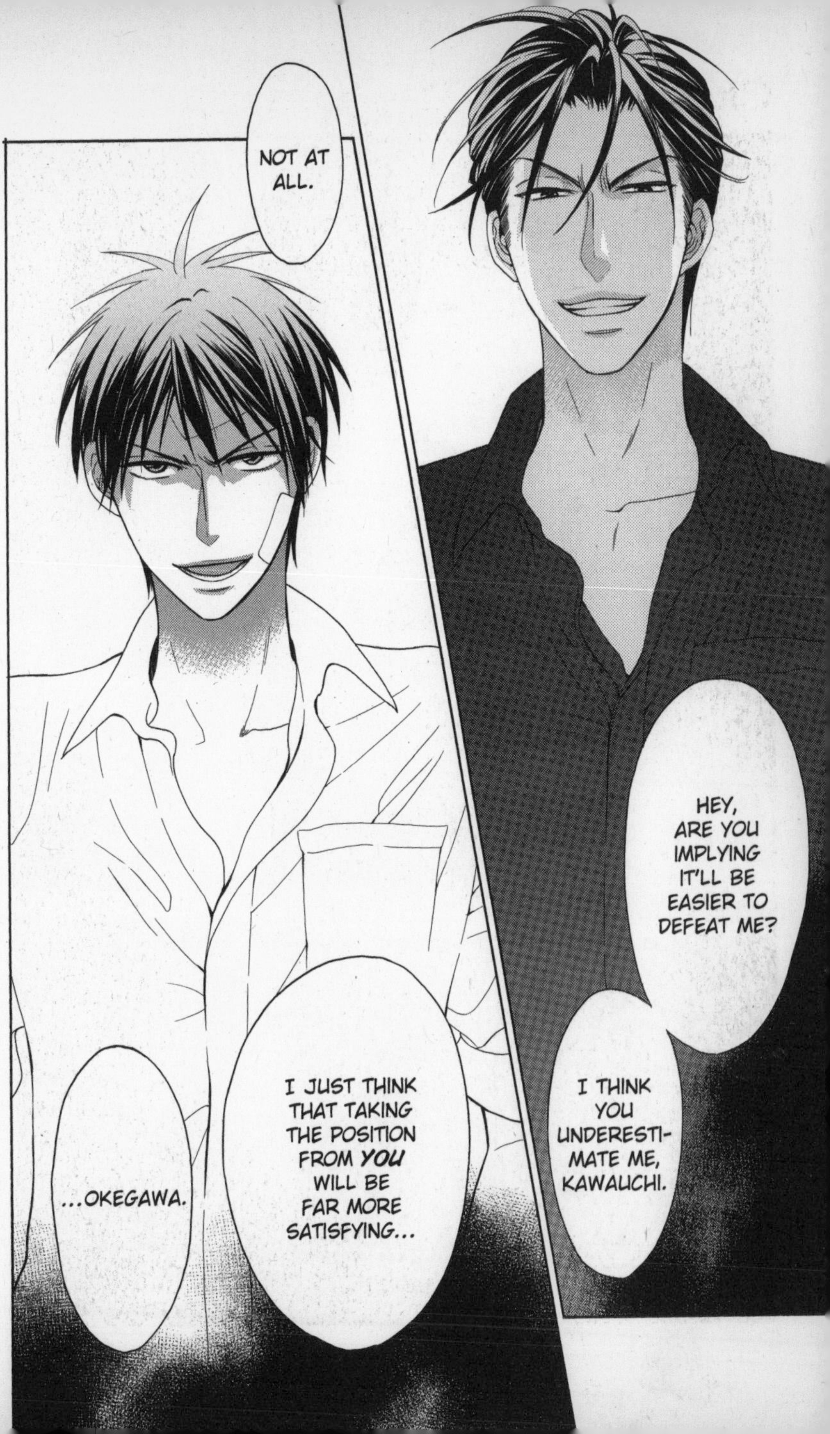
HEY, ARE YOU IMPLYING IT'LL BE EASIER TO DEFEAT ME?
I THINK YOU UNDERESTIMATE ME, KAWAUCHI.
NOT AT ALL.
I JUST THINK THAT TAKING THE POSITION FROM *YOU* WILL BE FAR MORE SATISFYING...
...OKEGAWA.

Chapter 50

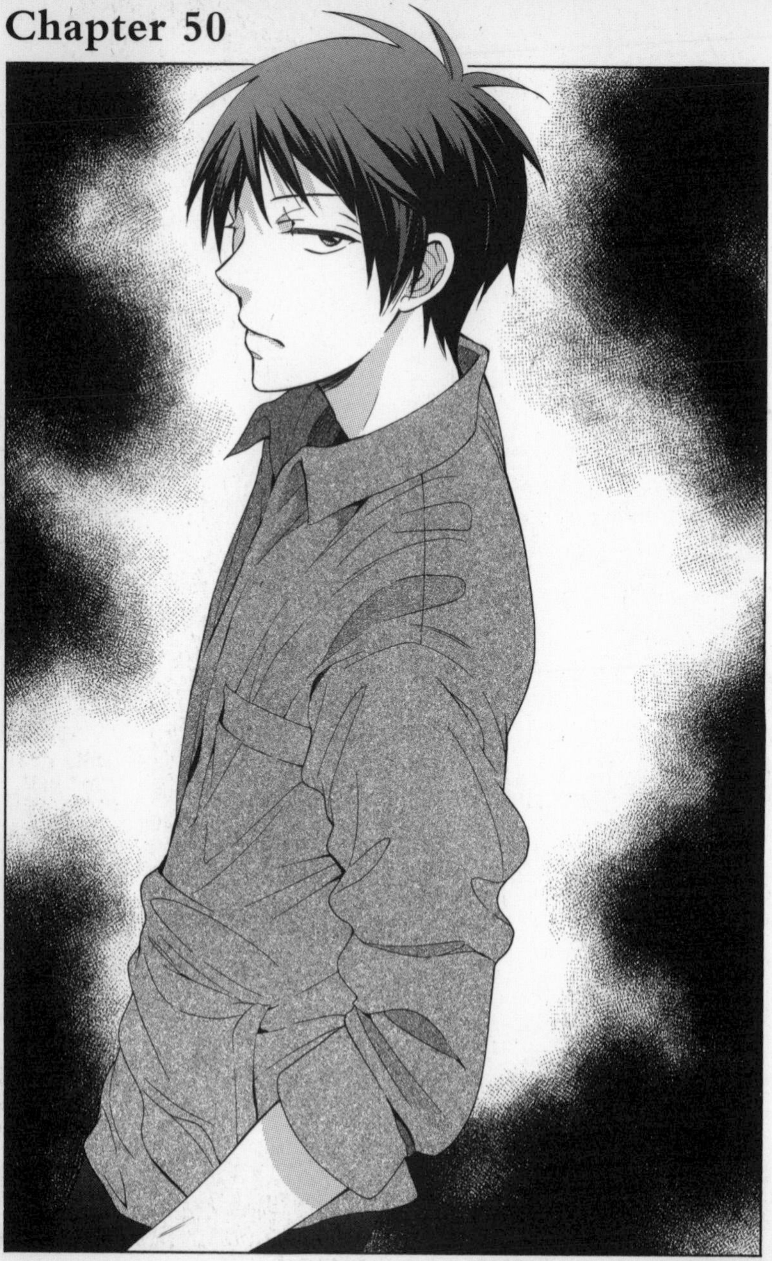

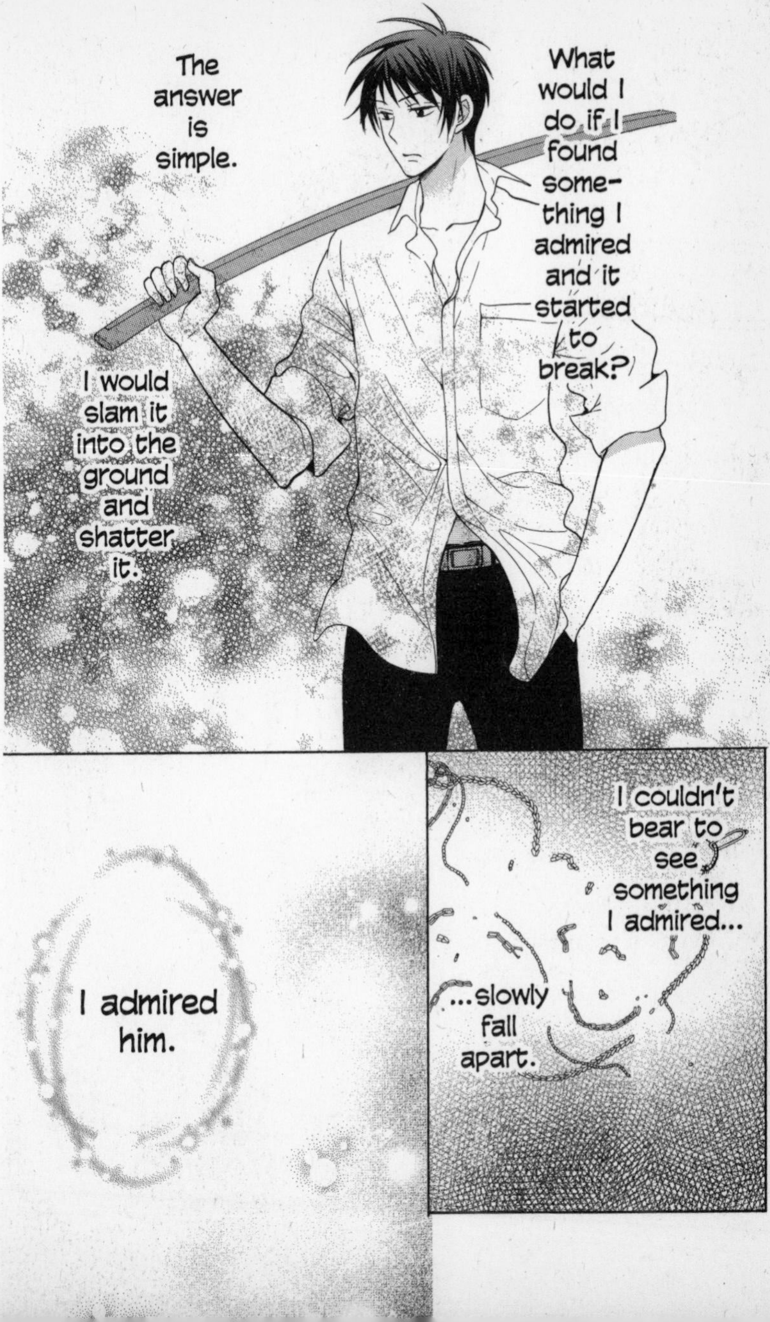
What would I do if I found something I admired and it started to break?
The answer is simple.
I would slam it into the ground and shatter it.
I couldn't bear to see something I admired...
...slowly fall apart.
I admired him.

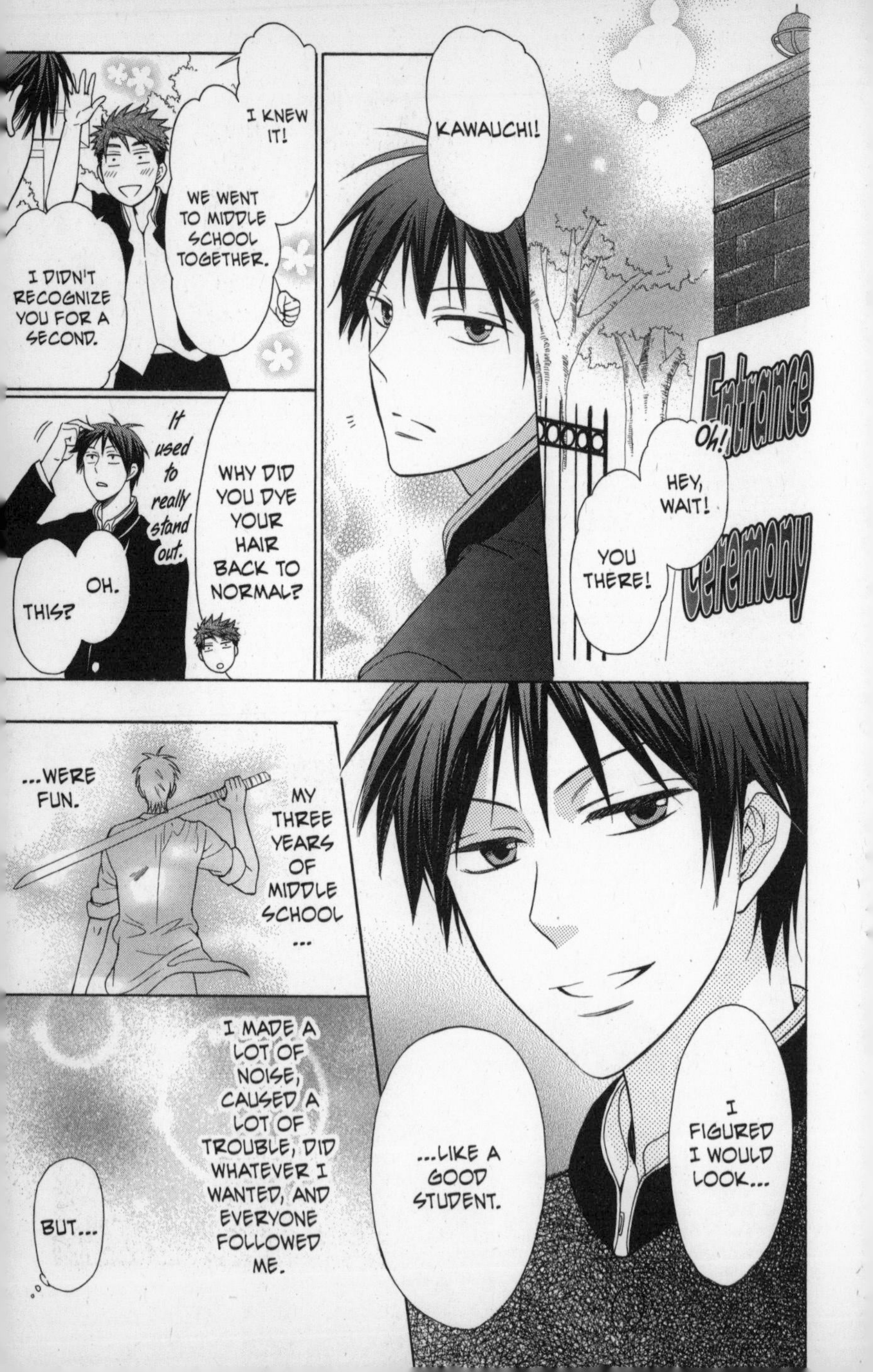
Entrance Ceremony
Oh!
HEY, WAIT!
YOU THERE!
KAWAUCHI!
I KNEW IT!
WE WENT TO MIDDLE SCHOOL TOGETHER.
I DIDN'T RECOGNIZE YOU FOR A SECOND.
WHY DID YOU DYE YOUR HAIR BACK TO NORMAL?
It used to really stand out.
OH. THIS?
I FIGURED I WOULD LOOK...
...LIKE A GOOD STUDENT.
MY THREE YEARS OF MIDDLE SCHOOL...
...WERE FUN.
I MADE A LOT OF NOISE, CAUSED A LOT OF TROUBLE, DID WHATEVER I WANTED, AND EVERYONE FOLLOWED ME.
BUT...

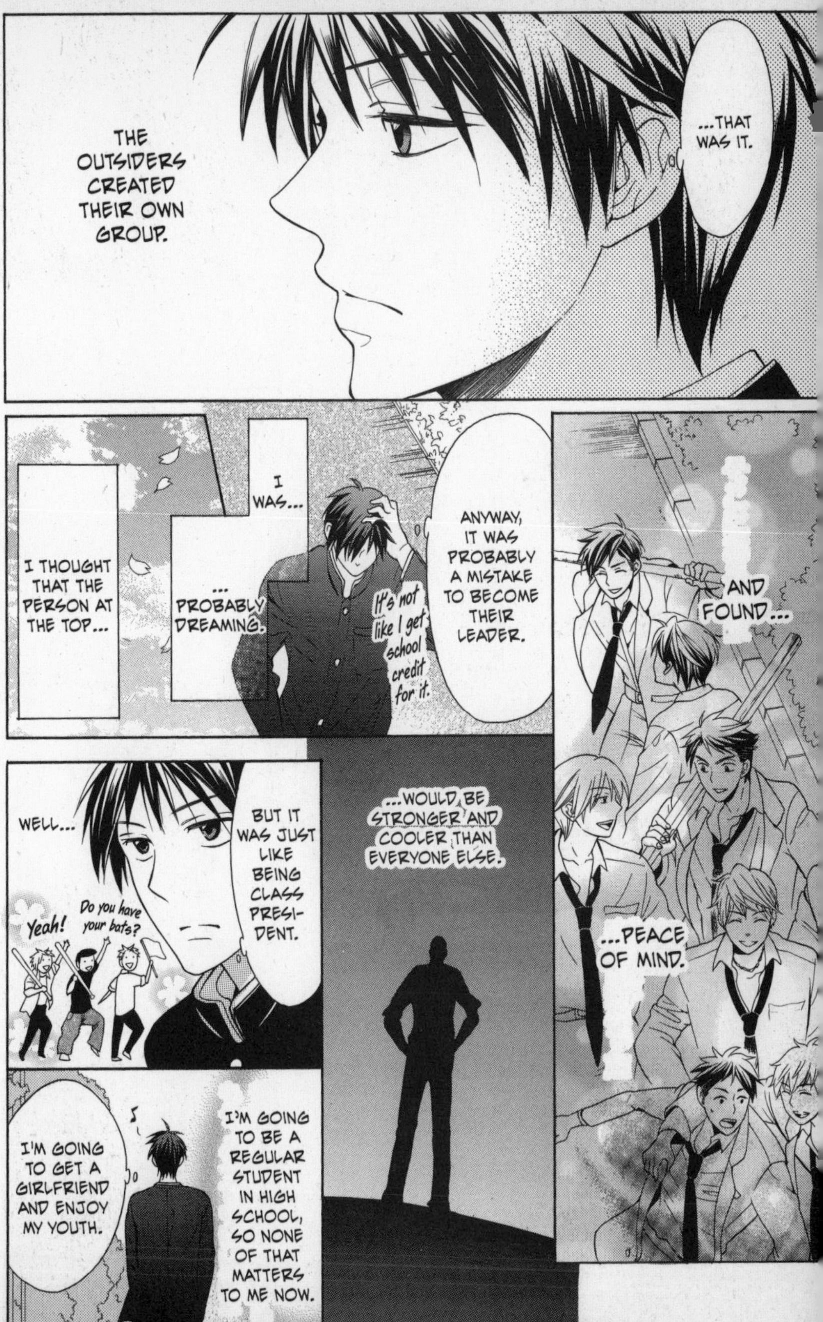
...THAT WAS IT.
THE OUTSIDERS CREATED THEIR OWN GROUP.
AND FOUND...
...PEACE OF MIND.
ANYWAY, IT WAS PROBABLY A MISTAKE TO BECOME THEIR LEADER.
It's not like I get school credit for it.
I WAS...
...PROBABLY DREAMING.
I THOUGHT THAT THE PERSON AT THE TOP...
...WOULD BE STRONGER AND COOLER THAN EVERYONE ELSE.
BUT IT WAS JUST LIKE BEING CLASS PRESIDENT.
WELL...
Do you have your bats?
Yeah!
I'M GOING TO BE A REGULAR STUDENT IN HIGH SCHOOL, SO NONE OF THAT MATTERS TO ME NOW.
I'M GOING TO GET A GIRLFRIEND AND ENJOY MY YOUTH.

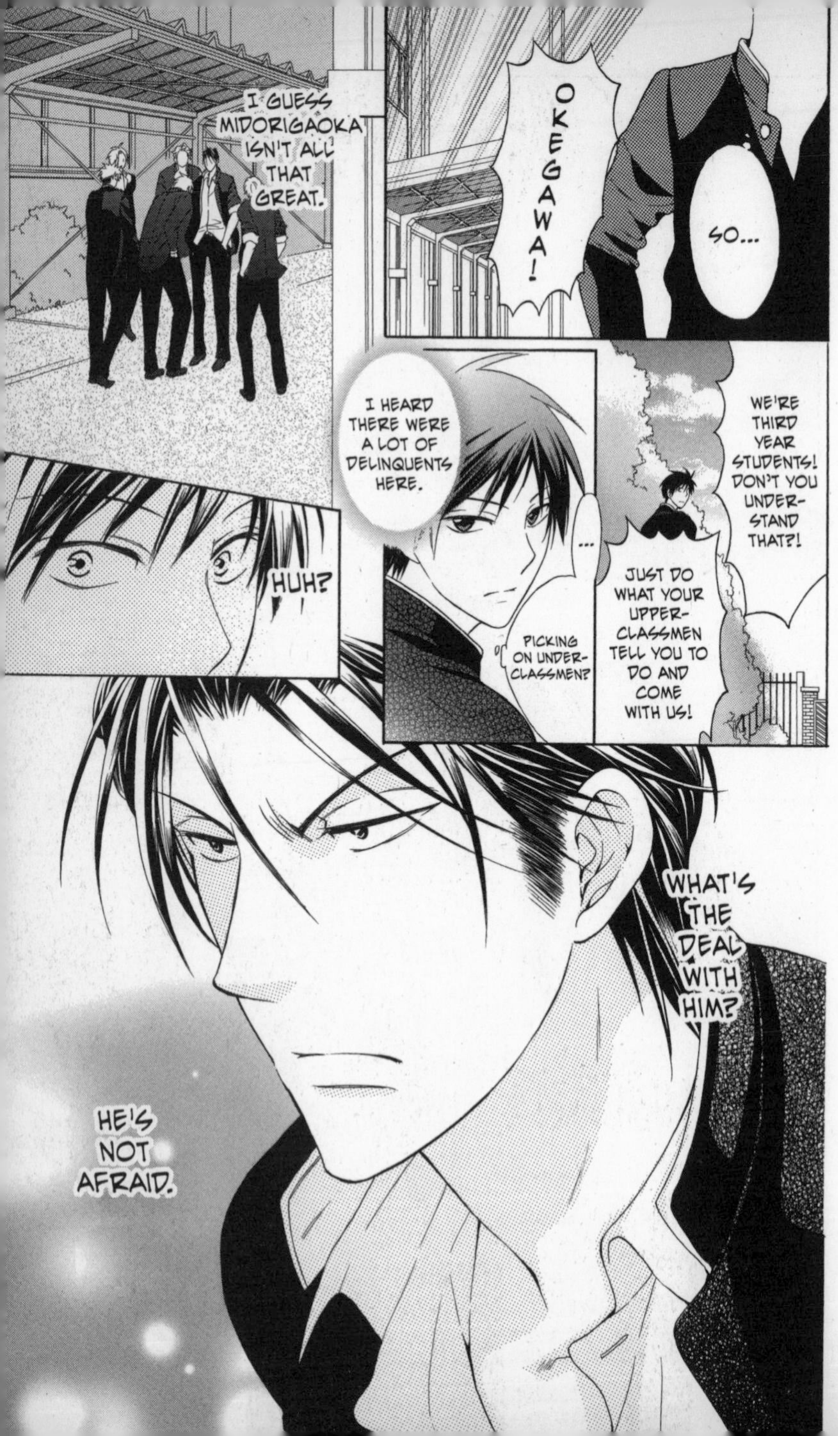
SO...
OKEGAWA!
WE'RE THIRD YEAR STUDENTS! DON'T YOU UNDER-STAND THAT?!
JUST DO WHAT YOUR UPPER-CLASSMEN TELL YOU TO DO AND COME WITH US!
I HEARD THERE WERE A LOT OF DELINQUENTS HERE.
...
PICKING ON UNDER-CLASSMEN?
I GUESS MIDORIGAOKA ISN'T ALL THAT GREAT.
HUH?
WHAT'S THE DEAL WITH HIM?
HE'S NOT AFRAID.

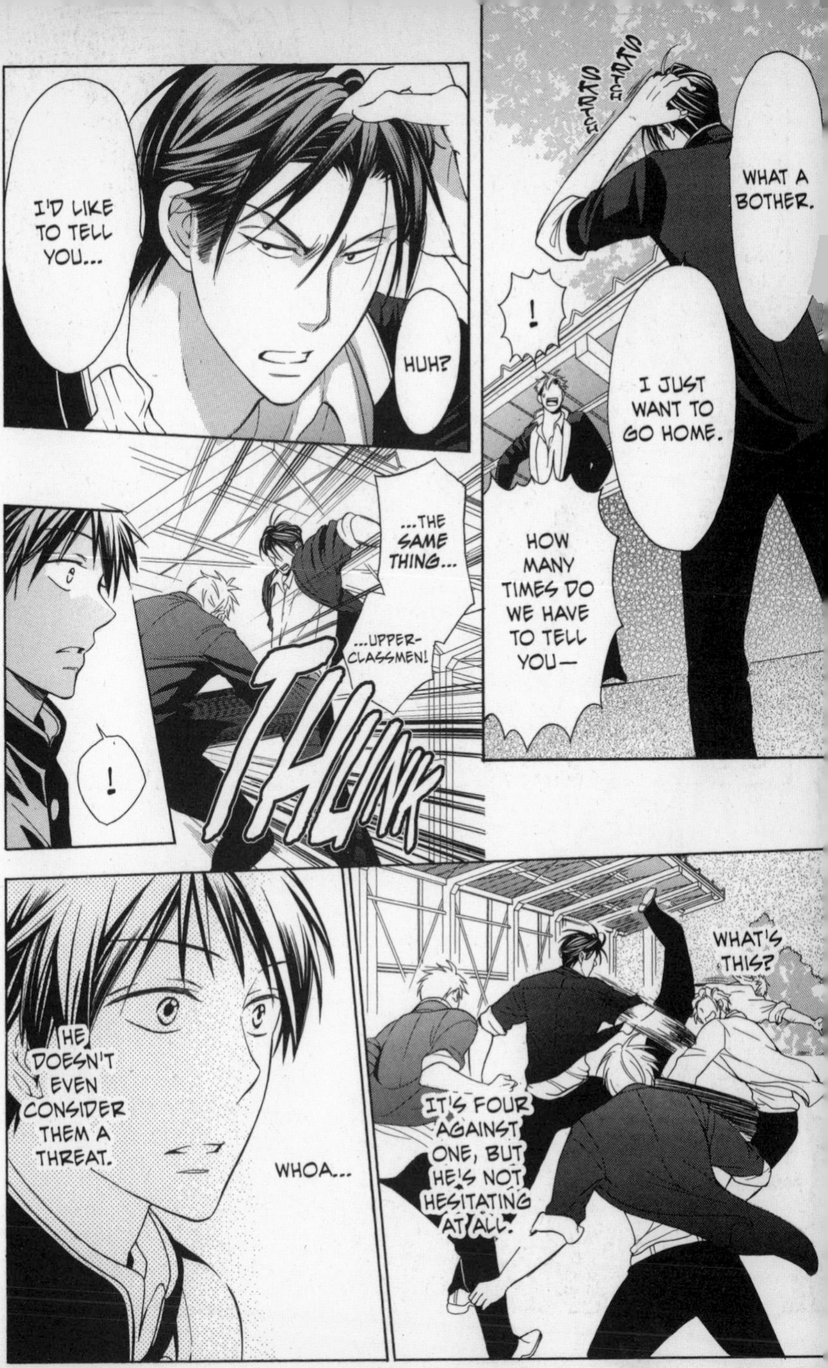
SKRTCH SKRTCH
WHAT A BOTHER.
!
I JUST WANT TO GO HOME.
HOW MANY TIMES DO WE HAVE TO TELL YOU—
HUH?
I'D LIKE TO TELL YOU...
...THE SAME THING...
...UPPER-CLASSMEN!
THUNK
!
WHAT'S THIS?
IT'S FOUR AGAINST ONE, BUT HE'S NOT HESITATING AT ALL.
WHOA...
HE DOESN'T EVEN CONSIDER THEM A THREAT.

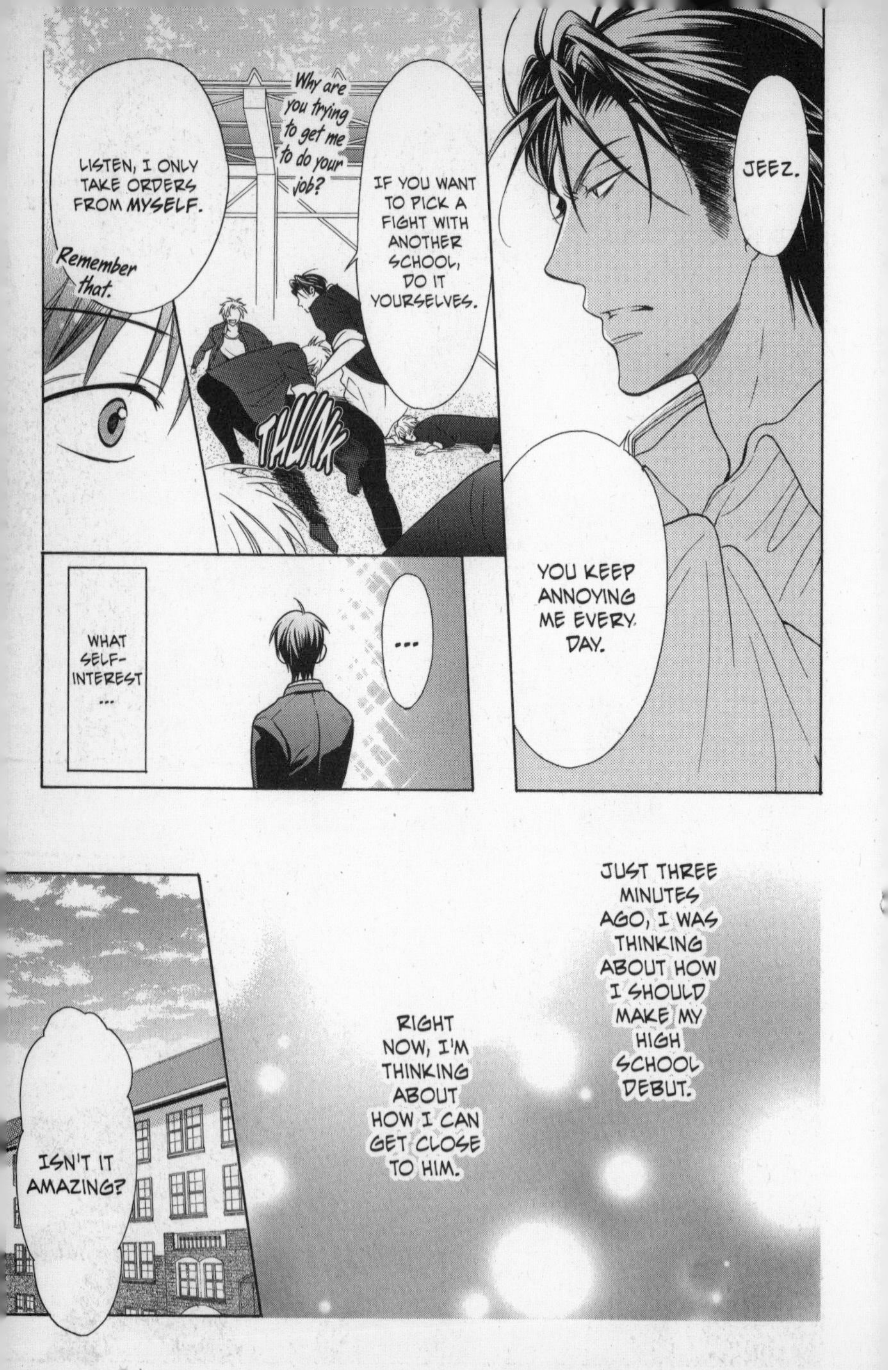

JEEZ.
YOU KEEP ANNOYING ME EVERY DAY.
IF YOU WANT TO PICK A FIGHT WITH ANOTHER SCHOOL, DO IT YOURSELVES.
Why are you trying to get me to do your job?
THUNK
LISTEN, I ONLY TAKE ORDERS FROM MYSELF.
Remember that.
...
WHAT SELF-INTEREST...
JUST THREE MINUTES AGO, I WAS THINKING ABOUT HOW I SHOULD MAKE MY HIGH SCHOOL DEBUT.
RIGHT NOW, I'M THINKING ABOUT HOW I CAN GET CLOSE TO HIM.
ISN'T IT AMAZING?

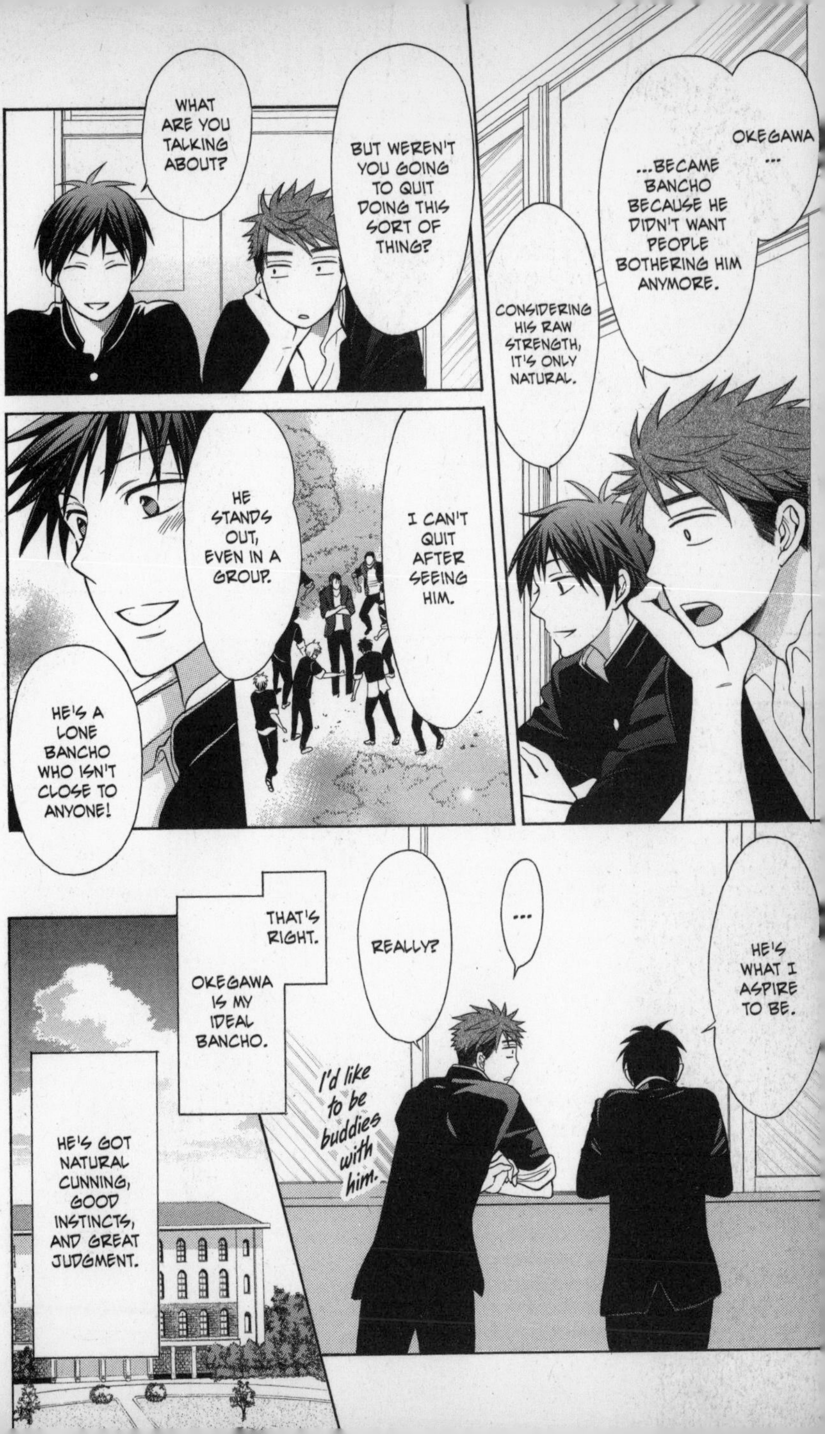
OKEGAWA ...
...BECAME BANCHO BECAUSE HE DIDN'T WANT PEOPLE BOTHERING HIM ANYMORE.
CONSIDERING HIS RAW STRENGTH, IT'S ONLY NATURAL.
BUT WEREN'T YOU GOING TO QUIT DOING THIS SORT OF THING?
WHAT ARE YOU TALKING ABOUT?
I CAN'T QUIT AFTER SEEING HIM.
HE STANDS OUT, EVEN IN A GROUP.
HE'S A LONE BANCHO WHO ISN'T CLOSE TO ANYONE!
HE'S WHAT I ASPIRE TO BE.
...
REALLY?
THAT'S RIGHT.
OKEGAWA IS MY IDEAL BANCHO.
I'd like to be buddies with him.
HE'S GOT NATURAL CUNNING, GOOD INSTINCTS, AND GREAT JUDGMENT.

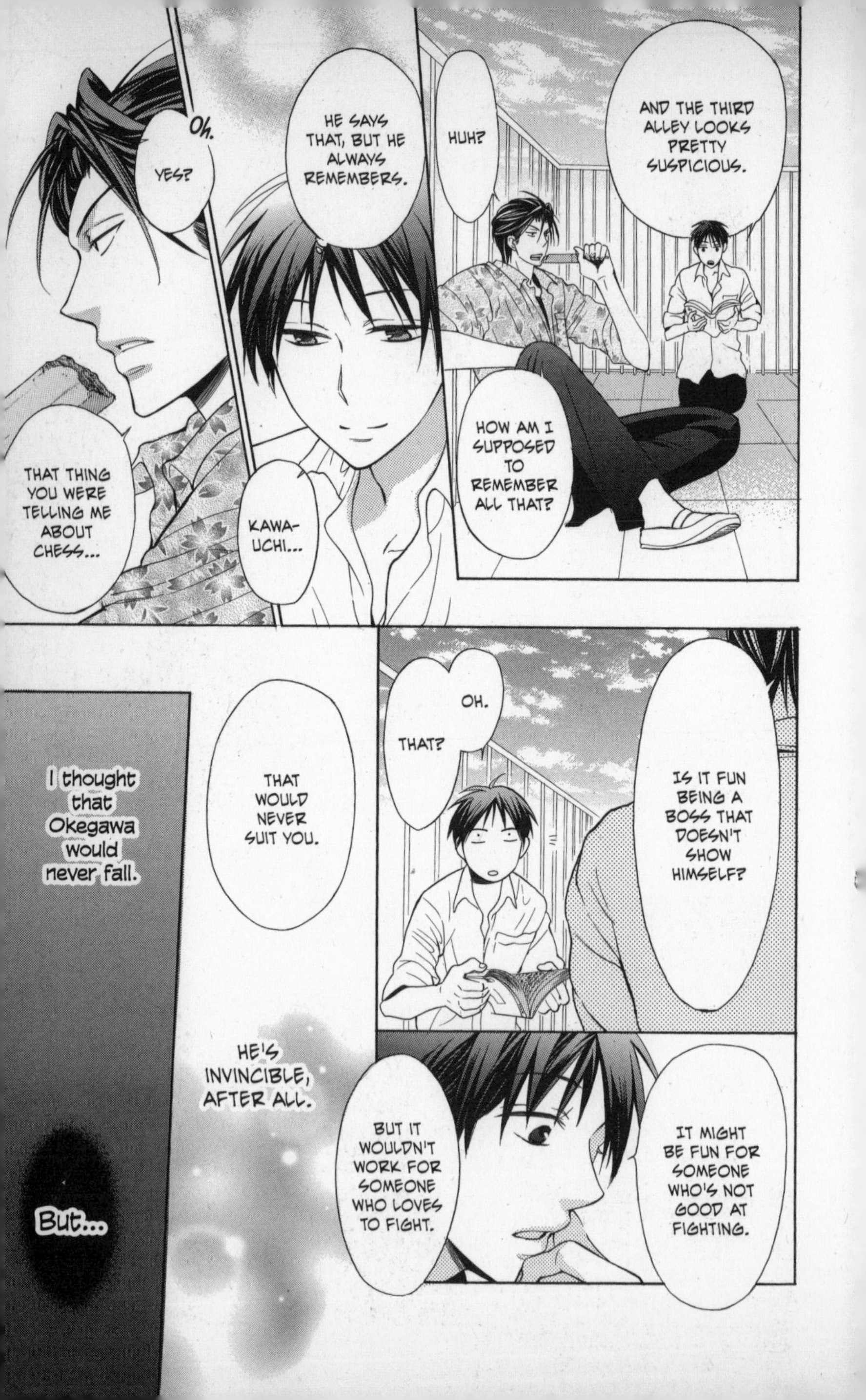
AND THE THIRD ALLEY LOOKS PRETTY SUSPICIOUS.
HUH?
HOW AM I SUPPOSED TO REMEMBER ALL THAT?
HE SAYS THAT, BUT HE ALWAYS REMEMBERS.
KAWA-UCHI...
Oh.
YES?
THAT THING YOU WERE TELLING ME ABOUT CHESS...
IS IT FUN BEING A BOSS THAT DOESN'T SHOW HIMSELF?
OH.
THAT?
THAT WOULD NEVER SUIT YOU.
IT MIGHT BE FUN FOR SOMEONE WHO'S NOT GOOD AT FIGHTING.
BUT IT WOULDN'T WORK FOR SOMEONE WHO LOVES TO FIGHT.
I thought that Okegawa would never fall.
HE'S INVINCIBLE, AFTER ALL.
But...

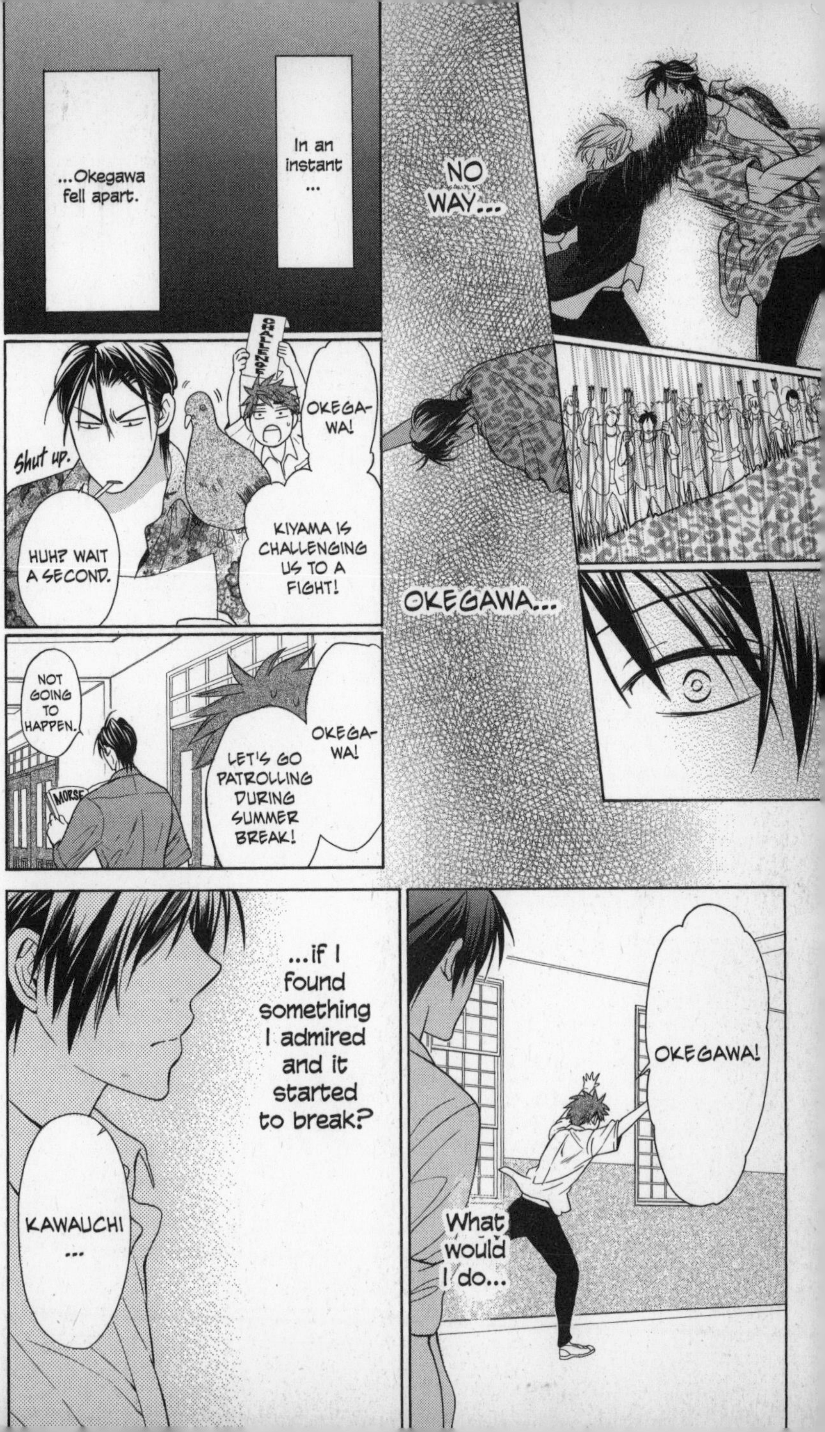
NO WAY...
OKEGAWA...
In an instant ...
...Okegawa fell apart.
CHALLENGE
OKEGA-WA!
KIYAMA IS CHALLENGING US TO A FIGHT!
Shut up.
HUH? WAIT A SECOND.
OKEGA-WA!
LET'S GO PATROLLING DURING SUMMER BREAK!
MORSE
NOT GOING TO HAPPEN.
OKEGAWA!
What would I do...
...if I found something I admired and it started to break?
KAWAUCHI ...

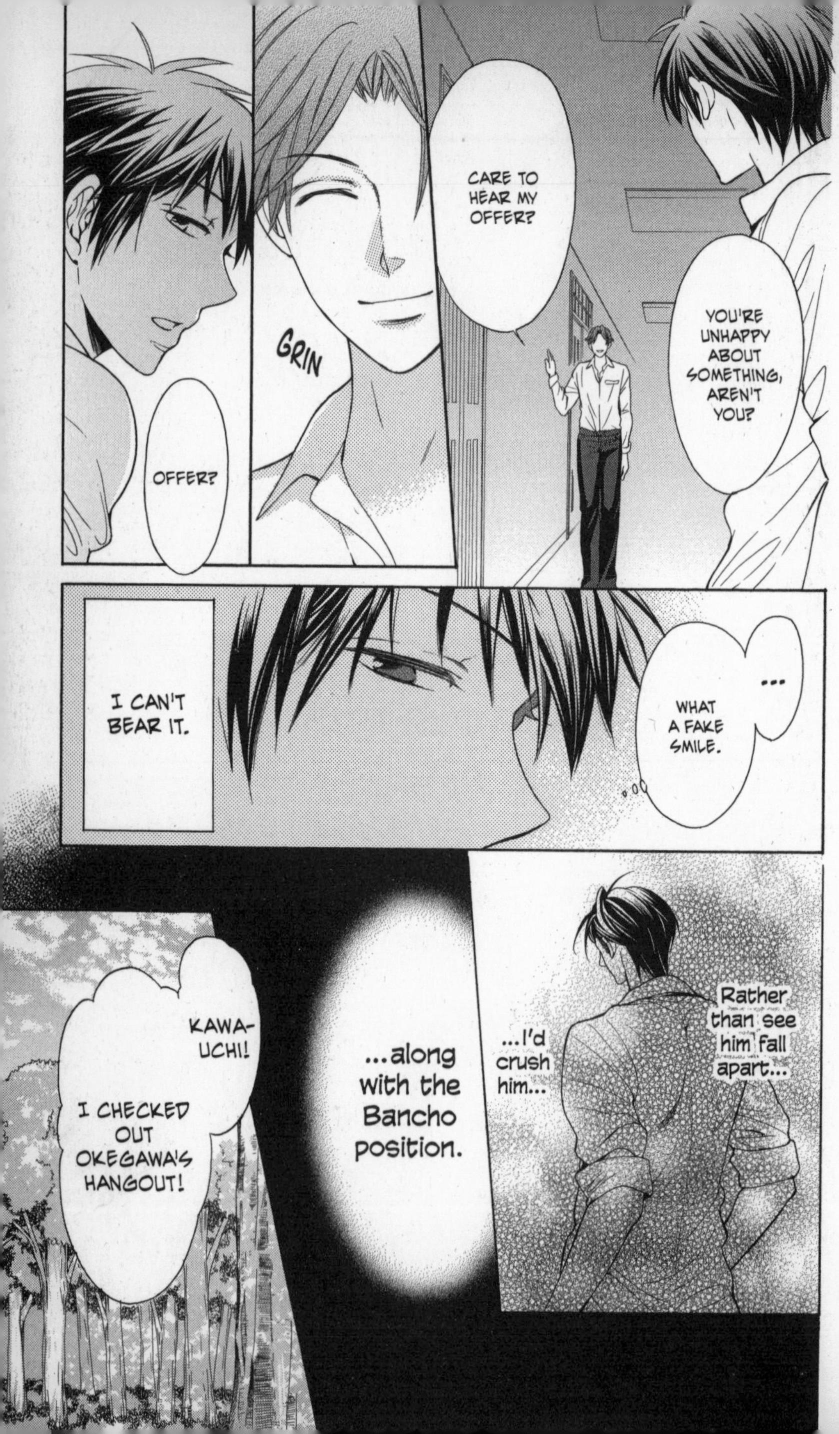
YOU'RE UNHAPPY ABOUT SOMETHING, AREN'T YOU?
CARE TO HEAR MY OFFER?
GRIN
OFFER?
...
WHAT A FAKE SMILE.
I CAN'T BEAR IT.
Rather than see him fall apart...
...I'd crush him...
...along with the Bancho position.
KAWA-UCHI!
I CHECKED OUT OKEGAWA'S HANGOUT!

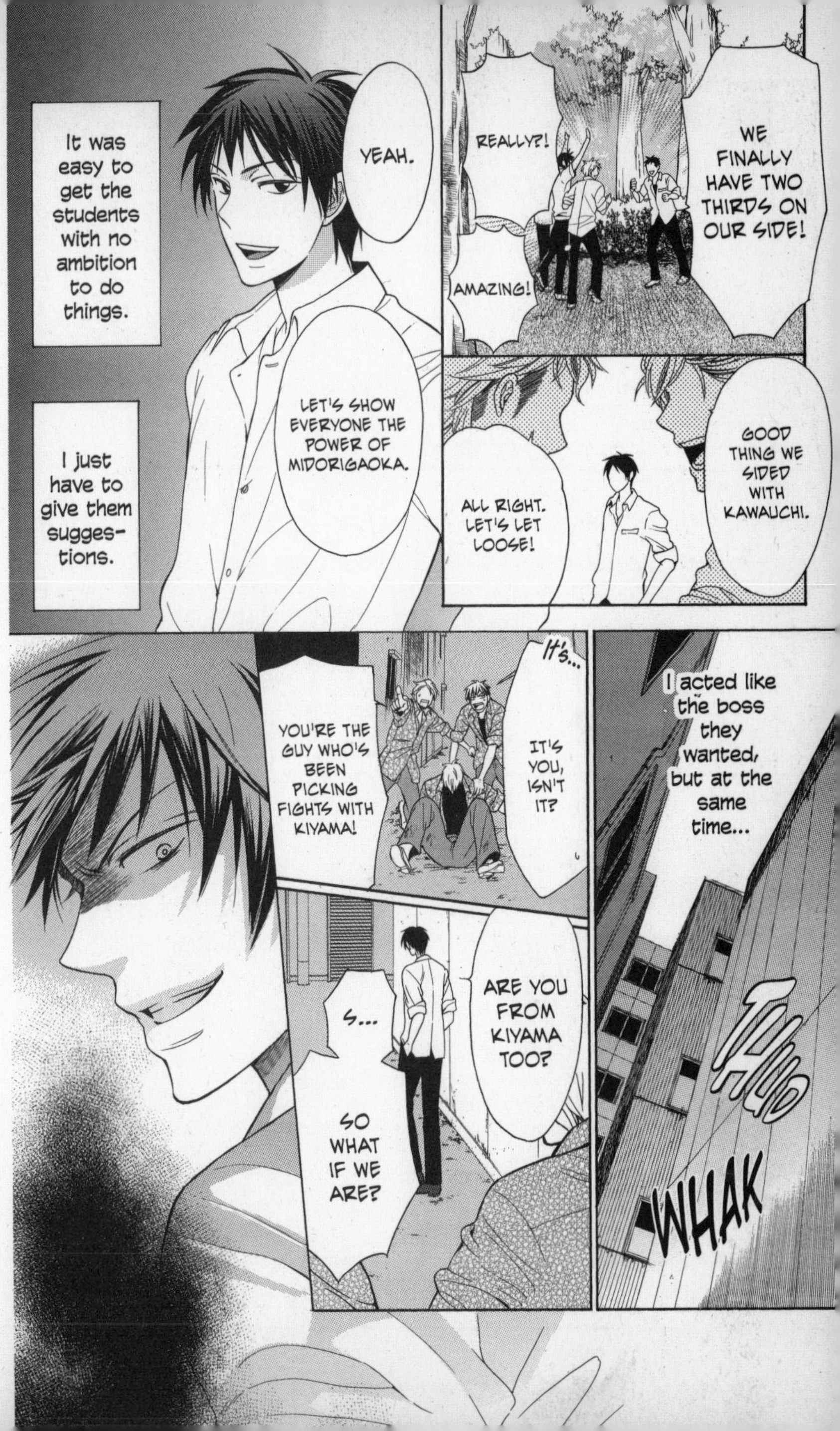
WE FINALLY HAVE TWO THIRDS ON OUR SIDE!
REALLY?!
AMAZING!
GOOD THING WE SIDED WITH KAWAUCHI.
ALL RIGHT. LET'S LET LOOSE!
YEAH.
It was easy to get the students with no ambition to do things.
LET'S SHOW EVERYONE THE POWER OF MIDORIGAOKA.
I just have to give them sugges-tions.
I acted like the boss they wanted, but at the same time...
THUD
WHAK
It's...
IT'S YOU, ISN'T IT?
YOU'RE THE GUY WHO'S BEEN PICKING FIGHTS WITH KIYAMA!
ARE YOU FROM KIYAMA TOO?
S...
SO WHAT IF WE ARE?

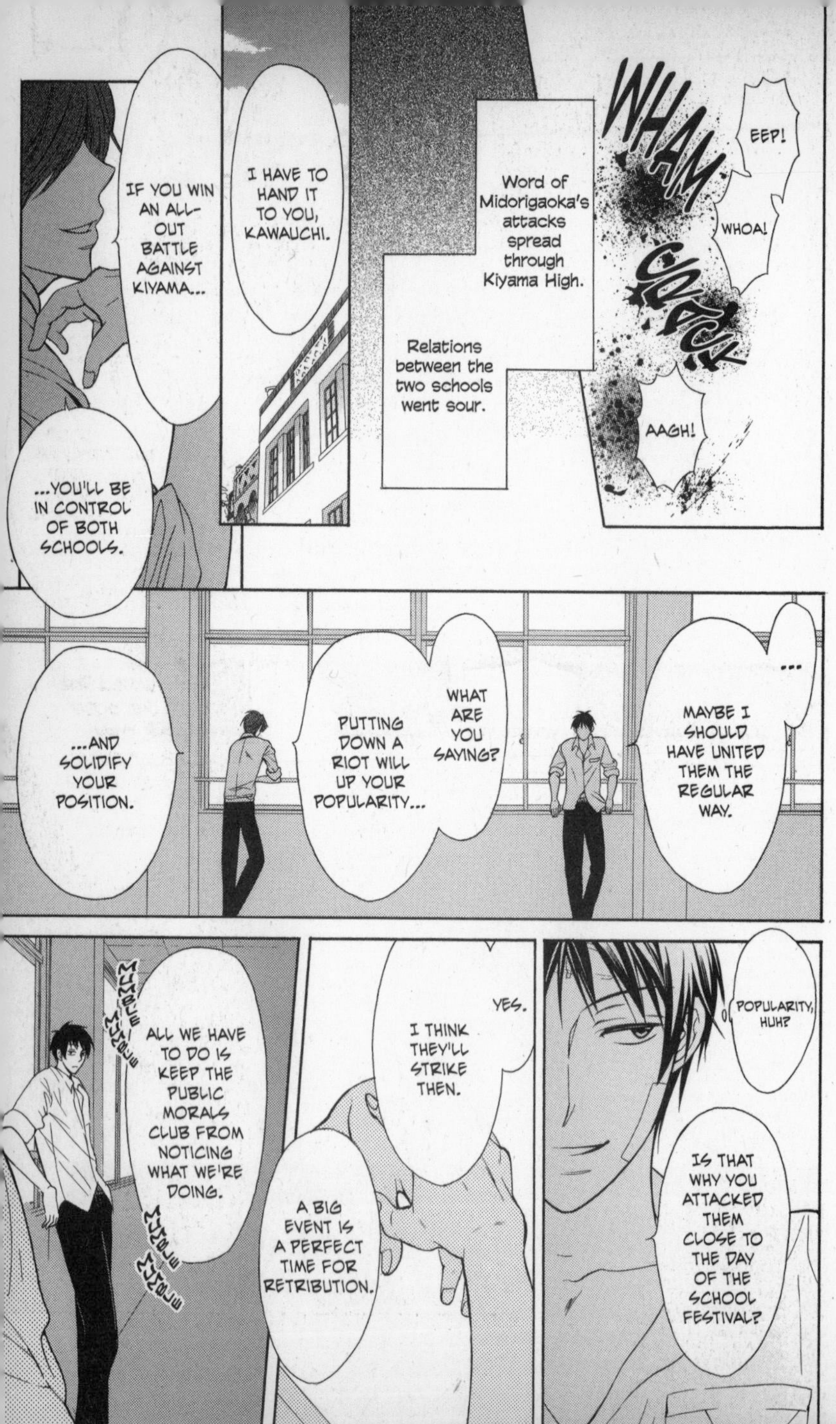
WHAM
EEP!
WHOA!
AAGH!
Word of Midorigaoka's attacks spread through Kiyama High.
Relations between the two schools went sour.
I HAVE TO HAND IT TO YOU, KAWAUCHI.
IF YOU WIN AN ALL-OUT BATTLE AGAINST KIYAMA...
...YOU'LL BE IN CONTROL OF BOTH SCHOOLS.
...
MAYBE I SHOULD HAVE UNITED THEM THE REGULAR WAY.
WHAT ARE YOU SAYING?
PUTTING DOWN A RIOT WILL UP YOUR POPULARITY...
...AND SOLIDIFY YOUR POSITION.
POPULARITY, HUH?
IS THAT WHY YOU ATTACKED THEM CLOSE TO THE DAY OF THE SCHOOL FESTIVAL?
YES.
I THINK THEY'LL STRIKE THEN.
A BIG EVENT IS A PERFECT TIME FOR RETRIBUTION.
ALL WE HAVE TO DO IS KEEP THE PUBLIC MORALS CLUB FROM NOTICING WHAT WE'RE DOING.
MUMBLE MUMBLE
MUMBLE MUMBLE

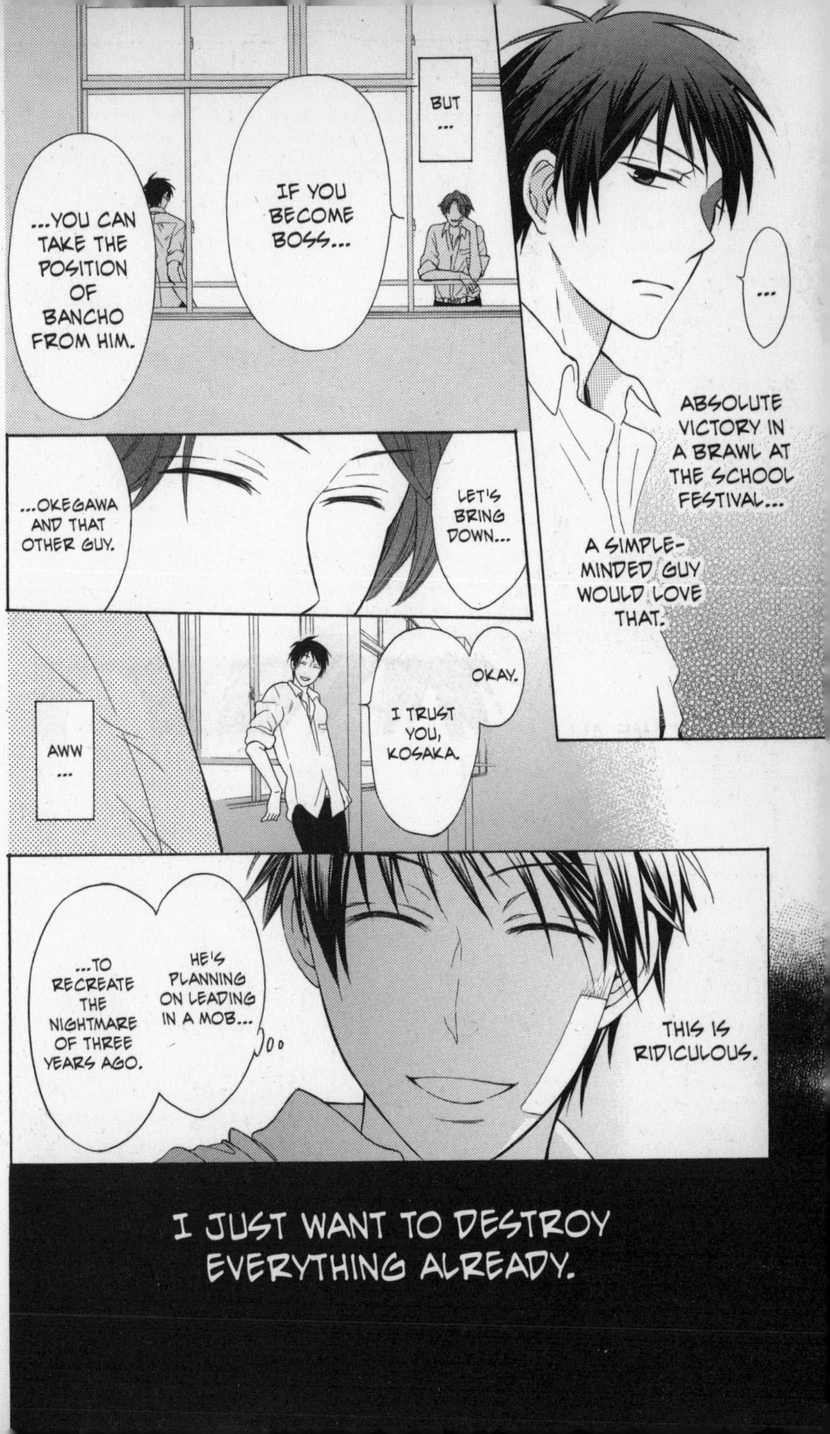
...
ABSOLUTE VICTORY IN A BRAWL AT THE SCHOOL FESTIVAL...
A SIMPLE-MINDED GUY WOULD LOVE THAT.
BUT...
IF YOU BECOME BOSS...
...YOU CAN TAKE THE POSITION OF BANCHO FROM HIM.
LET'S BRING DOWN...
...OKEGAWA AND THAT OTHER GUY.
OKAY.
I TRUST YOU, KOSAKA.
AWW...
THIS IS RIDICULOUS.
HE'S PLANNING ON LEADING IN A MOB...
...TO RECREATE THE NIGHTMARE OF THREE YEARS AGO.
I JUST WANT TO DESTROY EVERYTHING ALREADY.

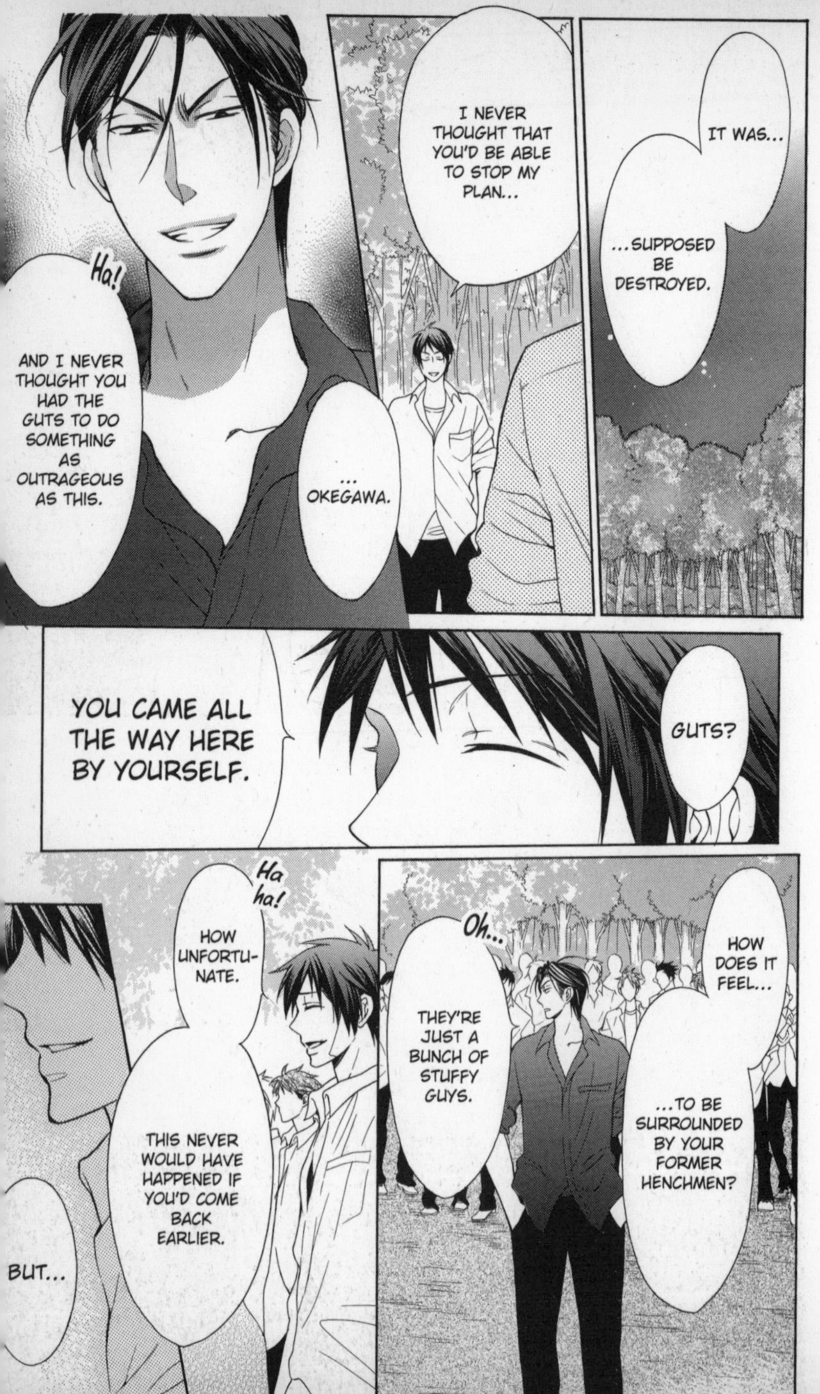
IT WAS...
...SUPPOSED BE DESTROYED.
I NEVER THOUGHT THAT YOU'D BE ABLE TO STOP MY PLAN...
...OKEGAWA.
Ha!
AND I NEVER THOUGHT YOU HAD THE GUTS TO DO SOMETHING AS OUTRAGEOUS AS THIS.
GUTS?
YOU CAME ALL THE WAY HERE BY YOURSELF.
HOW DOES IT FEEL...
...TO BE SURROUNDED BY YOUR FORMER HENCHMEN?
Oh...
THEY'RE JUST A BUNCH OF STUFFY GUYS.
Ha ha!
HOW UNFORTU-NATE.
THIS NEVER WOULD HAVE HAPPENED IF YOU'D COME BACK EARLIER.
BUT...

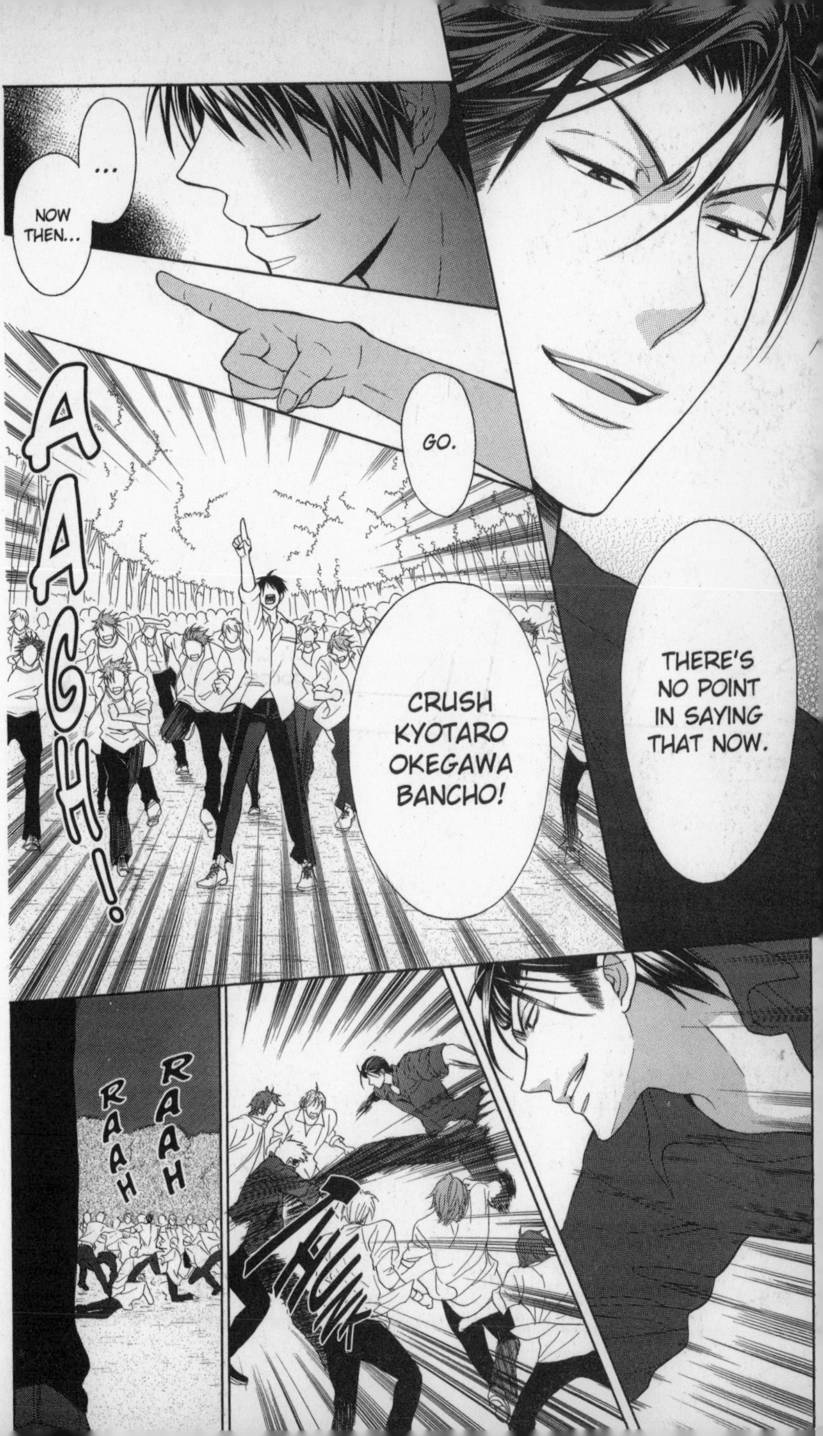
THERE'S NO POINT IN SAYING THAT NOW.
...
NOW THEN...
GO.
CRUSH KYOTARO OKEGAWA BANCHO!
AAGH!!
THUNK
RAAAH RAAAH

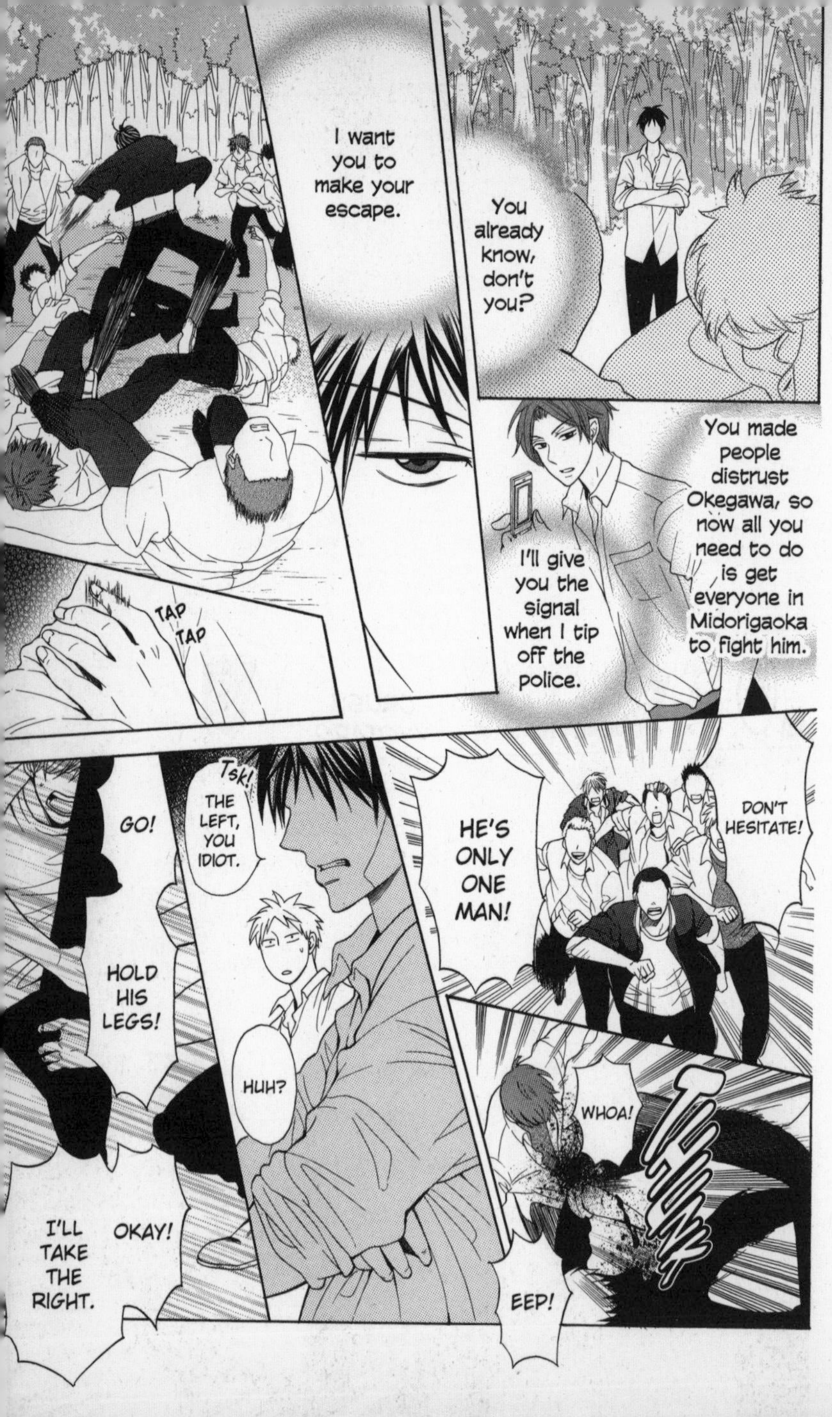
You already know, don't you?
I want you to make your escape.
You made people distrust Okegawa, so now all you need to do is get everyone in Midorigaoka to fight him.
I'll give you the signal when I tip off the police.
TAP
TAP
DON'T HESITATE!
HE'S ONLY ONE MAN!
WHOA!
EEP!
Tsk!
THE LEFT, YOU IDIOT.
HUH?
GO!
HOLD HIS LEGS!
OKAY!
I'LL TAKE THE RIGHT.

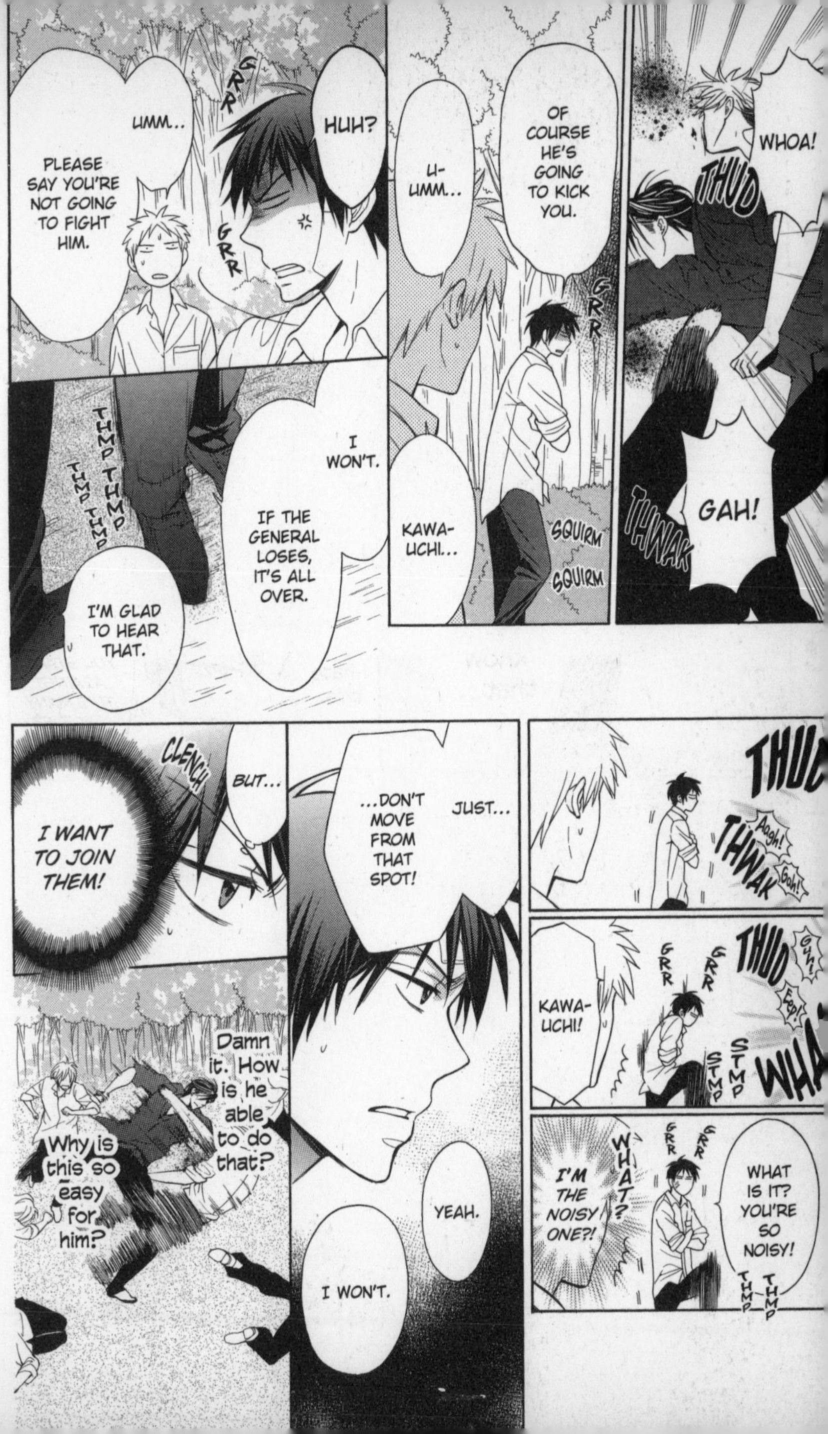
WHOA!
THUD
GAH!
THWAK
OF COURSE HE'S GOING TO KICK YOU.
U-UMM...
GRR
KAWA-UCHI...
SQUIRM
SQUIRM
HUH?
GRR
UMM...
PLEASE SAY YOU'RE NOT GOING TO FIGHT HIM.
GRR
I WON'T.
IF THE GENERAL LOSES, IT'S ALL OVER.
THMP THMP
THMP THMP
I'M GLAD TO HEAR THAT.
THUD
THWAK
Aagh!
Gah!
GRR
GRR
KAWA-UCHI!
THUD
Guh!
Eep!
STMP
STMP
WHA
WHAT IS IT? YOU'RE SO NOISY!
GRR
GRR
WHAT?
I'M THE NOISY ONE?!
THMP
THMP
JUST...
...DON'T MOVE FROM THAT SPOT!
YEAH.
I WON'T.
BUT...
CLENCH
I WANT TO JOIN THEM!
Damn it. How is he able to do that?
Why is this so easy for him?

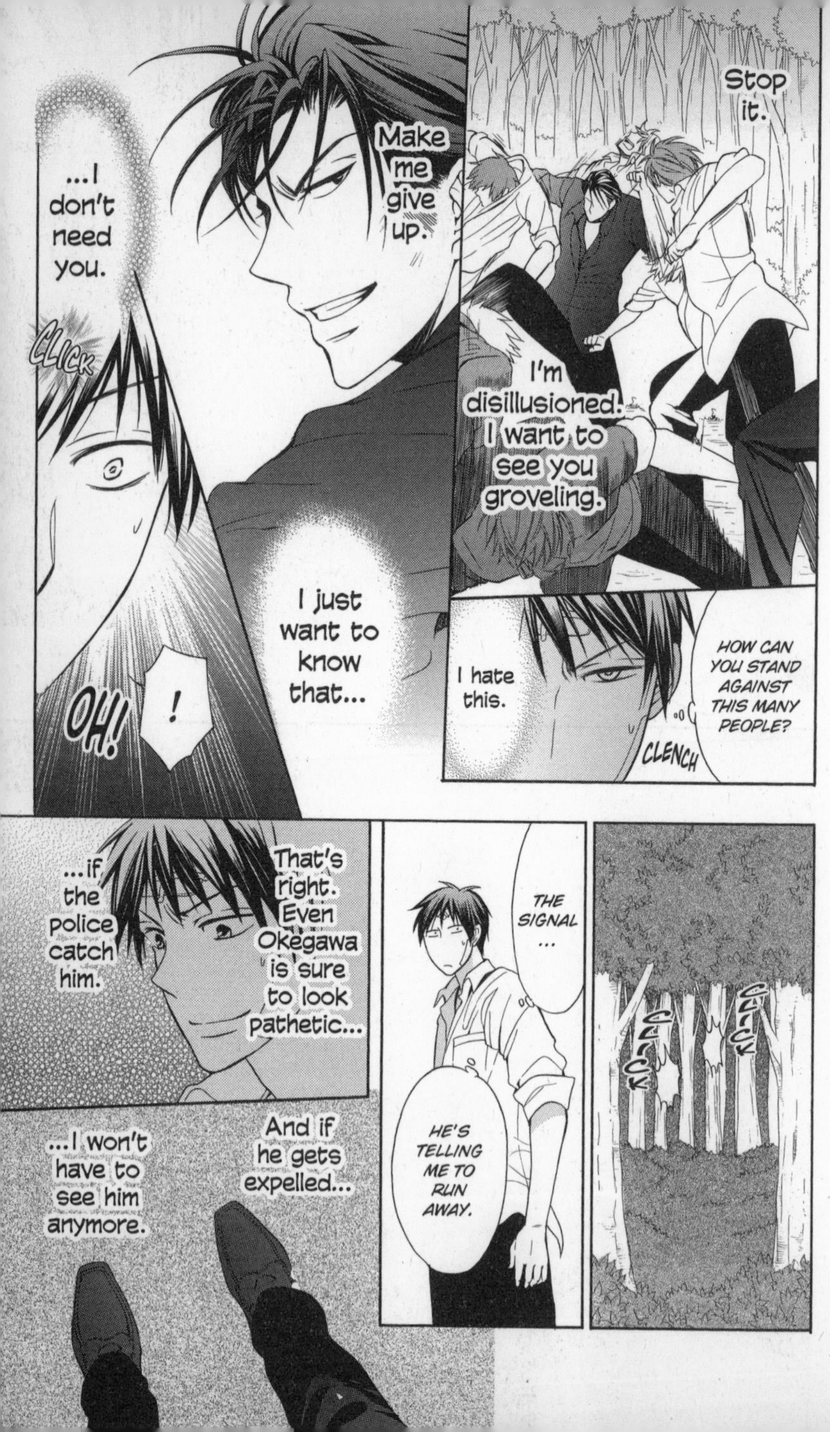
Stop it.
I'm disillusioned. I want to see you groveling.
HOW CAN YOU STAND AGAINST THIS MANY PEOPLE?
I hate this.
CLENCH
Make me give up.
...I don't need you.
CLICK
I just want to know that...
!
OH!
CLICK
CLICK
THE SIGNAL...
HE'S TELLING ME TO RUN AWAY.
That's right. Even Okegawa is sure to look pathetic...
...if the police catch him.
And if he gets expelled...
...I won't have to see him anymore.

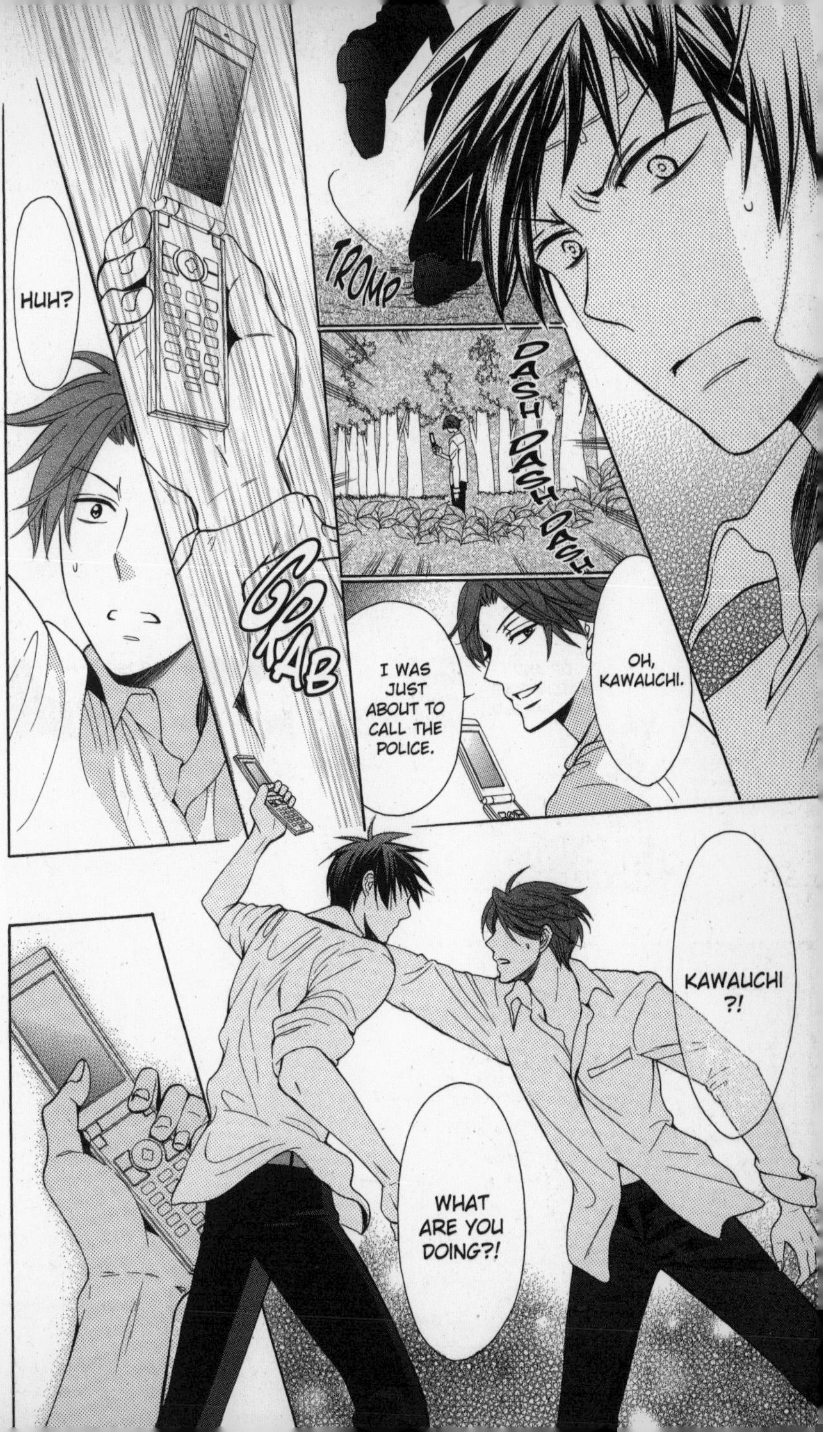
TROMP
DASH DASH DASH
OH, KAWAUCHI.
I WAS JUST ABOUT TO CALL THE POLICE.
HUH?
GRAB
KAWAUCHI?!
WHAT ARE YOU DOING?!

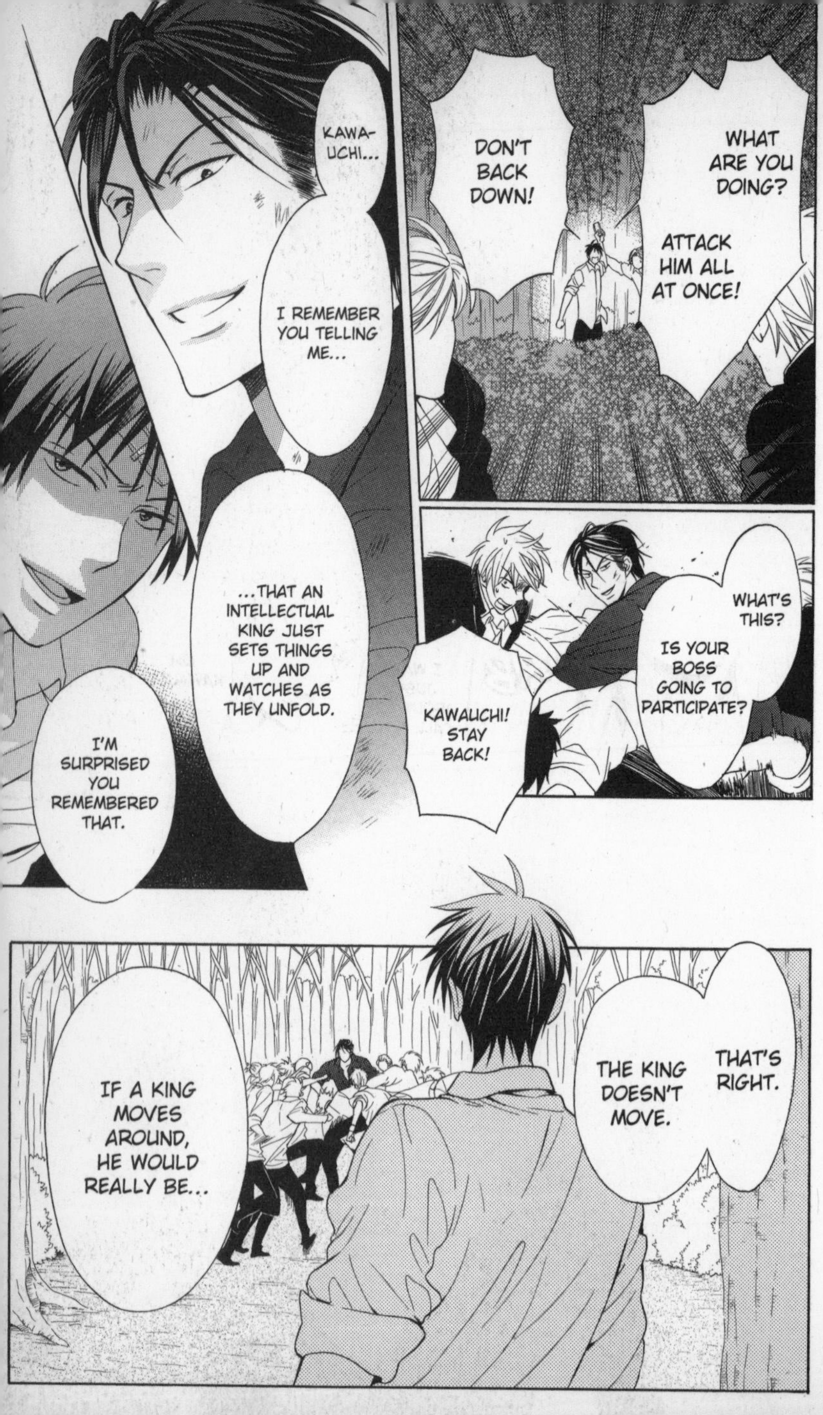
WHAT ARE YOU DOING?
DON'T BACK DOWN!
ATTACK HIM ALL AT ONCE!
WHAT'S THIS? IS YOUR BOSS GOING TO PARTICIPATE?
KAWAUCHI! STAY BACK!
KAWA-UCHI...
I REMEMBER YOU TELLING ME...
...THAT AN INTELLECTUAL KING JUST SETS THINGS UP AND WATCHES AS THEY UNFOLD.
I'M SURPRISED YOU REMEMBERED THAT.
THAT'S RIGHT.
THE KING DOESN'T MOVE.
IF A KING MOVES AROUND, HE WOULD REALLY BE...

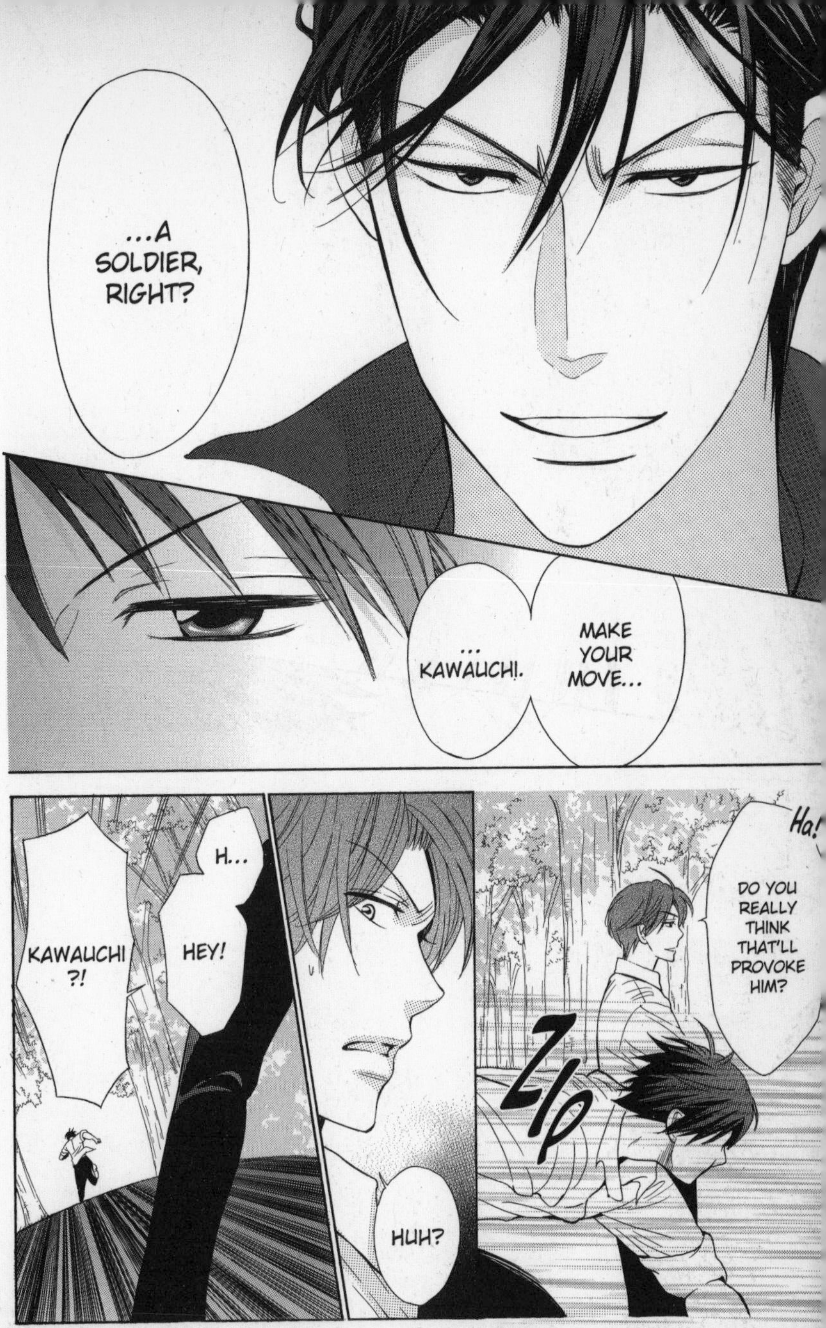
...A SOLDIER, RIGHT?
MAKE YOUR MOVE...
... KAWAUCHI.
Ha!
DO YOU REALLY THINK THAT'LL PROVOKE HIM?
ZIP
HUH?
H...
HEY!
KAWAUCHI ?!

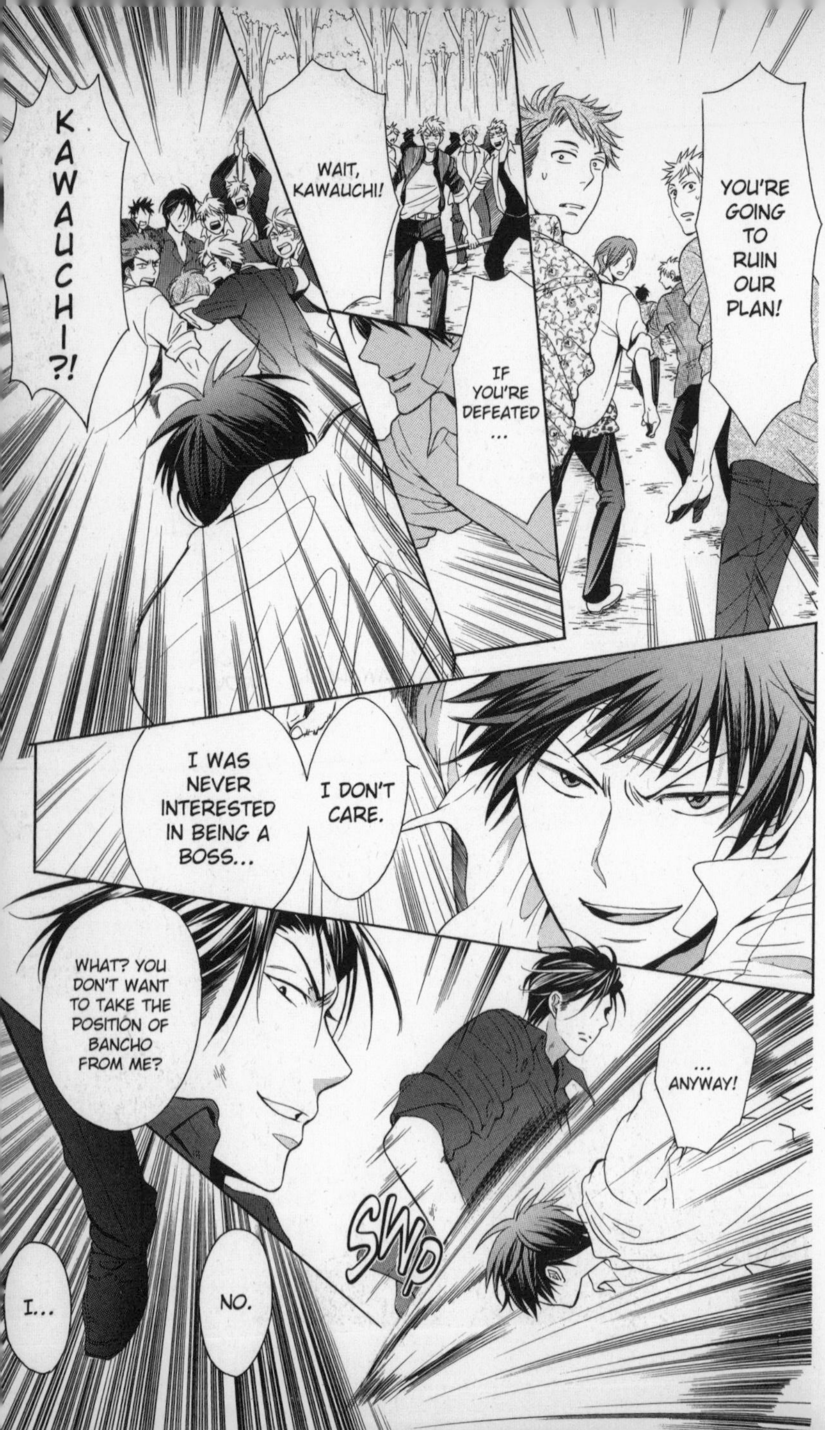
YOU'RE GOING TO RUIN OUR PLAN!
IF YOU'RE DEFEATED ...
WAIT, KAWAUCHI!
KAWAUCHI?!
I DON'T CARE.
I WAS NEVER INTERESTED IN BEING A BOSS...
... ANYWAY!
WHAT? YOU DON'T WANT TO TAKE THE POSITION OF BANCHO FROM ME?
SWP
NO.
I...

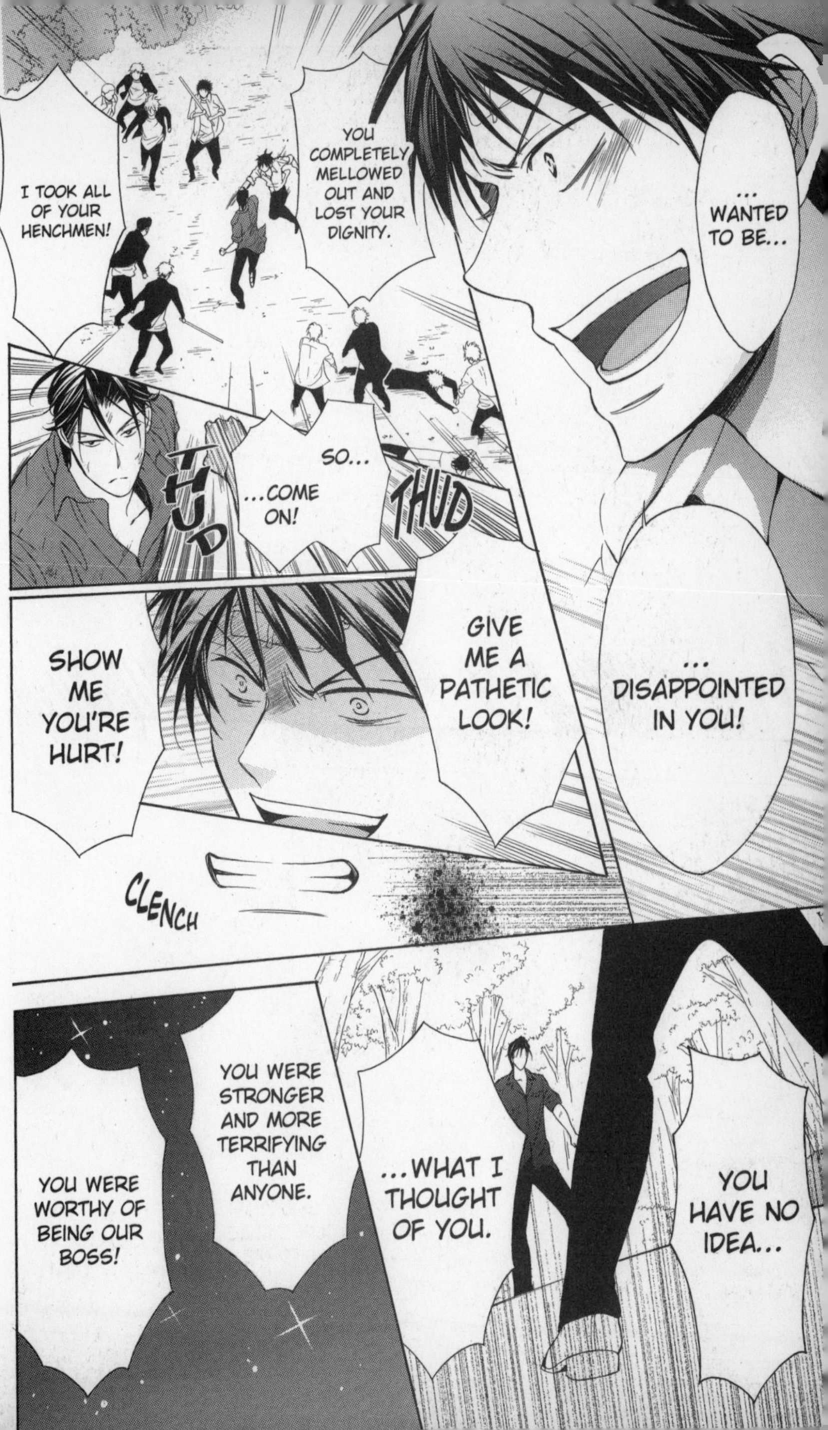
...WANTED TO BE...
...DISAPPOINTED IN YOU!
YOU COMPLETELY MELLOWED OUT AND LOST YOUR DIGNITY.
I TOOK ALL OF YOUR HENCHMEN!
THUD
SO...
...COME ON!
THUD
GIVE ME A PATHETIC LOOK!
SHOW ME YOU'RE HURT!
CLENCH
YOU HAVE NO IDEA...
...WHAT I THOUGHT OF YOU.
YOU WERE STRONGER AND MORE TERRIFYING THAN ANYONE.
YOU WERE WORTHY OF BEING OUR BOSS!

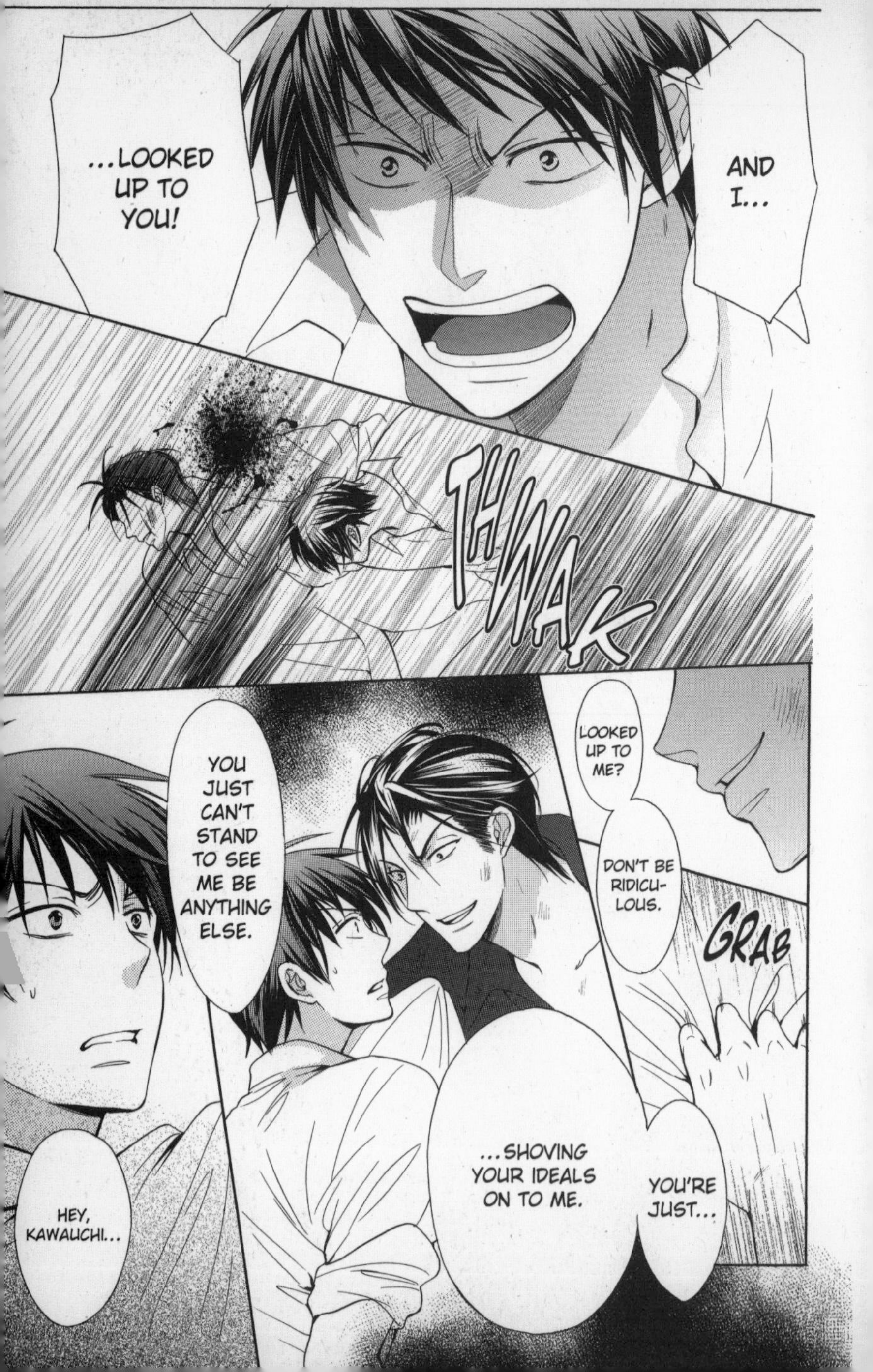
AND I...
...LOOKED UP TO YOU!
THWAK
LOOKED UP TO ME?
DON'T BE RIDICULOUS.
GRAB
YOU'RE JUST...
...SHOVING YOUR IDEALS ON TO ME.
YOU JUST CAN'T STAND TO SEE ME BE ANYTHING ELSE.
HEY, KAWAUCHI...

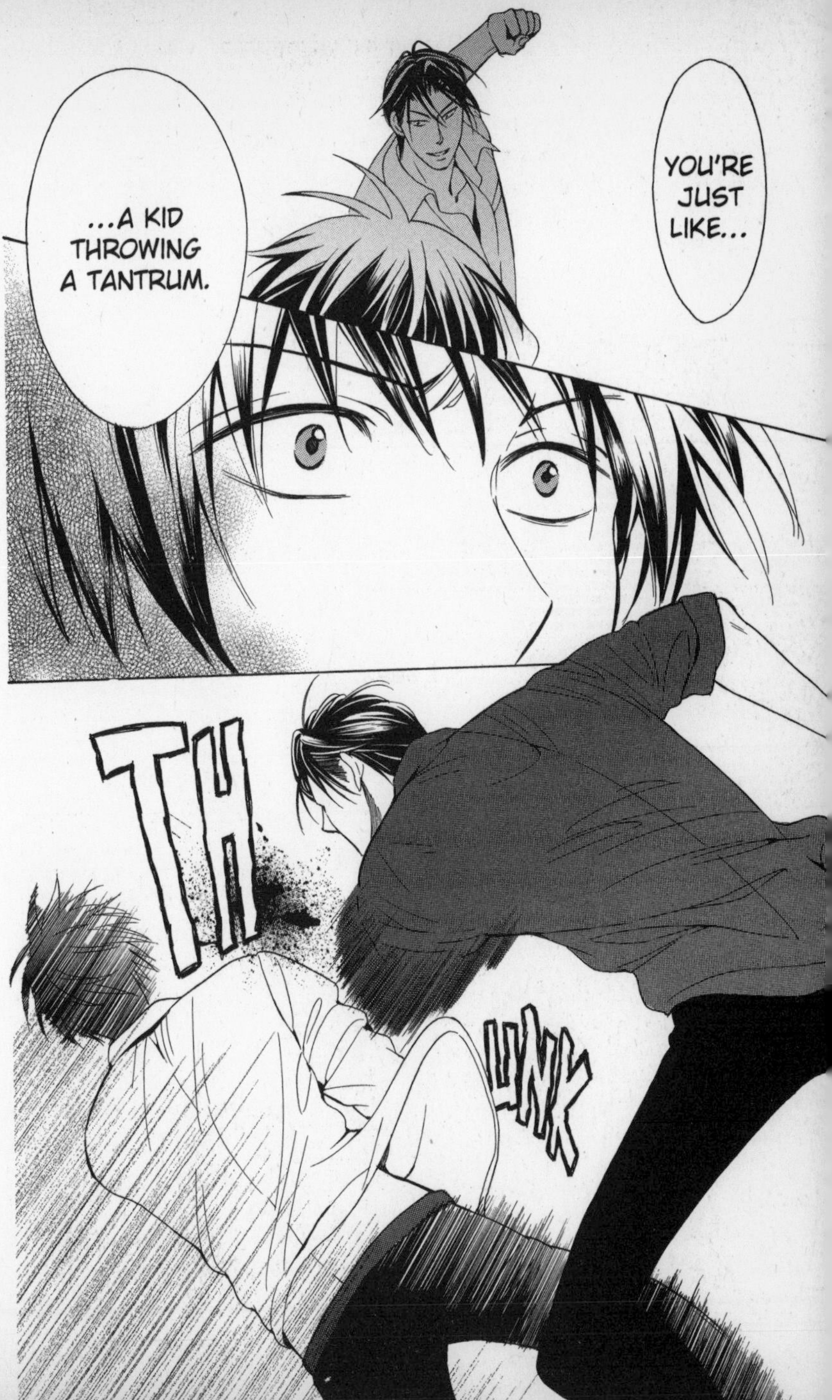
YOU'RE JUST LIKE...
...A KID THROWING A TANTRUM.
THUNK

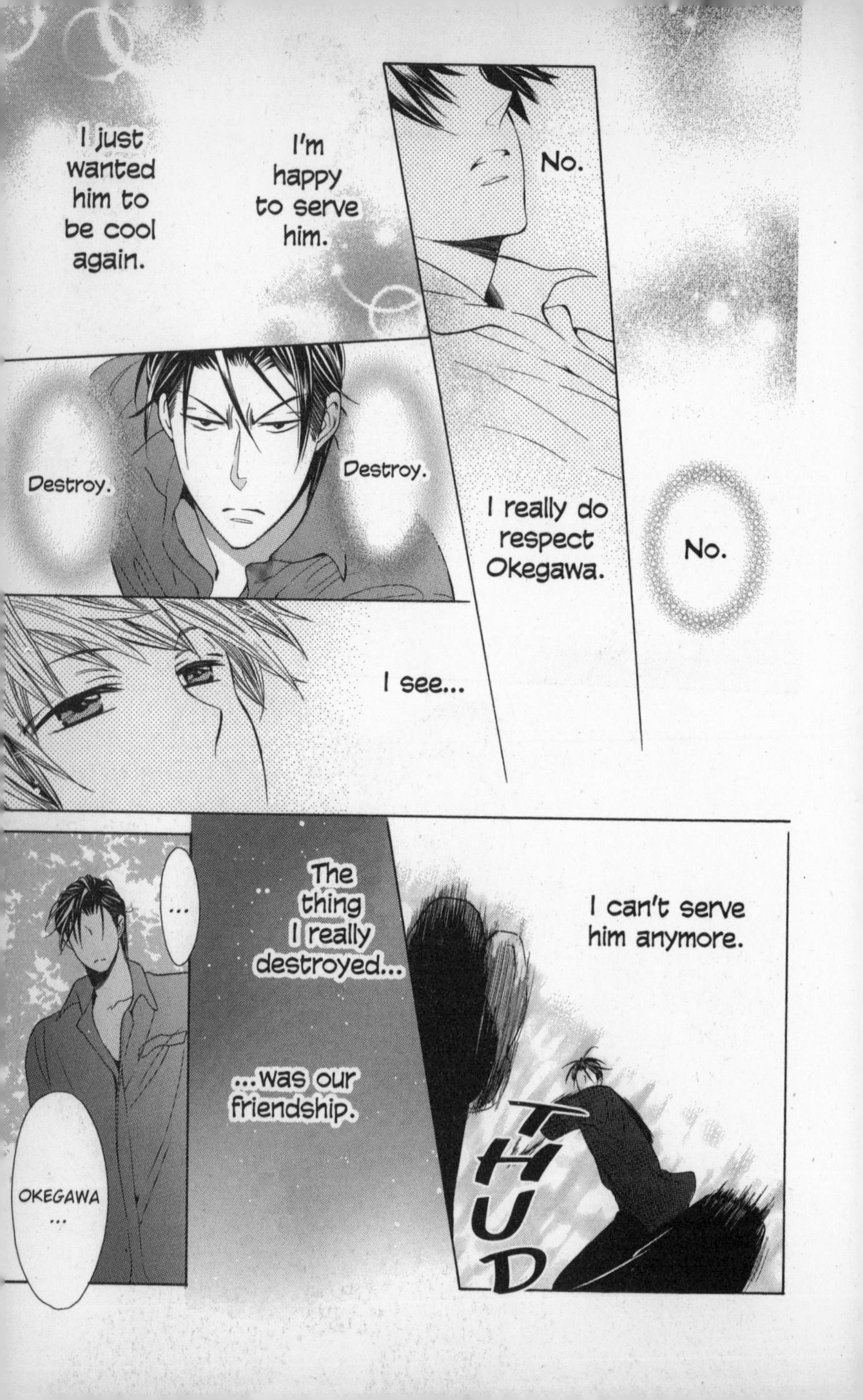
No.
I'm happy to serve him.
I just wanted him to be cool again.
No.
I really do respect Okegawa.
Destroy.
Destroy.
I see...
I can't serve him anymore.
THUD
The thing I really destroyed...
...was our friendship.
...
OKEGAWA ...

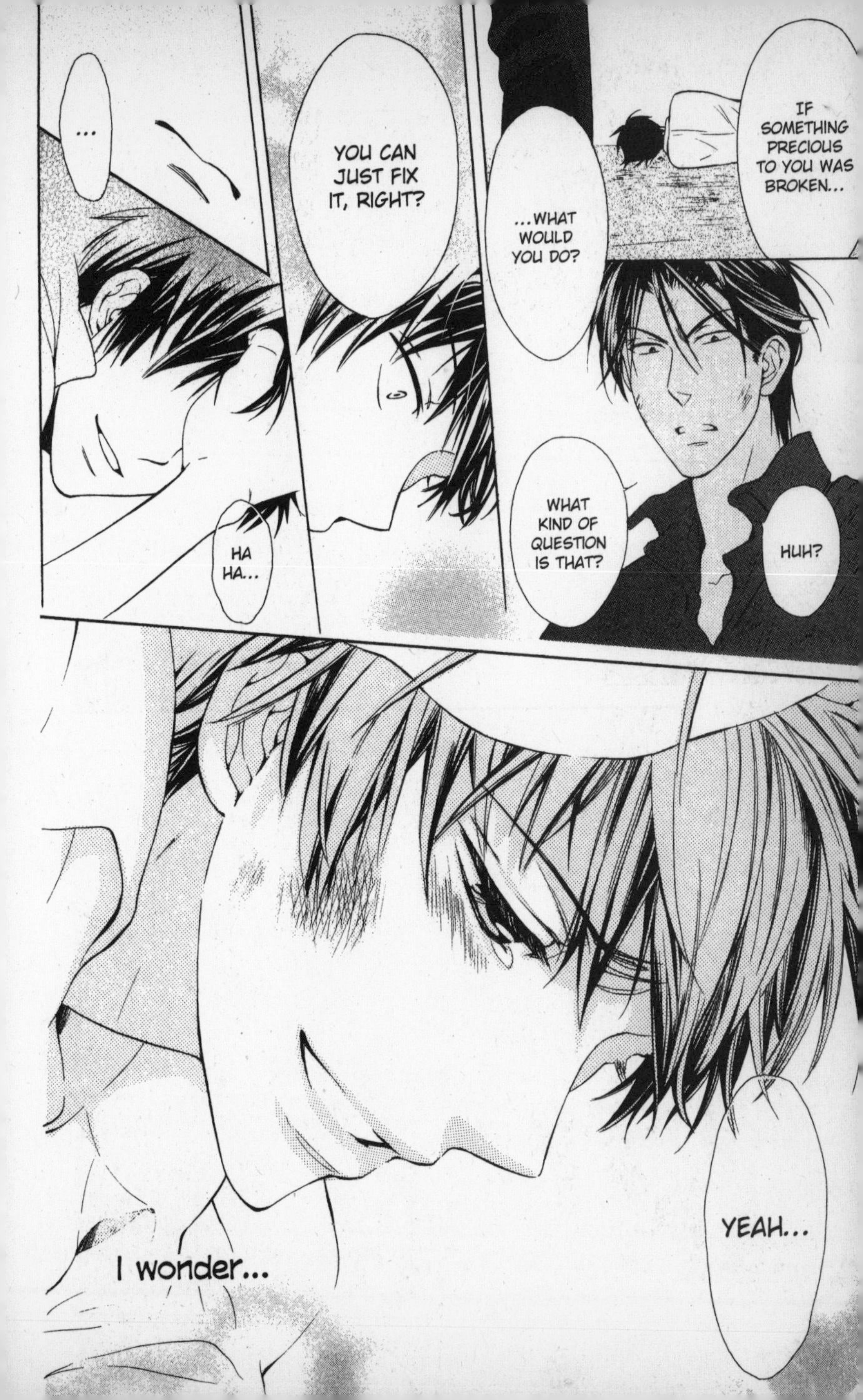
IF SOMETHING PRECIOUS TO YOU WAS BROKEN...
...WHAT WOULD YOU DO?
HUH?
WHAT KIND OF QUESTION IS THAT?
YOU CAN JUST FIX IT, RIGHT?
...
HA HA...
YEAH...
I wonder...

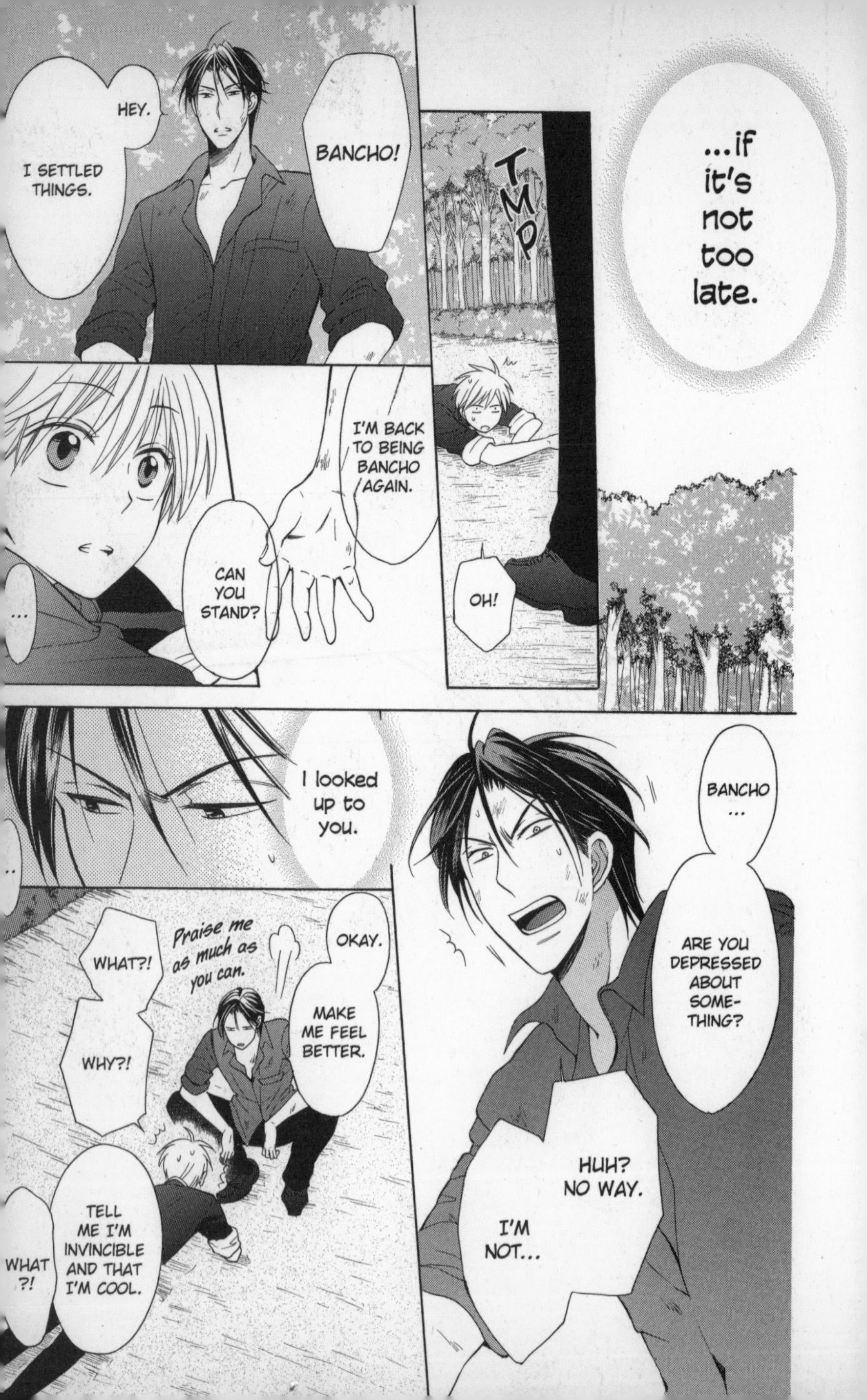
...if it's not too late.
TMP
OH!
BANCHO!
HEY.
I SETTLED THINGS.
I'M BACK TO BEING BANCHO AGAIN.
CAN YOU STAND?
...
BANCHO ...
ARE YOU DEPRESSED ABOUT SOME-THING?
HUH? NO WAY.
I'M NOT...
I looked up to you.
...
OKAY.
MAKE ME FEEL BETTER.
Praise me as much as you can.
WHAT?!
WHY?!
TELL ME I'M INVINCIBLE AND THAT I'M COOL.
WHAT ?!

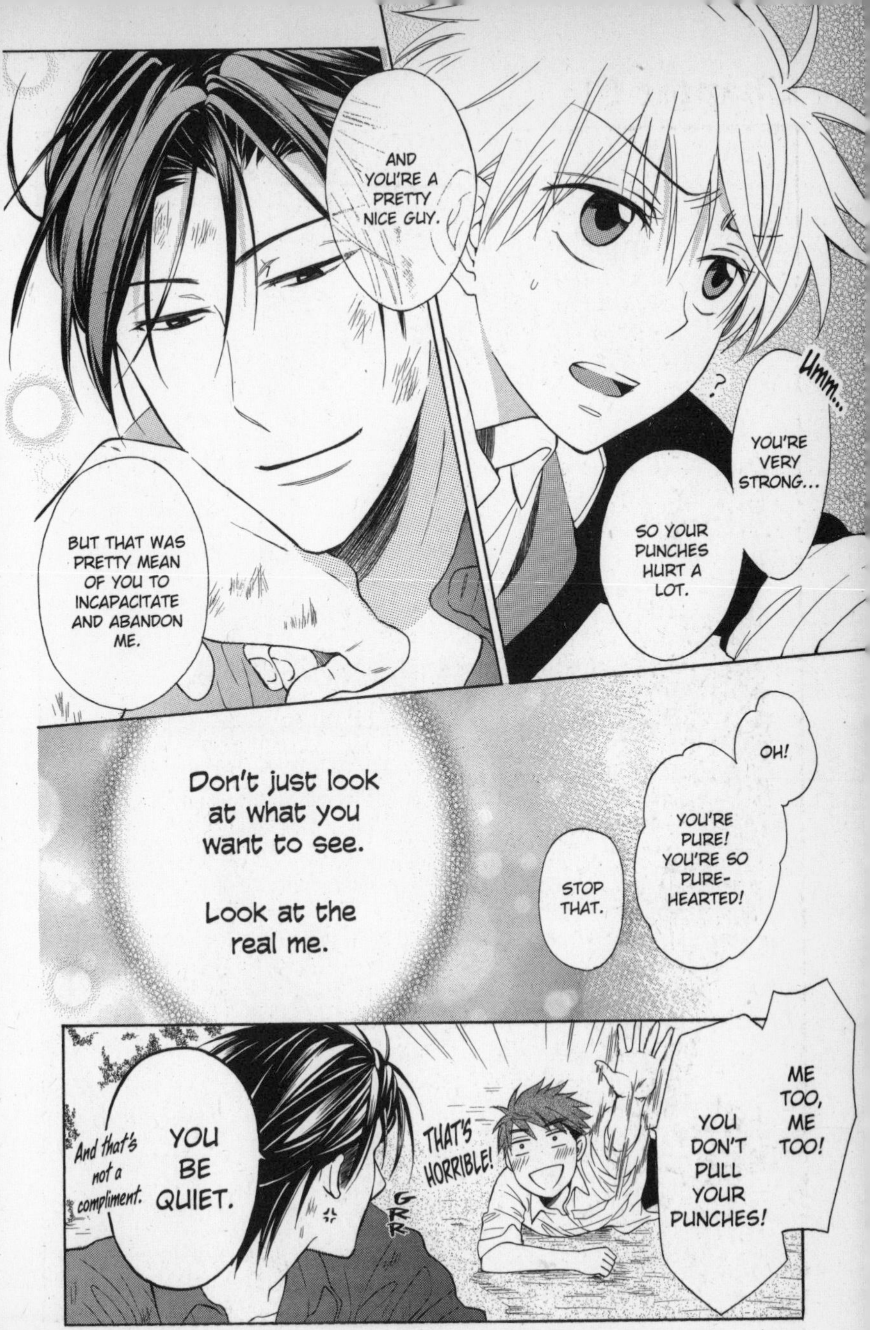
Umm...
YOU'RE VERY STRONG...
SO YOUR PUNCHES HURT A LOT.
AND YOU'RE A PRETTY NICE GUY.
BUT THAT WAS PRETTY MEAN OF YOU TO INCAPACITATE AND ABANDON ME.
OH!
YOU'RE PURE! YOU'RE SO PURE-HEARTED!
STOP THAT.
Don't just look at what you want to see.
Look at the real me.
ME TOO, ME TOO!
YOU DON'T PULL YOUR PUNCHES!
THAT'S HORRIBLE!
GRR
YOU BE QUIET.
And that's not a compliment.

Chapter 51

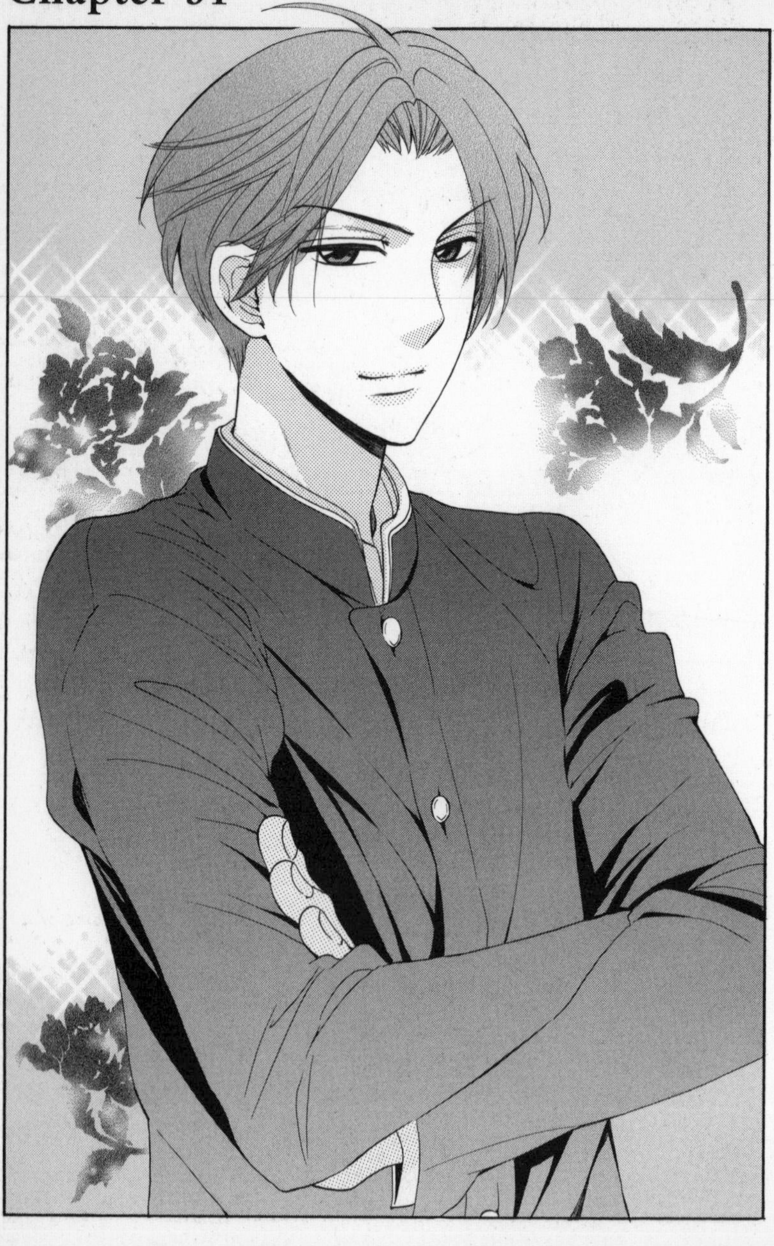

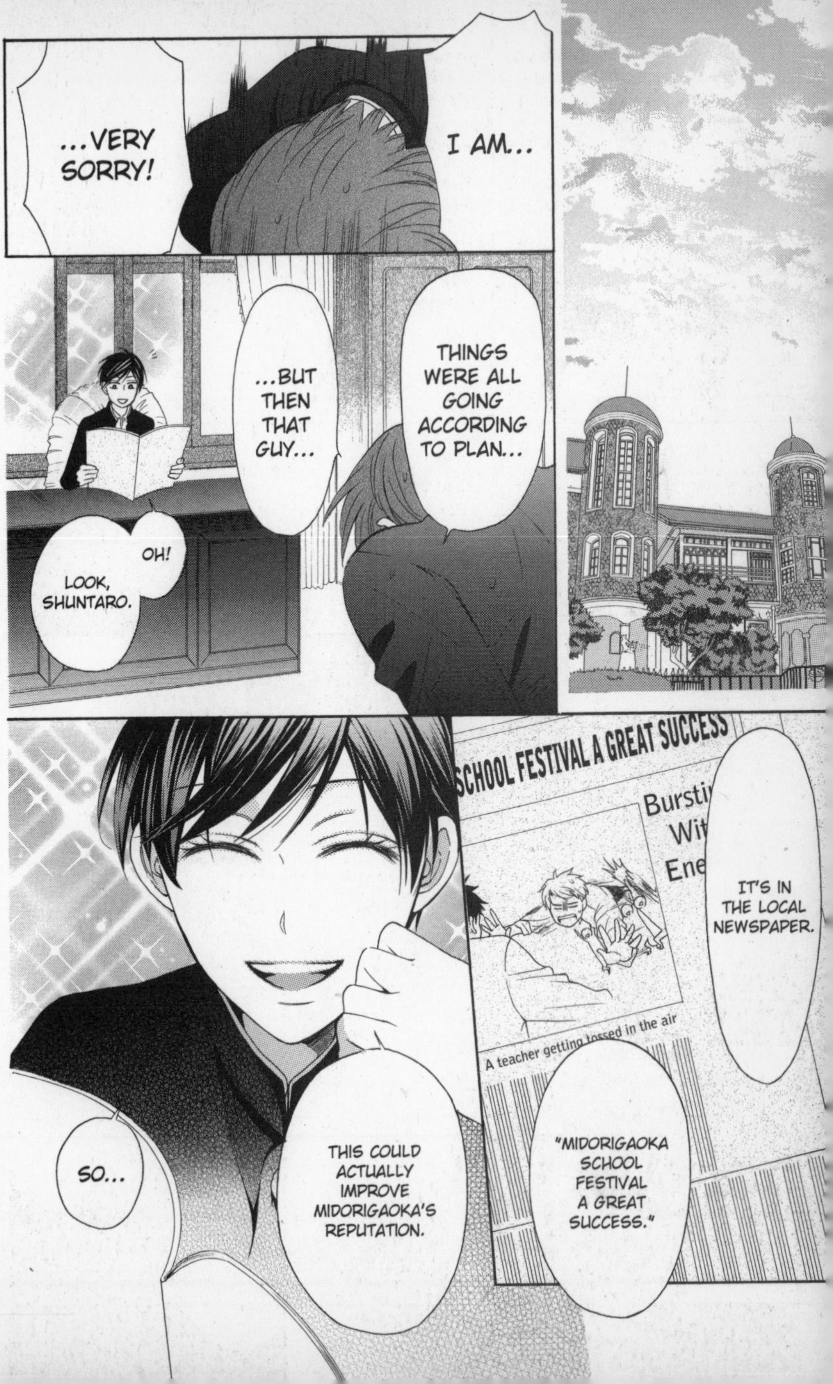
I AM...
...VERY SORRY!
THINGS WERE ALL GOING ACCORDING TO PLAN...
...BUT THEN THAT GUY...
OH! LOOK, SHUNTARO.
SCHOOL FESTIVAL A GREAT SUCCESS
A teacher getting tossed in the air
IT'S IN THE LOCAL NEWSPAPER.
"MIDORIGAOKA SCHOOL FESTIVAL A GREAT SUCCESS."
THIS COULD ACTUALLY IMPROVE MIDORIGAOKA'S REPUTATION.
SO...

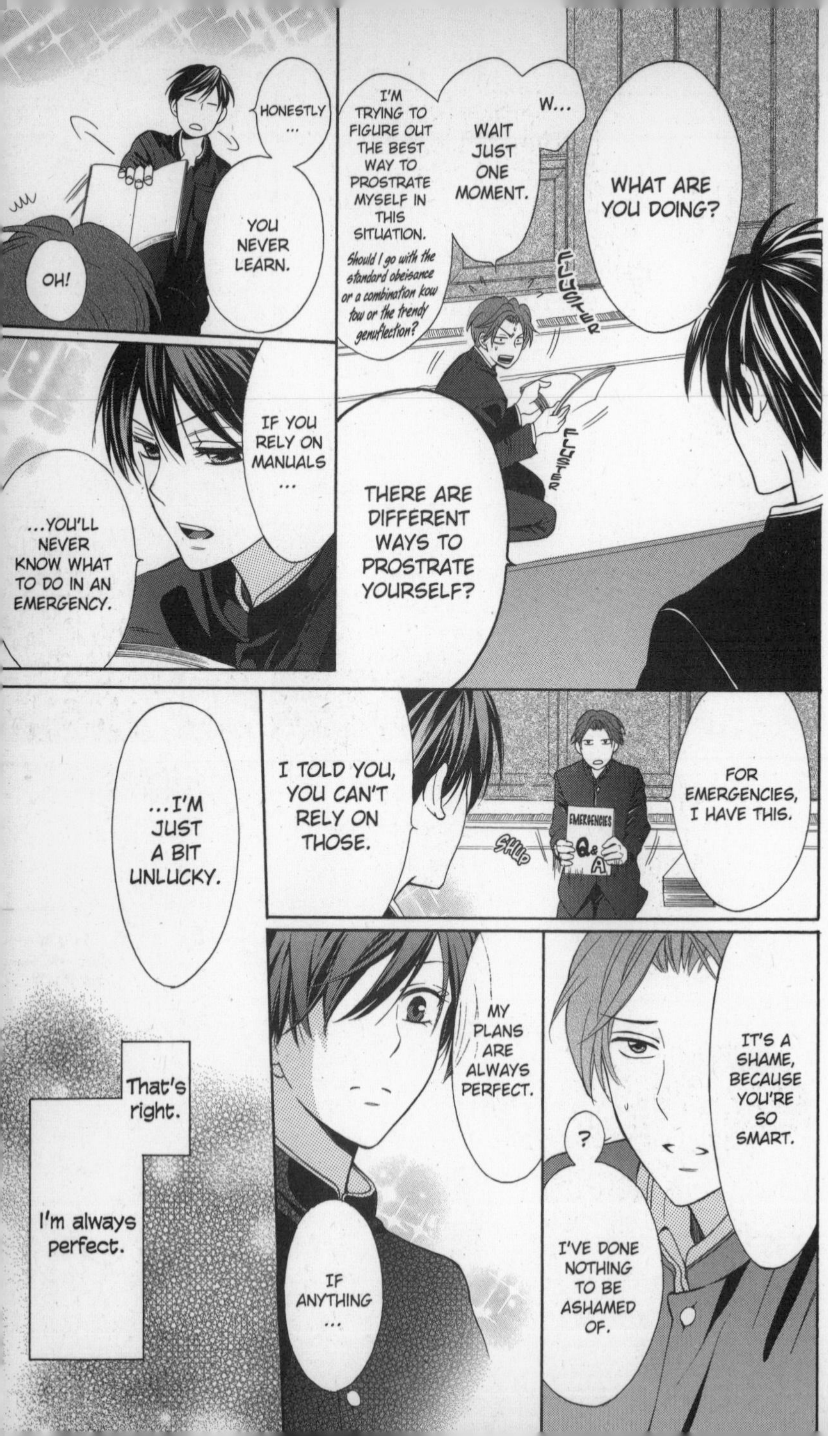
WHAT ARE YOU DOING?
W...
WAIT JUST ONE MOMENT.
I'M TRYING TO FIGURE OUT THE BEST WAY TO PROSTRATE MYSELF IN THIS SITUATION.
Should I go with the standard obeisance or a combination kow tow or the trendy genuflection?
FLUSTER
FLUSTER
THERE ARE DIFFERENT WAYS TO PROSTRATE YOURSELF?
HONESTLY ...
YOU NEVER LEARN.
OH!
IF YOU RELY ON MANUALS ...
...YOU'LL NEVER KNOW WHAT TO DO IN AN EMERGENCY.
FOR EMERGENCIES, I HAVE THIS.
EMERGENCIES
Q&A
SHUP
I TOLD YOU, YOU CAN'T RELY ON THOSE.
...I'M JUST A BIT UNLUCKY.
IT'S A SHAME, BECAUSE YOU'RE SO SMART.
?
I'VE DONE NOTHING TO BE ASHAMED OF.
MY PLANS ARE ALWAYS PERFECT.
IF ANYTHING ...
That's right.
I'm always perfect.

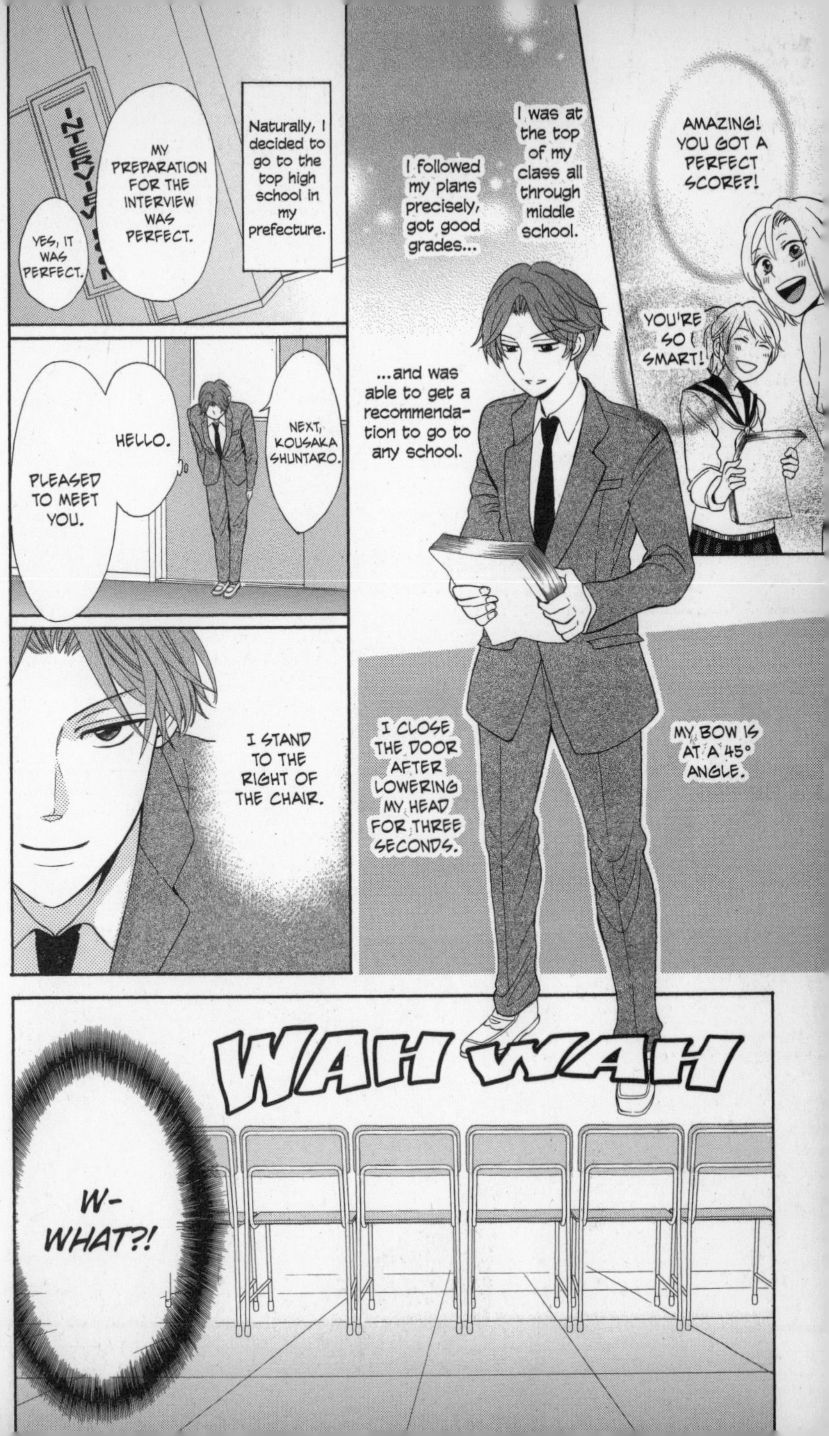
AMAZING! YOU GOT A PERFECT SCORE?!
YOU'RE SO SMART!
I was at the top of my class all through middle school.
I followed my plans precisely, got good grades...
...and was able to get a recommendation to go to any school.
Naturally, I decided to go to the top high school in my prefecture.
INTERVIEW
MY PREPARATION FOR THE INTERVIEW WAS PERFECT.
YES, IT WAS PERFECT.
NEXT, KOUSAKA SHUNTARO.
HELLO.
PLEASED TO MEET YOU.
MY BOW IS AT A 45° ANGLE.
I CLOSE THE DOOR AFTER LOWERING MY HEAD FOR THREE SECONDS.
I STAND TO THE RIGHT OF THE CHAIR.
WAH WAH
W-WHAT?!

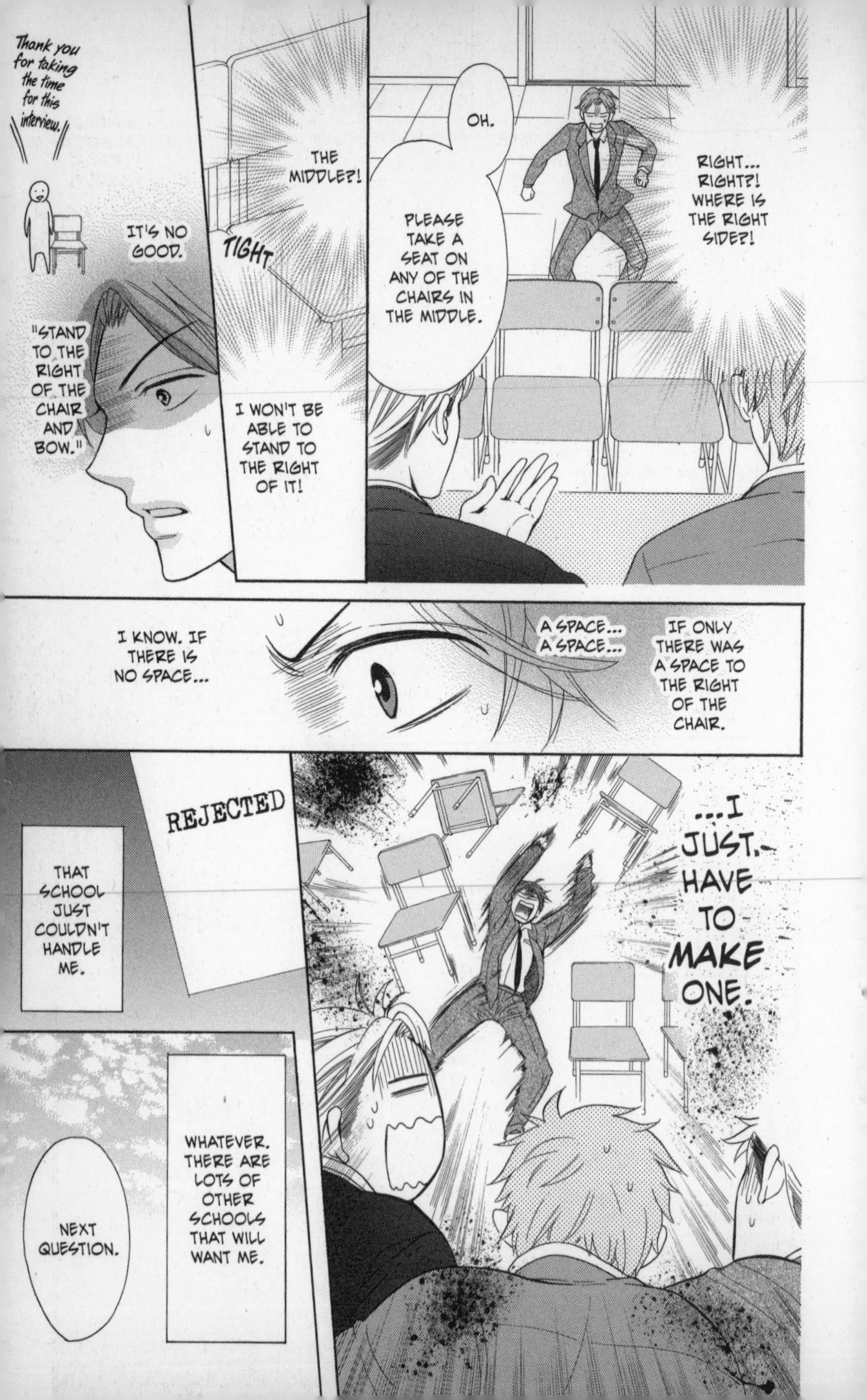
PLEASE TAKE A SEAT ON ANY OF THE CHAIRS IN THE MIDDLE.
OH.
RIGHT... RIGHT?! WHERE IS THE RIGHT SIDE?!
THE MIDDLE?!
TIGHT
I WON'T BE ABLE TO STAND TO THE RIGHT OF IT!
Thank you for taking the time for this interview.
IT'S NO GOOD.
"STAND TO THE RIGHT OF THE CHAIR AND BOW."
IF ONLY THERE WAS A SPACE TO THE RIGHT OF THE CHAIR.
A SPACE... A SPACE...
I KNOW. IF THERE IS NO SPACE...
...I JUST HAVE TO MAKE ONE.
REJECTED
THAT SCHOOL JUST COULDN'T HANDLE ME.
WHATEVER. THERE ARE LOTS OF OTHER SCHOOLS THAT WILL WANT ME.
NEXT QUESTION.

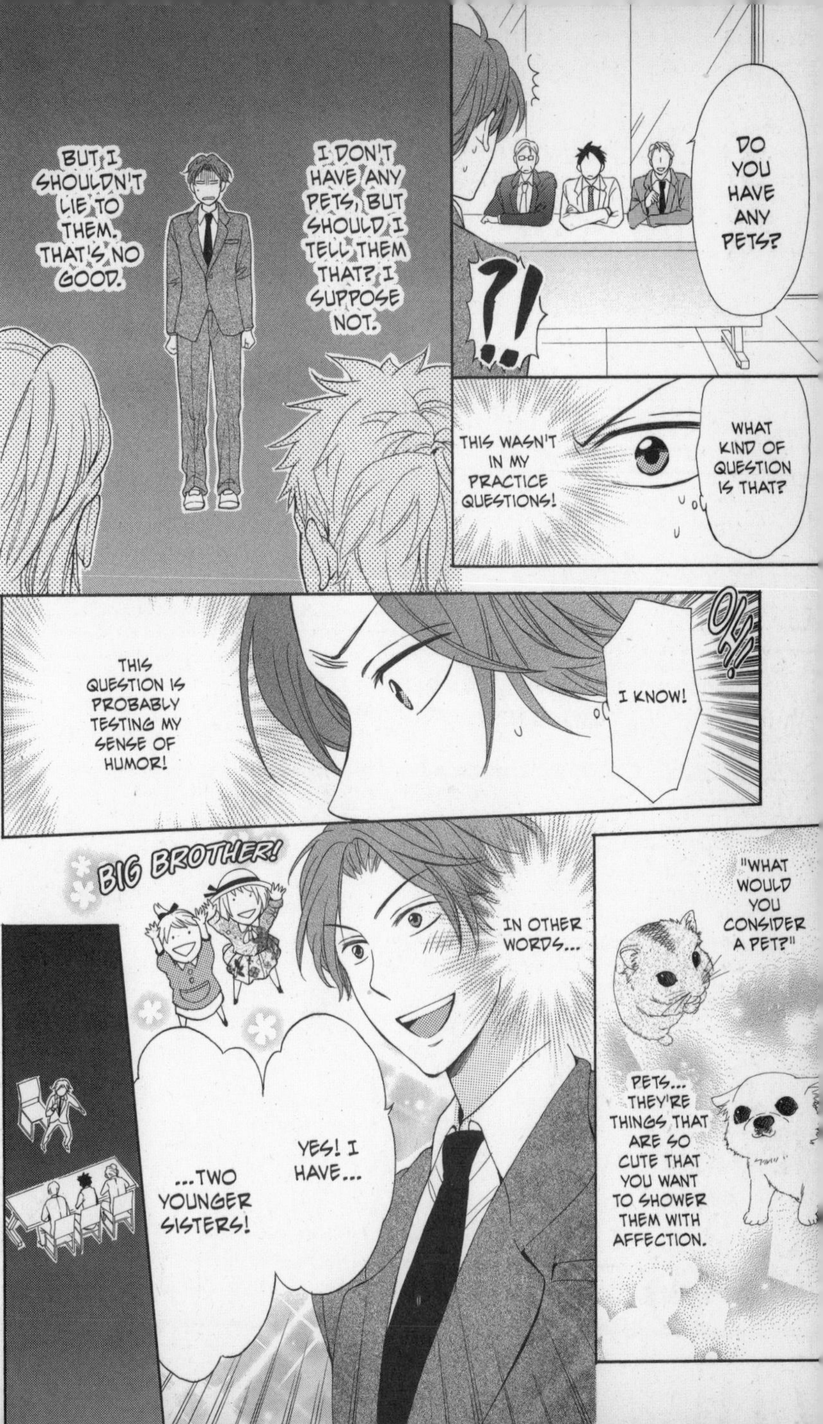
DO YOU HAVE ANY PETS?
?!
WHAT KIND OF QUESTION IS THAT?
THIS WASN'T IN MY PRACTICE QUESTIONS!
I DON'T HAVE ANY PETS, BUT SHOULD I TELL THEM THAT? I SUPPOSE NOT.
BUT I SHOULDN'T LIE TO THEM. THAT'S NO GOOD.
OH!
I KNOW!
THIS QUESTION IS PROBABLY TESTING MY SENSE OF HUMOR!
"WHAT WOULD YOU CONSIDER A PET?"
PETS... THEY'RE THINGS THAT ARE SO CUTE THAT YOU WANT TO SHOWER THEM WITH AFFECTION.
IN OTHER WORDS...
BIG BROTHER!
YES! I HAVE...
...TWO YOUNGER SISTERS!

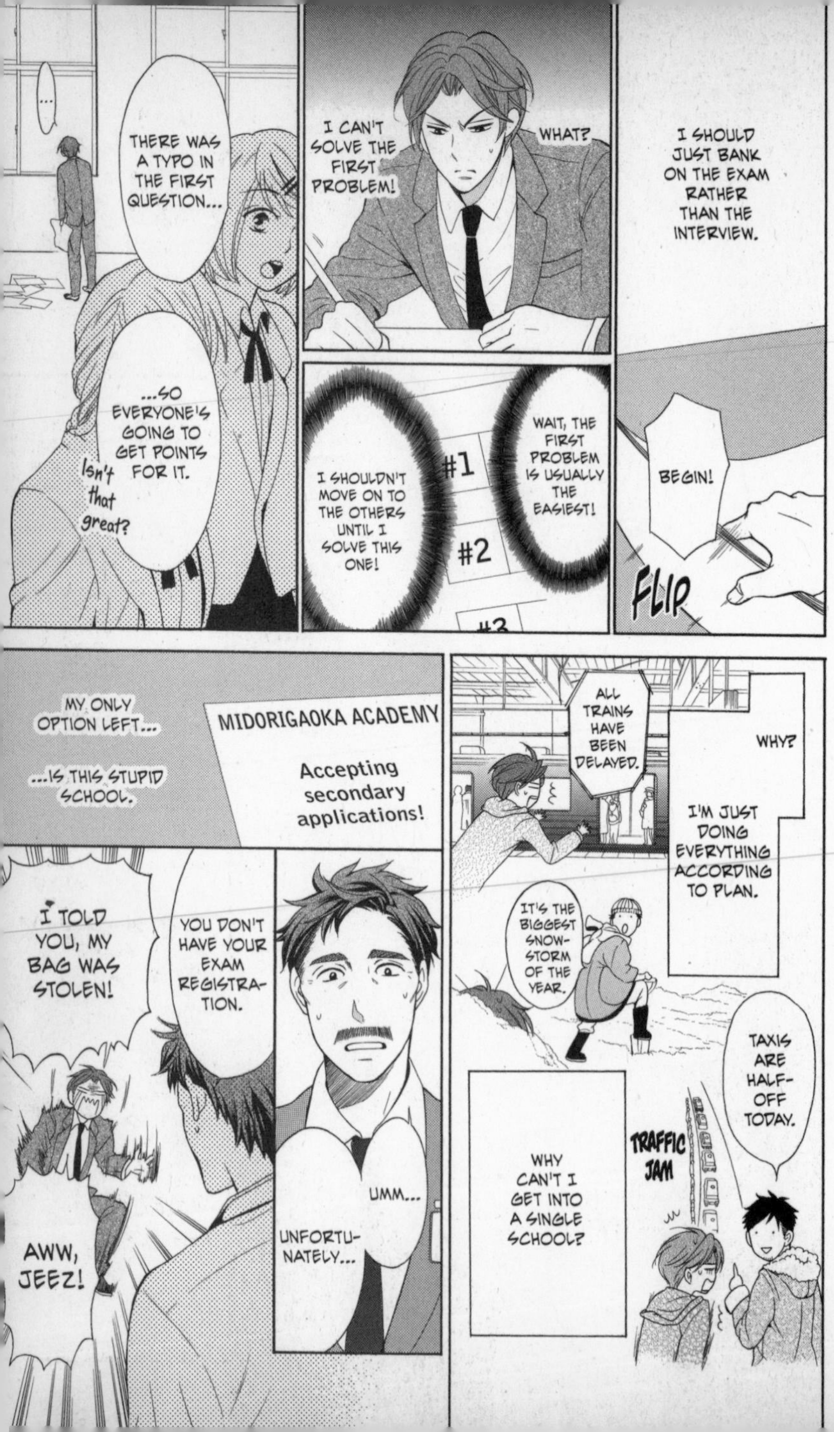
I SHOULD JUST BANK ON THE EXAM RATHER THAN THE INTERVIEW.
BEGIN!
FLIP
WHAT?
I CAN'T SOLVE THE FIRST PROBLEM!
WAIT, THE FIRST PROBLEM IS USUALLY THE EASIEST!
#1
#2
#3
I SHOULDN'T MOVE ON TO THE OTHERS UNTIL I SOLVE THIS ONE!
...
THERE WAS A TYPO IN THE FIRST QUESTION...
...SO EVERYONE'S GOING TO GET POINTS FOR IT.
Isn't that great?
WHY?
I'M JUST DOING EVERYTHING ACCORDING TO PLAN.
ALL TRAINS HAVE BEEN DELAYED.
IT'S THE BIGGEST SNOW-STORM OF THE YEAR.
TAXIS ARE HALF-OFF TODAY.
TRAFFIC JAM
WHY CAN'T I GET INTO A SINGLE SCHOOL?
MIDORIGAOKA ACADEMY
Accepting secondary applications!
MY ONLY OPTION LEFT...
...IS THIS STUPID SCHOOL.
YOU DON'T HAVE YOUR EXAM REGISTRA-TION.
UMM...
UNFORTU-NATELY...
I TOLD YOU, MY BAG WAS STOLEN!
AWW, JEEZ!

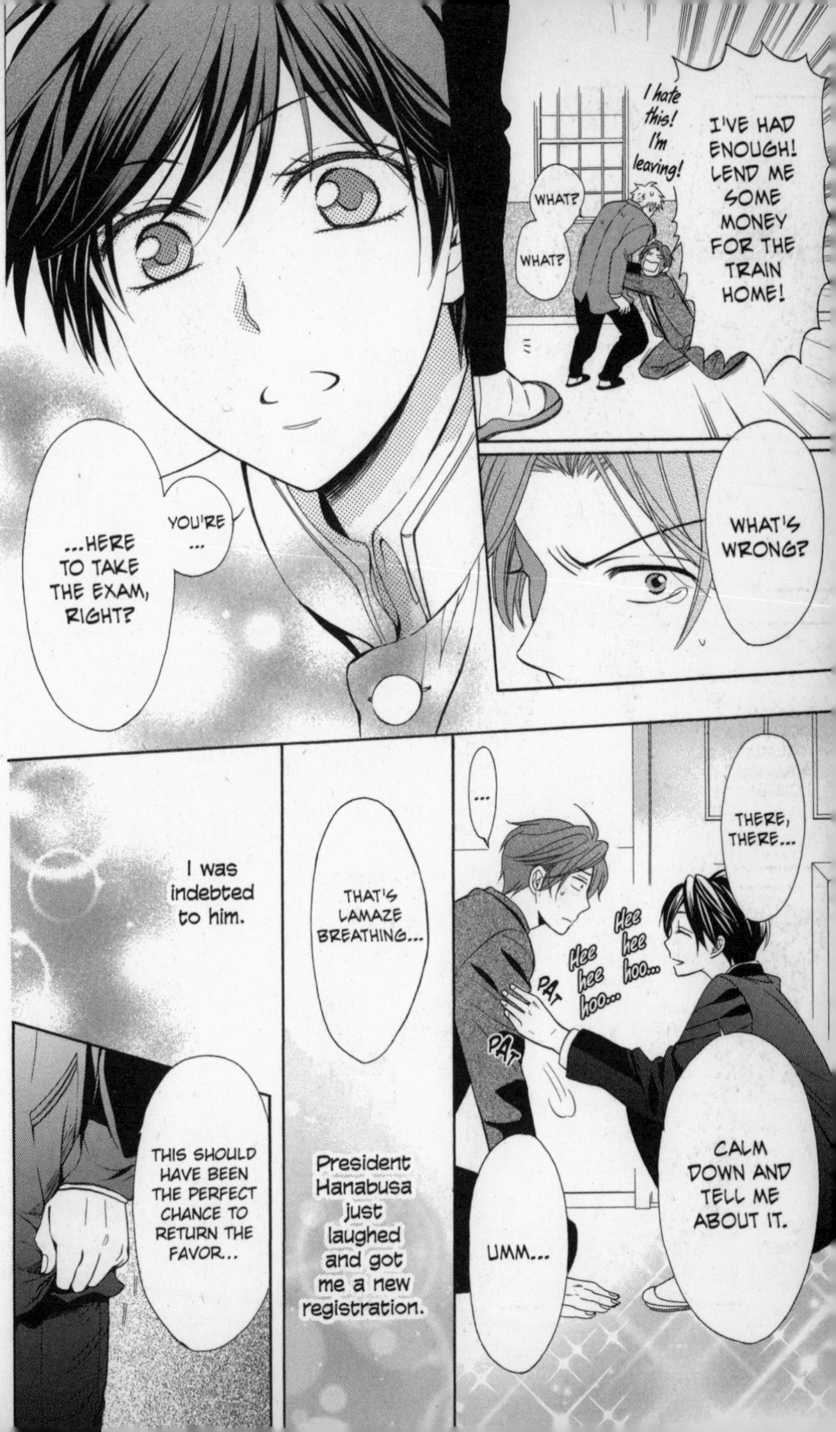
I'VE HAD ENOUGH! LEND ME SOME MONEY FOR THE TRAIN HOME!
I hate this! I'm leaving!
WHAT?
WHAT?
WHAT'S WRONG?
YOU'RE ...
...HERE TO TAKE THE EXAM, RIGHT?
THERE, THERE...
...
Hee hee hoo...
Hee hee hoo...
PAT
PAT
CALM DOWN AND TELL ME ABOUT IT.
UMM...
THAT'S LAMAZE BREATHING...
President Hanabusa just laughed and got me a new registration.
I was indebted to him.
THIS SHOULD HAVE BEEN THE PERFECT CHANCE TO RETURN THE FAVOR...

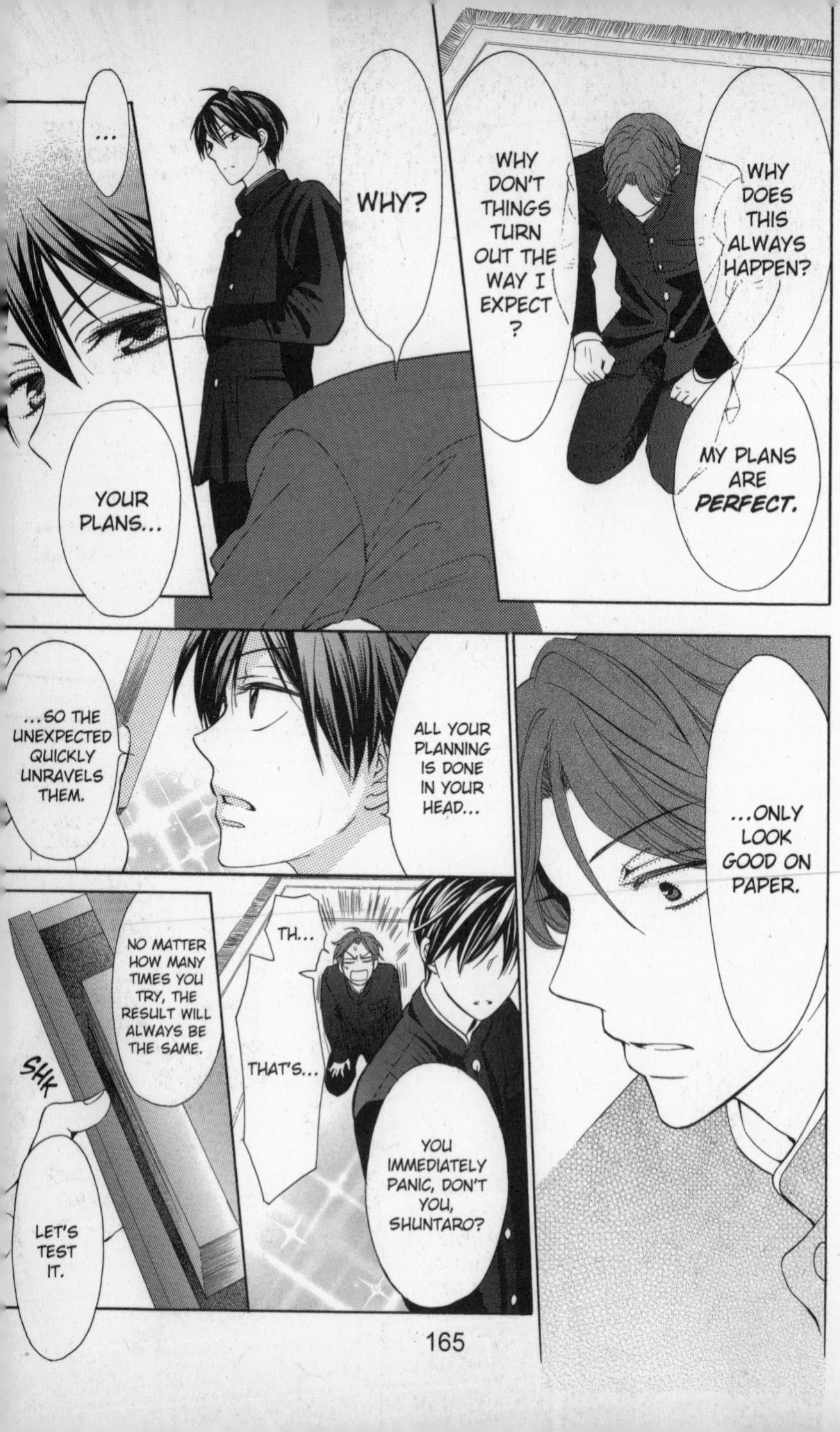
WHY DOES THIS ALWAYS HAPPEN?
MY PLANS ARE PERFECT.
WHY DON'T THINGS TURN OUT THE WAY I EXPECT?
WHY?
...
YOUR PLANS...
...ONLY LOOK GOOD ON PAPER.
ALL YOUR PLANNING IS DONE IN YOUR HEAD...
...SO THE UNEXPECTED QUICKLY UNRAVELS THEM.
YOU IMMEDIATELY PANIC, DON'T YOU, SHUNTARO?
TH...
THAT'S...
NO MATTER HOW MANY TIMES YOU TRY, THE RESULT WILL ALWAYS BE THE SAME.
SHK
LET'S TEST IT.

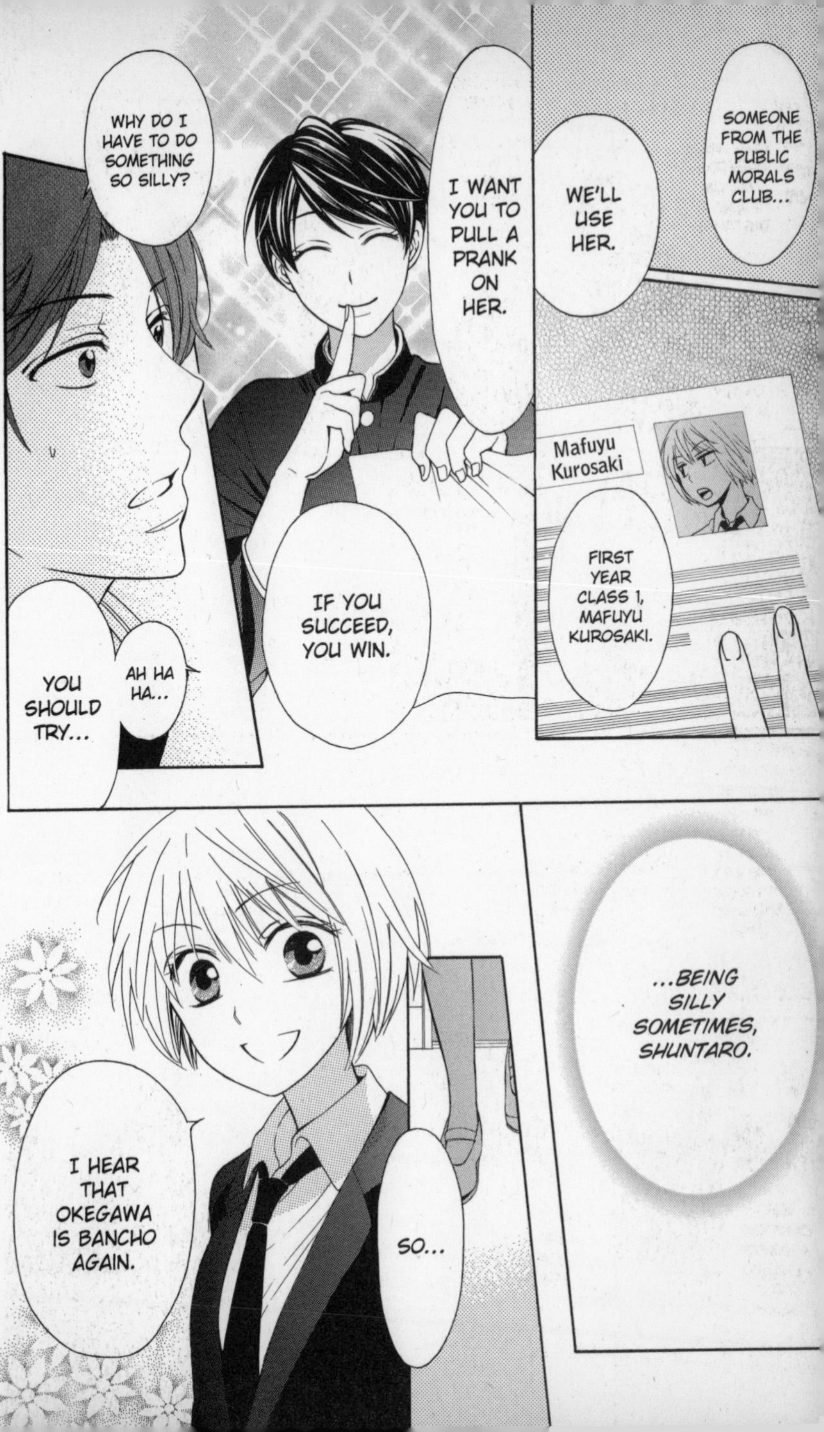
SOMEONE FROM THE PUBLIC MORALS CLUB...
WE'LL USE HER.
Mafuyu Kurosaki
FIRST YEAR CLASS 1, MAFUYU KUROSAKI.
I WANT YOU TO PULL A PRANK ON HER.
WHY DO I HAVE TO DO SOMETHING SO SILLY?
IF YOU SUCCEED, YOU WIN.
AH HA HA...
YOU SHOULD TRY...
...BEING SILLY SOMETIMES, SHUNTARO.
SO...
I HEAR THAT OKEGAWA IS BANCHO AGAIN.

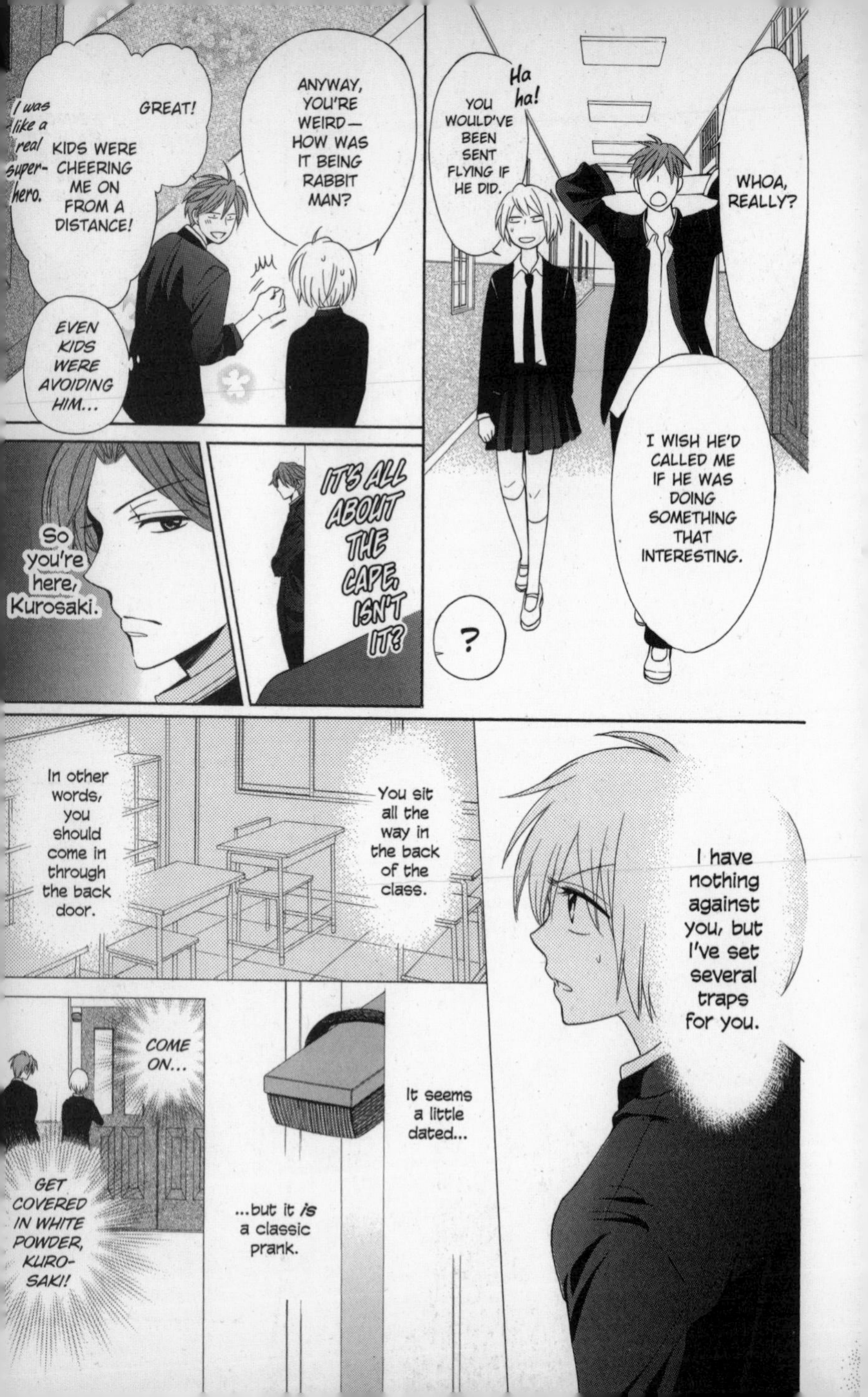
WHOA, REALLY?
Ha ha!
YOU WOULD'VE BEEN SENT FLYING IF HE DID.
I WISH HE'D CALLED ME IF HE WAS DOING SOMETHING THAT INTERESTING.
?
ANYWAY, YOU'RE WEIRD—HOW WAS IT BEING RABBIT MAN?
GREAT! KIDS WERE CHEERING ME ON FROM A DISTANCE!
I was like a real super-hero.
EVEN KIDS WERE AVOIDING HIM...
IT'S ALL ABOUT THE CAPE, ISN'T IT?
So you're here, Kurosaki.
I have nothing against you, but I've set several traps for you.
You sit all the way in the back of the class.
In other words, you should come in through the back door.
It seems a little dated...
...but it *is* a classic prank.
COME ON...
GET COVERED IN WHITE POWDER, KURO-SAKI!

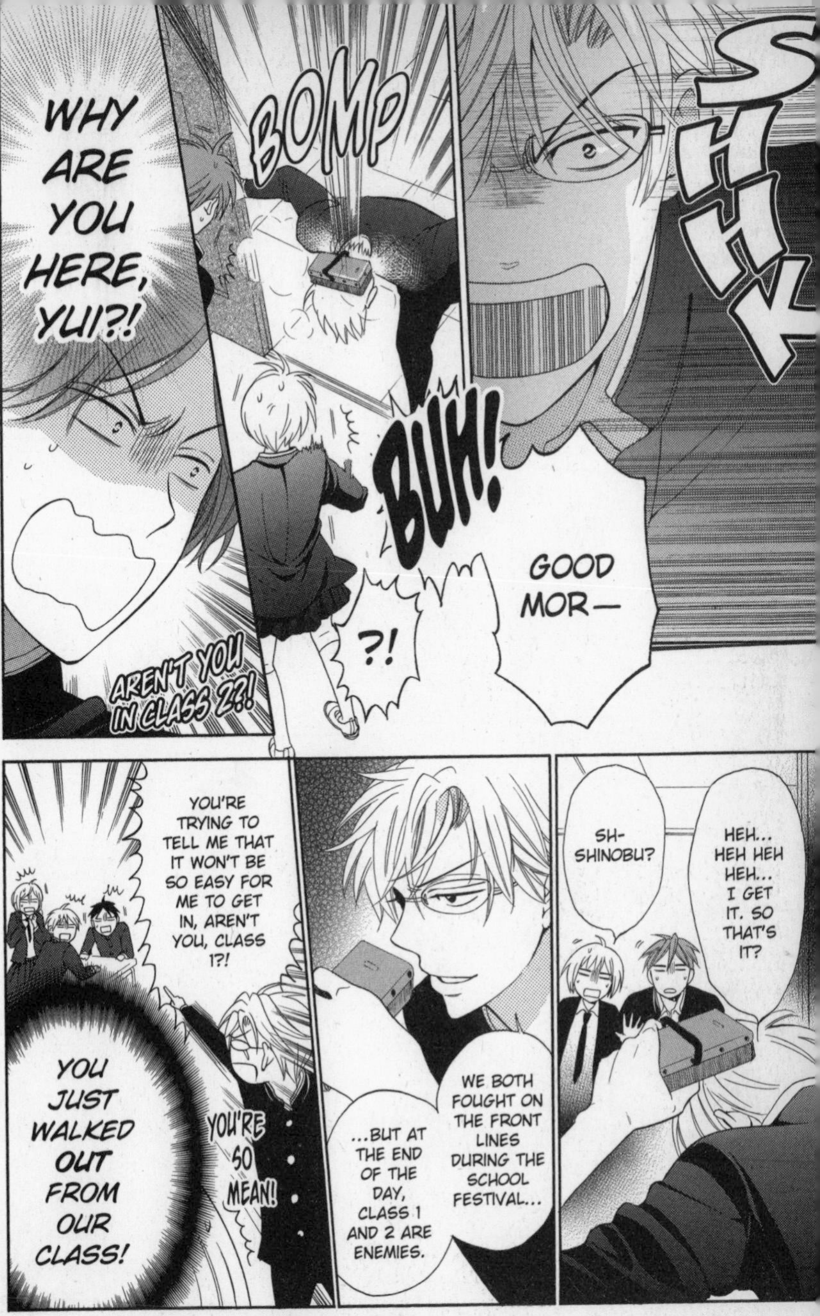
SHHK
GOOD MOR—
BOMP
BUH!
?!
WHY ARE YOU HERE, YUI?!
AREN'T YOU IN CLASS 2?!
HEH... HEH HEH HEH... I GET IT. SO THAT'S IT?
SH-SHINOBU?
WE BOTH FOUGHT ON THE FRONT LINES DURING THE SCHOOL FESTIVAL...
...BUT AT THE END OF THE DAY, CLASS 1 AND 2 ARE ENEMIES.
YOU'RE TRYING TO TELL ME THAT IT WON'T BE SO EASY FOR ME TO GET IN, AREN'T YOU, CLASS 1?!
YOU JUST WALKED OUT FROM OUR CLASS!
YOU'RE SO MEAN!

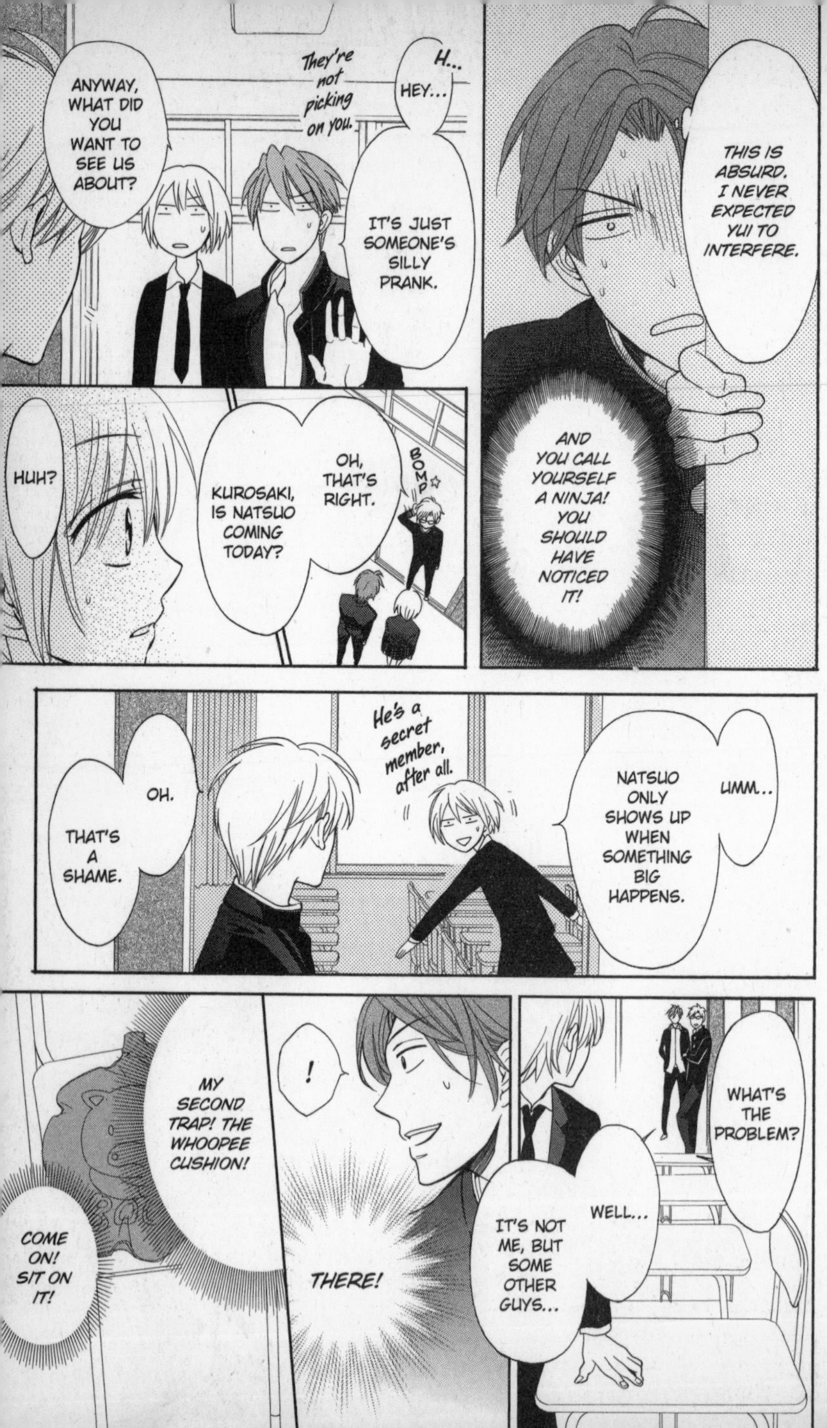
THIS IS ABSURD. I NEVER EXPECTED YUI TO INTERFERE.
AND YOU CALL YOURSELF A NINJA! YOU SHOULD HAVE NOTICED IT!
H...
HEY...
IT'S JUST SOMEONE'S SILLY PRANK.
They're not picking on you.
ANYWAY, WHAT DID YOU WANT TO SEE US ABOUT?
OH, THAT'S RIGHT.
BOMP☆
KUROSAKI, IS NATSUO COMING TODAY?
HUH?
UMM...
NATSUO ONLY SHOWS UP WHEN SOMETHING BIG HAPPENS.
He's a secret member, after all.
OH.
THAT'S A SHAME.
WHAT'S THE PROBLEM?
WELL...
IT'S NOT ME, BUT SOME OTHER GUYS...
!
THERE!
MY SECOND TRAP! THE WHOOPEE CUSHION!
COME ON! SIT ON IT!

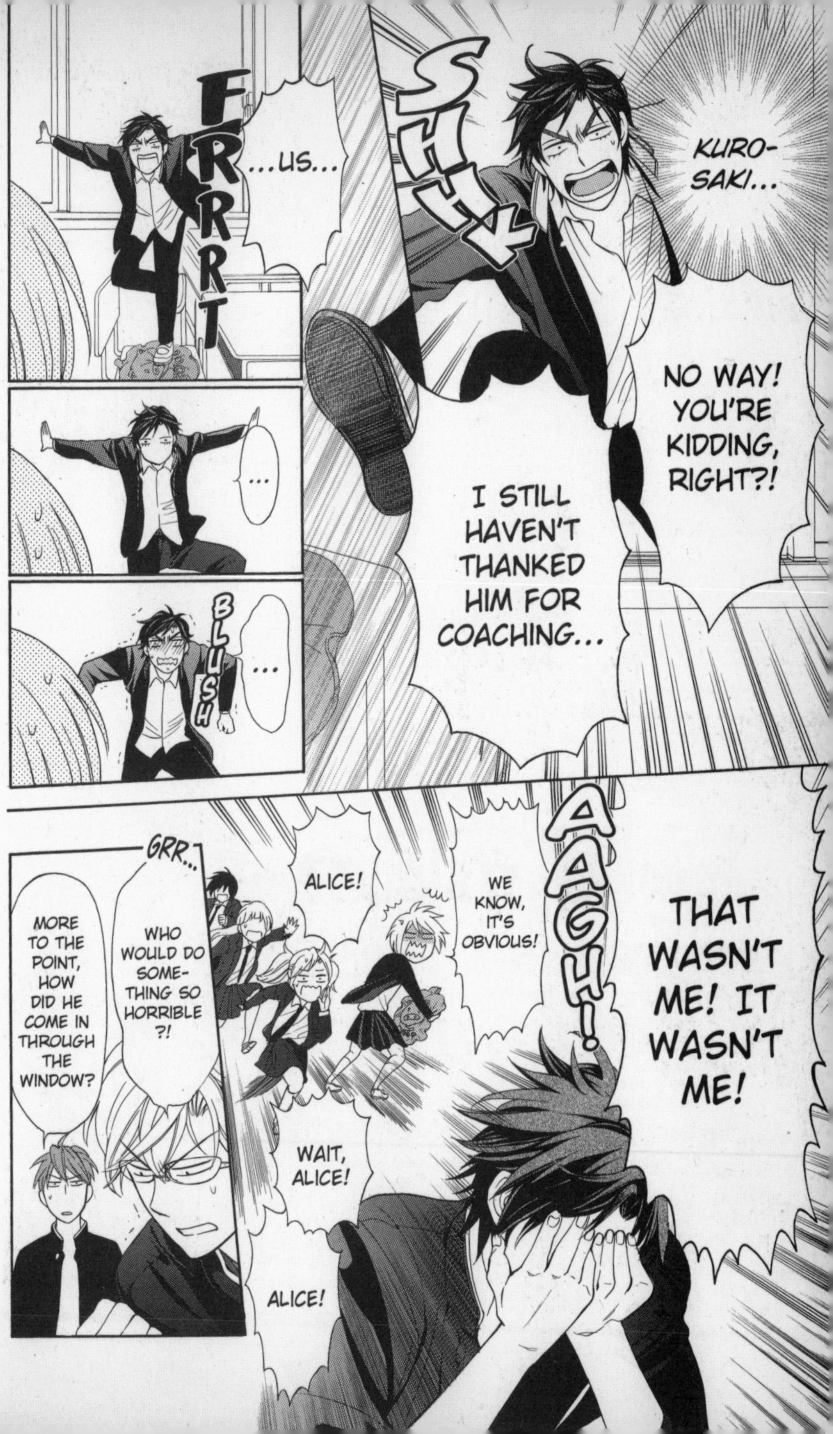
KURO-SAKI...
SHHK
NO WAY! YOU'RE KIDDING, RIGHT?!
I STILL HAVEN'T THANKED HIM FOR COACHING...
FRRRT
...US...
...
BLUSH
...
AAGH!
THAT WASN'T ME! IT WASN'T ME!
WE KNOW, IT'S OBVIOUS!
ALICE!
WAIT, ALICE!
ALICE!
GRR...
WHO WOULD DO SOME-THING SO HORRIBLE?!
MORE TO THE POINT, HOW DID HE COME IN THROUGH THE WINDOW?

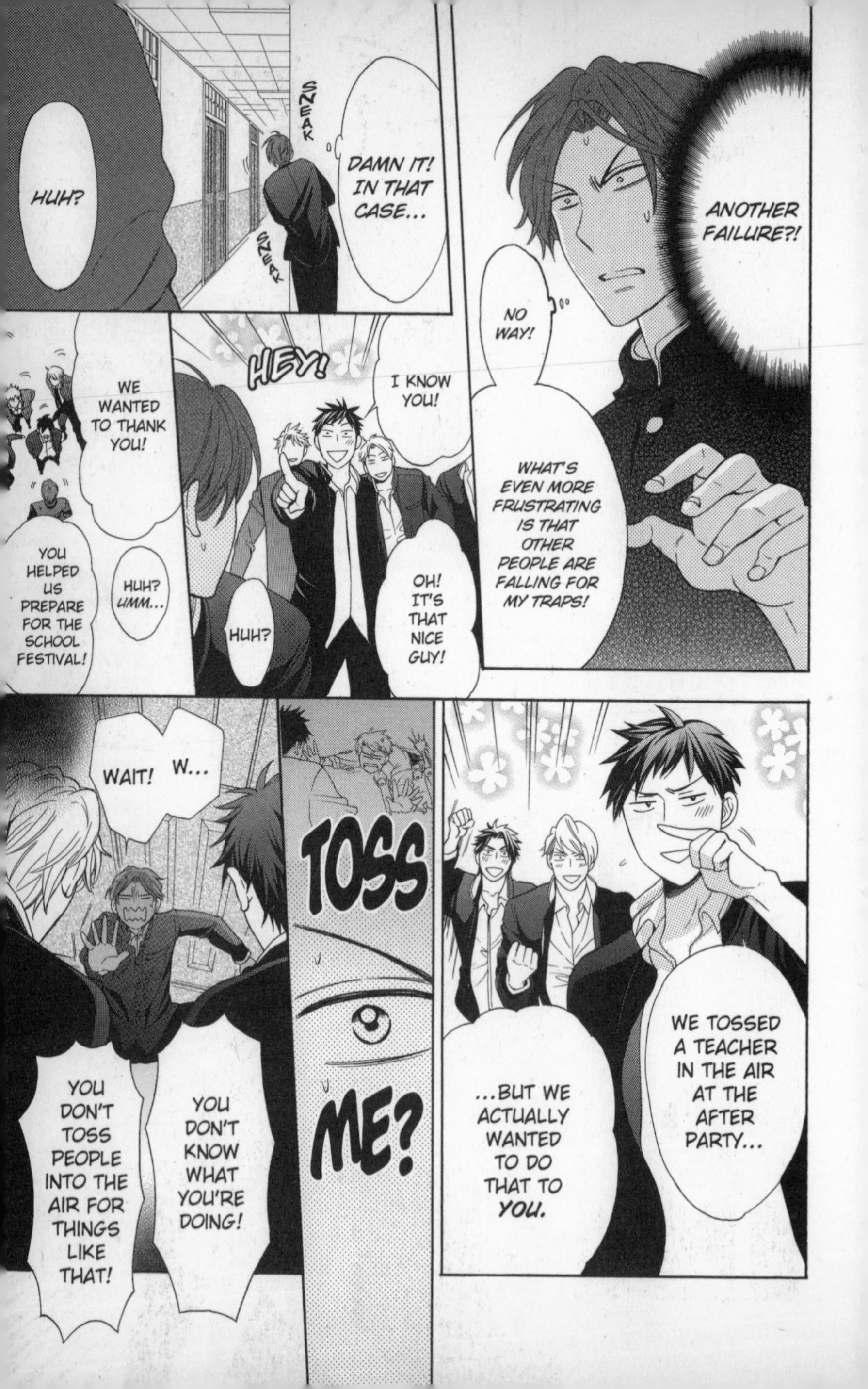
ANOTHER FAILURE?!
NO WAY!
WHAT'S EVEN MORE FRUSTRATING IS THAT OTHER PEOPLE ARE FALLING FOR MY TRAPS!
SNEAK
DAMN IT! IN THAT CASE...
SNEAK
HUH?
HEY!
I KNOW YOU!
OH! IT'S THAT NICE GUY!
HUH?
WE WANTED TO THANK YOU!
HUH? UMM...
YOU HELPED US PREPARE FOR THE SCHOOL FESTIVAL!
WE TOSSED A TEACHER IN THE AIR AT THE AFTER PARTY...
...BUT WE ACTUALLY WANTED TO DO THAT TO YOU.
TOSS
ME?
W...
WAIT!
YOU DON'T KNOW WHAT YOU'RE DOING!
YOU DON'T TOSS PEOPLE INTO THE AIR FOR THINGS LIKE THAT!

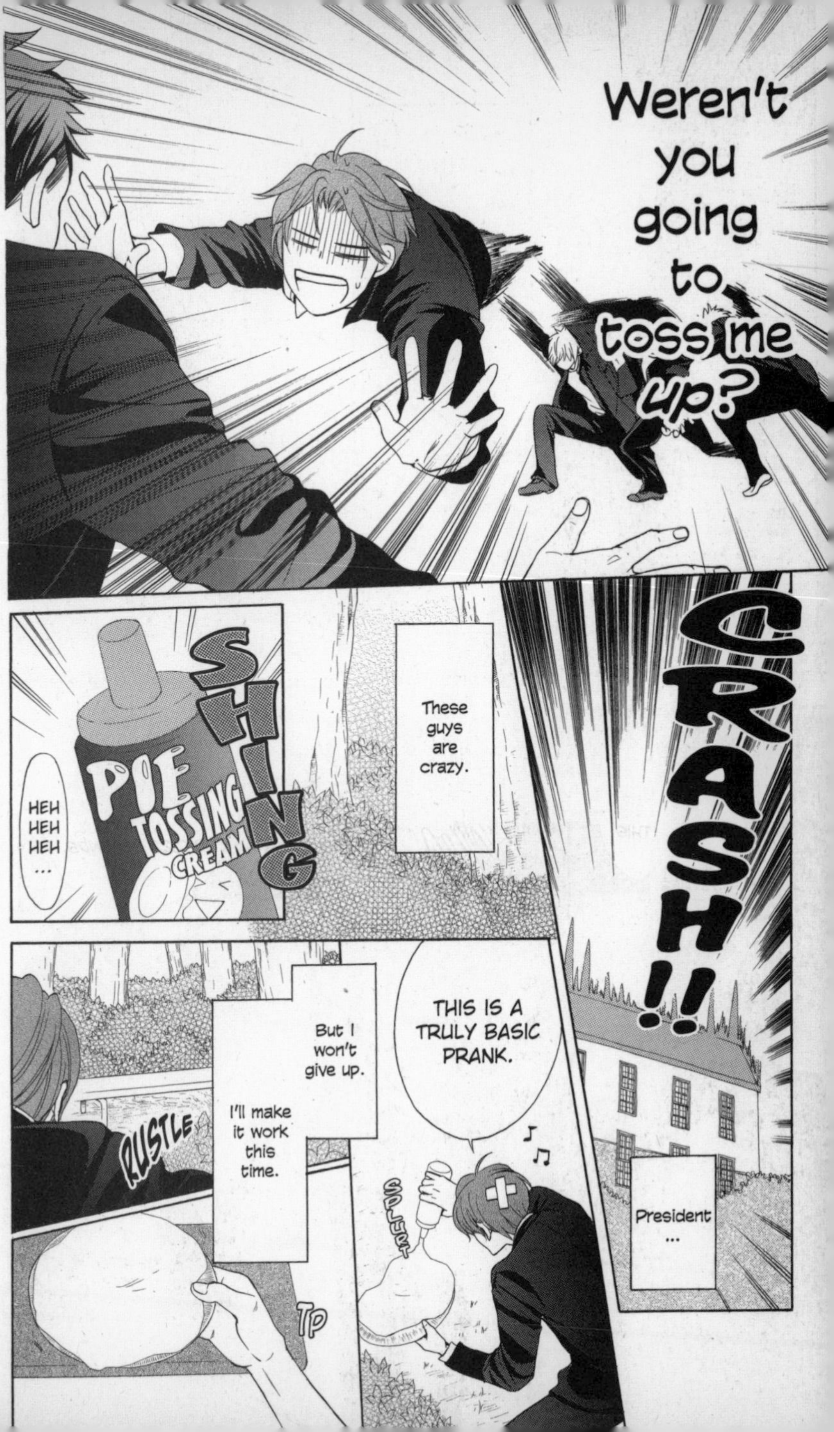
Weren't you going to toss me up?
CRASH!!
President ...
These guys are crazy.
SHING
PIE TOSSING CREAM
HEH HEH HEH ...
THIS IS A TRULY BASIC PRANK.
SPLURT
But I won't give up.
I'll make it work this time.
RUSTLE
TP

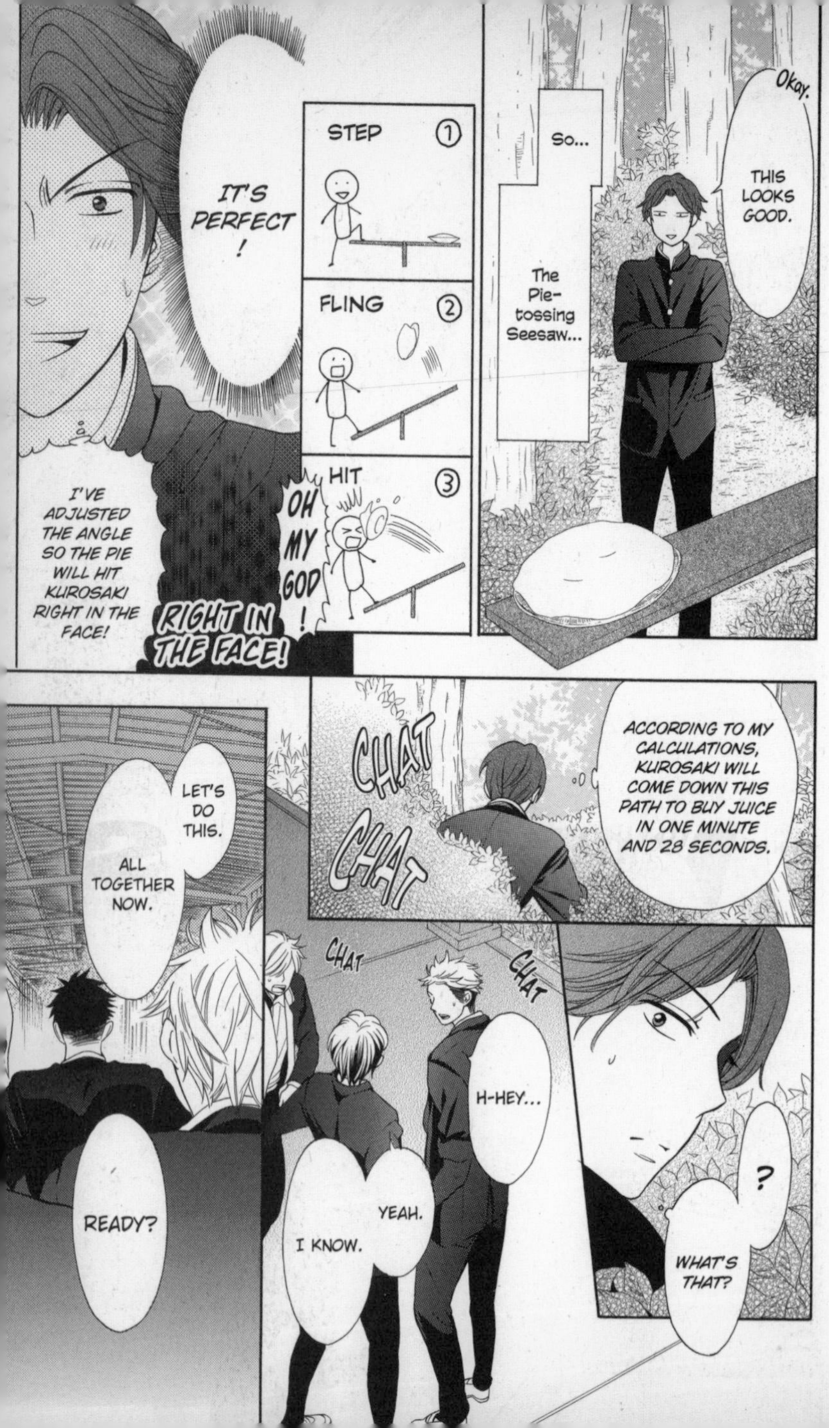
Okay.
THIS LOOKS GOOD.
So...
The Pie-tossing Seesaw...
STEP ①
FLING ②
HIT ③
OH MY GOD!
IT'S PERFECT!
I'VE ADJUSTED THE ANGLE SO THE PIE WILL HIT KUROSAKI RIGHT IN THE FACE!
RIGHT IN THE FACE!
CHAT CHAT
ACCORDING TO MY CALCULATIONS, KUROSAKI WILL COME DOWN THIS PATH TO BUY JUICE IN ONE MINUTE AND 28 SECONDS.
?
WHAT'S THAT?
CHAT CHAT
H-HEY...
YEAH.
I KNOW.
LET'S DO THIS.
ALL TOGETHER NOW.
READY?

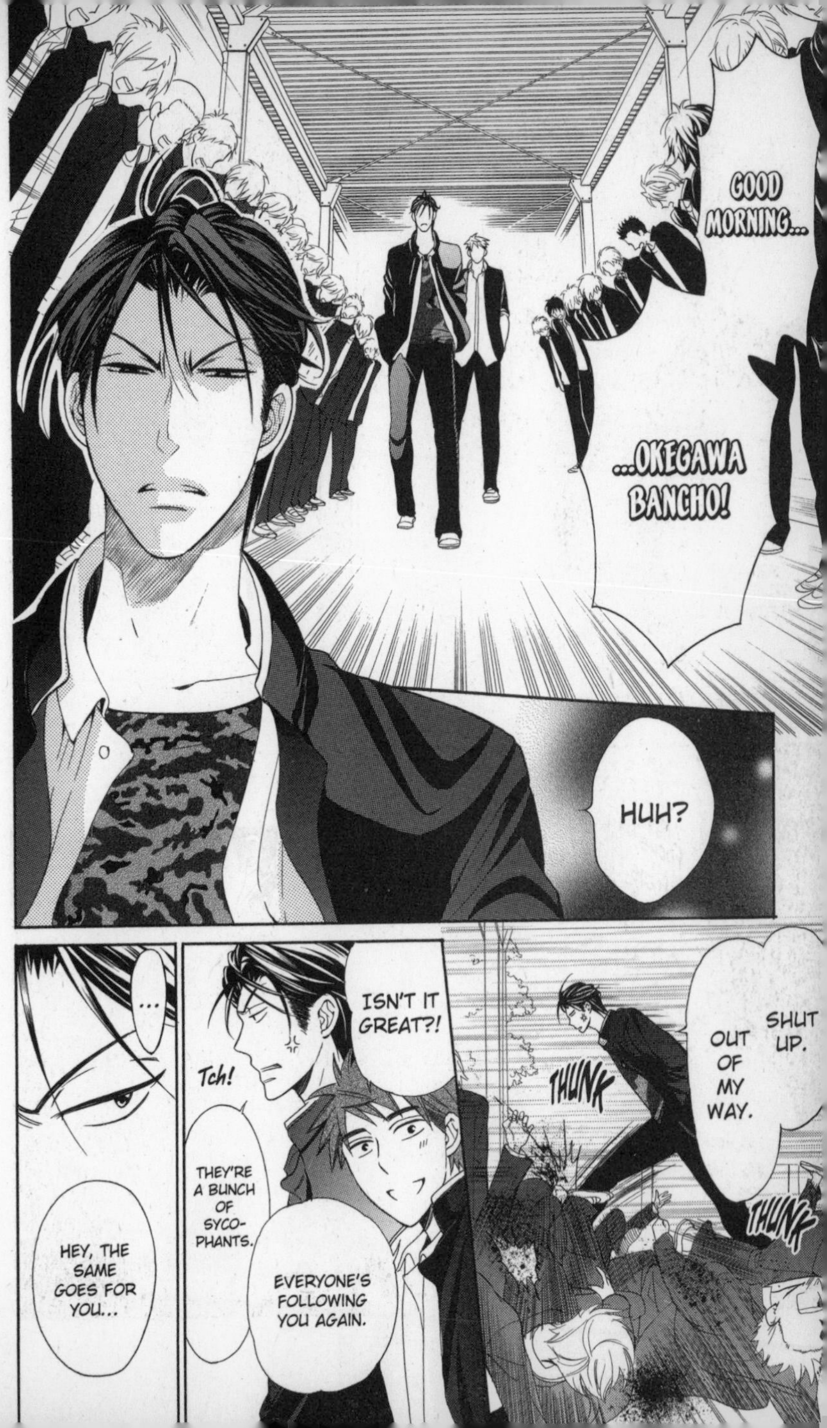
GOOD MORNING...
...OKEGAWA BANCHO!
HUH?
SHUT UP.
OUT OF MY WAY.
THUNK
THUNK
ISN'T IT GREAT?!
Tch!
THEY'RE A BUNCH OF SYCO-PHANTS.
EVERYONE'S FOLLOWING YOU AGAIN.
...
HEY, THE SAME GOES FOR YOU...

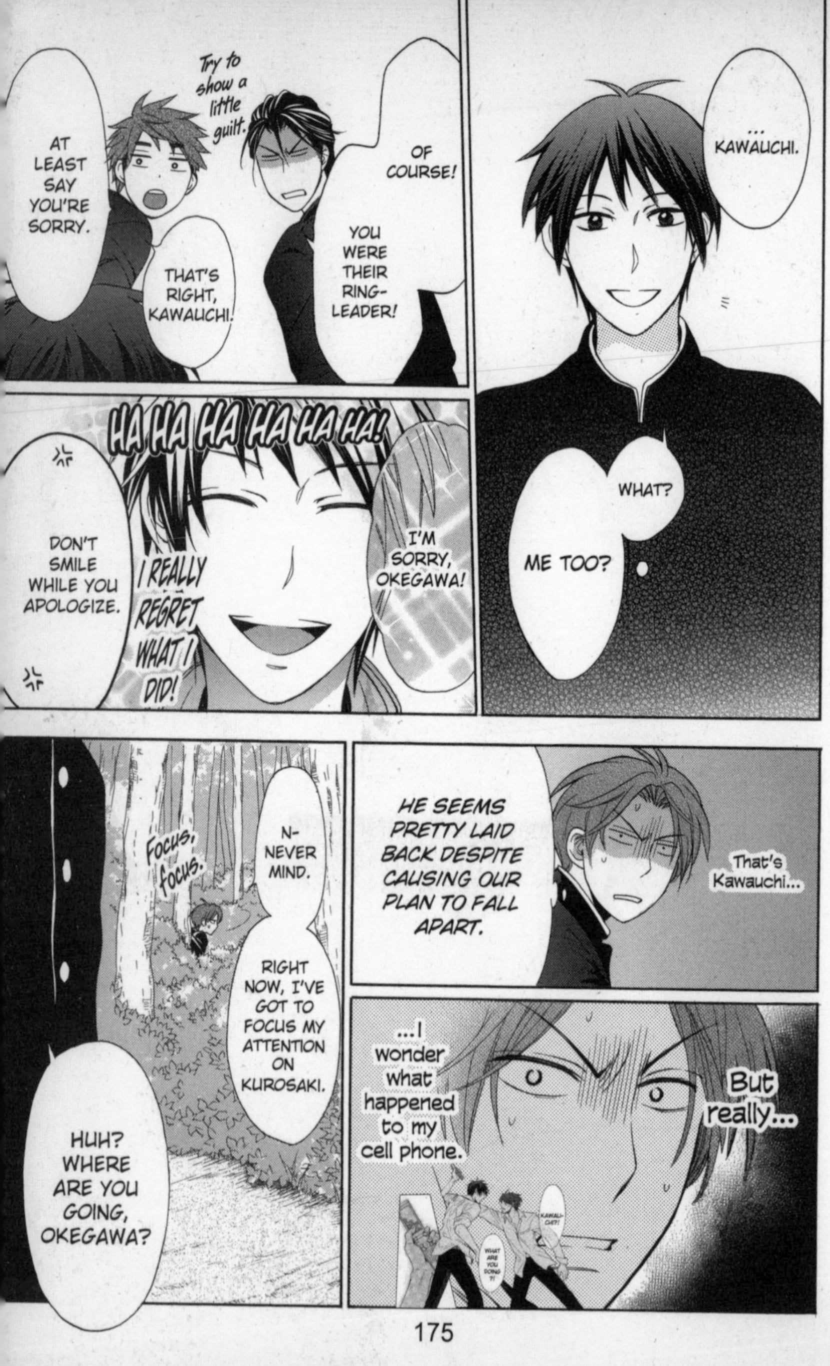

...KAWAUCHI.
WHAT?
ME TOO?
OF COURSE!
YOU WERE THEIR RING-LEADER!
Try to show a little guilt.
AT LEAST SAY YOU'RE SORRY.
THAT'S RIGHT, KAWAUCHI!
HA HA HA HA HA HA!
I'M SORRY, OKEGAWA!
I REALLY REGRET WHAT I DID!
DON'T SMILE WHILE YOU APOLOGIZE.
That's Kawauchi...
HE SEEMS PRETTY LAID BACK DESPITE CAUSING OUR PLAN TO FALL APART.
But really...
...I wonder what happened to my cell phone.
KAWAUCHI?!
WHAT ARE YOU DOING?!
N-NEVER MIND.
RIGHT NOW, I'VE GOT TO FOCUS MY ATTENTION ON KUROSAKI.
Focus, focus.
HUH? WHERE ARE YOU GOING, OKEGAWA?

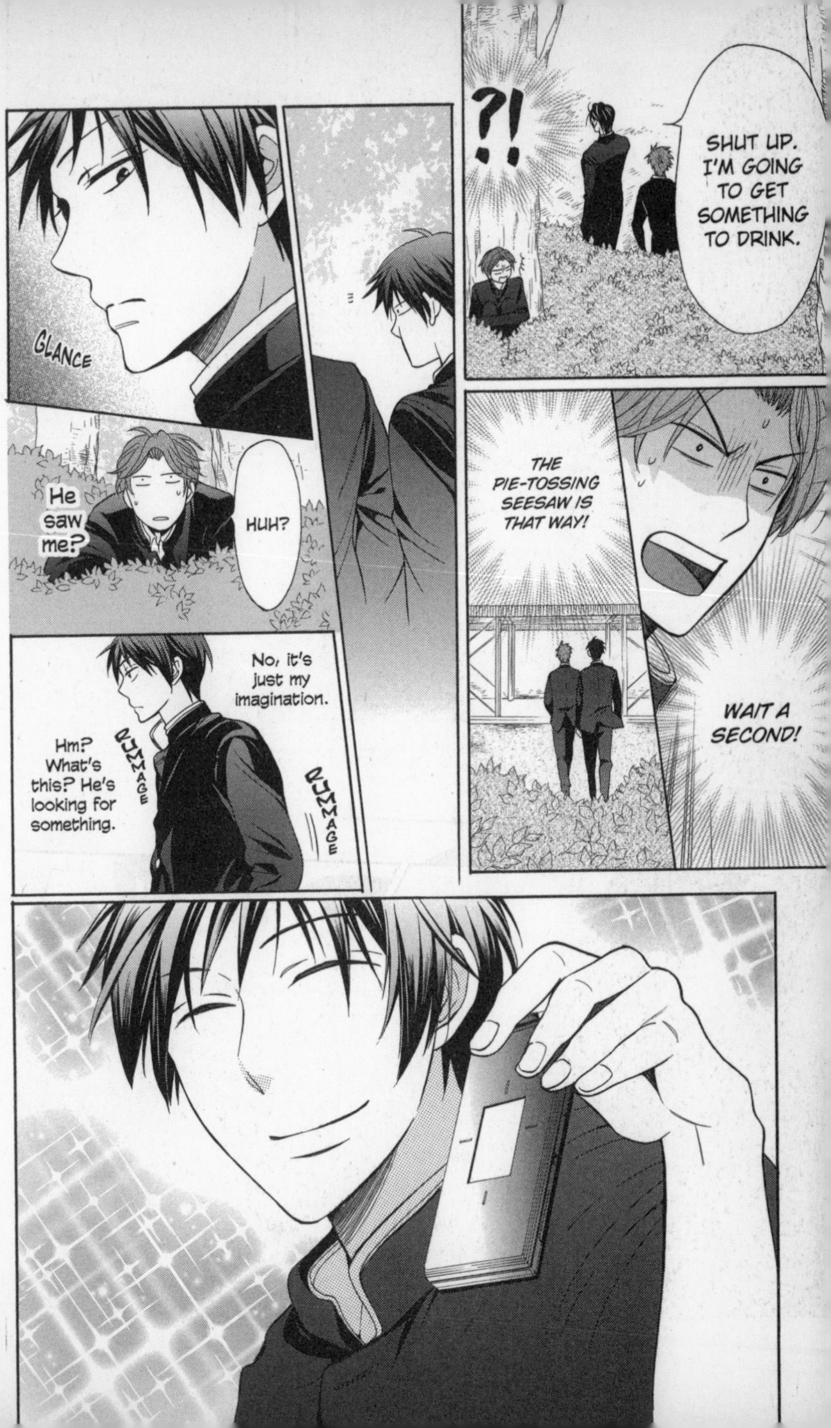
?!
SHUT UP. I'M GOING TO GET SOMETHING TO DRINK.
THE PIE-TOSSING SEESAW IS THAT WAY!
WAIT A SECOND!
GLANCE
HUH?
He saw me?
No, it's just my imagination.
RUMMAGE
RUMMAGE
Hm? What's this? He's looking for something.

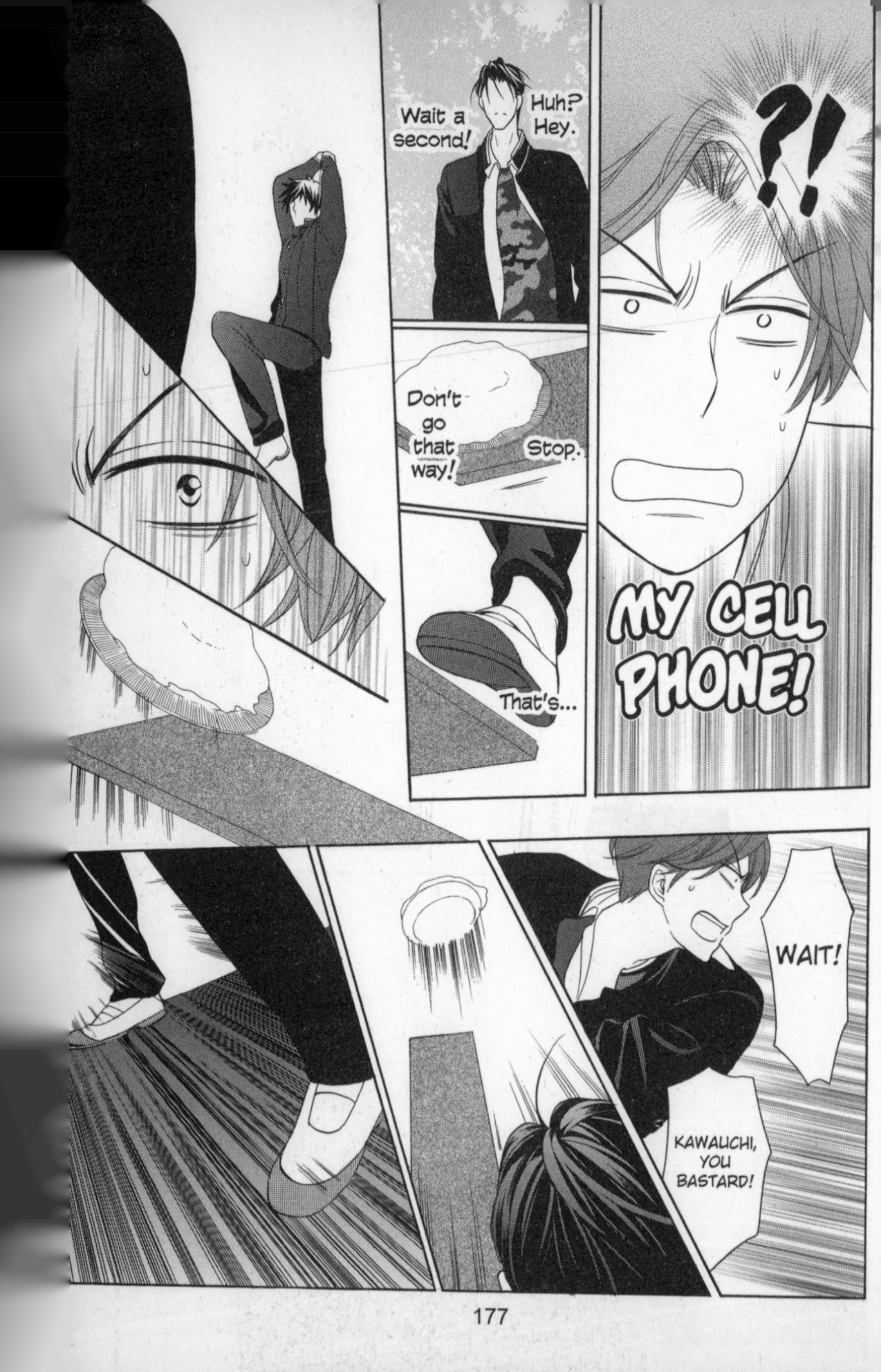
?!
MY CELL PHONE!
Huh? Hey.
Wait a second!
Stop.
Don't go that way!
That's...
WAIT!
KAWAUCHI, YOU BASTARD!

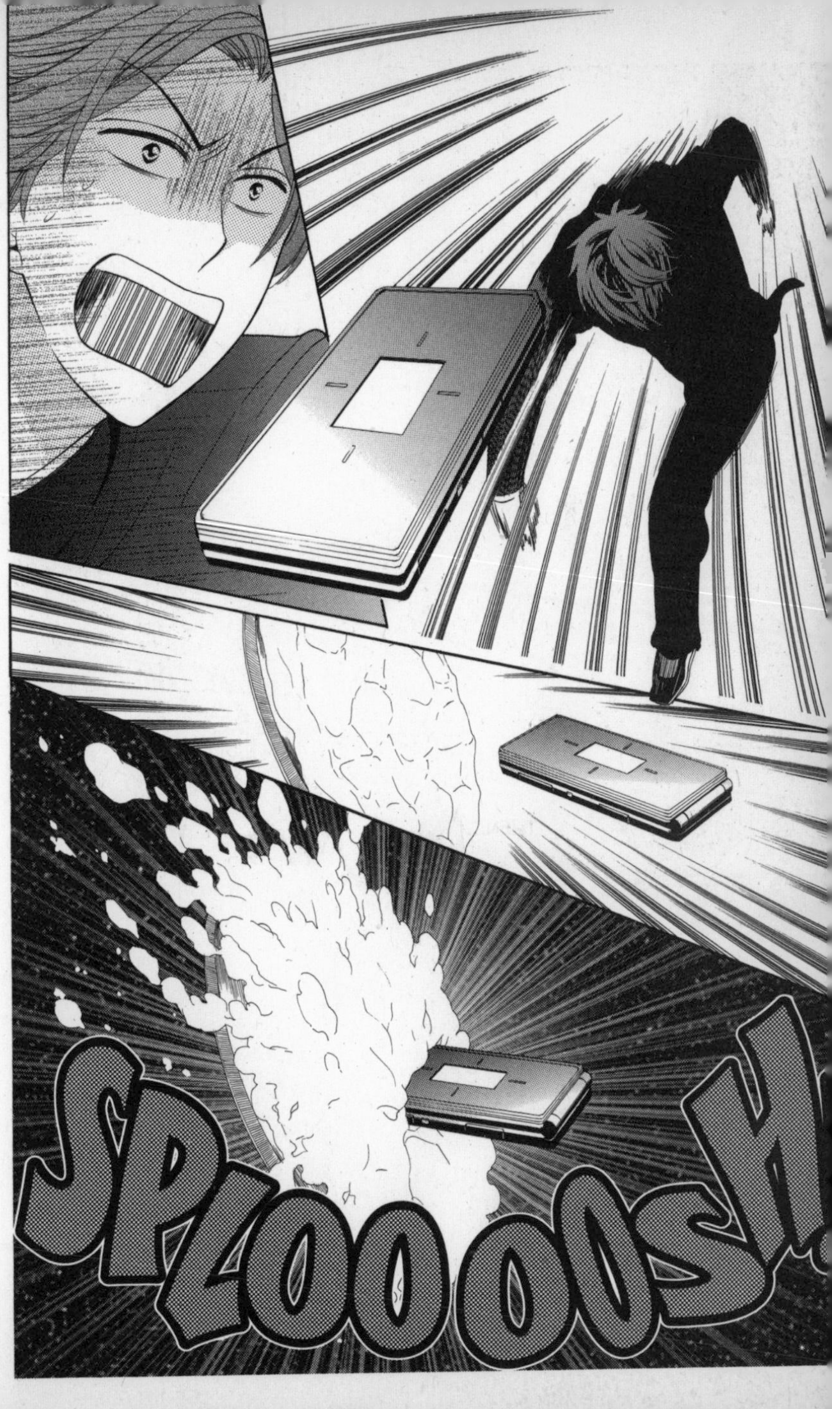
SPLOOOOSH!

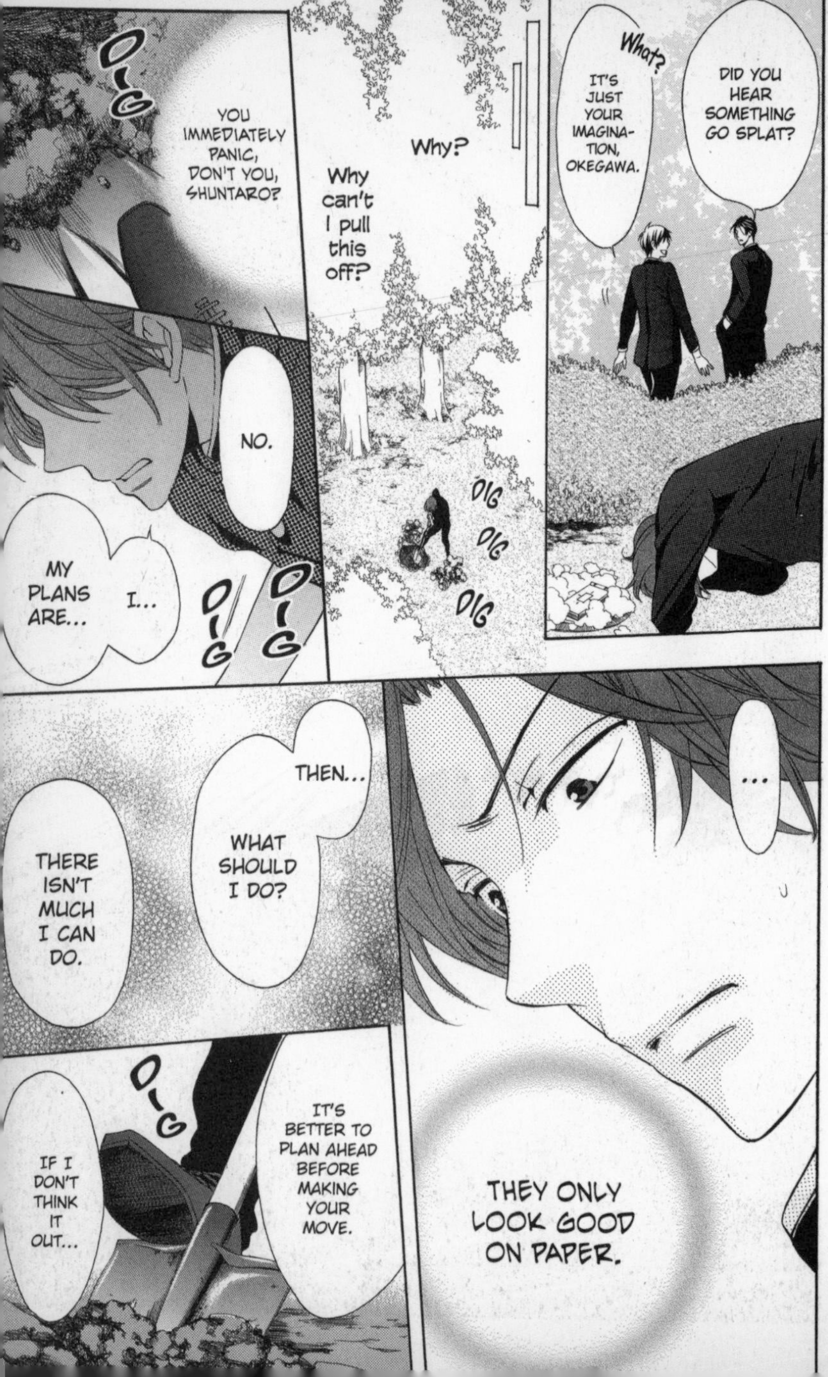
DID YOU HEAR SOMETHING GO SPLAT?
What?
IT'S JUST YOUR IMAGINATION, OKEGAWA.
Why?
Why can't I pull this off?
DIG DIG DIG
DIG
YOU IMMEDIATELY PANIC, DON'T YOU, SHUNTARO?
NO.
DIG DIG
I...
MY PLANS ARE...
...
THEY ONLY LOOK GOOD ON PAPER.
THEN...
WHAT SHOULD I DO?
THERE ISN'T MUCH I CAN DO.
DIG
IT'S BETTER TO PLAN AHEAD BEFORE MAKING YOUR MOVE.
IF I DON'T THINK IT OUT...

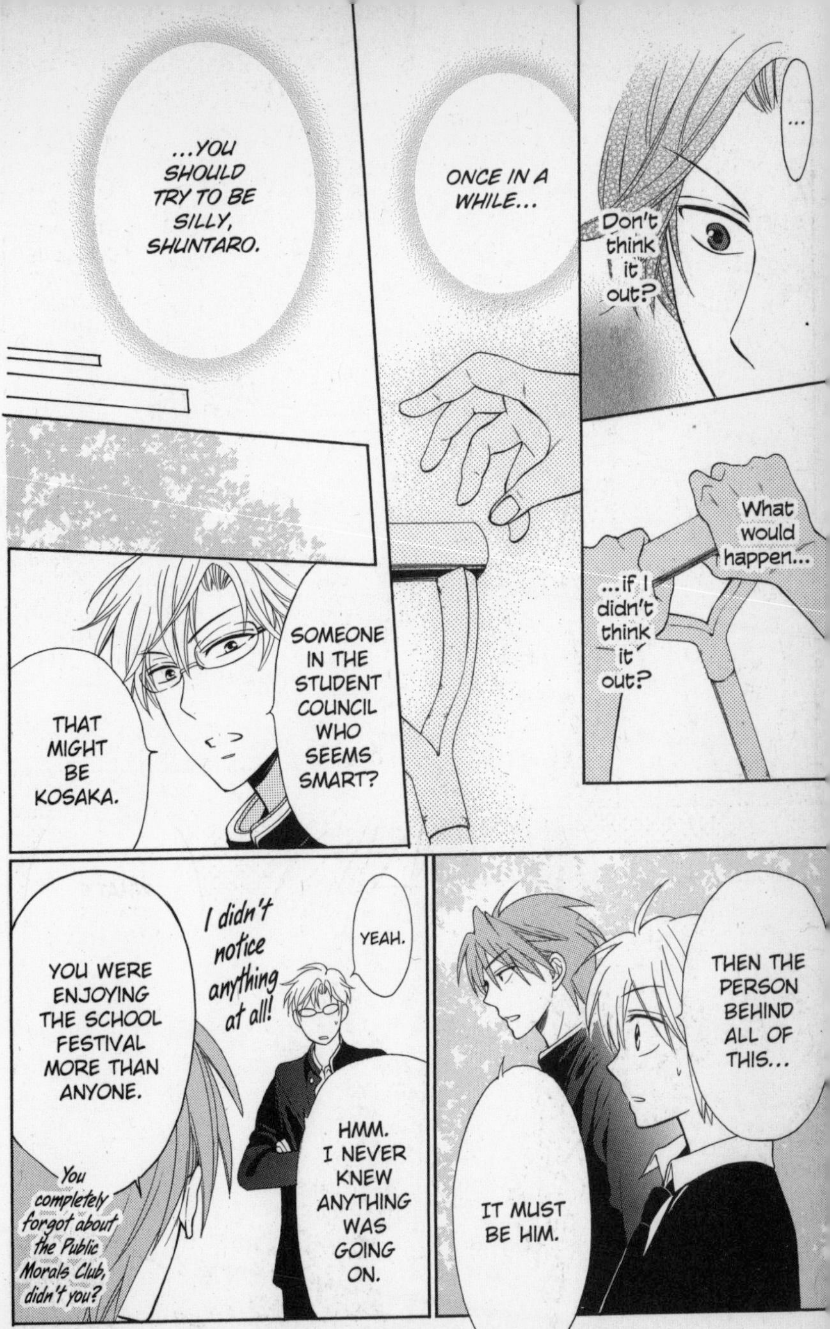
...
Don't think it out?
What would happen...
...if I didn't think it out?
ONCE IN A WHILE...
...YOU SHOULD TRY TO BE SILLY, SHUNTARO.
SOMEONE IN THE STUDENT COUNCIL WHO SEEMS SMART?
THAT MIGHT BE KOSAKA.
THEN THE PERSON BEHIND ALL OF THIS...
IT MUST BE HIM.
YEAH.
I didn't notice anything at all!
HMM. I NEVER KNEW ANYTHING WAS GOING ON.
YOU WERE ENJOYING THE SCHOOL FESTIVAL MORE THAN ANYONE.
You completely forgot about the Public Morals Club, didn't you?

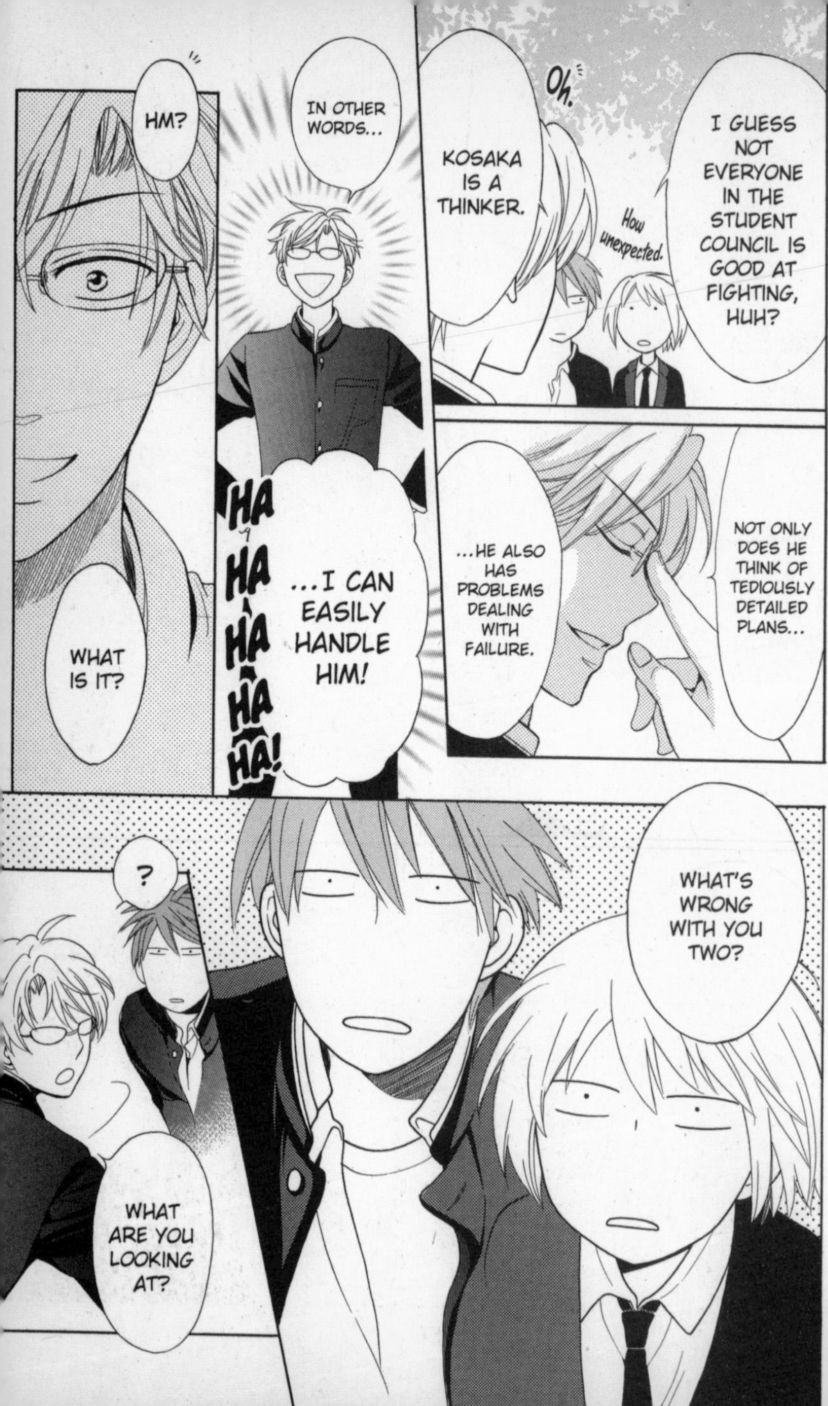
I GUESS NOT EVERYONE IN THE STUDENT COUNCIL IS GOOD AT FIGHTING, HUH?
Oh.
How unexpected.
KOSAKA IS A THINKER.
NOT ONLY DOES HE THINK OF TEDIOUSLY DETAILED PLANS...
...HE ALSO HAS PROBLEMS DEALING WITH FAILURE.
IN OTHER WORDS...
...I CAN EASILY HANDLE HIM!
HA HA HA HA HA HA!
HM?
WHAT IS IT?
WHAT'S WRONG WITH YOU TWO?
?
WHAT ARE YOU LOOKING AT?

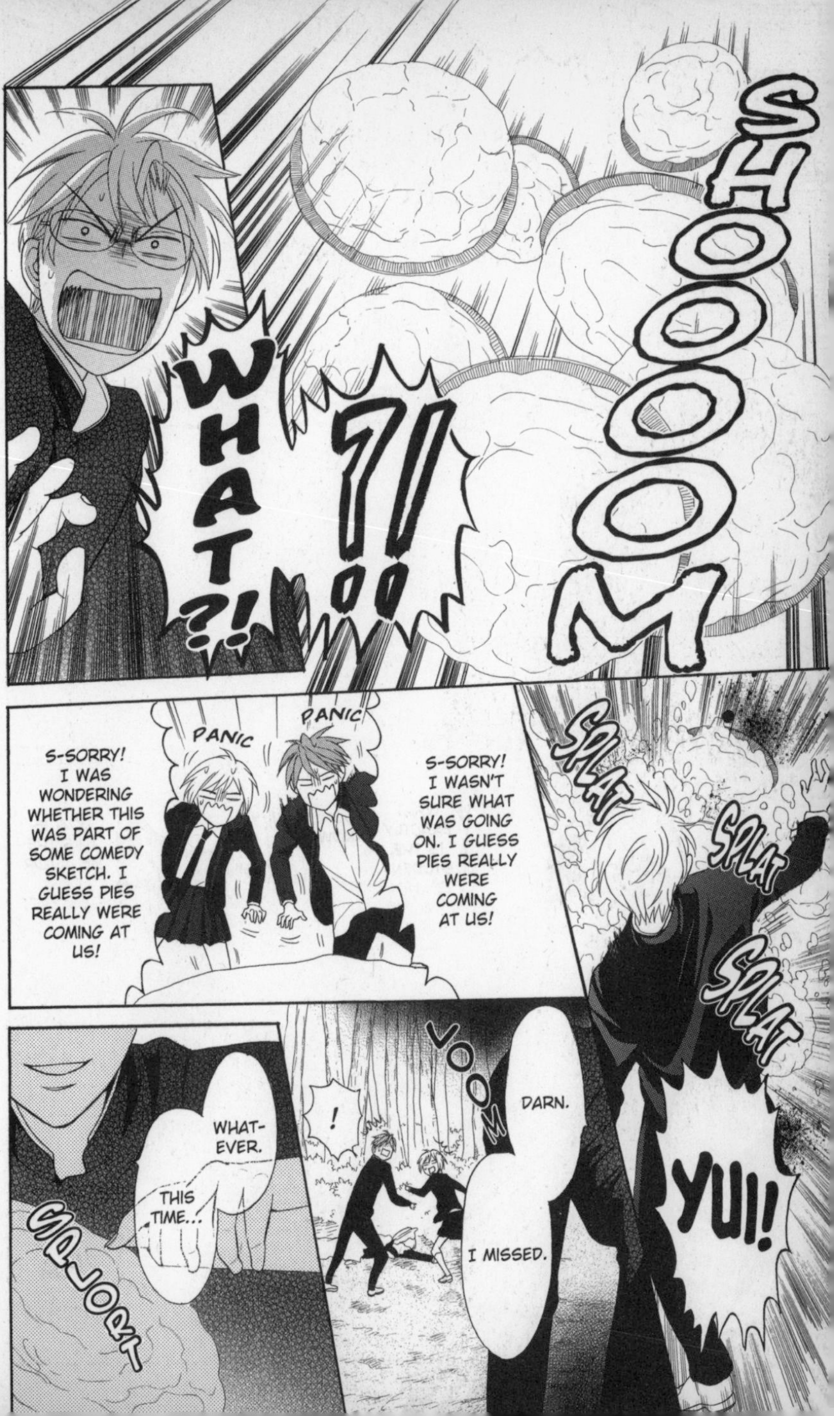
SHOOOOOM
?!
WHAT?!
SPLAT
SPLAT
SPLAT
S-SORRY! I WASN'T SURE WHAT WAS GOING ON. I GUESS PIES REALLY WERE COMING AT US!
PANIC
PANIC
S-SORRY! I WAS WONDERING WHETHER THIS WAS PART OF SOME COMEDY SKETCH. I GUESS PIES REALLY WERE COMING AT US!
YUI!
DARN.
I MISSED.
VOOOM
!
WHAT-EVER.
THIS TIME...
SQUORT

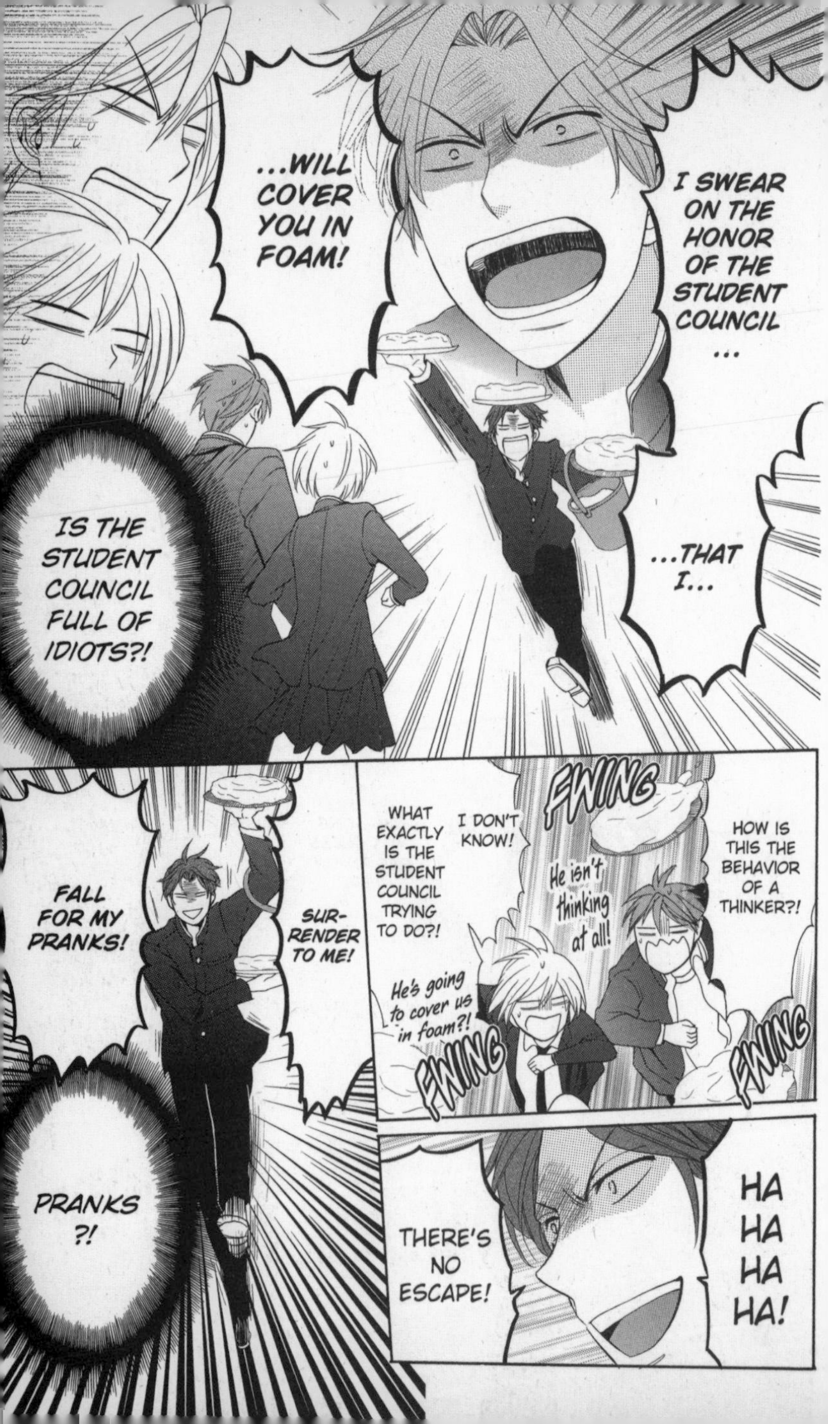
I SWEAR ON THE HONOR OF THE STUDENT COUNCIL...
...THAT I...
...WILL COVER YOU IN FOAM!
IS THE STUDENT COUNCIL FULL OF IDIOTS?!
FWING
HOW IS THIS THE BEHAVIOR OF A THINKER?!
He isn't thinking at all!
I DON'T KNOW!
WHAT EXACTLY IS THE STUDENT COUNCIL TRYING TO DO?!
He's going to cover us in foam?!
FWING
FWING
HA HA HA HA!
THERE'S NO ESCAPE!
SUR-RENDER TO ME!
FALL FOR MY PRANKS!
PRANKS?!

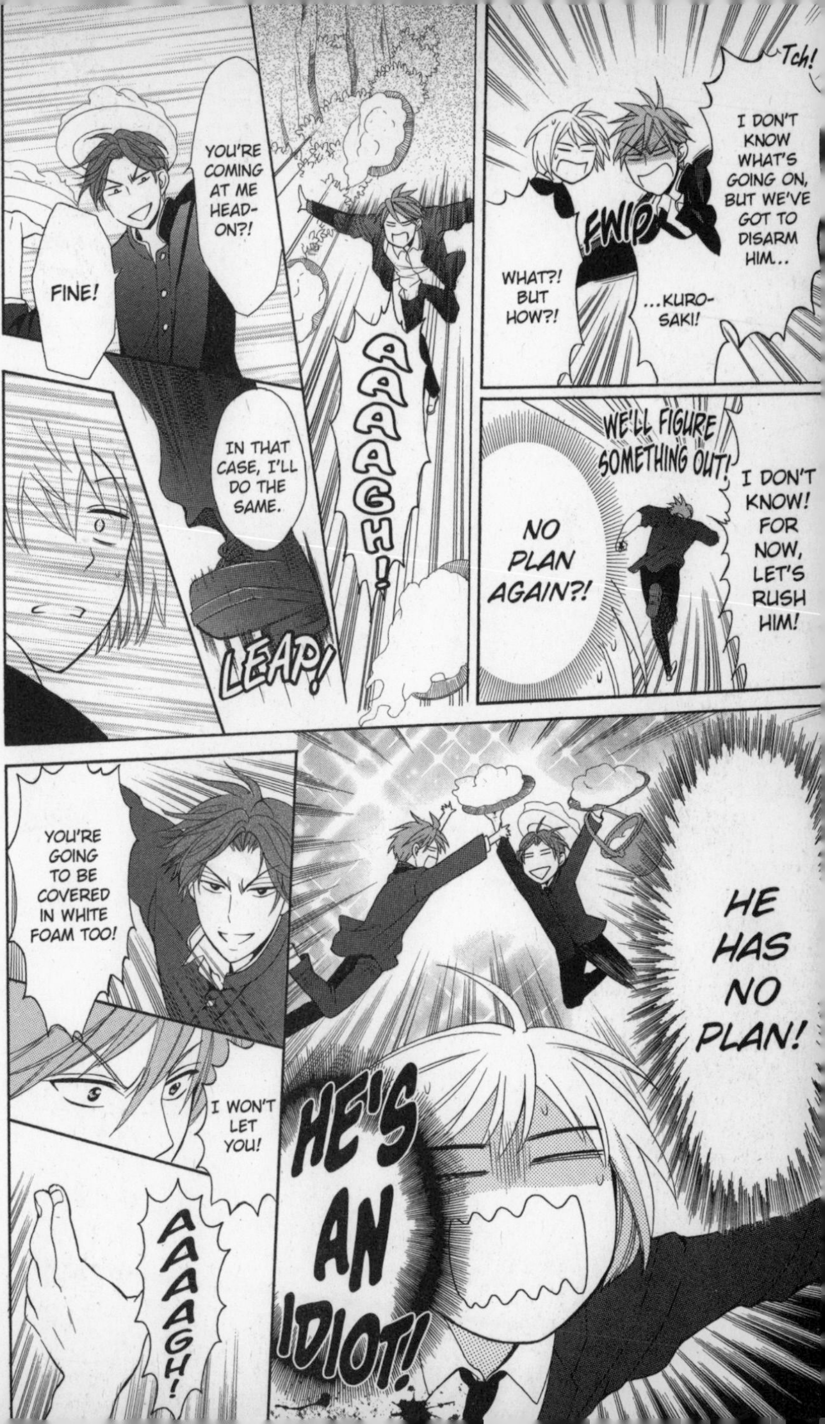
Tch!
I DON'T KNOW WHAT'S GOING ON, BUT WE'VE GOT TO DISARM HIM...
FWIP
...KURO-SAKI!
WHAT?! BUT HOW?!
I DON'T KNOW! FOR NOW, LET'S RUSH HIM!
WE'LL FIGURE SOMETHING OUT!
NO PLAN AGAIN?!
AAAAAGH!
YOU'RE COMING AT ME HEAD-ON?!
FINE!
IN THAT CASE, I'LL DO THE SAME.
LEAP!
HE HAS NO PLAN!
HE'S AN IDIOT!
YOU'RE GOING TO BE COVERED IN WHITE FOAM TOO!
I WON'T LET YOU!
AAAAAGH!

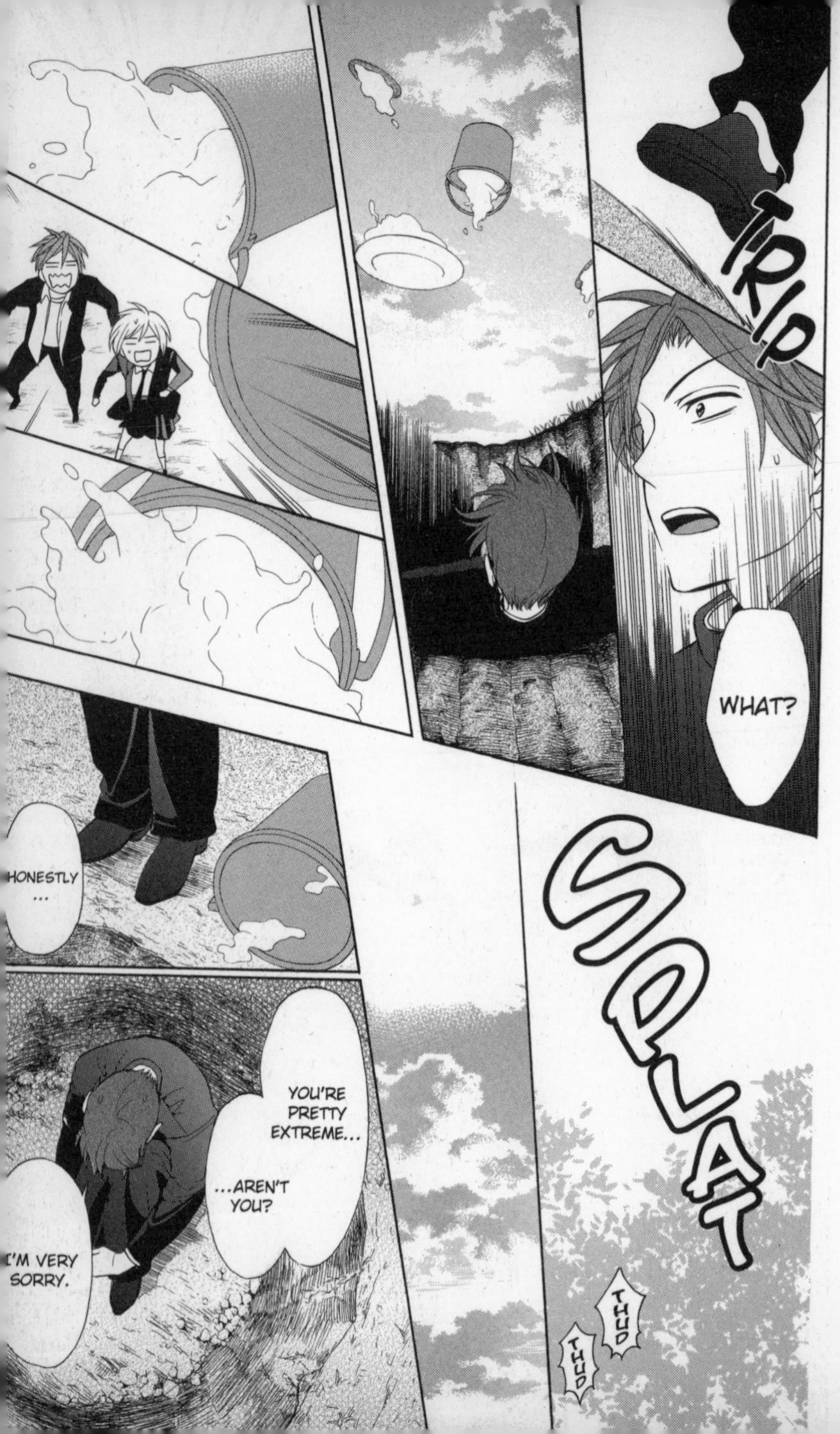
TRIP
WHAT?
SPLAT
THUD
THUD
HONESTLY...
YOU'RE PRETTY EXTREME...
...AREN'T YOU?
I'M VERY SORRY.

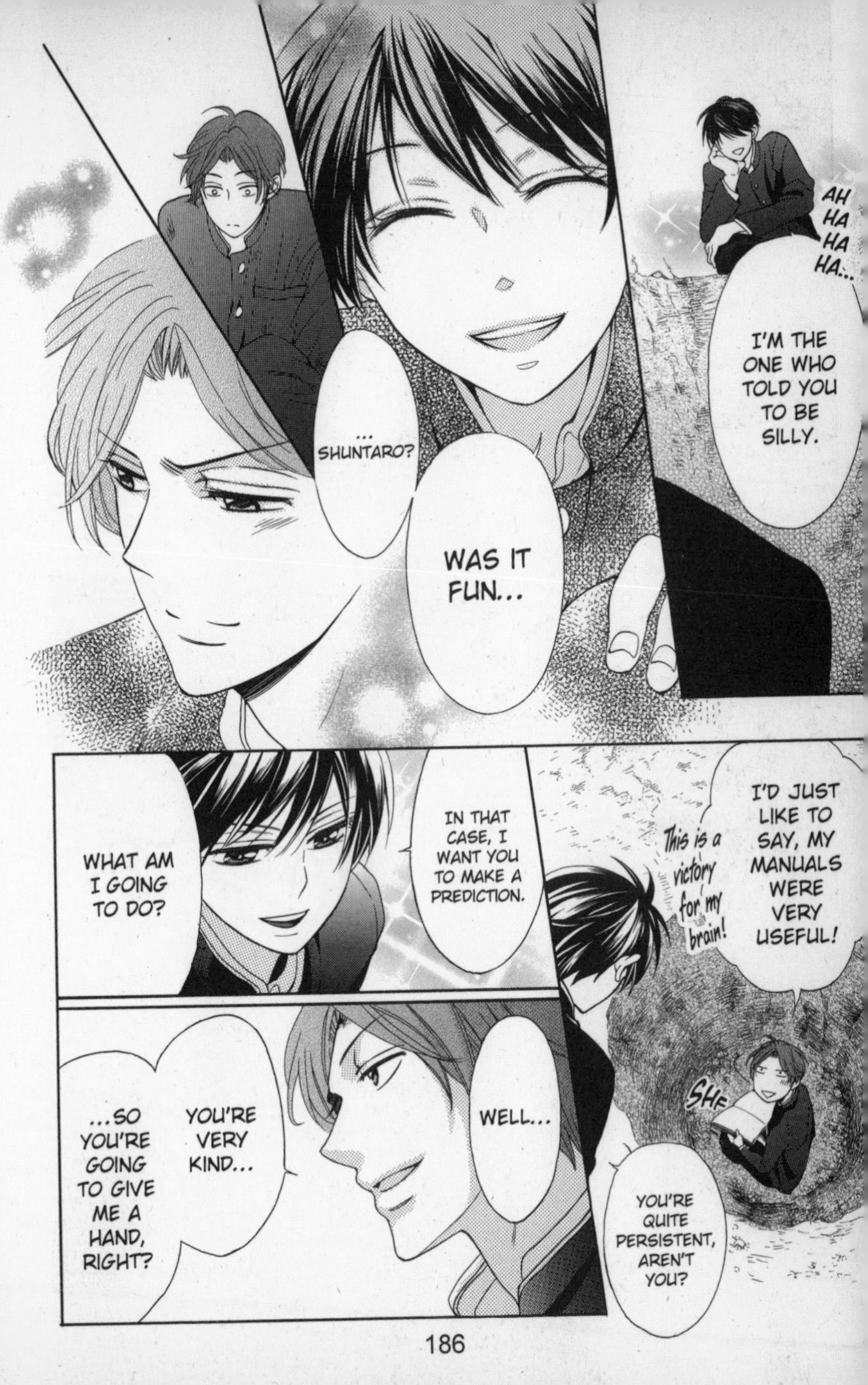
AH HA HA HA...
I'M THE ONE WHO TOLD YOU TO BE SILLY.
WAS IT FUN...
...SHUNTARO?
I'D JUST LIKE TO SAY, MY MANUALS WERE VERY USEFUL!
This is a victory for my brain!
SHF
YOU'RE QUITE PERSISTENT, AREN'T YOU?
IN THAT CASE, I WANT YOU TO MAKE A PREDICTION.
WHAT AM I GOING TO DO?
WELL...
YOU'RE VERY KIND...
...SO YOU'RE GOING TO GIVE ME A HAND, RIGHT?

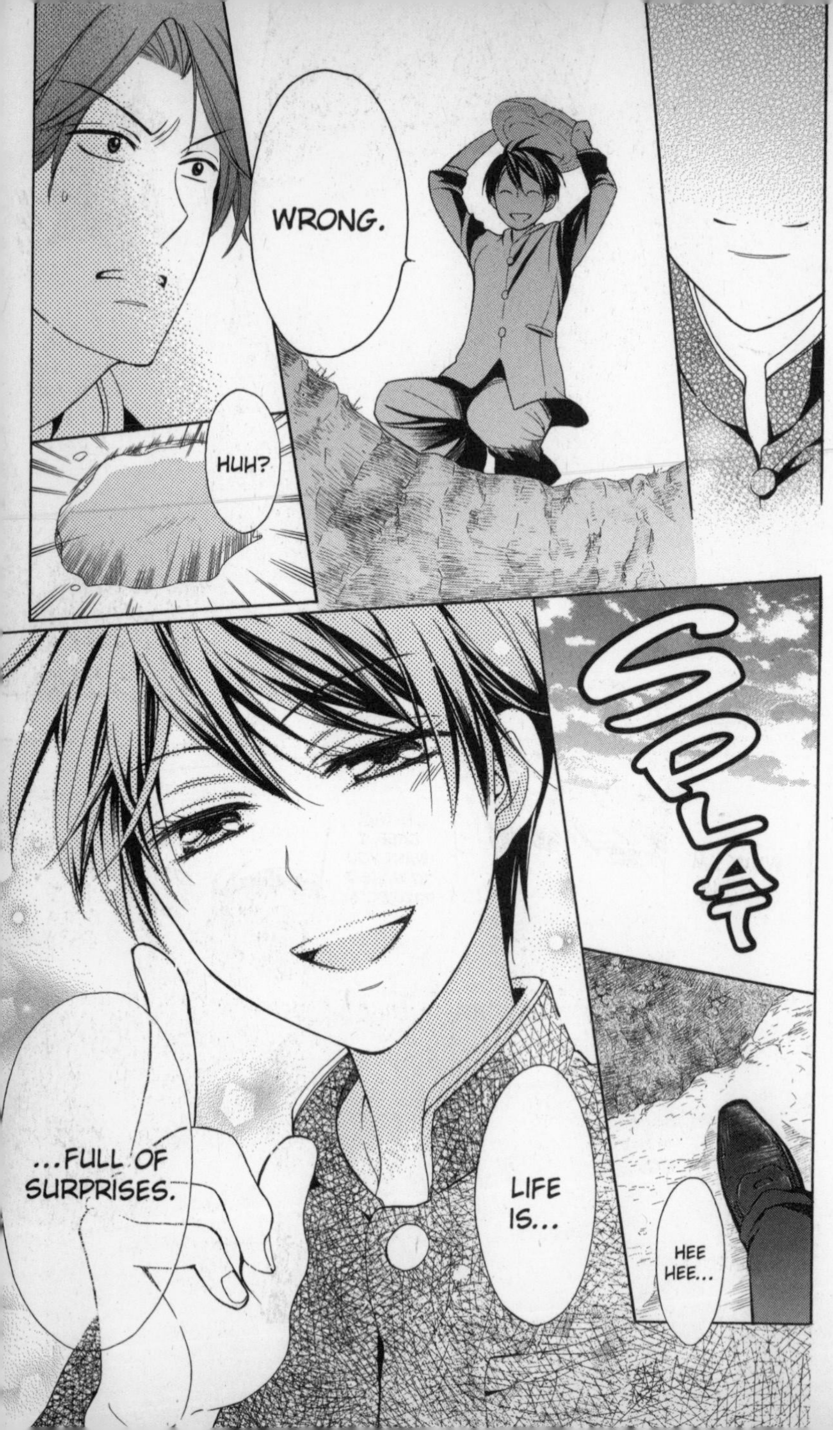
WRONG.
HUH?
SPLAT
HEE HEE...
LIFE IS...
...FULL OF SURPRISES.

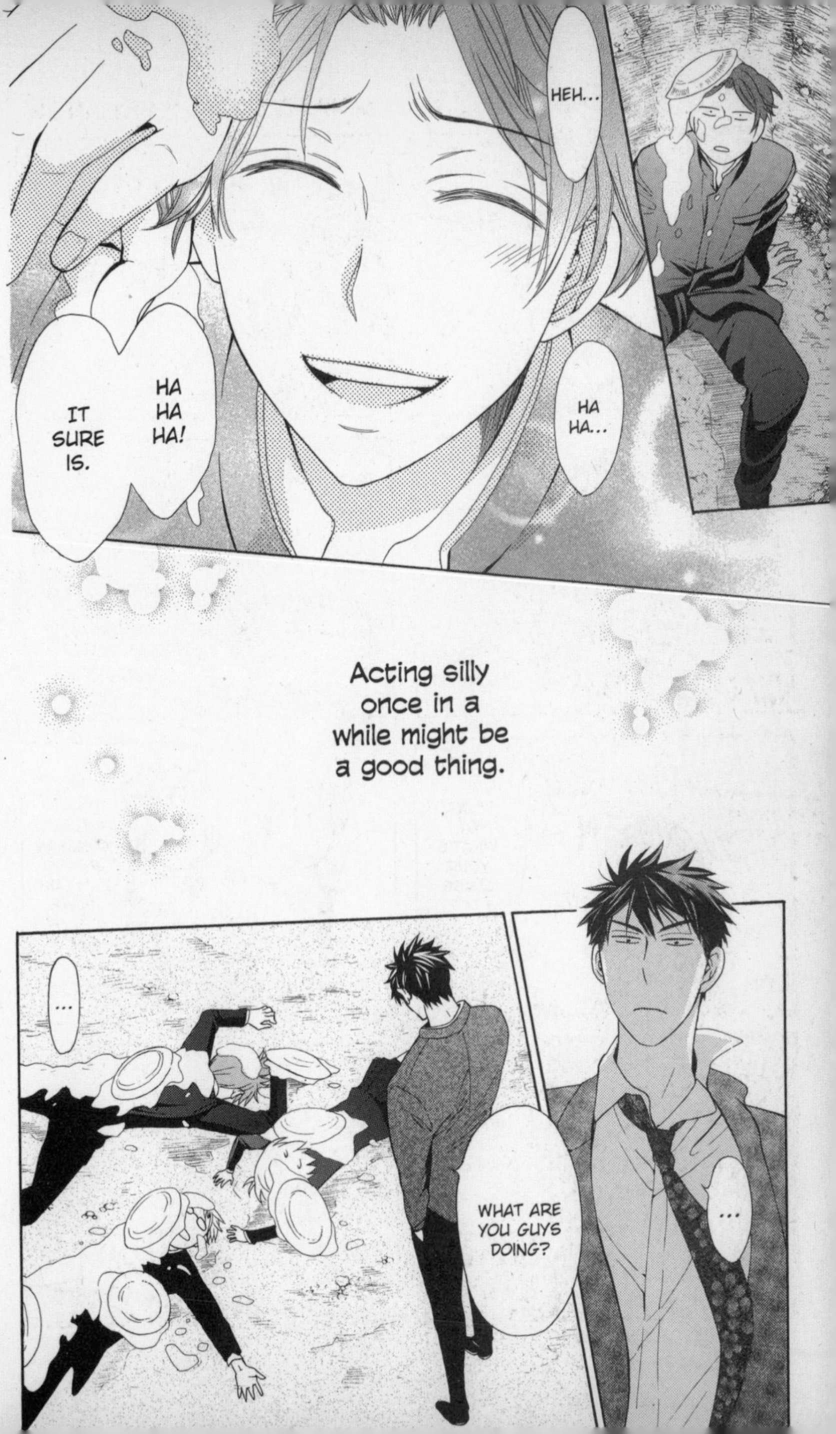
HEH...
HA HA...
HA HA HA!
IT SURE IS.
Acting silly once in a while might be a good thing.
...
WHAT ARE YOU GUYS DOING?
...

MINATO'S GIRLY FEELINGS

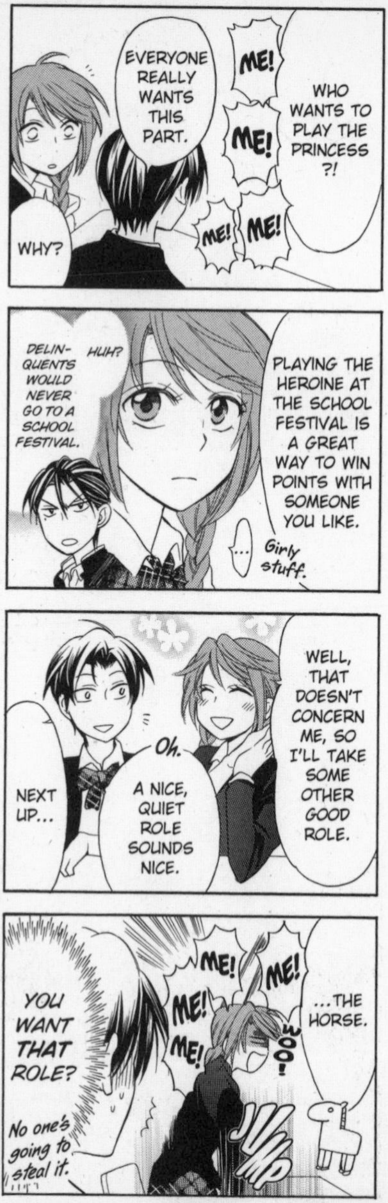
WHO WANTS TO PLAY THE PRINCESS?!
ME!
ME!
ME!
ME!
EVERYONE REALLY WANTS THIS PART.
WHY?
PLAYING THE HEROINE AT THE SCHOOL FESTIVAL IS A GREAT WAY TO WIN POINTS WITH SOMEONE YOU LIKE.
HUH?
DELINQUENTS WOULD NEVER GO TO A SCHOOL FESTIVAL.
...
Girly stuff.
WELL, THAT DOESN'T CONCERN ME, SO I'LL TAKE SOME OTHER GOOD ROLE.
Oh.
A NICE, QUIET ROLE SOUNDS NICE.
NEXT UP...
...THE HORSE.
ME!
ME!
ME!
ME!
WOO!
YOU WANT THAT ROLE?
JUMP
No one's going to steal it.

THE DAY OF THE FESTIVAL

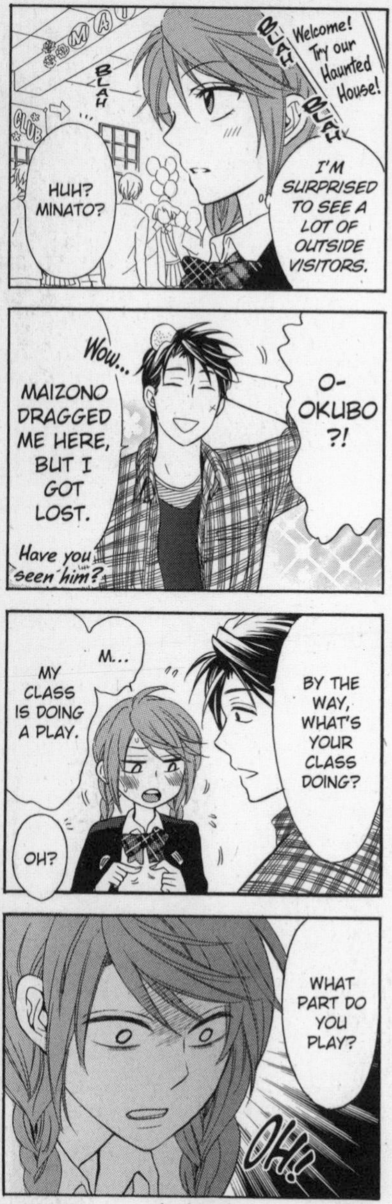
I'M SURPRISED TO SEE A LOT OF OUTSIDE VISITORS.
Welcome! Try our Haunted House!
BLAH
BLAH
BLAH
HUH? MINATO?
O-OKUBO?!
Wow...
MAIZONO DRAGGED ME HERE, BUT I GOT LOST.
Have you seen him?
BY THE WAY, WHAT'S YOUR CLASS DOING?
M...
MY CLASS IS DOING A PLAY.
OH?
WHAT PART DO YOU PLAY?
OH!

The horse!

FERVENT STARE

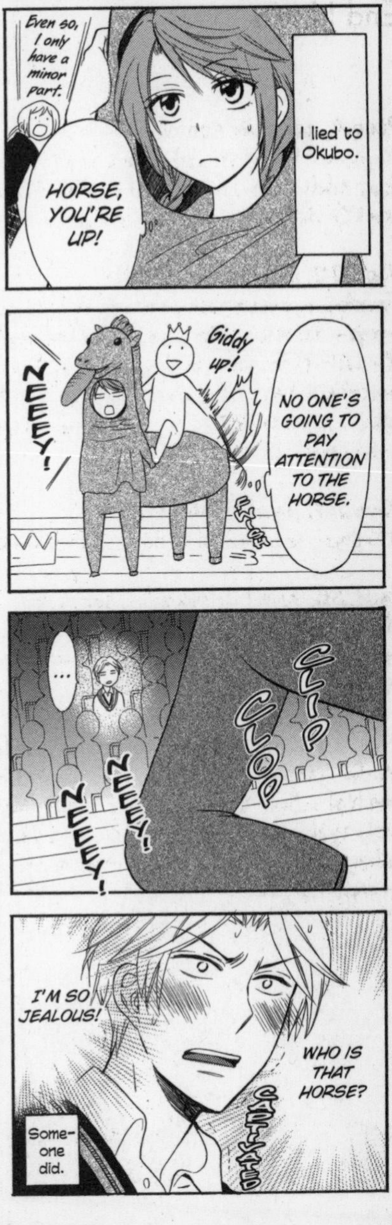
I lied to Okubo.
Even so, I only have a minor part.
HORSE, YOU'RE UP!
NO ONE'S GOING TO PAY ATTENTION TO THE HORSE.
Giddy up!
NEEEY!
CLIP CLOP
NEEEY!
NEEEY!
...
WHO IS THAT HORSE?
CAPTIVATED
I'M SO JEALOUS!
Someone did.

ACTOR OF INTEREST

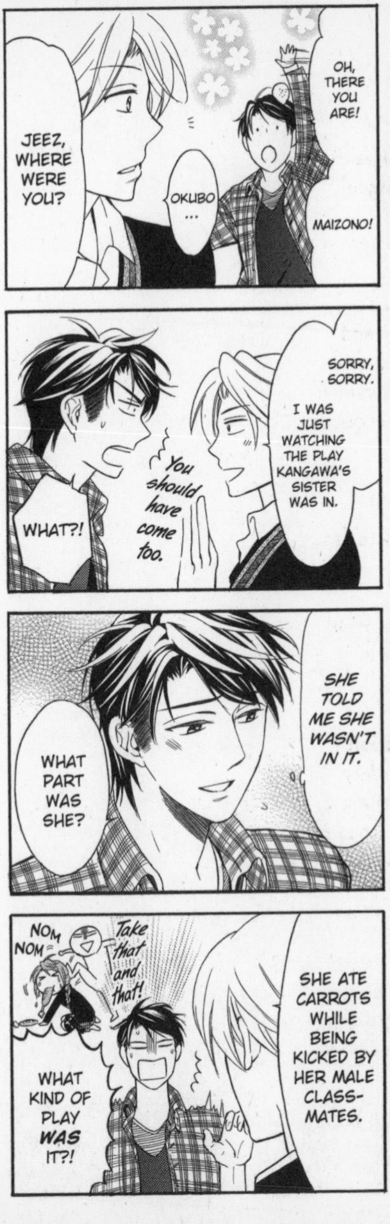
OH, THERE YOU ARE!
MAIZONO!
OKUBO...
JEEZ, WHERE WERE YOU?
SORRY, SORRY.
I WAS JUST WATCHING THE PLAY KANGAWA'S SISTER WAS IN.
You should have come too.
WHAT?!
SHE TOLD ME SHE WASN'T IN IT.
WHAT PART WAS SHE?
SHE ATE CARROTS WHILE BEING KICKED BY HER MALE CLASS-MATES.
Take that and that!
NOM NOM
WHAT KIND OF PLAY WAS IT?!

End Notes

Page 4, panel 4: Konnyaku
Konnyaku is a traditional Japanese jelly-like health food made from the starch of the "devil's tongue" plant (a relative of the sweet potato).

Page 30, panel 2: Tsundere
Tsundere is a term that combines two Japanese words—*tsuntsun* (which means "unfriendly") and *deredere* (which means "lovestruck"). It is used to describe people who are rather unfriendly at first sight but gradually become more lovely as you get to know them.

Page 55, panel 6: Monjayaki
Monjayaki is a type of griddle cake with vegetables.

Page 56, panel 2: Yakisoba, takoyaki
Yakisoba is pan-fried noodles and *takoyaki* are fried octopus balls. Both are popular festival foods in Japan.

Page 160, panel 2: School recommendation
Students in Japan don't automatically matriculate into high school like they do in the U.S. They must apply to the high school they wish to attend, through either a recommendation from their middle school or an entrance test.

Izumi Tsubaki began drawing manga in her first year of high school. She was soon selected to be in the top ten of *Hana to Yume*'s HMC (*Hana to Yume* Mangaka Course), and subsequently won *Hana to Yume*'s Big Challenge contest. Her debut title, *Chijimete Distance* (Shrink the Distance), ran in 2002 in *Hana to Yume* magazine, issue 17. Her other works include *The Magic Touch* (*Oyayubi kara Romance*) and *Oresama Teacher*, which she is currently working on.

ORESAMA TEACHER
Vol. 9
Shojo Beat Edition

STORY AND ART BY
Izumi Tsubaki

English Translation & Adaptation/JN Productions
Touch-up Art & Lettering/Eric Erbes
Design/Yukiko Whitley
Editor/Pancha Diaz

ORESAMA TEACHER by Izumi Tsubaki © Izumi Tsubaki 2010
All rights reserved. First published in Japan in 2010 by HAKUSENSHA, Inc., Tokyo.
English language translation rights arranged with HAKUSENSHA, Inc., Tokyo.

The stories, characters and incidents mentioned in this publication are
entirely fictional.

Printed in Canada

Published by VIZ Media, LLC
P.O. Box 77010
San Francisco, CA 94107

10 9 8 7 6 5 4 3 2 1
First printing, July 2012

www.viz.com   www.shojobeat.com

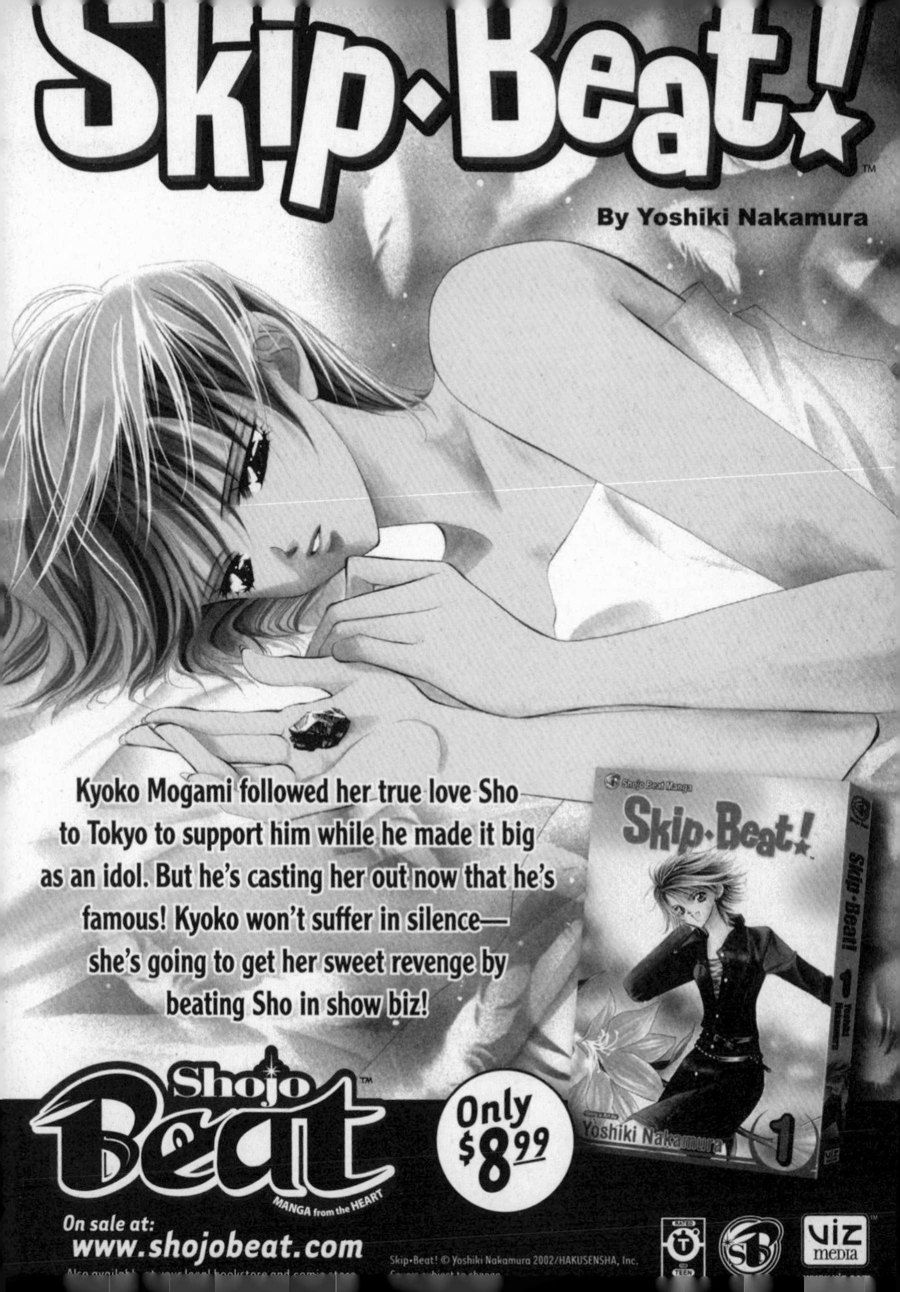

Skip·Beat!
By Yoshiki Nakamura
Kyoko Mogami followed her true love Sho to Tokyo to support him while he made it big as an idol. But he's casting her out now that he's famous! Kyoko won't suffer in silence—she's going to get her sweet revenge by beating Sho in show biz!
Shojo Beat
MANGA from the HEART
Only $8.99
Skip·Beat!
Yoshiki Nakamura
1
On sale at:
www.shojobeat.com
Skip·Beat! © Yoshiki Nakamura 2002/HAKUSENSHA, Inc.
TEEN
viz media

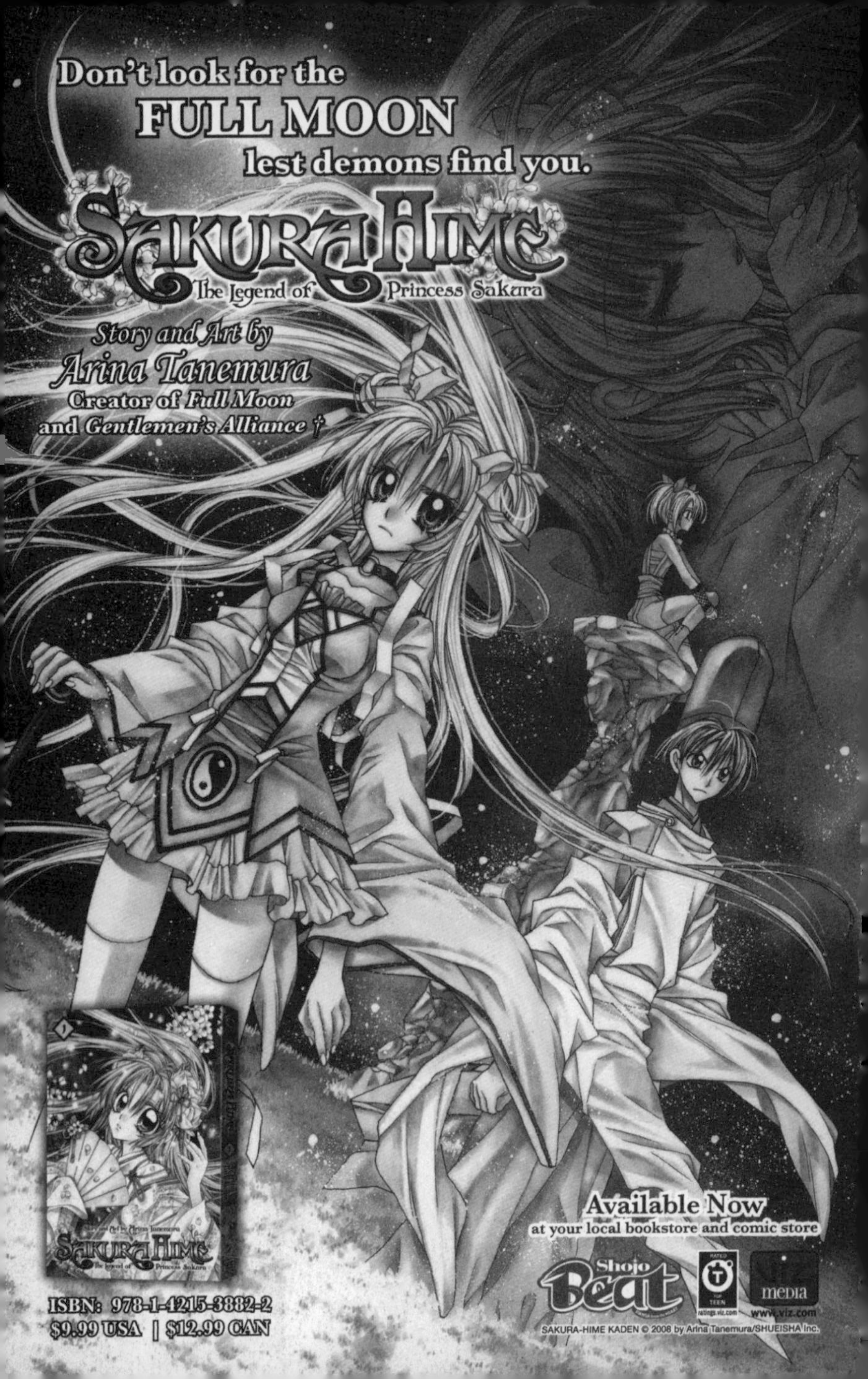

Don't look for the
FULL MOON
lest demons find you.
SAKURA HIME
The Legend of Princess Sakura
Story and Art by
Arina Tanemura
Creator of Full Moon
and Gentlemen's Alliance †
ISBN: 978-1-4215-3882-2
$9.99 USA | $12.99 CAN
Available Now
at your local bookstore and comic store
Shojo Beat
media
www.viz.com
SAKURA-HIME KADEN © 2008 by Arina Tanemura/SHUEISHA Inc.

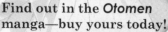
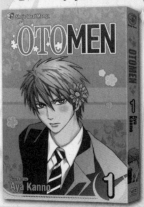
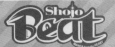

Kisaki is called out to California—
to fight aliens!

Mistress Fortune

Story and Art by Arina Tanemura

Creator of *Gentlemen's Alliance †* and *Full Moon*

Fourteen-year-old Kisaki Tachibana has psychic powers. She works for PSI, a secret government agency that fights aliens. She's in love with her partner Giniro, but PSI won't allow operatives to get involved. Just when Kisaki thinks she may be getting closer to Giniro, she finds out she's going to be transferred to California!

Bonus Color Poster Inside

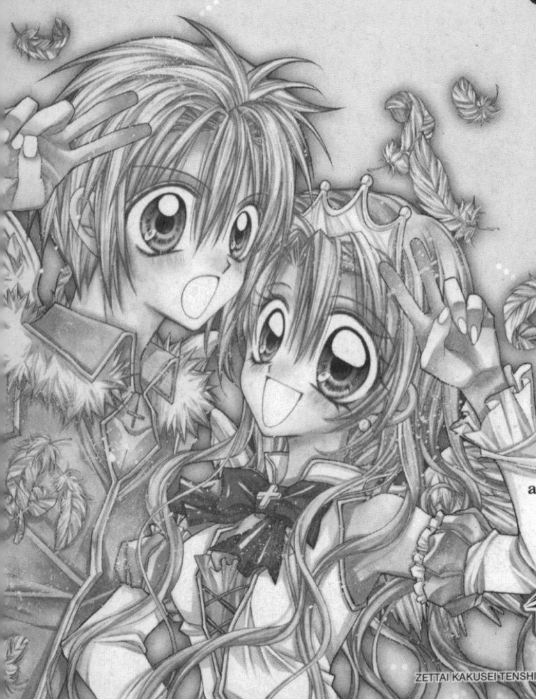

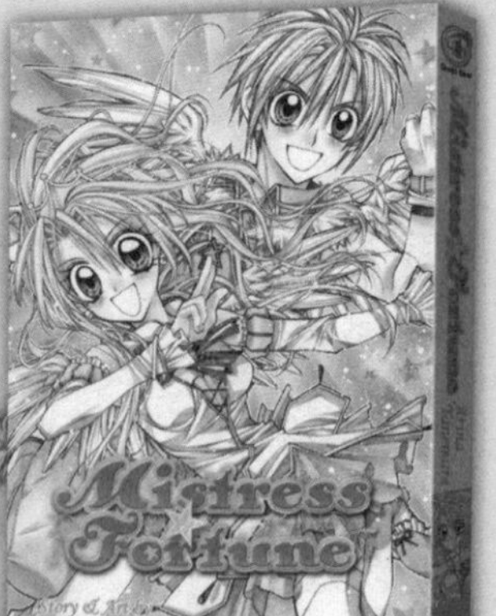
Mistress Fortune
Arina Tanemura

Available Now

at your local bookstore or comic store

ISBN: 978-1-4215-3881-5
$9.99 USA | $12.99 CAN

Shojo Beat
RATED T FOR TEEN ratings.viz.com
VIZ media www.viz.com

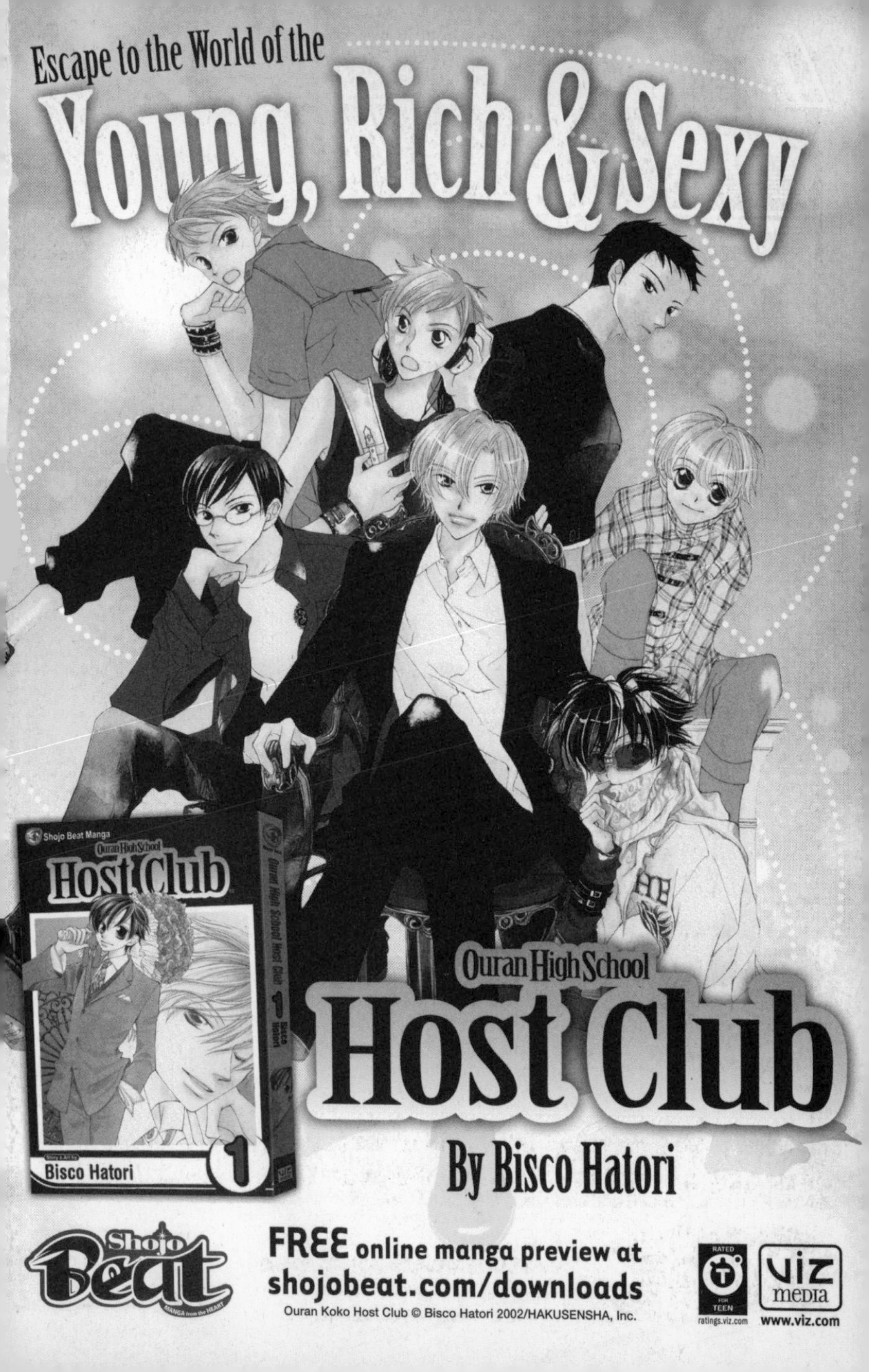

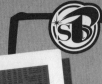
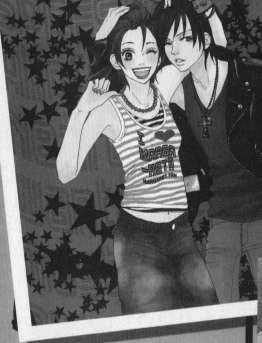
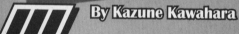
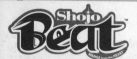

Surprise!

S0-BAW-580

You may be reading the wrong way!

It's true: In keeping with the original Japanese comic format, this book reads from right to left—so action, sound effects, and word balloons are completely reversed. This preserves the orientation of the original artwork—plus, it's fun! Check out the diagram shown here to get the hang of things, and then turn to the other side of the book to get started!

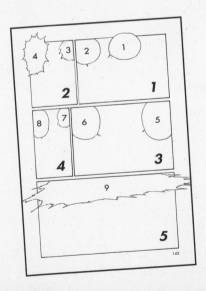